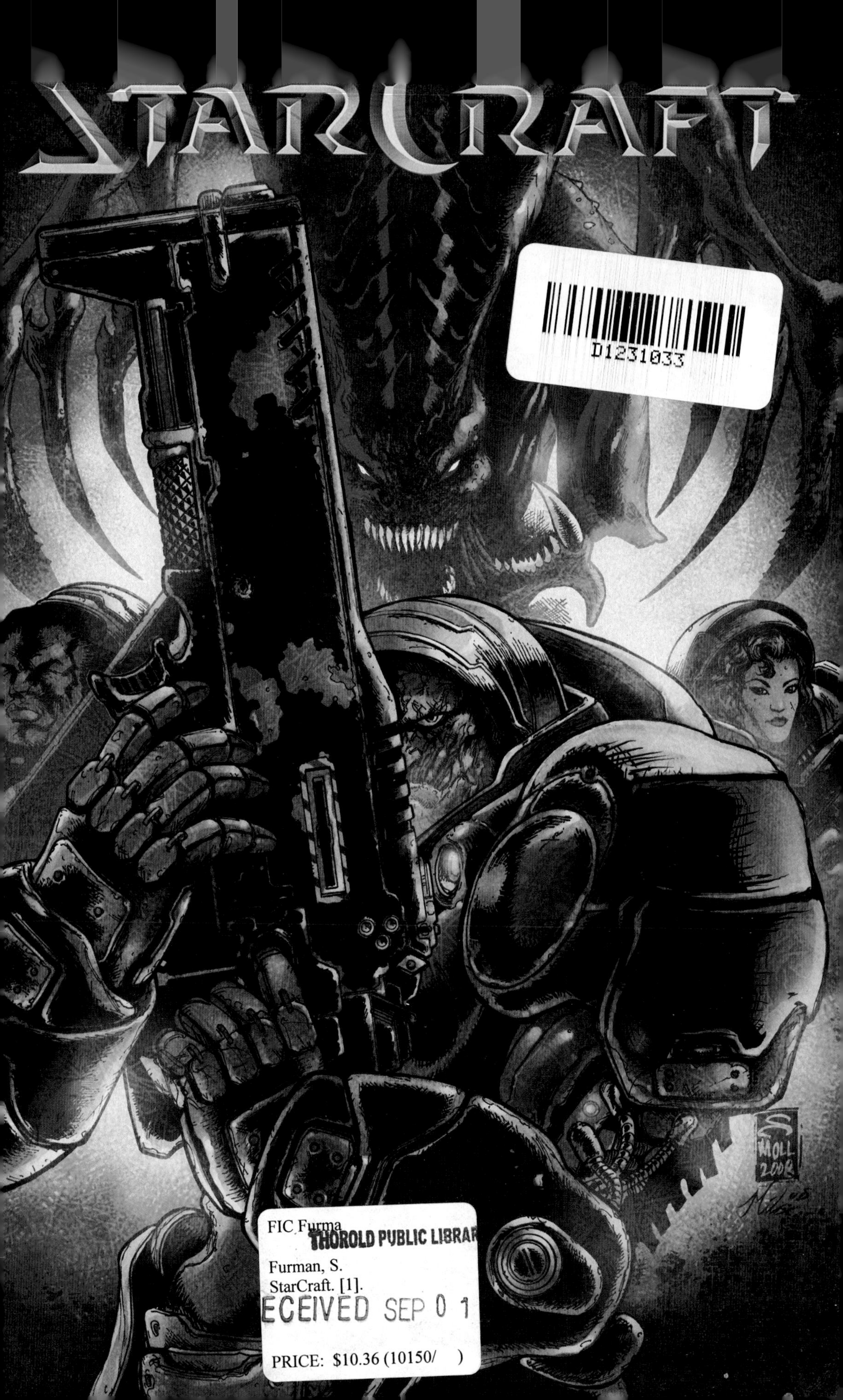
STARCRAFT

Story by
SIMON FURMAN

Art by
**FEDERICO DALLOCCHIO
BRIAN DENHAM
CARLOS D'ANDA
and MIKE S. MILLER**

Colors by
**MILEN PARVANOV, CARRIE STRACHAN
and WILDSTORM FX**

Letters by
SAIDA TEMOFONTE

Cover and original series covers by
**FEDERICO DALLOCCHIO
with MILEN PARVANOV and JONNY RENCH**

Variant covers and pinups by
**SHAWN MOLL, SHAWN MOLL & DOUG MAHNKE
SHAWN MOLL & SANDRA HOPE, CARLOS D'ANDA
FEDERICO DALLOCCHIO**

Story consultants:
**CHRIS METZEN, MICKY NEILSON,
ANDY CHAMBERS & JAMES WAUGH**

War Pigs concept by **JASON BISCHOFF**

Special thanks to **KEITH GIFFEN**

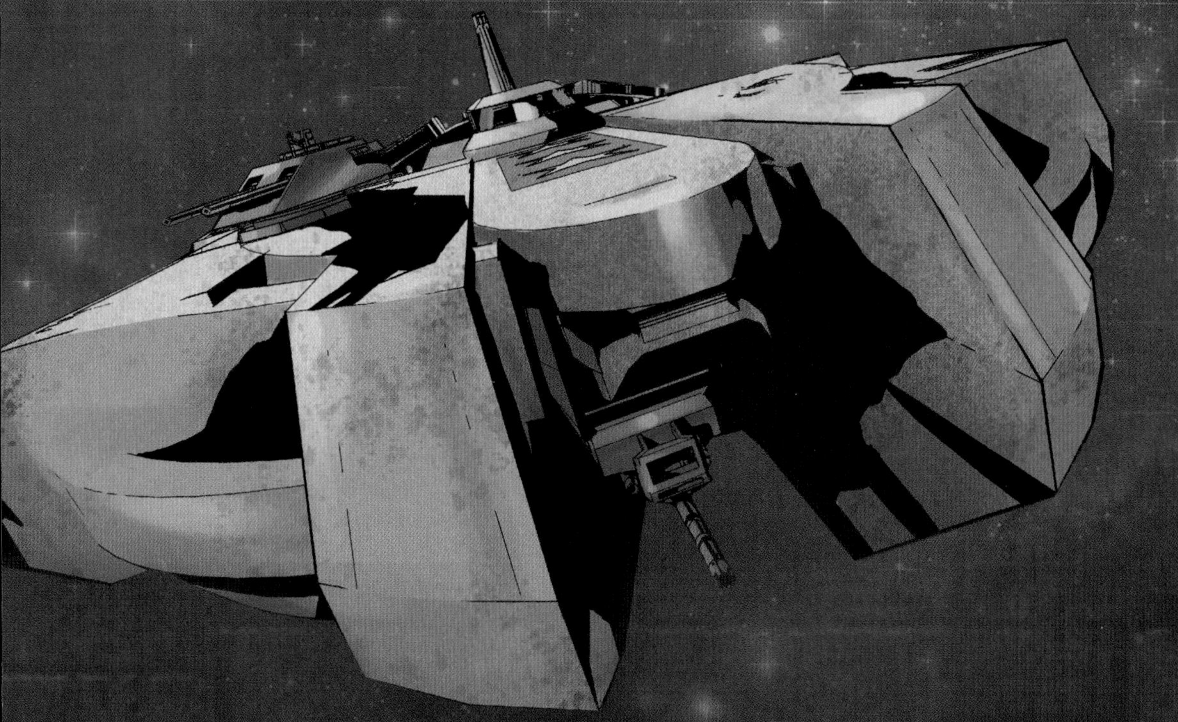

For Blizzard Entertainment:

Chris Metzen	Senior VP - Creative Development
Jeff Donais	Director - Creative Development
Micky Neilson	Story Consultant and Development
Glenn Rane	Art Director
Cory Jones	Director - Global Business Development and Licensing
Jason Bischoff	Associate Licensing Manager
Tommy Newcomer	Additional Development
Cameron Dayton	Additional Development

For DC Comics:

Ben Abernathy	Editor - Original Series
Ian Sattler	Director, Editorial - Archival Editions
Kristy Quinn	Editor
Robbin Brosterman	Design Director - Books
Eddie Berganza	Executive Editor
Bob Harras	VP - Editor in Chief
Diane Nelson	President
Dan DiDio and Jim Lee	Co-Publishers
Geoff Johns	Chief Creative Officer
John Rood	Executive VP - Sales, Marketing and Business Development
Amy Genkins	Senior VP - Business and Legal Affairs
Nairi Gardiner	Senior VP - Finance
Jeff Boison	VP - Publishing Operations
Mark Chiarello	VP - Art Direction and Design
John Cunningham	VP - Marketing
Terri Cunningham	VP - Talent Relations and Services
Alison Gill	Senior VP - Manufacturing and Operations
David Hyde	VP - Publicity
Hank Kanalz	Senior VP - Digital
Jay Kogan	VP - Business and Legal Affairs, Publishing
Jack Mahan	VP - Business Affairs, Talent
Nick Napolitano	VP - Manufacturing Administration
Ron Perazza	VP - Online
Sue Pohja	VP - Book Sales
Courtney Simmons	Senior VP - Publicity
Bob Wayne	Senior VP - Sales

STARCRAFT

DC Comics, 1700 Broadway, New York, NY 10019
A Warner Bros. Entertainment Company
Printed by RR Donnelley, Salem, VA, USA. 4/8/11. First Printing
ISBN: 978-1-4012-3167-5

SUSTAINABLE FORESTRY INITIATIVE
Certified Chain of Custody
Fiber used in this product line meets the sourcing requirements of the SFI program. www.sfiprogram.org SGS-SFI/COC-US10/81072

LICENSED BLIZZARD ENTERTAINMENT PRODUCT

INTRODUCTION

StarCraft.

It is a strange little universe.

Since the original game's launch back in 1998, we've been actively finding ways to continue the stories of the protoss, zerg and terrans—each locked in their seemingly endless war for dominance. Being a huge fan of comics myself, I always figured we'd get around to doing a comic—so long as we found the right creative partners. It took awhile (y'know—ten years or so), but the exceptional team at WildStorm proved to be the perfect match for what we had envisioned.

The book you hold in your hands started taking shape about two years ago. At that point, we were knee-deep in the development of *Starcraft 2: Wings of Liberty*—and still defining the characters and story elements that would form the narrative of that long-awaited sequel. Since there were still some lingering questions as to the fate of our major franchise characters (ie: Jim Raynor, Kerrigan, Zeratul, etc.), we decided to take a different track with the comic series and focus on characters and areas of the universe that would be fun to explore and be a bit less complicated to wrangle (*given the myriad plot complexities on the game-side*).

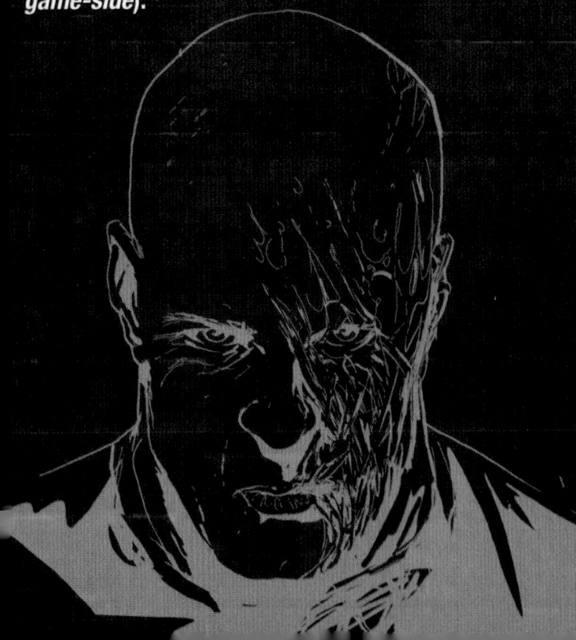

We realized very quickly that this choice provided us a great opportunity to show our fans the broader scope of the IP, giving them a glimpse at the political machinations at play inside the Dominion, letting them feel the plight of the rugged fringe world colonist, and all around really showcase what life in the Koprulu Sector is like when you're not harvesting crystals or trying to get your firebats to counter a massive zerg rush.

It was Blizzard's own Jason Bischoff wh stepped up to the plate and pitched the idea a group of grim and gritty mercenaries makir their way through terran space—one ste ahead of the law (*personally, I think Jase watched a little too much* A-Team *as a kid- but then again…is there such a thing as to much* A-Team?). Jason and the conce team immediately jumped on this idea ar helped to flesh out the broad strokes of th story—and define the various personalitie (and fatal hang-ups) of the War Pigs.

Based on the brilliant scripts from Simon Furma (Mister *Transformers* himself) and the gritty, hea artwork from Federico Dallocchio—the STARCRA comic proved to be a fast-paced, hyper-kinetic ron through the seedy, morally-compromised underbel of the *Starcraft* universe.

Mission accomplished, indeed.

Chris Metzen
SVP, Creative Development
Blizzard Entertainment

INTRODUCTION

"They let you in the door?" (The honest-to-goodness first words spoken to me when I came [to] interview at Blizzard.)

Tell someone you work in video games and [yo]u're the "bee's knees." Follow with the fact [th]at you're the licensing guy, and suddenly [yo]u're just another "business jerk."

Don't get me wrong, this strange industry I [ru]n around in is full of the above-mentioned [st]ereotype. They can be the worm to the [cr]eative apple and sadly, at surface glance, [yo]u'd think me one of them. It's typecasting, [I a]ssure you, but an easy mistake.

My name's not in the title, nor found on [th]e cover. On occasion (if I'm lucky), [ch]eck inside, near the legal. I hide [th]ere beside: "Associate Licensing [M]anager." It's a veil, a ruse to lead [yo]u off my path. I'm just a busi-[ne]ss jerk after all, like Bruce [W]ayne perhaps? Second glances [wo]n't be necessary. But don't [be]lieve it, don't buy into it for [th]e second. Deep inside this façade lies a furnace [bu]rning for the chance to really creatively flex. You, [my fri]end, have just thrown a log onto that hungry fire.

[... W]hy? Skim the credits again: "War Pigs Concept [by]." I'm shaking as I type this. I feel the floodgates of [ch]emical emotion swim in my face as I am thankful [an]d unworthy, anxious and shell-shocked. *World of [W]arcraft*, *Diablo* and *StarCraft* have always been [me]ans of lore to me. How could I have expected to [tr]averse even one of these worlds safely, nonetheless [sh]aped them in some way? How could an "Associate [Li]censing Manager" have managed court-time with a [ca]bal like Simon Furman, Chris Metzen and *New York*

Times Best Selling Graphic Novel author Micky Neilson? (Sorry, Mick, I had to.)

Many years ago, in the primordial days of the mid 2000s, I silently contributed content to some of the biggest brands in pop culture. I cast off those gloves to do what I do now, never thinking that my writing ambitions would be encouraged once again in my new role. Little did I know it would be like being adopted by the family that had wanted me all along. Their patience was saintly. Their welcome astounding. Their opportunity generous. Cheers, guys. Thanks for letting me play.

The broken mess of Terran waste you are about to meet, the WarPigs, were born in seat 31 J (a sixteen-hour prison of my choosing as I flew to Hong Kong in the Spring of '08 for, you guessed it, business). You'll never find the original document that I entitled "Penance Detail" (what was I thinking?), but I can assure you that much of the setup and its stars survived the translation into the ride you're about to take. They were perfected in the weeks to come in Metzen's "Lab." Micky renamed Cole and made Turfa glow (literally). Chris christened the 'Pigs with a name (based off an early SC1 cinematic) and set them off into the fringe worlds on their own ship, the *General Lee*, and Simon—dear "Nemesis Part 2" Simon Furman—made them flipping fantastic.

For the seven issues that comprise this collection (of which I am extremely proud), I've been given a rare taste at what it is that a Senior Vice President of Creative Development does across the hundred-odd feet between our offices. I've got to say it, Mr. Metzen, I'm hooked. Wanna trade for a day…or a lifetime?

Jason Bischoff
Associate Licensing Manager
Blizzard Entertainment

Special thanks to Cory, Hank and James for your enduring wisdom and encouragement!

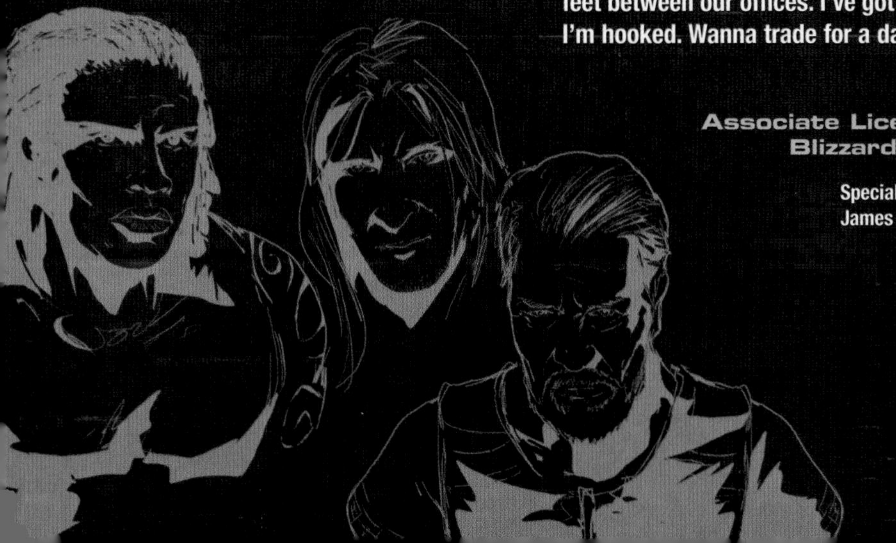

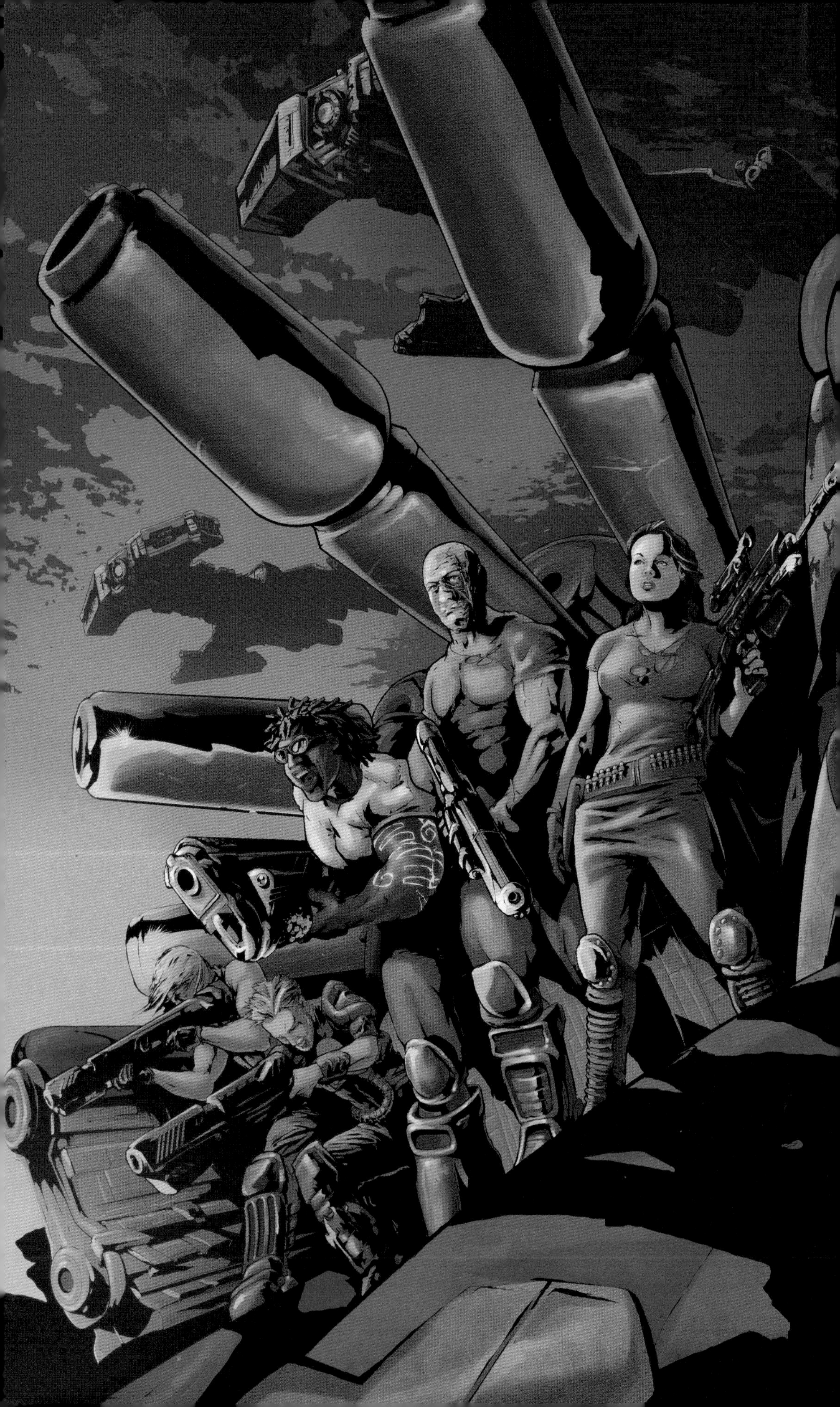

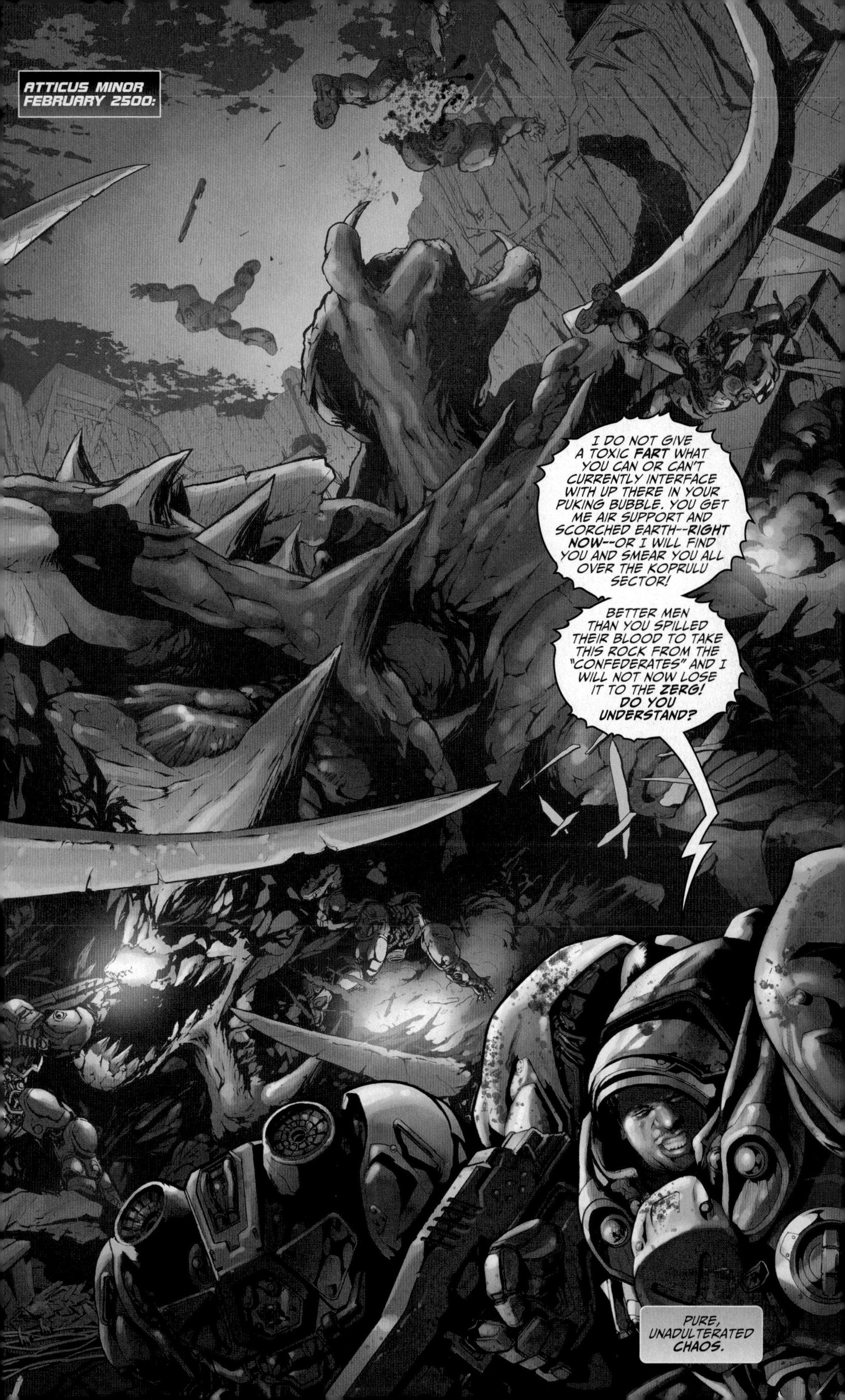
ATTICUS MINOR FEBRUARY 2500:
I DO NOT GIVE A TOXIC FART WHAT YOU CAN OR CAN'T CURRENTLY INTERFACE WITH UP THERE IN YOUR PUKING BUBBLE. YOU GET ME AIR SUPPORT AND SCORCHED EARTH--RIGHT NOW--OR I WILL FIND YOU AND SMEAR YOU ALL OVER THE KOPRULU SECTOR!
BETTER MEN THAN YOU SPILLED THEIR BLOOD TO TAKE THIS ROCK FROM THE "CONFEDERATES" AND I WILL NOT NOW LOSE IT TO THE ZERG! DO YOU UNDERSTAND?
PURE, UNADULTERATED CHAOS.

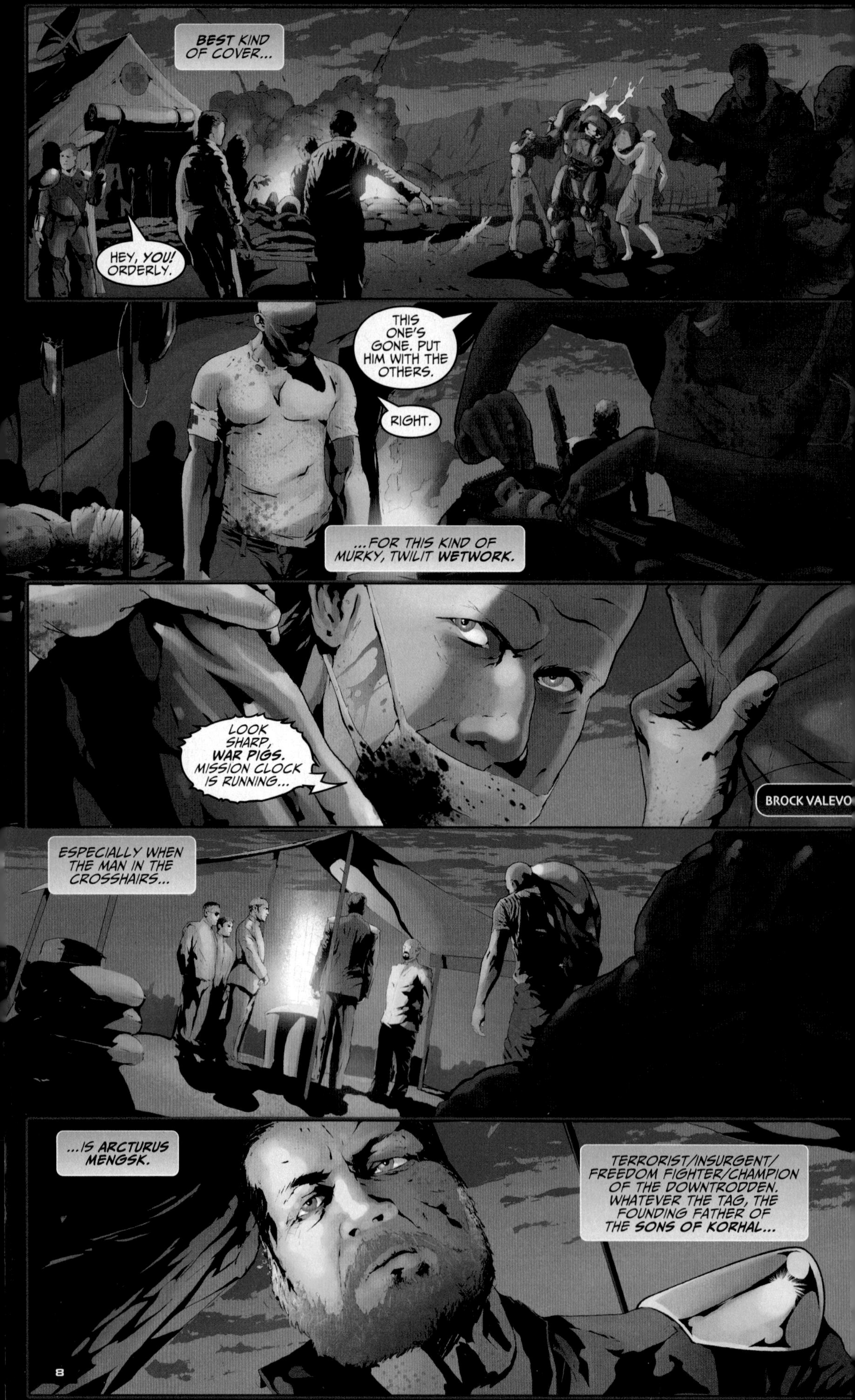

BEST KIND OF COVER...
HEY, YOU! ORDERLY.
THIS ONE'S GONE. PUT HIM WITH THE OTHERS.
RIGHT.
...FOR THIS KIND OF MURKY, TWILIT WETWORK.
LOOK SHARP, WAR PIGS. MISSION CLOCK IS RUNNING...
BROCK VALEVO
ESPECIALLY WHEN THE MAN IN THE CROSSHAIRS...
...IS ARCTURUS MENGSK.
TERRORIST/INSURGENT/FREEDOM FIGHTER/CHAMPION OF THE DOWNTRODDEN. WHATEVER THE TAG, THE FOUNDING FATHER OF THE SONS OF KORHAL...

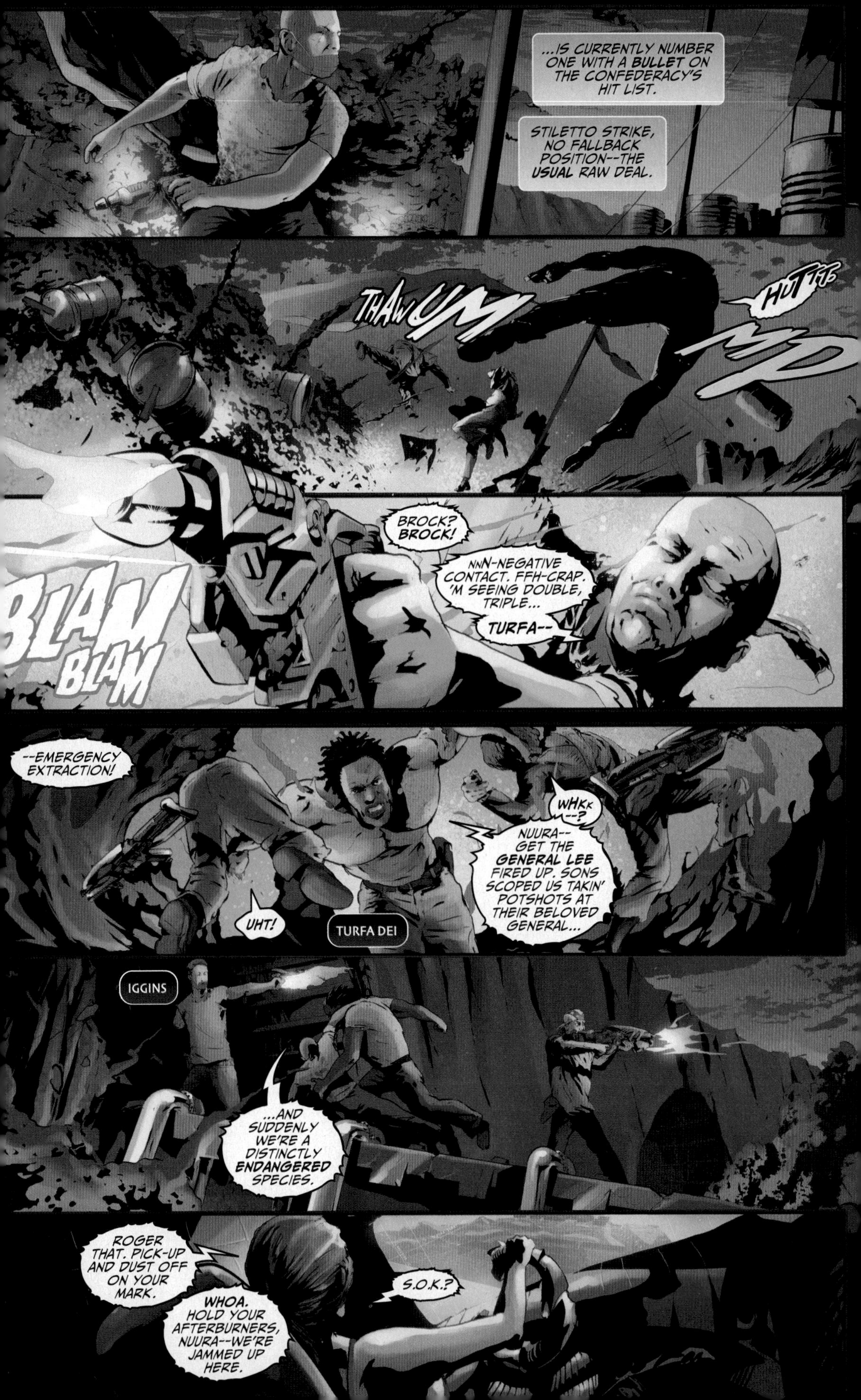
...IS CURRENTLY NUMBER ONE WITH A BULLET ON THE CONFEDERACY'S HIT LIST.
STILETTO STRIKE, NO FALLBACK POSITION--THE USUAL RAW DEAL.
THAWUMMP
HUT
BROCK? BROCK!
NNN-NEGATIVE CONTACT. FFH-CRAP. 'M SEEING DOUBLE, TRIPLE...
TURFA--
BLAM BLAM
--EMERGENCY EXTRACTION!
WHKK--?
NUURA-- GET THE GENERAL LEE FIRED UP. SONS SCOPED US TAKIN' POTSHOTS AT THEIR BELOVED GENERAL...
UHT!
TURFA DEI
IGGINS
...AND SUDDENLY WE'RE A DISTINCTLY ENDANGERED SPECIES.
ROGER THAT. PICK-UP AND DUST OFF ON YOUR MARK.
S.O.K.?
WHOA. HOLD YOUR AFTERBURNERS, NUURA--WE'RE JAMMED UP HERE.

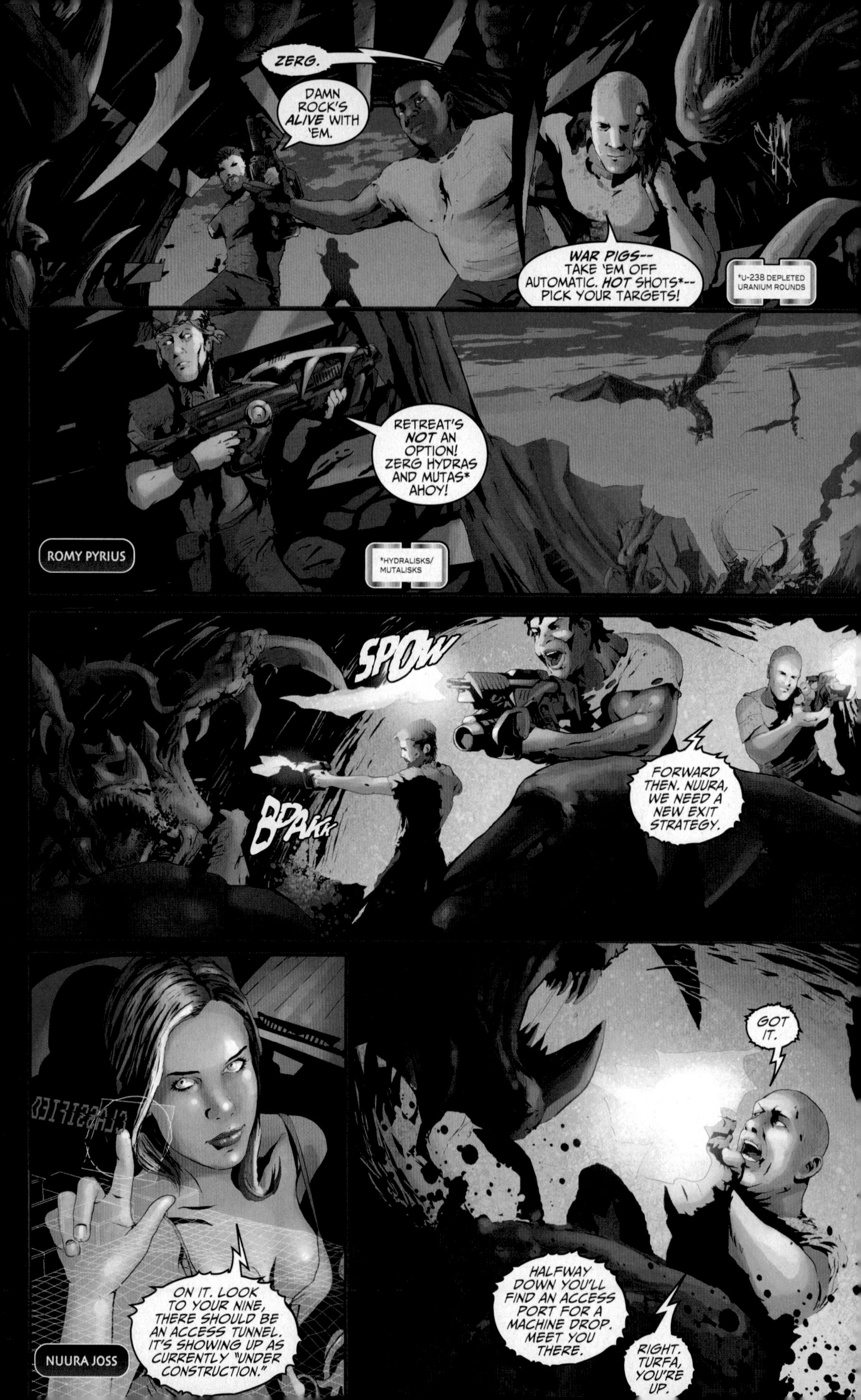

ZERG.
DAMN ROCK'S ALIVE WITH 'EM.
WAR PIGS-- TAKE 'EM OFF AUTOMATIC. HOT SHOTS*-- PICK YOUR TARGETS!
*U-238 DEPLETED URANIUM ROUNDS
ROMY PYRIUS
RETREAT'S NOT AN OPTION! ZERG HYDRAS AND MUTAS* AHOY!
*HYDRALISKS/ MUTALISKS
SPOW
BDAKK
FORWARD THEN. NUURA, WE NEED A NEW EXIT STRATEGY.
NUURA JOSS
ON IT. LOOK TO YOUR NINE, THERE SHOULD BE AN ACCESS TUNNEL. IT'S SHOWING UP AS CURRENTLY "UNDER CONSTRUCTION."
HALFWAY DOWN YOU'LL FIND AN ACCESS PORT FOR A MACHINE DROP. MEET YOU THERE.
RIGHT. TURFA, YOU'RE UP.
GOT IT.

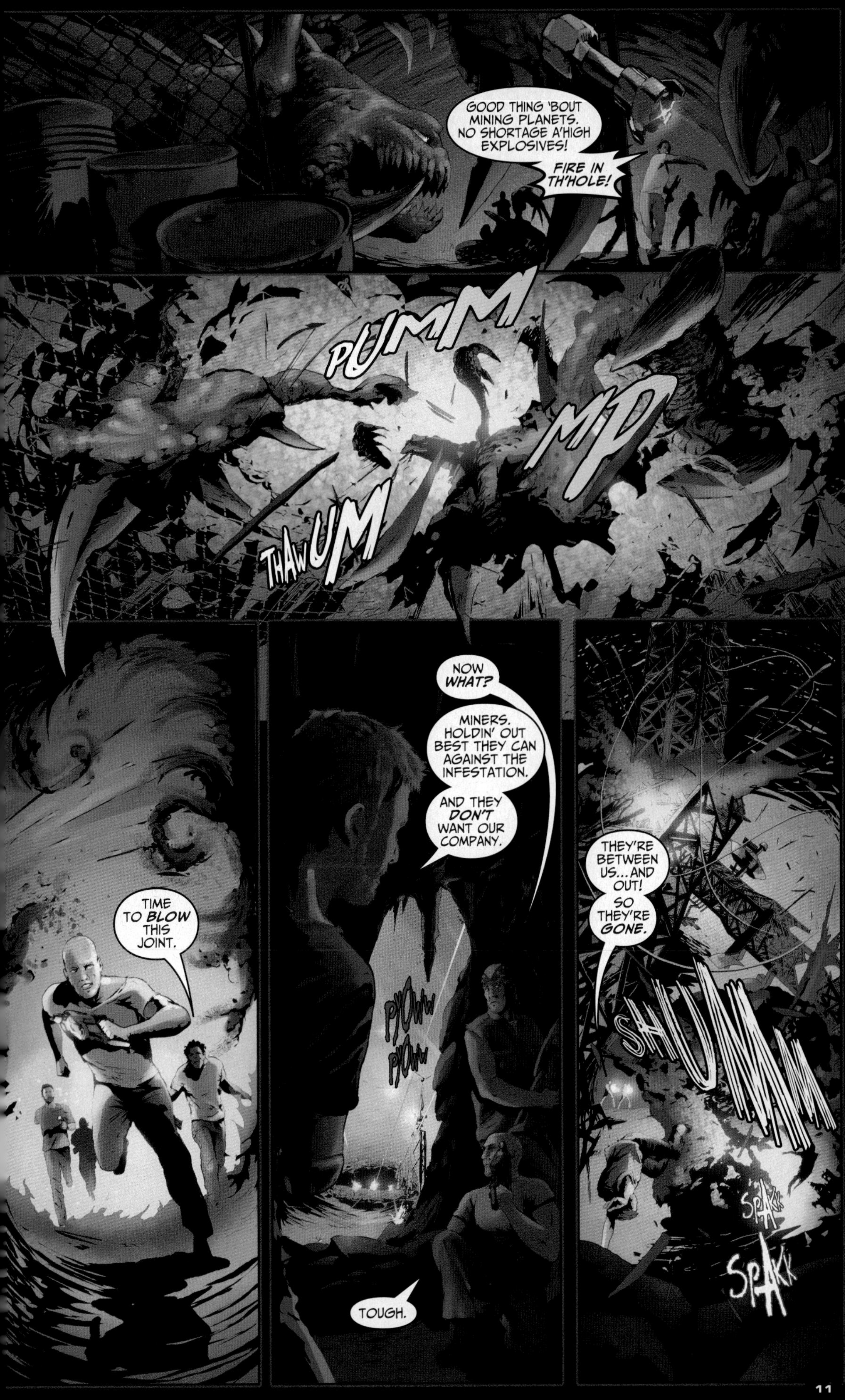
GOOD THING 'BOUT MINING PLANETS. NO SHORTAGE A'HIGH EXPLOSIVES!
FIRE IN TH'HOLE!
PUMM
THAWUMMP
TIME TO BLOW THIS JOINT.
NOW WHAT?
MINERS. HOLDIN' OUT BEST THEY CAN AGAINST THE INFESTATION.
AND THEY DON'T WANT OUR COMPANY.
PYOWW
PYOWW
TOUGH.
THEY'RE BETWEEN US...AND OUT! SO THEY'RE GONE.
SHUNAM
SPAKK
SPAKK

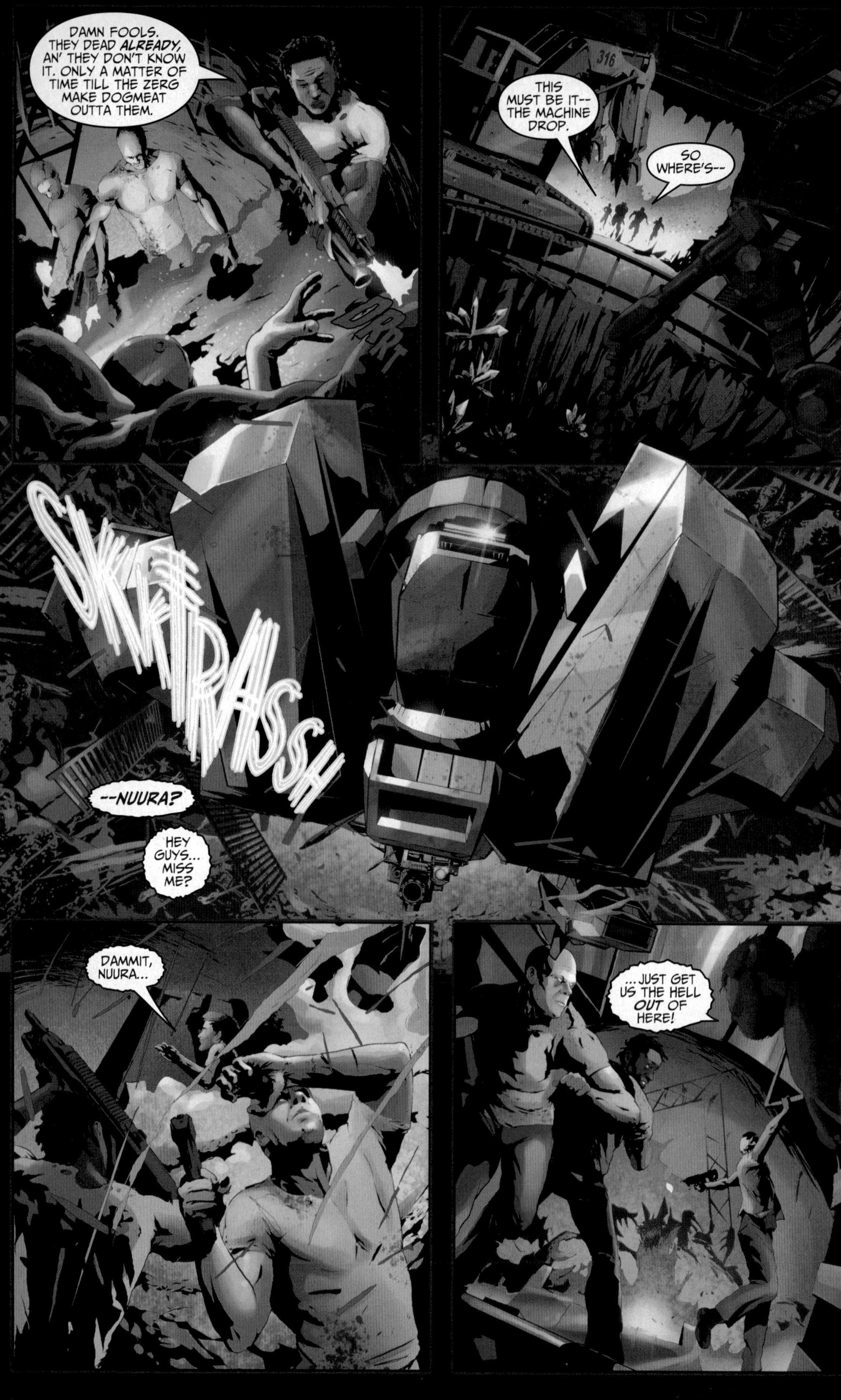
DAMN FOOLS. THEY DEAD ALREADY, AN' THEY DON'T KNOW IT. ONLY A MATTER OF TIME TILL THE ZERG MAKE DOGMEAT OUTTA THEM.
DRRT
THIS MUST BE IT-- THE MACHINE DROP.
SO WHERE'S--
SKRRASSH
--NUURA?
HEY GUYS... MISS ME?
DAMMIT, NUURA...
...JUST GET US THE HELL OUT OF HERE!

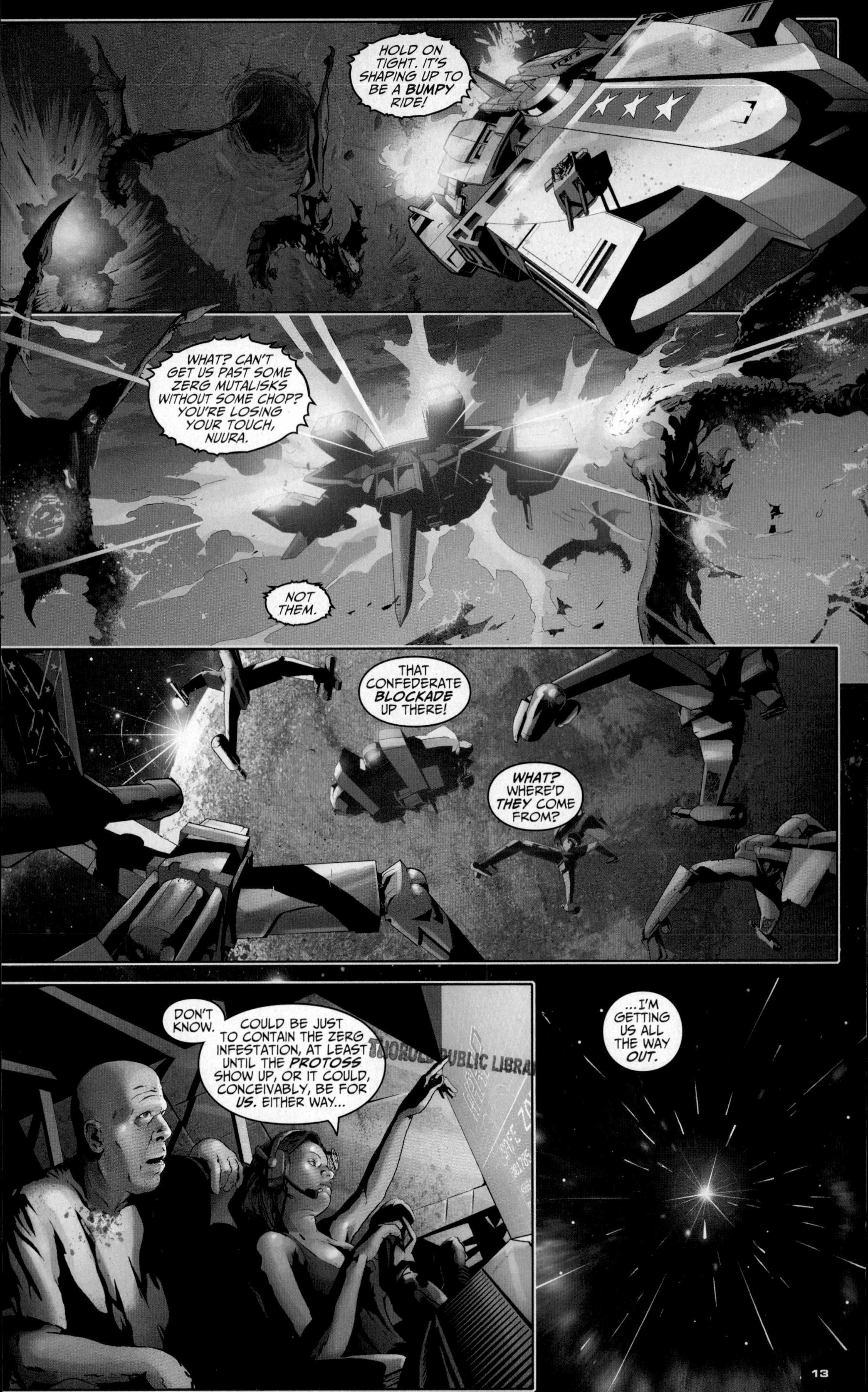
HOLD ON TIGHT. IT'S SHAPING UP TO BE A BUMPY RIDE!
WHAT? CAN'T GET US PAST SOME ZERG MUTALISKS WITHOUT SOME CHOP? YOU'RE LOSING YOUR TOUCH, NUURA.
NOT THEM.
THAT CONFEDERATE BLOCKADE UP THERE!
WHAT? WHERE'D THEY COME FROM?
DON'T KNOW.
COULD BE JUST TO CONTAIN THE ZERG INFESTATION, AT LEAST UNTIL THE PROTOSS SHOW UP, OR IT COULD, CONCEIVABLY, BE FOR US. EITHER WAY...
...I'M GETTING US ALL THE WAY OUT.

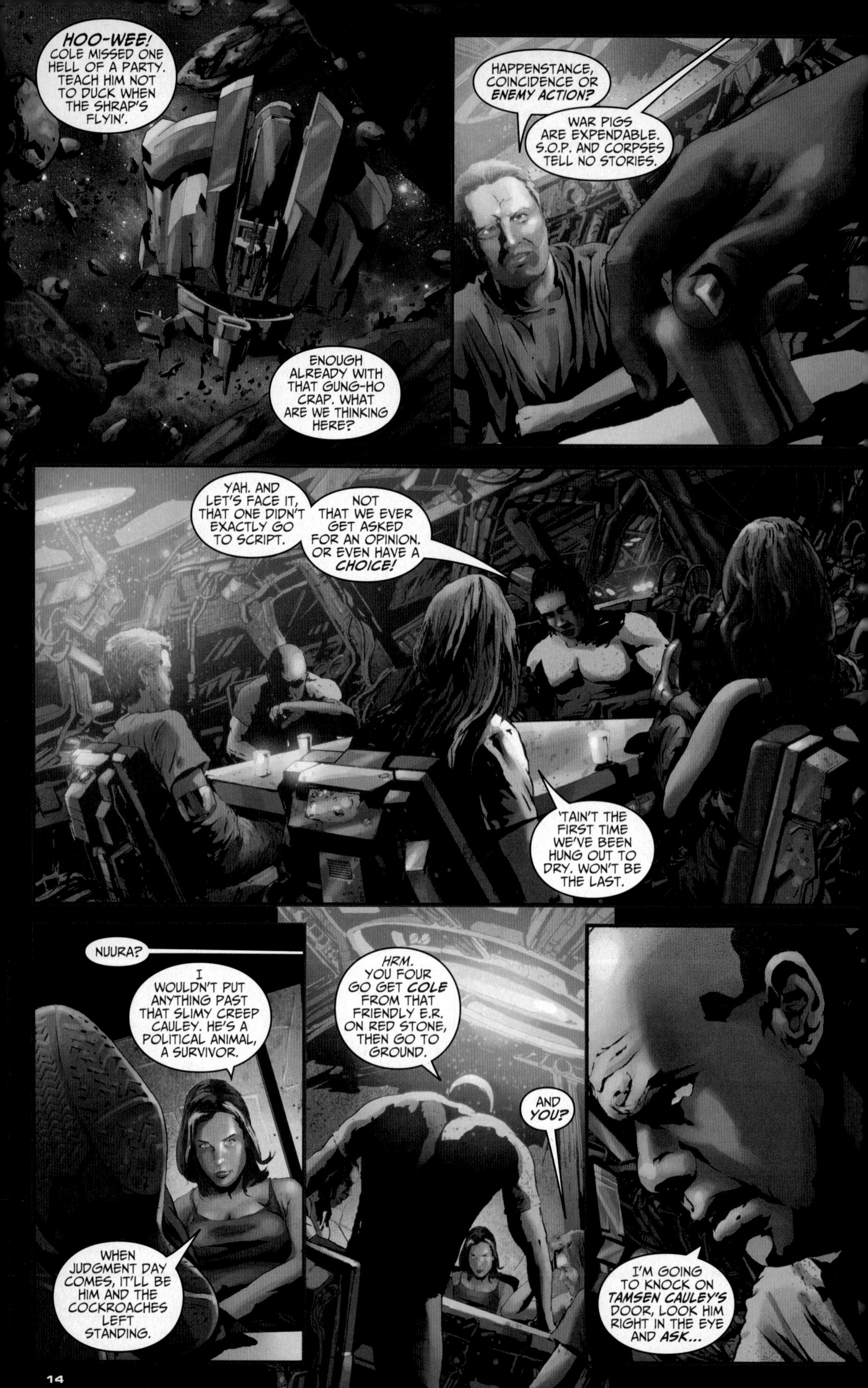
HOO-WEE! COLE MISSED ONE HELL OF A PARTY. TEACH HIM NOT TO DUCK WHEN THE SHRAP'S FLYIN'.
ENOUGH ALREADY WITH THAT GUNG-HO CRAP. WHAT ARE WE THINKING HERE?
HAPPENSTANCE, COINCIDENCE OR ENEMY ACTION?
WAR PIGS ARE EXPENDABLE. S.O.P. AND CORPSES TELL NO STORIES.
YAH. AND LET'S FACE IT, THAT ONE DIDN'T EXACTLY GO TO SCRIPT.
NOT THAT WE EVER GET ASKED FOR AN OPINION. OR EVEN HAVE A CHOICE!
'TAIN'T THE FIRST TIME WE'VE BEEN HUNG OUT TO DRY. WON'T BE THE LAST.
NUURA?
I WOULDN'T PUT ANYTHING PAST THAT SLIMY CREEP CAULEY. HE'S A POLITICAL ANIMAL, A SURVIVOR.
WHEN JUDGMENT DAY COMES, IT'LL BE HIM AND THE COCKROACHES LEFT STANDING.
HRM. YOU FOUR GO GET COLE FROM THAT FRIENDLY E.R. ON RED STONE, THEN GO TO GROUND.
AND YOU?
I'M GOING TO KNOCK ON TAMSEN CAULEY'S DOOR, LOOK HIM RIGHT IN THE EYE AND ASK...

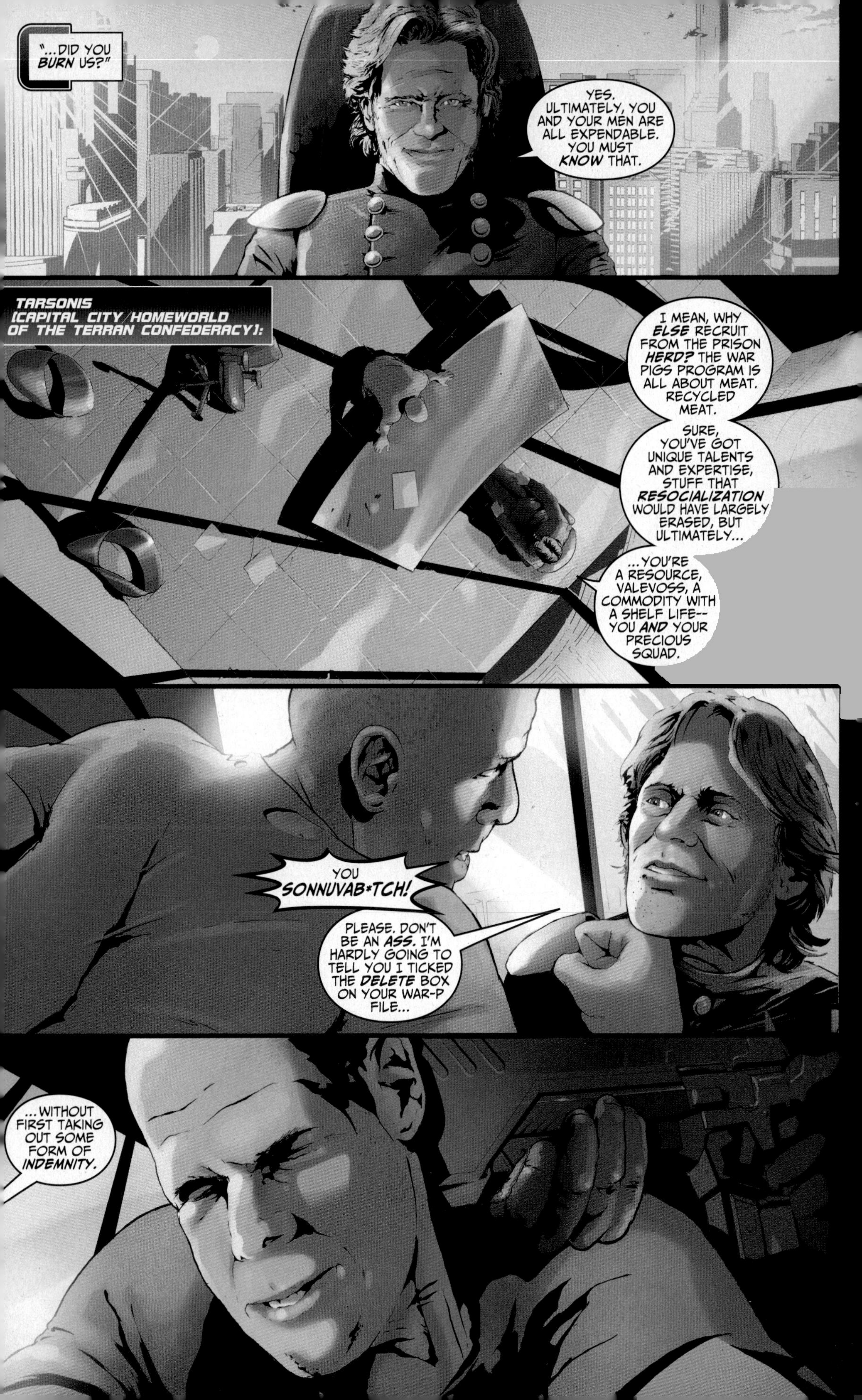
"...DID YOU BURN US?"
YES. ULTIMATELY, YOU AND YOUR MEN ARE ALL EXPENDABLE. YOU MUST KNOW THAT.
TARSONIS [CAPITAL CITY/HOMEWORLD OF THE TERRAN CONFEDERACY]:
I MEAN, WHY ELSE RECRUIT FROM THE PRISON HERD? THE WAR PIGS PROGRAM IS ALL ABOUT MEAT. RECYCLED MEAT.
SURE, YOU'VE GOT UNIQUE TALENTS AND EXPERTISE, STUFF THAT RESOCIALIZATION WOULD HAVE LARGELY ERASED, BUT ULTIMATELY...
...YOU'RE A RESOURCE, VALEVOSS, A COMMODITY WITH A SHELF LIFE-- YOU AND YOUR PRECIOUS SQUAD.
YOU SONNUVAB*TCH!
PLEASE. DON'T BE AN ASS. I'M HARDLY GOING TO TELL YOU I TICKED THE DELETE BOX ON YOUR WAR-P FILE...
...WITHOUT FIRST TAKING OUT SOME FORM OF INDEMNITY.

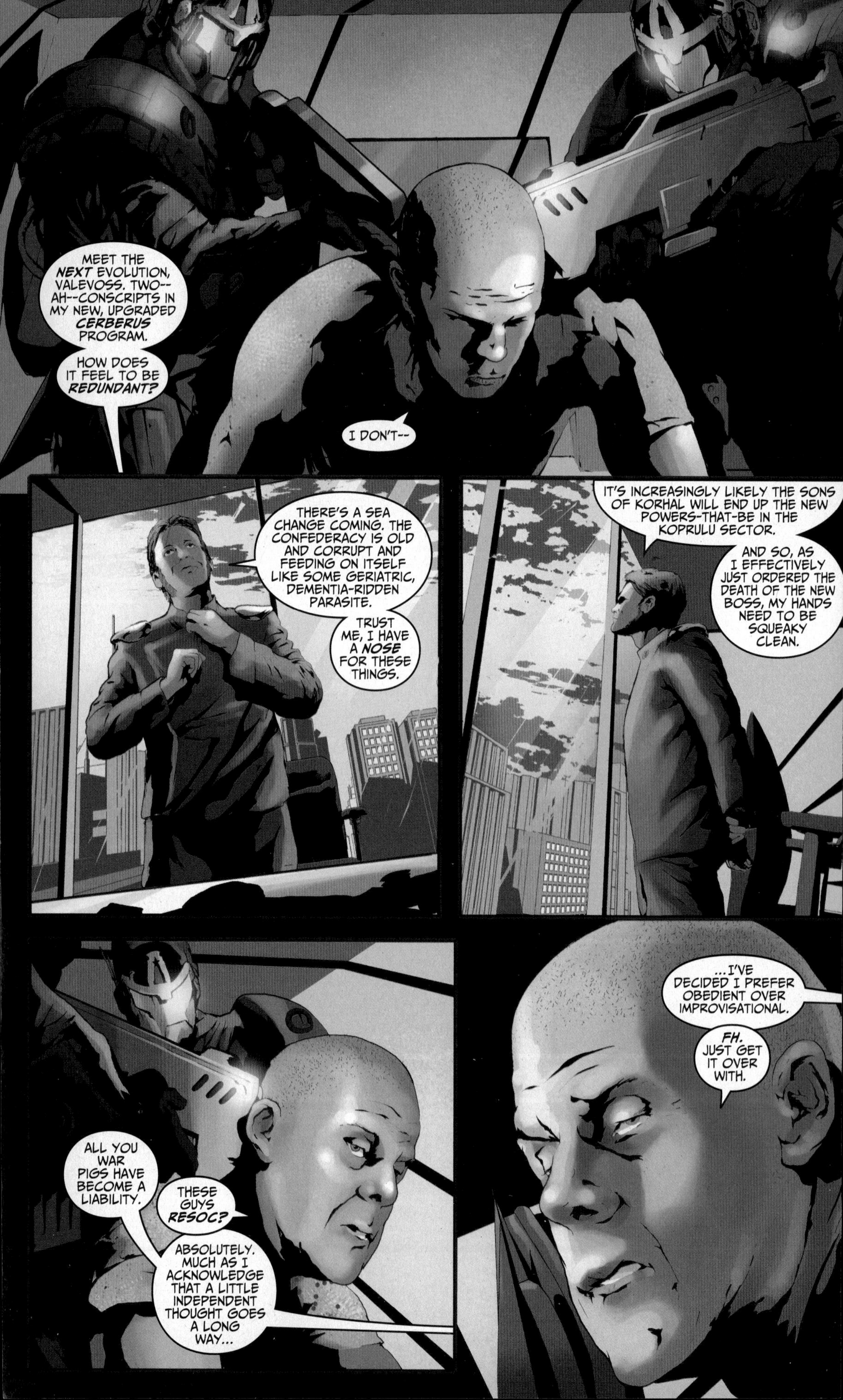
MEET THE NEXT EVOLUTION, VALEVOSS. TWO--AH--CONSCRIPTS IN MY NEW, UPGRADED CERBERUS PROGRAM.
HOW DOES IT FEEL TO BE REDUNDANT?
I DON'T--
THERE'S A SEA CHANGE COMING. THE CONFEDERACY IS OLD AND CORRUPT AND FEEDING ON ITSELF LIKE SOME GERIATRIC, DEMENTIA-RIDDEN PARASITE.
TRUST ME, I HAVE A NOSE FOR THESE THINGS.
IT'S INCREASINGLY LIKELY THE SONS OF KORHAL WILL END UP THE NEW POWERS-THAT-BE IN THE KOPRULU SECTOR.
AND SO, AS I EFFECTIVELY JUST ORDERED THE DEATH OF THE NEW BOSS, MY HANDS NEED TO BE SQUEAKY CLEAN.
ALL YOU WAR PIGS HAVE BECOME A LIABILITY.
THESE GUYS RESOC?
ABSOLUTELY. MUCH AS I ACKNOWLEDGE THAT A LITTLE INDEPENDENT THOUGHT GOES A LONG WAY...
...I'VE DECIDED I PREFER OBEDIENT OVER IMPROVISATIONAL.
FH. JUST GET IT OVER WITH.

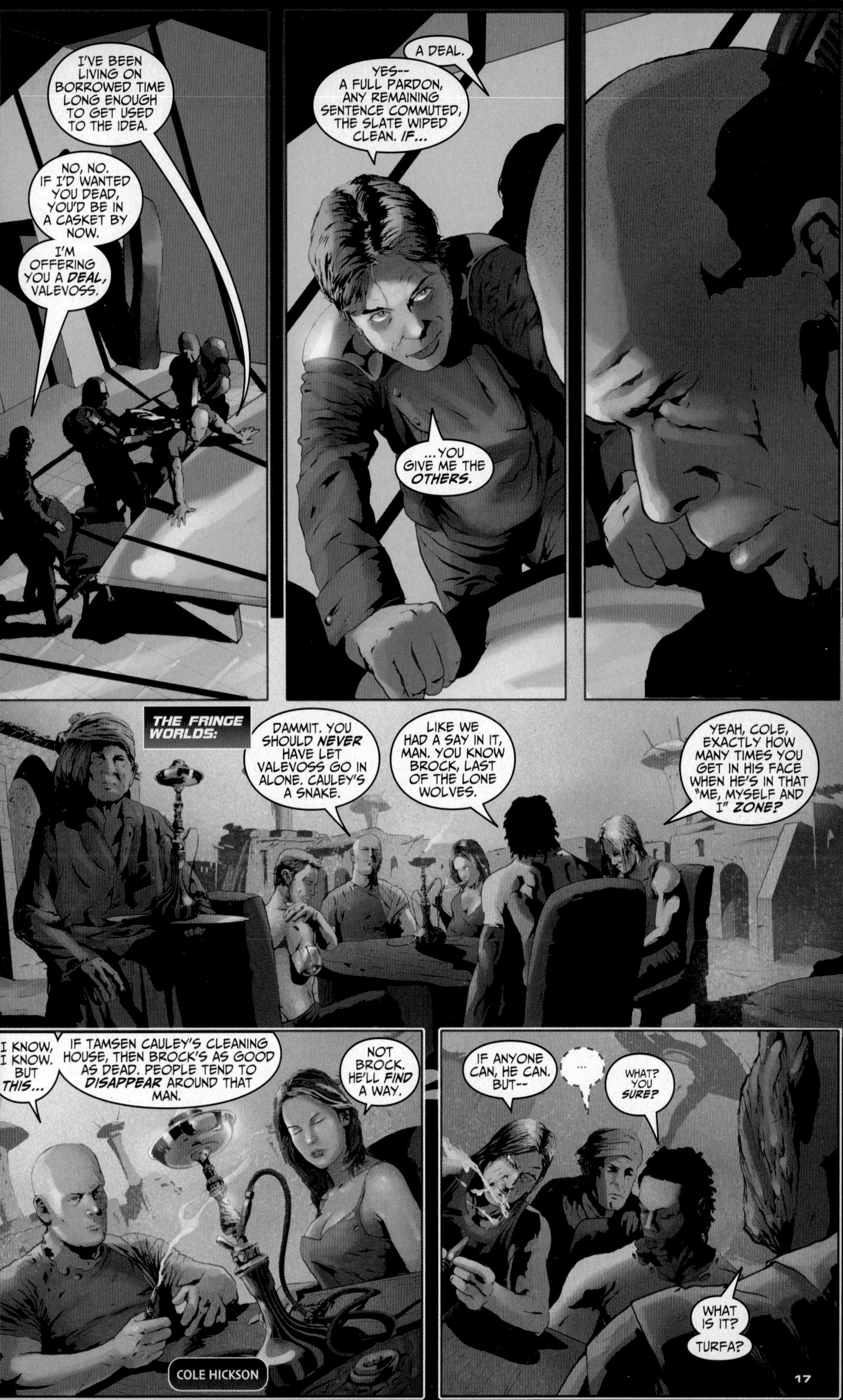

I'VE BEEN LIVING ON BORROWED TIME LONG ENOUGH TO GET USED TO THE IDEA.
NO, NO. IF I'D WANTED YOU DEAD, YOU'D BE IN A CASKET BY NOW.
I'M OFFERING YOU A DEAL, VALEVOSS.
A DEAL.
YES-- A FULL PARDON, ANY REMAINING SENTENCE COMMUTED, THE SLATE WIPED CLEAN. IF...
...YOU GIVE ME THE OTHERS.
THE FRINGE WORLDS:
DAMMIT. YOU SHOULD NEVER HAVE LET VALEVOSS GO IN ALONE. CAULEY'S A SNAKE.
LIKE WE HAD A SAY IN IT, MAN. YOU KNOW BROCK, LAST OF THE LONE WOLVES.
YEAH, COLE, EXACTLY HOW MANY TIMES YOU GET IN HIS FACE WHEN HE'S IN THAT "ME, MYSELF AND I" ZONE?
I KNOW, I KNOW. BUT THIS...
IF TAMSEN CAULEY'S CLEANING HOUSE, THEN BROCK'S AS GOOD AS DEAD. PEOPLE TEND TO DISAPPEAR AROUND THAT MAN.
NOT BROCK. HE'LL FIND A WAY.
COLE HICKSON
IF ANYONE CAN, HE CAN. BUT--
...
WHAT? YOU SURE?
WHAT IS IT?
TURFA?

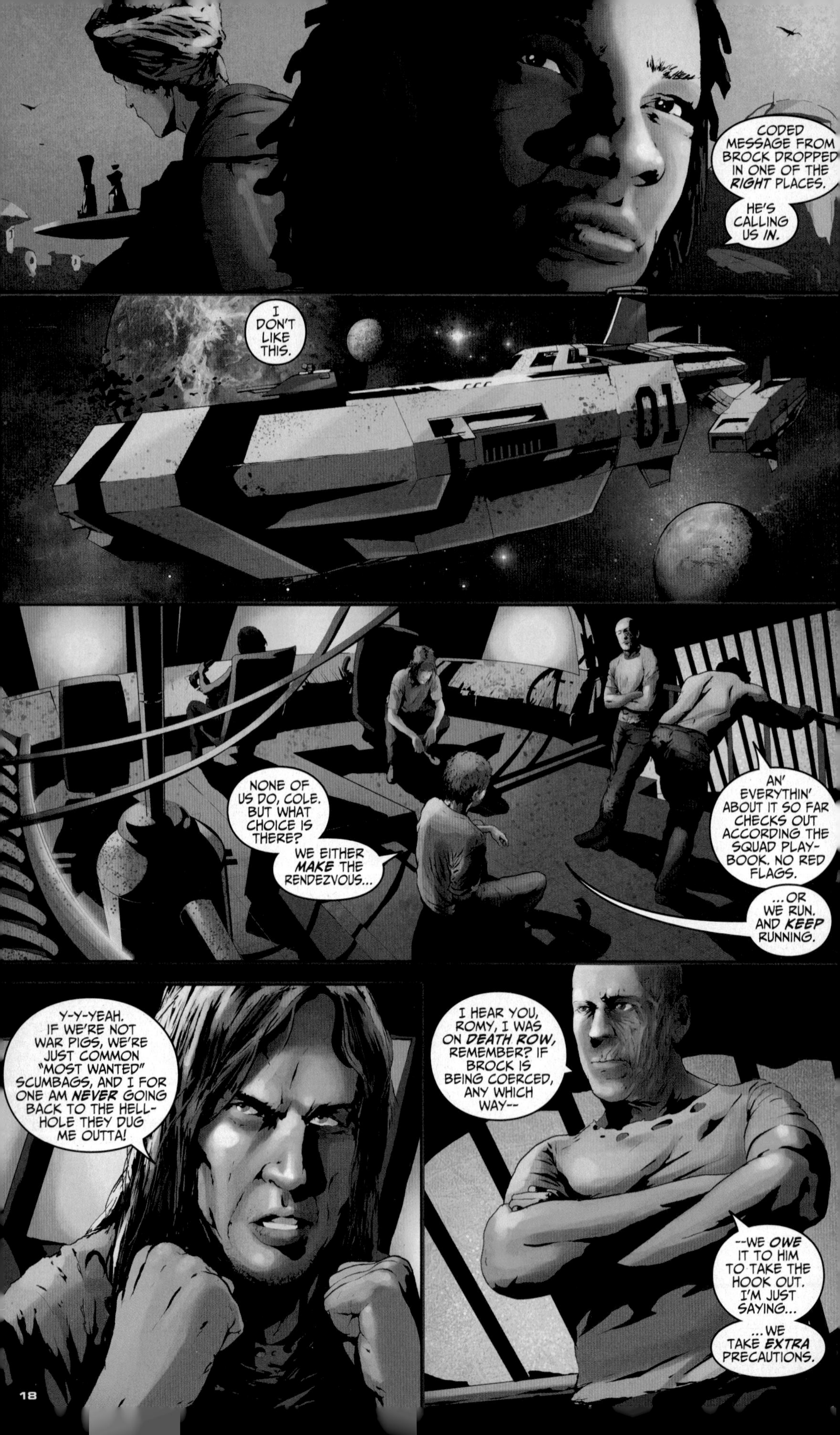
CODED MESSAGE FROM BROCK DROPPED IN ONE OF THE RIGHT PLACES.
HE'S CALLING US IN.
I DON'T LIKE THIS.
NONE OF US DO, COLE. BUT WHAT CHOICE IS THERE?
WE EITHER MAKE THE RENDEZVOUS...
AN' EVERYTHIN' ABOUT IT SO FAR CHECKS OUT ACCORDING THE SQUAD PLAY-BOOK. NO RED FLAGS.
...OR WE RUN. AND KEEP RUNNING.
Y-Y-YEAH. IF WE'RE NOT WAR PIGS, WE'RE JUST COMMON "MOST WANTED" SCUMBAGS, AND I FOR ONE AM NEVER GOING BACK TO THE HELL-HOLE THEY DUG ME OUTTA!
I HEAR YOU, ROMY, I WAS ON DEATH ROW, REMEMBER? IF BROCK IS BEING COERCED, ANY WHICH WAY--
--WE OWE IT TO HIM TO TAKE THE HOOK OUT. I'M JUST SAYING...
...WE TAKE EXTRA PRECAUTIONS.

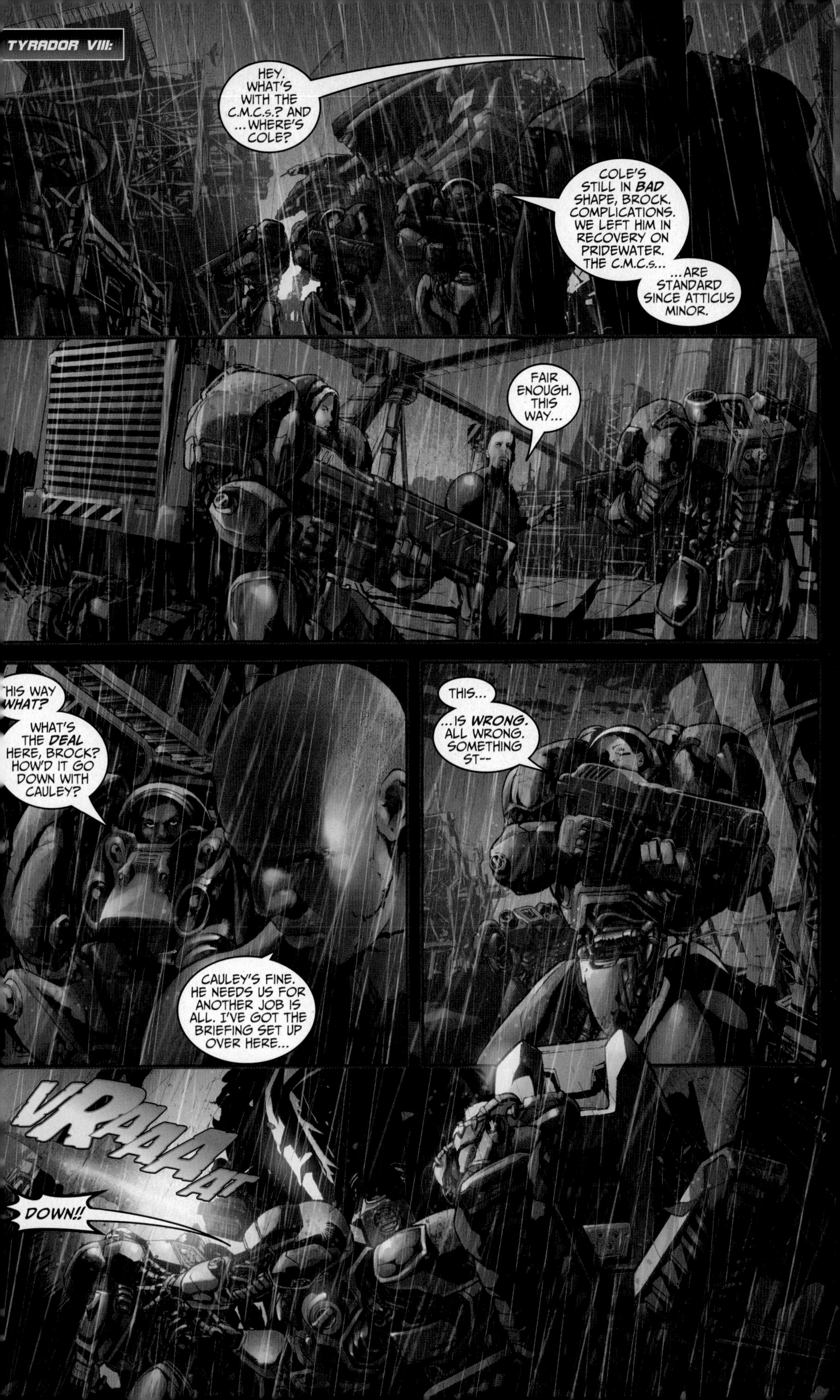
TYRADOR VIII:
HEY. WHAT'S WITH THE C.M.C.s.? AND ...WHERE'S COLE?
COLE'S STILL IN BAD SHAPE, BROCK. COMPLICATIONS. WE LEFT HIM IN RECOVERY ON PRIDEWATER. THE C.M.C.s...
...ARE STANDARD SINCE ATTICUS MINOR.
FAIR ENOUGH. THIS WAY...
THIS WAY WHAT?
WHAT'S THE DEAL HERE, BROCK? HOW'D IT GO DOWN WITH CAULEY?
CAULEY'S FINE. HE NEEDS US FOR ANOTHER JOB IS ALL. I'VE GOT THE BRIEFING SET UP OVER HERE...
THIS...
...IS WRONG. ALL WRONG. SOMETHING ST--
VRAAAAT
DOWN!!

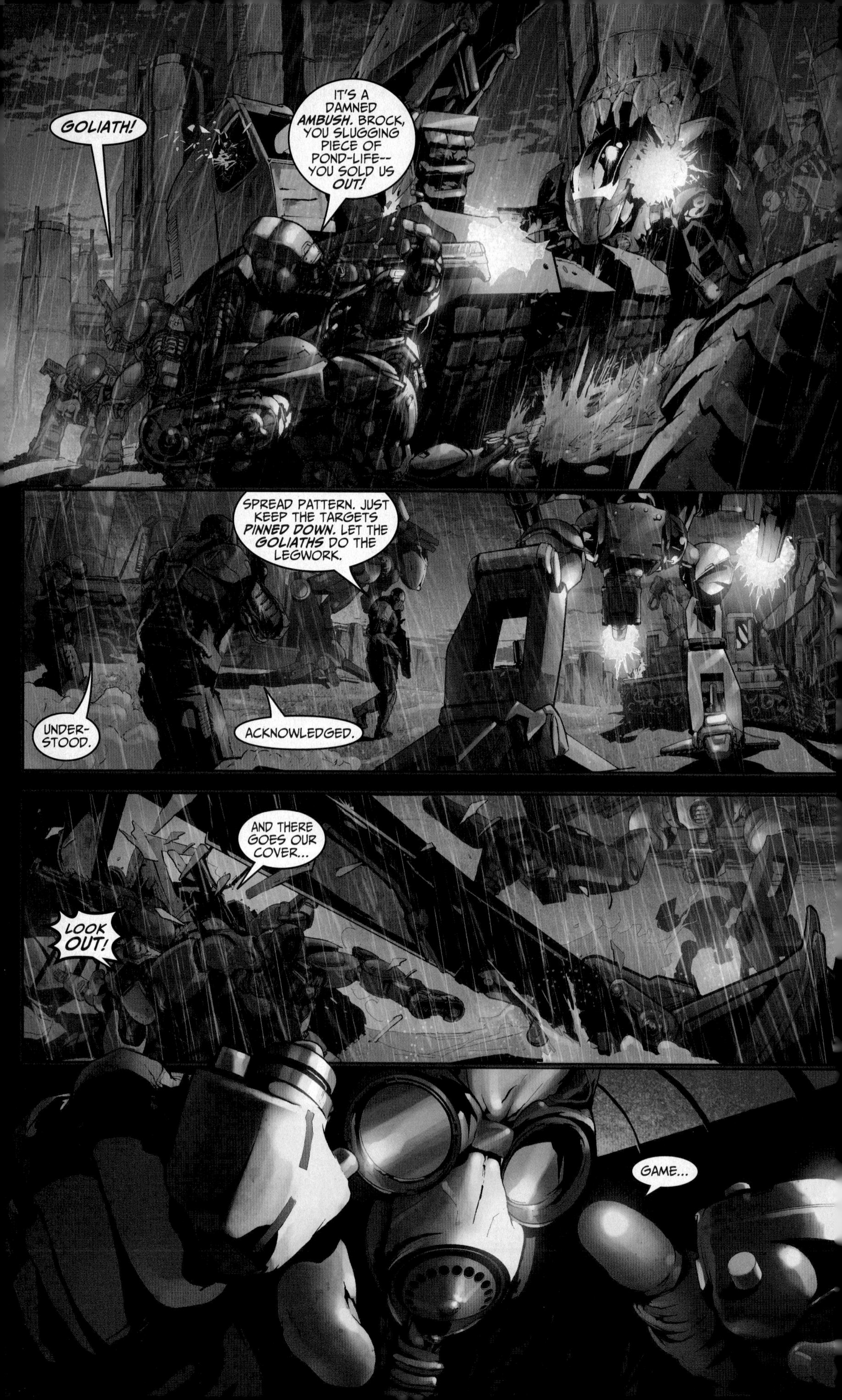
GOLIATH!
IT'S A DAMNED AMBUSH. BROCK, YOU SLUGGING PIECE OF POND-LIFE-- YOU SOLD US OUT!
SPREAD PATTERN. JUST KEEP THE TARGETS PINNED DOWN. LET THE GOLIATHS DO THE LEGWORK.
UNDER-STOOD.
ACKNOWLEDGED.
AND THERE GOES OUR COVER...
LOOK OUT!
GAME...

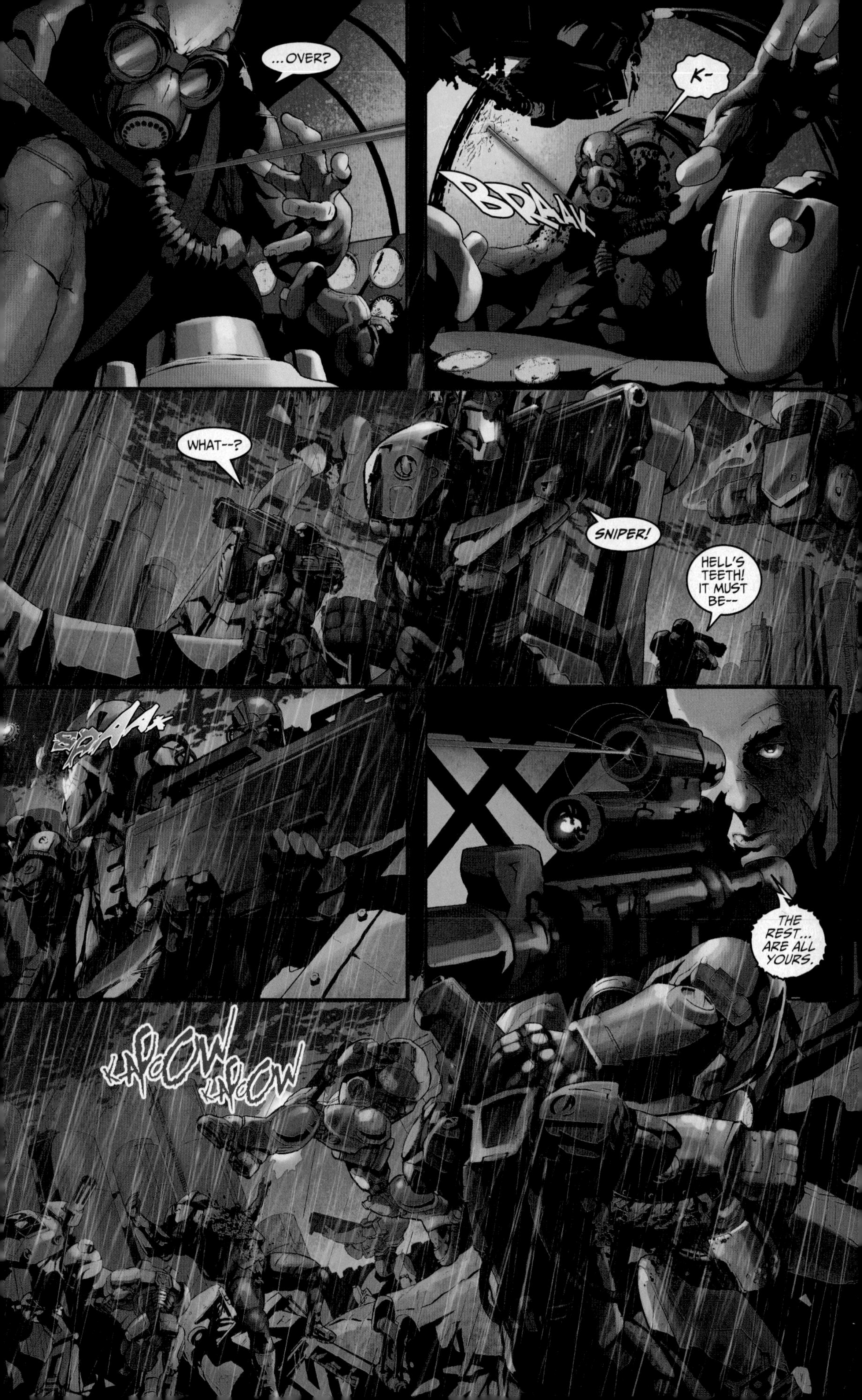
...OVER?
K-
BSRAAK
WHAT--?
SNIPER!
HELL'S TEETH! IT MUST BE--
THE REST... ARE ALL YOURS.

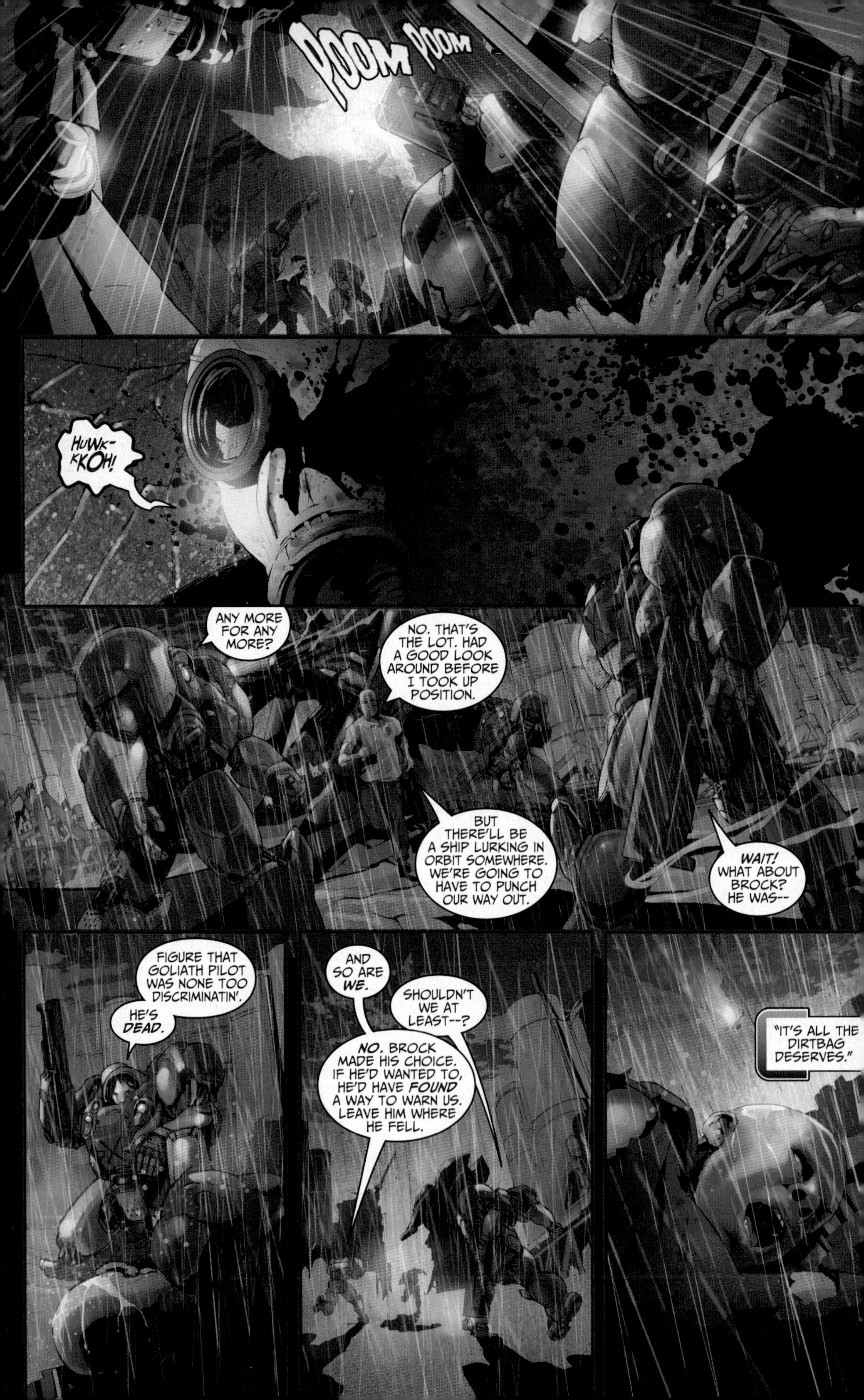
POOM POOM
HUWK-KKOH!
ANY MORE FOR ANY MORE?
NO. THAT'S THE LOT. HAD A GOOD LOOK AROUND BEFORE I TOOK UP POSITION.
BUT THERE'LL BE A SHIP LURKING IN ORBIT SOMEWHERE. WE'RE GOING TO HAVE TO PUNCH OUR WAY OUT.
WAIT! WHAT ABOUT BROCK? HE WAS--
HE'S DEAD.
FIGURE THAT GOLIATH PILOT WAS NONE TOO DISCRIMINATIN'.
AND SO ARE WE.
SHOULDN'T WE AT LEAST--?
NO. BROCK MADE HIS CHOICE. IF HE'D WANTED TO, HE'D HAVE FOUND A WAY TO WARN US. LEAVE HIM WHERE HE FELL.
"IT'S ALL THE DIRTBAG DESERVES."

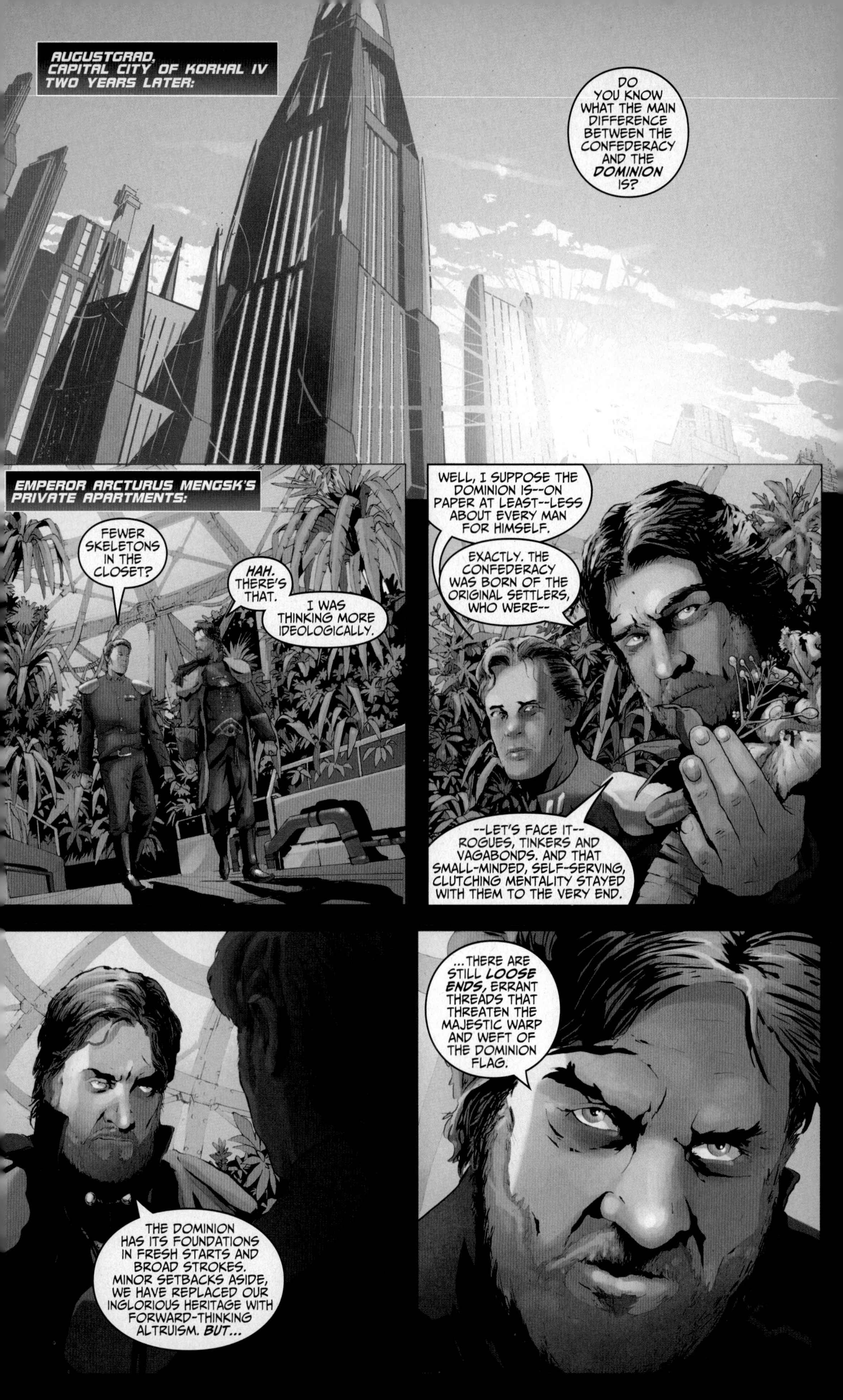
AUGUSTGRAD, CAPITAL CITY OF KORHAL IV TWO YEARS LATER:
DO YOU KNOW WHAT THE MAIN DIFFERENCE BETWEEN THE CONFEDERACY AND THE *DOMINION* IS?
EMPEROR ARCTURUS MENGSK'S PRIVATE APARTMENTS:
FEWER SKELETONS IN THE CLOSET?
HAH. THERE'S THAT.
I WAS THINKING MORE IDEOLOGICALLY.
WELL, I SUPPOSE THE DOMINION IS--ON PAPER AT LEAST--LESS ABOUT EVERY MAN FOR HIMSELF.
EXACTLY. THE CONFEDERACY WAS BORN OF THE ORIGINAL SETTLERS, WHO WERE--
--LET'S FACE IT-- ROGUES, TINKERS AND VAGABONDS. AND THAT SMALL-MINDED, SELF-SERVING, CLUTCHING MENTALITY STAYED WITH THEM TO THE VERY END.
THE DOMINION HAS ITS FOUNDATIONS IN FRESH STARTS AND BROAD STROKES. MINOR SETBACKS ASIDE, WE HAVE REPLACED OUR INGLORIOUS HERITAGE WITH FORWARD-THINKING ALTRUISM. *BUT...*
...THERE ARE STILL *LOOSE ENDS,* ERRANT THREADS THAT THREATEN THE MAJESTIC WARP AND WEFT OF THE DOMINION FLAG.

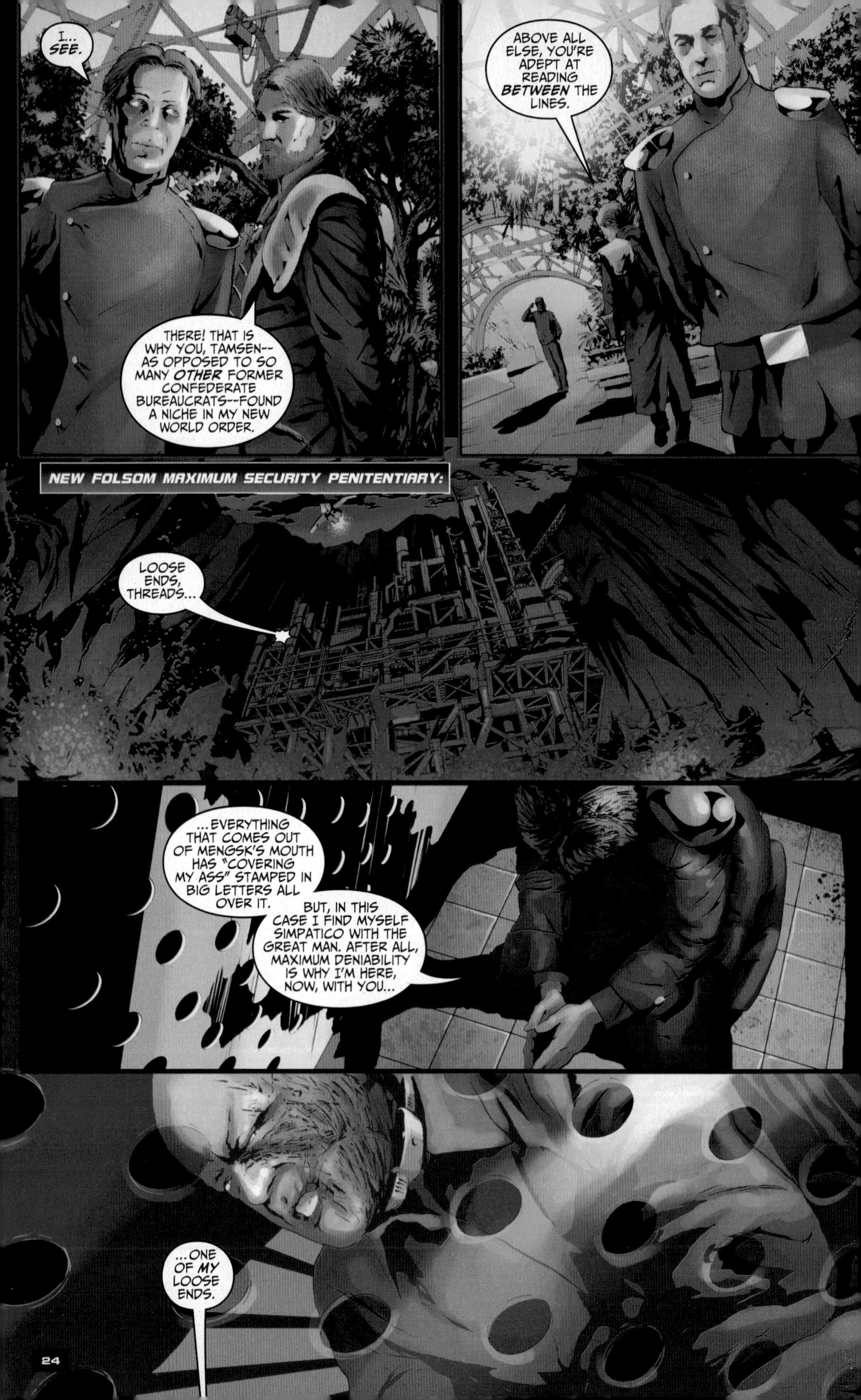
I... SEE.
THERE! THAT IS WHY YOU, TAMSEN--AS OPPOSED TO SO MANY OTHER FORMER CONFEDERATE BUREAUCRATS--FOUND A NICHE IN MY NEW WORLD ORDER.
ABOVE ALL ELSE, YOU'RE ADEPT AT READING BETWEEN THE LINES.
NEW FOLSOM MAXIMUM SECURITY PENITENTIARY:
LOOSE ENDS, THREADS...
...EVERYTHING THAT COMES OUT OF MENGSK'S MOUTH HAS "COVERING MY ASS" STAMPED IN BIG LETTERS ALL OVER IT.
BUT, IN THIS CASE I FIND MYSELF SIMPATICO WITH THE GREAT MAN. AFTER ALL, MAXIMUM DENIABILITY IS WHY I'M HERE, NOW, WITH YOU...
...ONE OF MY LOOSE ENDS.

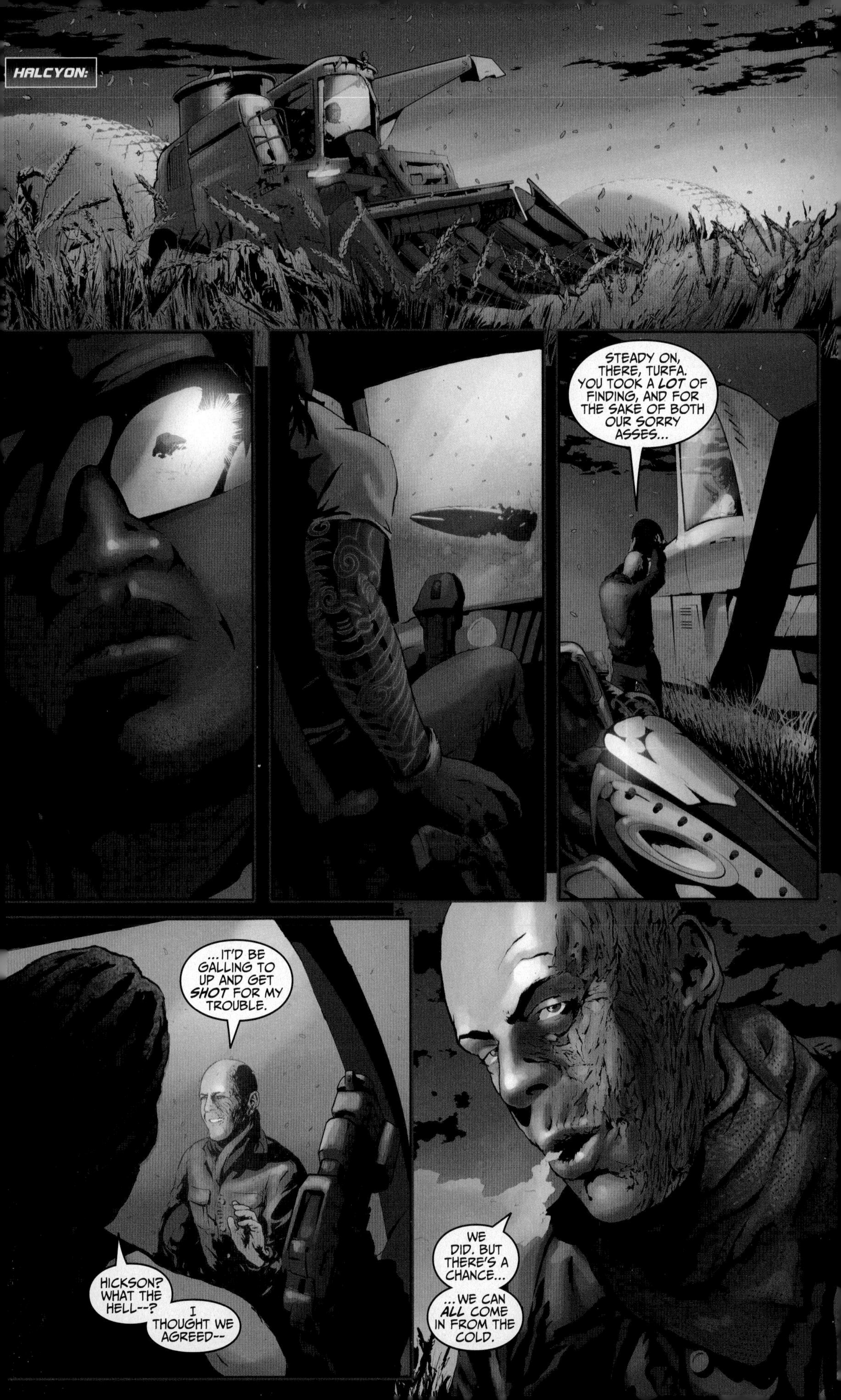
HALCYON:
STEADY ON, THERE, TURFA. YOU TOOK A LOT OF FINDING, AND FOR THE SAKE OF BOTH OUR SORRY ASSES...
...IT'D BE GALLING TO UP AND GET SHOT FOR MY TROUBLE.
HICKSON? WHAT THE HELL--?
I THOUGHT WE AGREED--
WE DID. BUT THERE'S A CHANCE...
...WE CAN ALL COME IN FROM THE COLD.

AND YOU *BELIEVE* HIM?

IT'S A BRAVE NEW WORLD, TURFA. CAULEY NO LONGER HAS HIS OWN DEDICATED AND LABYRINTHINE SUPPORT NETWORK.

MUCH AS HE MIGHT NOT LIKE IT, MENGSK HAS HIM ON A PRETTY TIGHT LEASH.

AND THE DEAL IS *WHAT* EXACTLY?

PUT OUR SQUAD BACK TOGETHER FOR ONE LAST MISSION. DO IT RIGHT AND WE'RE FREE MEN. FULL PARDON, BACK PAY, THE LOT.

ONE *BIG* HAPPY FAMILY, EH. REMEMBER WHAT HAPPENED *LAST* TIME?

I KNOW, I KNOW. THERE'S A LOT TO FORGIVE AND FORGET. WHEN CAULEY BROUGHT IT TO ME, MY FIRST REACTION WAS TO TELL HIM TO STUFF IT.

BUT THE ALTERNATIVE IS TO KEEP SCRAPING AROUND FOR PISS-AWFUL JOBS IN THE ASS END OF NOWHERE. I'M *TIRED*, TURFA...

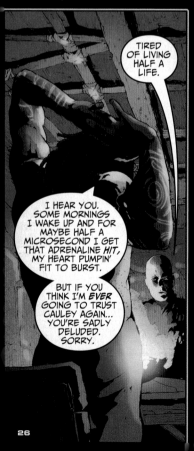

TIRED OF LIVING HALF A LIFE.

I HEAR YOU. SOME MORNINGS I WAKE UP AND FOR MAYBE HALF A MICROSECOND I GET THAT ADRENALINE *HIT*, MY HEART PUMPIN' FIT TO BURST.

BUT IF YOU THINK I'M *EVER* GOING TO TRUST CAULEY AGAIN... YOU'RE SADLY DELUDED. SORRY.

UM. JUST OUTTA CURIOSITY, WHAT'S THE JOB?

STANDARD. LOCATE AND ELIMINATE.

THE MARK?

EX-CONFEDERATE MARSHAL, RENEGADE, AND ALL ROUND THORN IN MENGSK'S BUTT.

JIM RAYNOR.

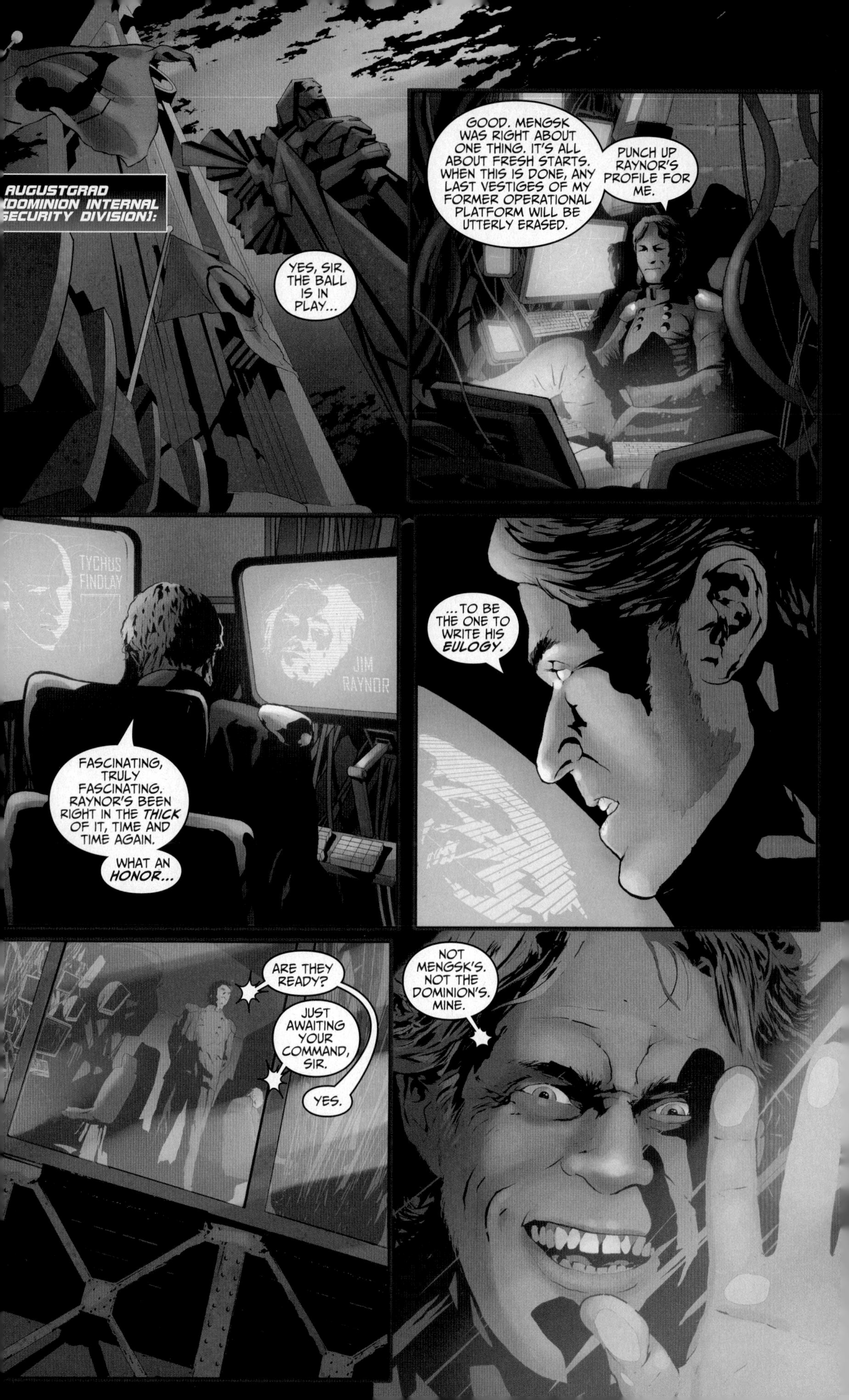
AUGUSTGRAD [DOMINION INTERNAL SECURITY DIVISION]:
YES, SIR. THE BALL IS IN PLAY...
GOOD. MENGSK WAS RIGHT ABOUT ONE THING. IT'S ALL ABOUT FRESH STARTS. WHEN THIS IS DONE, ANY LAST VESTIGES OF MY FORMER OPERATIONAL PLATFORM WILL BE UTTERLY ERASED.
PUNCH UP RAYNOR'S PROFILE FOR ME.
TYCHUS FINDLAY
JIM RAYNOR
FASCINATING, TRULY FASCINATING. RAYNOR'S BEEN RIGHT IN THE *THICK* OF IT, TIME AND TIME AGAIN.
WHAT AN *HONOR...*
...TO BE THE ONE TO WRITE HIS *EULOGY.*
ARE THEY READY?
JUST AWAITING YOUR COMMAND, SIR.
YES.
NOT MENGSK'S. NOT THE DOMINION'S. MINE.

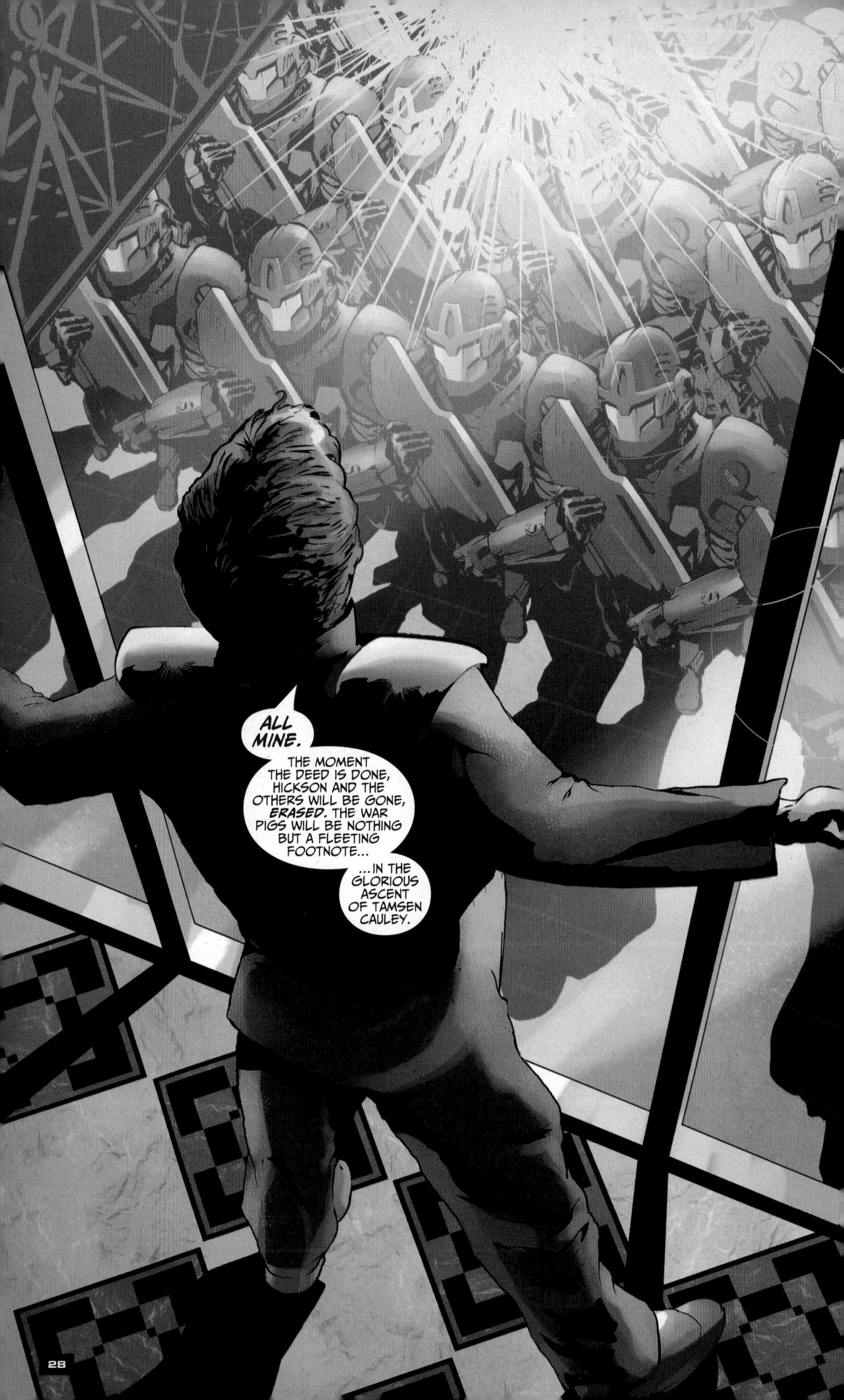
ALL MINE.
THE MOMENT THE DEED IS DONE, HICKSON AND THE OTHERS WILL BE GONE, ERASED. THE WAR PIGS WILL BE NOTHING BUT A FLEETING FOOTNOTE...
...IN THE GLORIOUS ASCENT OF TAMSEN CAULEY.

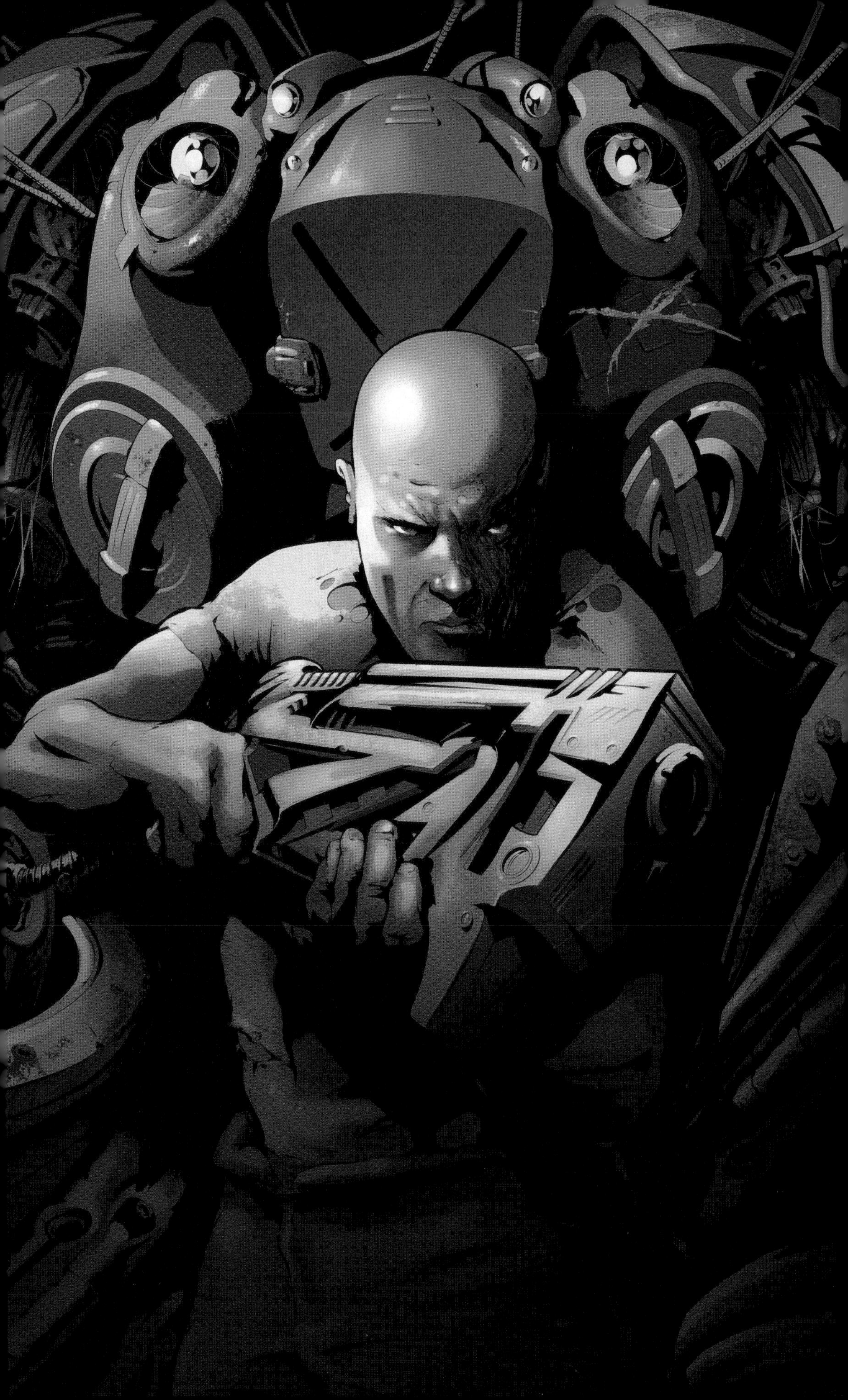

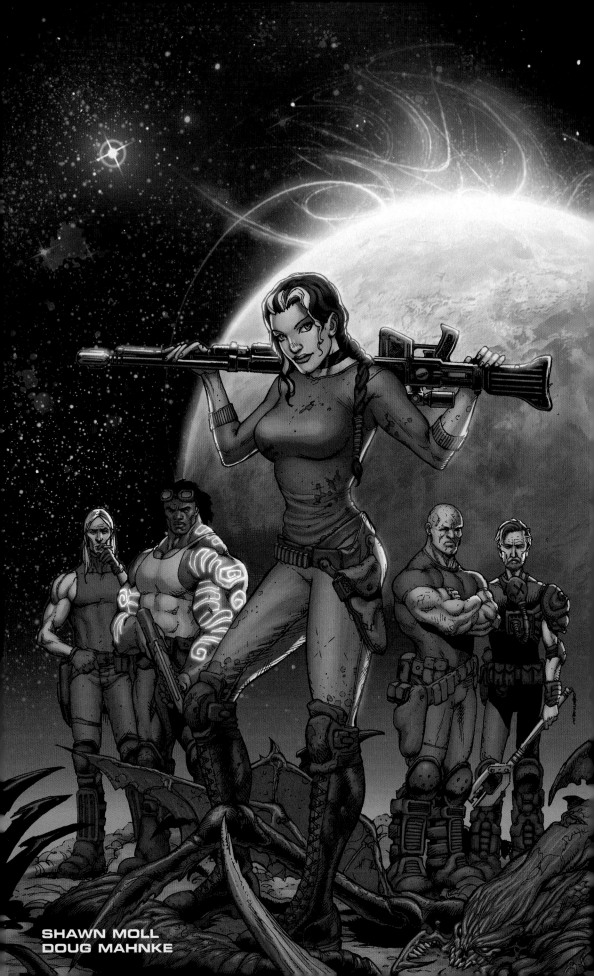

SHAWN MOLL
DOUG MAHNKE

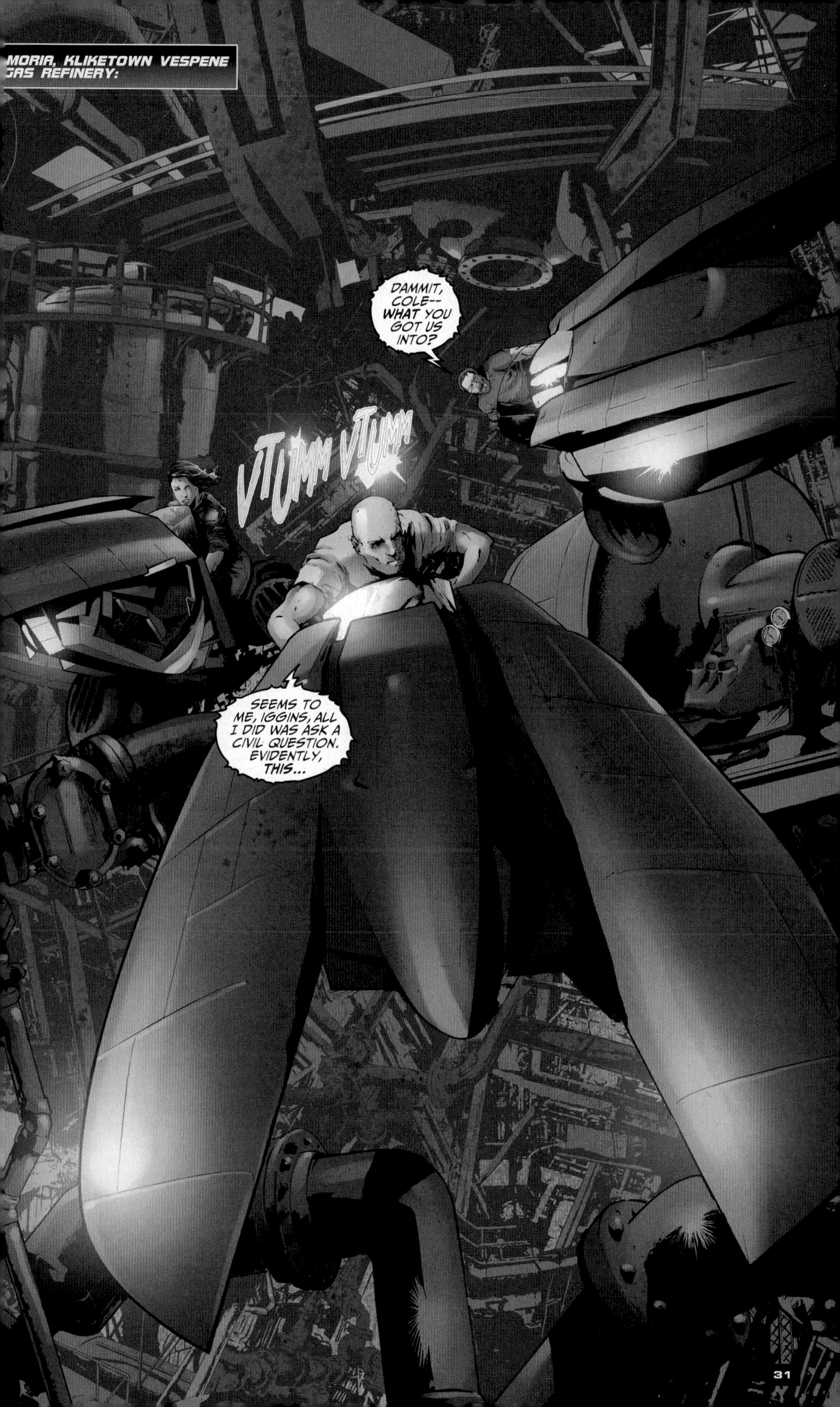
MORIA, KLIKETOWN VESPENE
GAS REFINERY:
DAMMIT, COLE-- WHAT YOU GOT US INTO?
VTUMM VTUMM
SEEMS TO ME, IGGINS, ALL I DID WAS ASK A CIVIL QUESTION. EVIDENTLY, THIS...

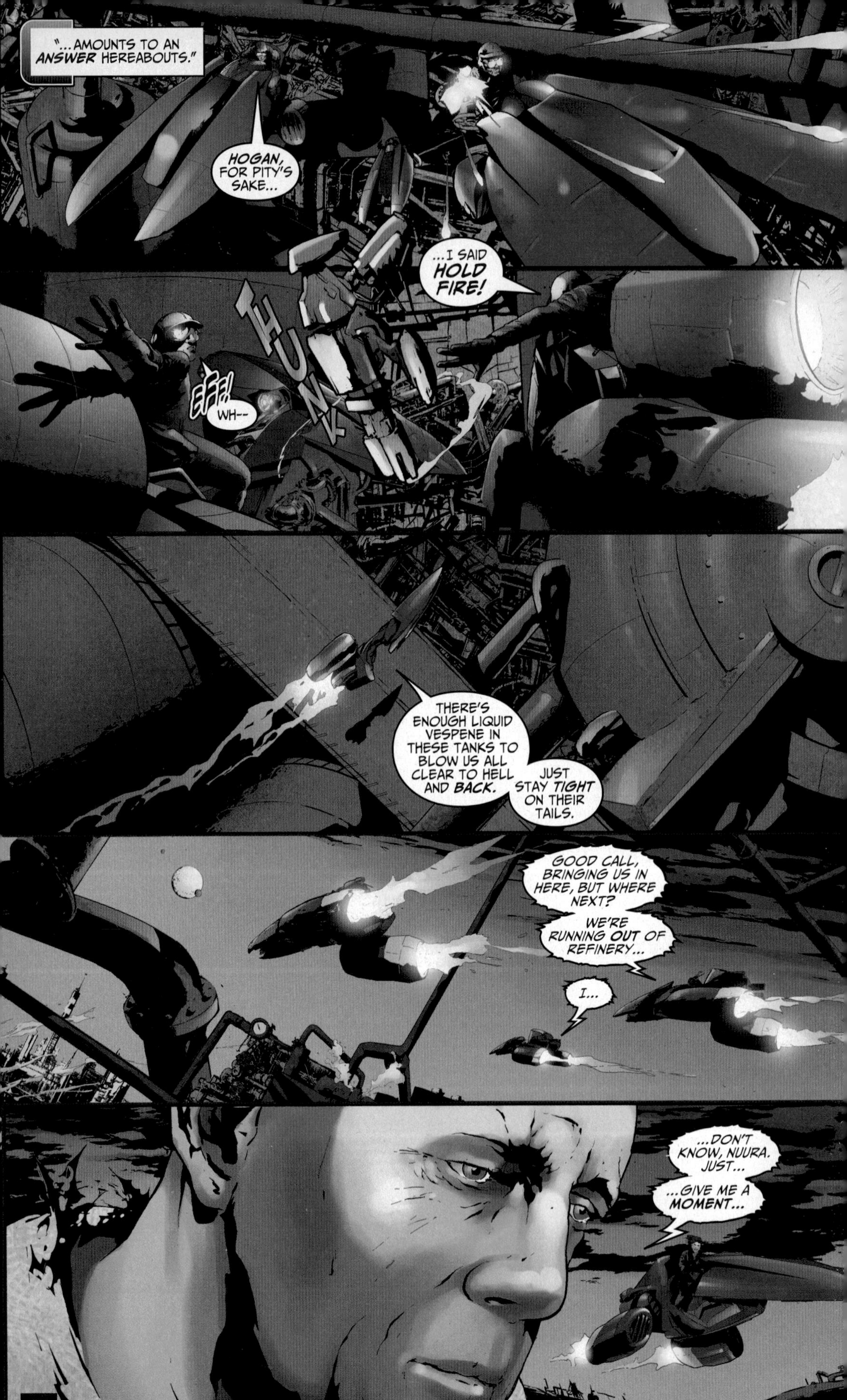
"...AMOUNTS TO AN ANSWER HEREABOUTS."
HOGAN, FOR PITY'S SAKE...
...I SAID HOLD FIRE!
THUNK
EFF! WH--
THERE'S ENOUGH LIQUID VESPENE IN THESE TANKS TO BLOW US ALL CLEAR TO HELL AND BACK.
JUST STAY TIGHT ON THEIR TAILS.
GOOD CALL, BRINGING US IN HERE, BUT WHERE NEXT?
WE'RE RUNNING OUT OF REFINERY...
I...
...DON'T KNOW, NUURA. JUST...
...GIVE ME A MOMENT...

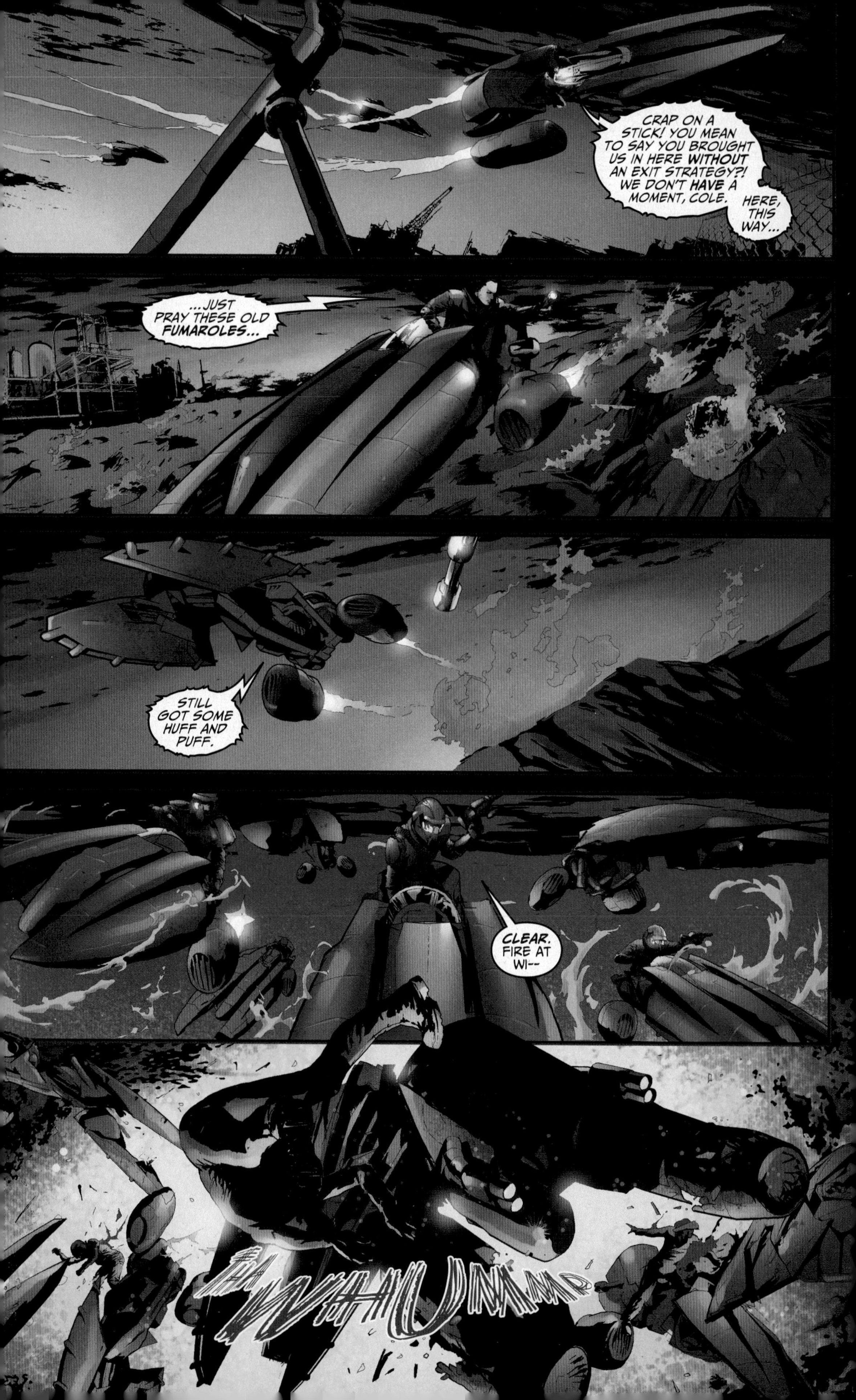
CRAP ON A STICK! YOU MEAN TO SAY YOU BROUGHT US IN HERE **WITHOUT** AN EXIT STRATEGY?! WE DON'T **HAVE** A MOMENT, COLE.
HERE, THIS WAY...
...JUST PRAY THESE OLD **FUMAROLES...**
STILL GOT SOME HUFF AND PUFF.
CLEAR. FIRE AT WI--
THAWHUNMMP

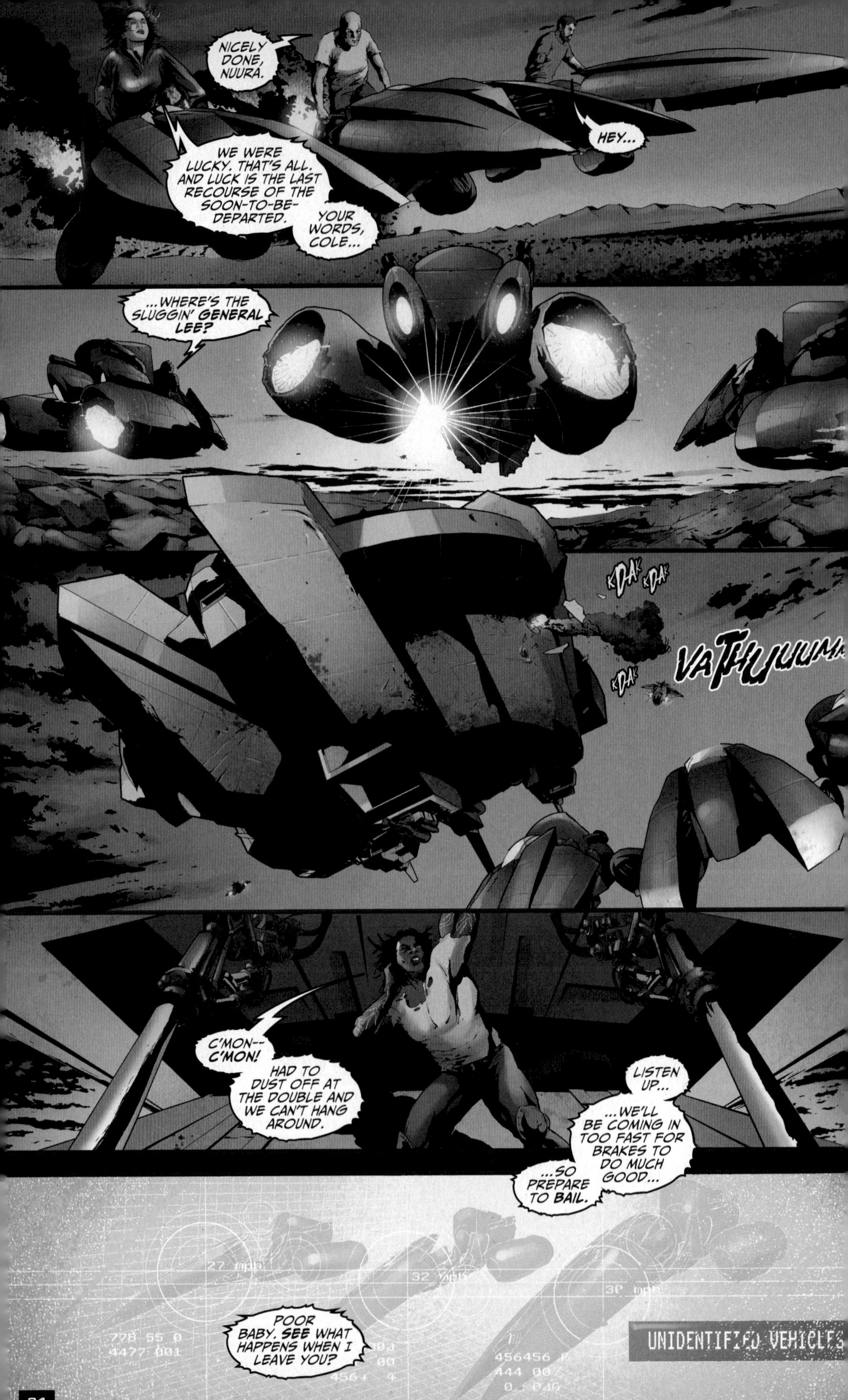
NICELY DONE, NUURA.
WE WERE LUCKY. THAT'S ALL. AND LUCK IS THE LAST RECOURSE OF THE SOON-TO-BE-DEPARTED.
YOUR WORDS, COLE...
HEY...
...WHERE'S THE SLUGGIN' GENERAL LEE?
KDAK KDAK
VATHUUUM
KDAK
C'MON-- C'MON!
HAD TO DUST OFF AT THE DOUBLE AND WE CAN'T HANG AROUND.
LISTEN UP...
...WE'LL BE COMING IN TOO FAST FOR BRAKES TO DO MUCH GOOD...
...SO PREPARE TO BAIL.
27 mph
32 mph
30 mph
POOR BABY. SEE WHAT HAPPENS WHEN I LEAVE YOU?
UNIDENTIFIED VEHICLES

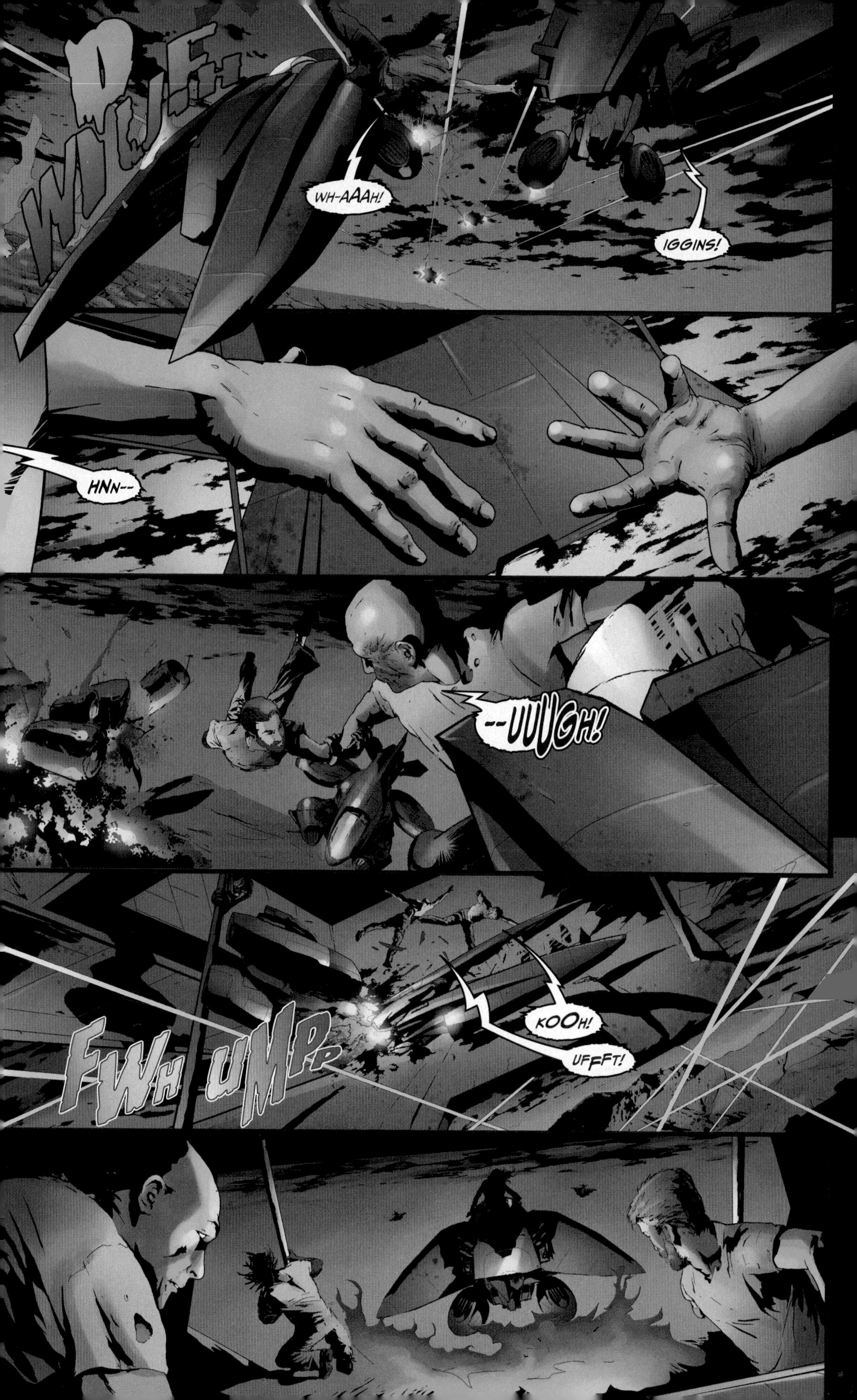
WHUFF
WH-AAAH!
IGGINS!
HNn--
--UUUGH!
FWH UMPP
KOOH!
UFFFT!

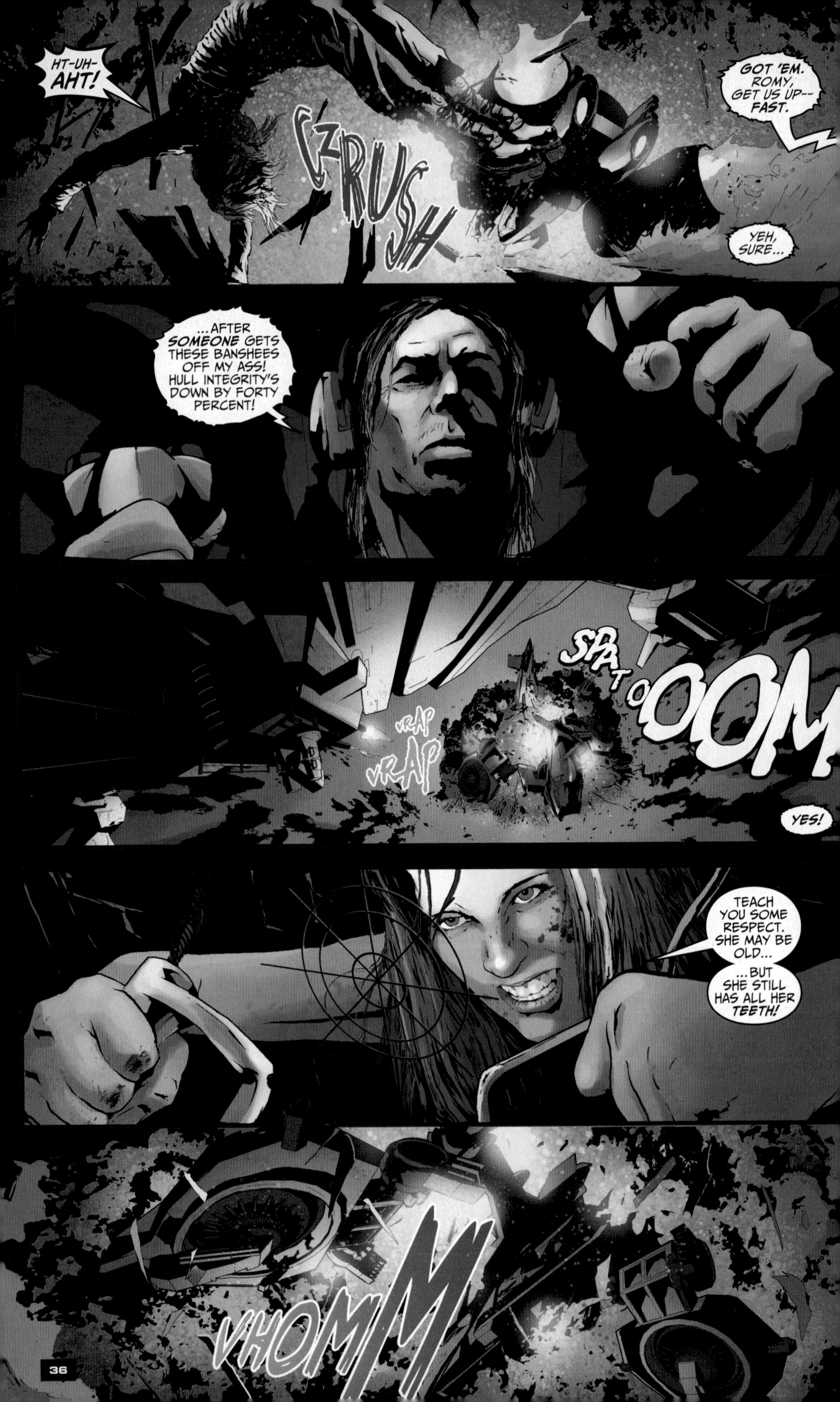
HT-UH-AHT!
CZRUSH
GOT 'EM. ROMY, GET US UP-- FAST.
YEH, SURE...
...AFTER SOMEONE GETS THESE BANSHEES OFF MY ASS! HULL INTEGRITY'S DOWN BY FORTY PERCENT!
SPATOOOM
VRAP VRAP
YES!
TEACH YOU SOME RESPECT. SHE MAY BE OLD...
...BUT SHE STILL HAS ALL HER TEETH!
VHOMM

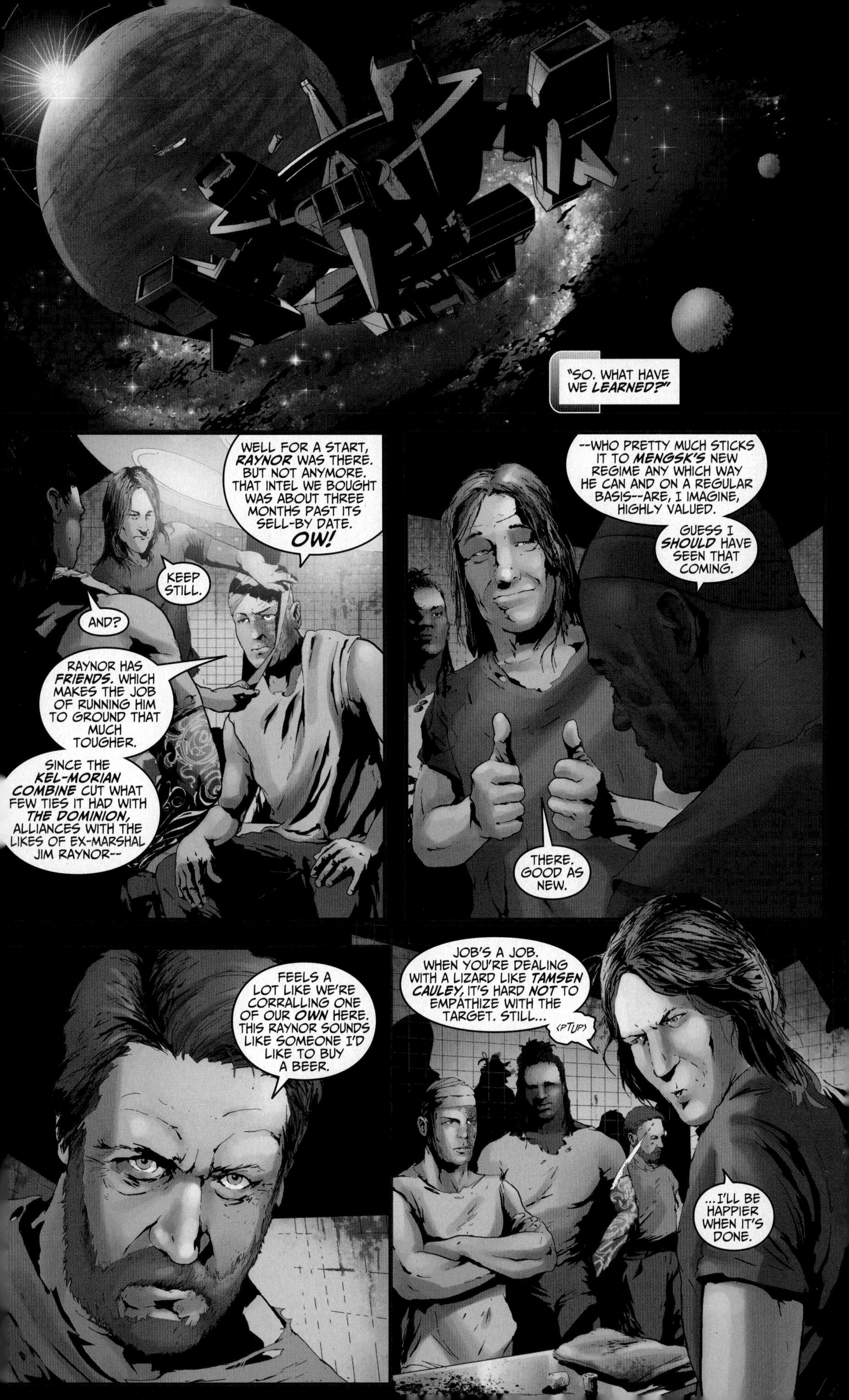
"SO. WHAT HAVE WE LEARNED?"
WELL FOR A START, RAYNOR WAS THERE. BUT NOT ANYMORE. THAT INTEL WE BOUGHT WAS ABOUT THREE MONTHS PAST ITS SELL-BY DATE. OW!
KEEP STILL.
AND?
RAYNOR HAS FRIENDS. WHICH MAKES THE JOB OF RUNNING HIM TO GROUND THAT MUCH TOUGHER.
SINCE THE KEL-MORIAN COMBINE CUT WHAT FEW TIES IT HAD WITH THE DOMINION, ALLIANCES WITH THE LIKES OF EX-MARSHAL JIM RAYNOR--
--WHO PRETTY MUCH STICKS IT TO MENGSK'S NEW REGIME ANY WHICH WAY HE CAN AND ON A REGULAR BASIS--ARE, I IMAGINE, HIGHLY VALUED.
GUESS I SHOULD HAVE SEEN THAT COMING.
THERE. GOOD AS NEW.
FEELS A LOT LIKE WE'RE CORRALLING ONE OF OUR OWN HERE. THIS RAYNOR SOUNDS LIKE SOMEONE I'D LIKE TO BUY A BEER.
JOB'S A JOB. WHEN YOU'RE DEALING WITH A LIZARD LIKE TAMSEN CAULEY, IT'S HARD NOT TO EMPATHIZE WITH THE TARGET. STILL...
<PTUP>
...I'LL BE HAPPIER WHEN IT'S DONE.

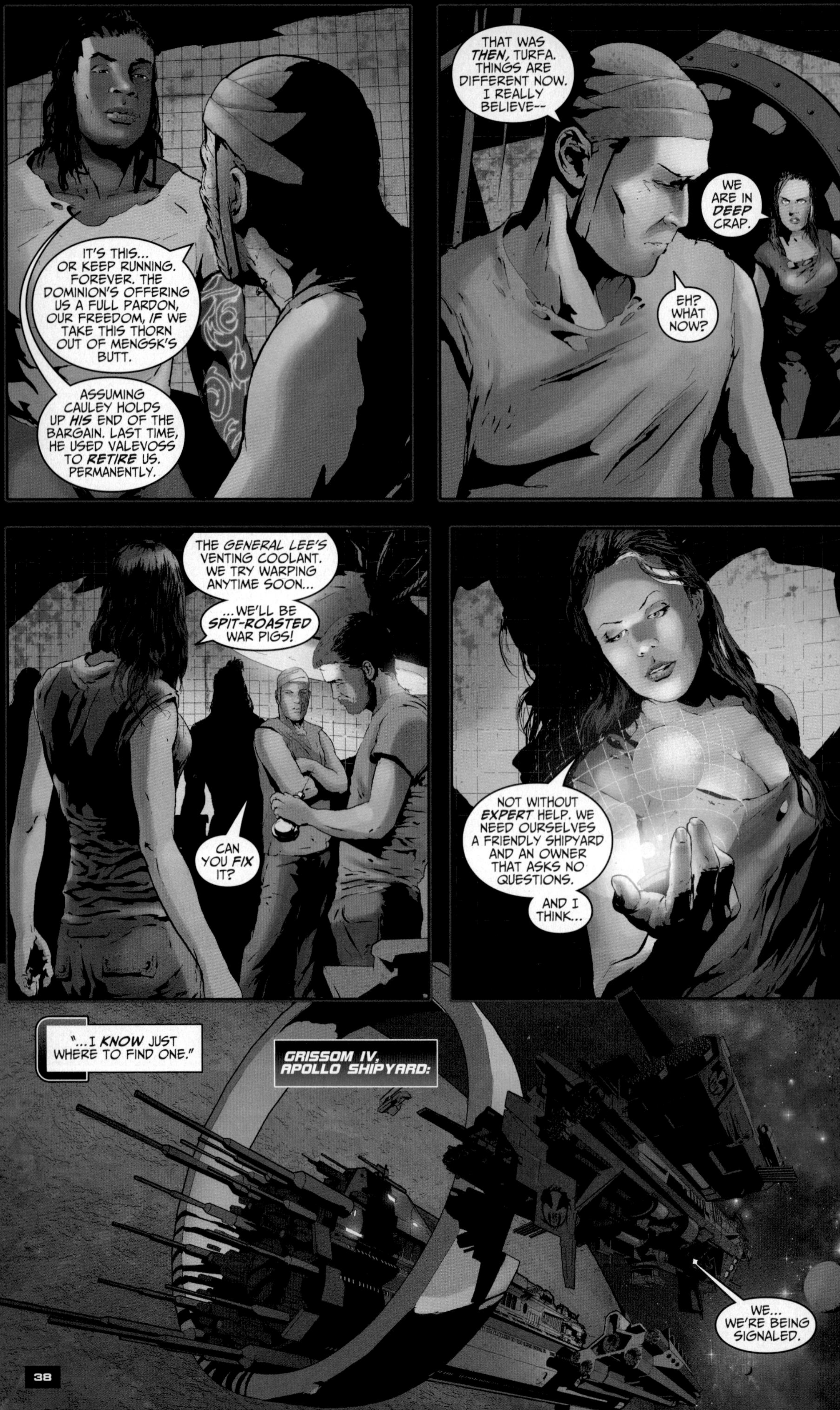
IT'S THIS... OR KEEP RUNNING. FOREVER. THE DOMINION'S OFFERING US A FULL PARDON, OUR FREEDOM, IF WE TAKE THIS THORN OUT OF MENGSK'S BUTT.
ASSUMING CAULEY HOLDS UP HIS END OF THE BARGAIN. LAST TIME, HE USED VALEVOSS TO RETIRE US. PERMANENTLY.
THAT WAS THEN, TURFA. THINGS ARE DIFFERENT NOW. I REALLY BELIEVE--
WE ARE IN DEEP CRAP.
EH? WHAT NOW?
THE GENERAL LEE'S VENTING COOLANT. WE TRY WARPING ANYTIME SOON...
...WE'LL BE SPIT-ROASTED WAR PIGS!
CAN YOU FIX IT?
NOT WITHOUT EXPERT HELP. WE NEED OURSELVES A FRIENDLY SHIPYARD AND AN OWNER THAT ASKS NO QUESTIONS.
AND I THINK...
"...I KNOW JUST WHERE TO FIND ONE."
GRISSOM IV, APOLLO SHIPYARD:
WE... WE'RE BEING SIGNALED.

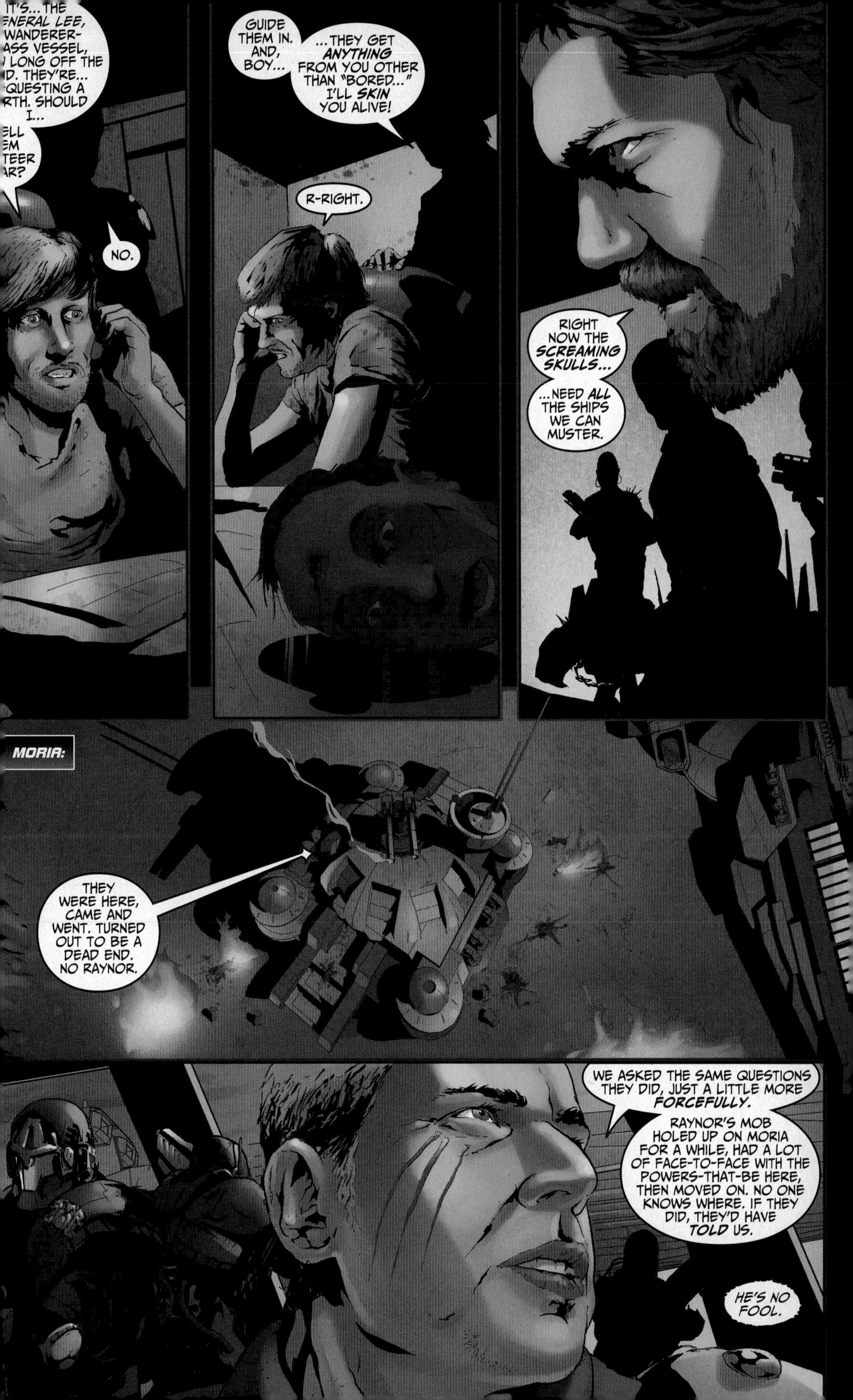

IT'S... THE ENERAL LEE, WANDERER- ASS VESSEL, LONG OFF THE D. THEY'RE... QUESTING A RTH. SHOULD I...
ELL EM TEER AR?
NO.
GUIDE THEM IN. AND, BOY...
...THEY GET ANYTHING FROM YOU OTHER THAN "BORED..." I'LL SKIN YOU ALIVE!
R-RIGHT.
RIGHT NOW THE SCREAMING SKULLS...
...NEED ALL THE SHIPS WE CAN MUSTER.
MORIA:
THEY WERE HERE, CAME AND WENT. TURNED OUT TO BE A DEAD END. NO RAYNOR.
WE ASKED THE SAME QUESTIONS THEY DID, JUST A LITTLE MORE FORCEFULLY.
RAYNOR'S MOB HOLED UP ON MORIA FOR A WHILE, HAD A LOT OF FACE-TO-FACE WITH THE POWERS-THAT-BE HERE, THEN MOVED ON. NO ONE KNOWS WHERE. IF THEY DID, THEY'D HAVE TOLD US.
HE'S NO FOOL.

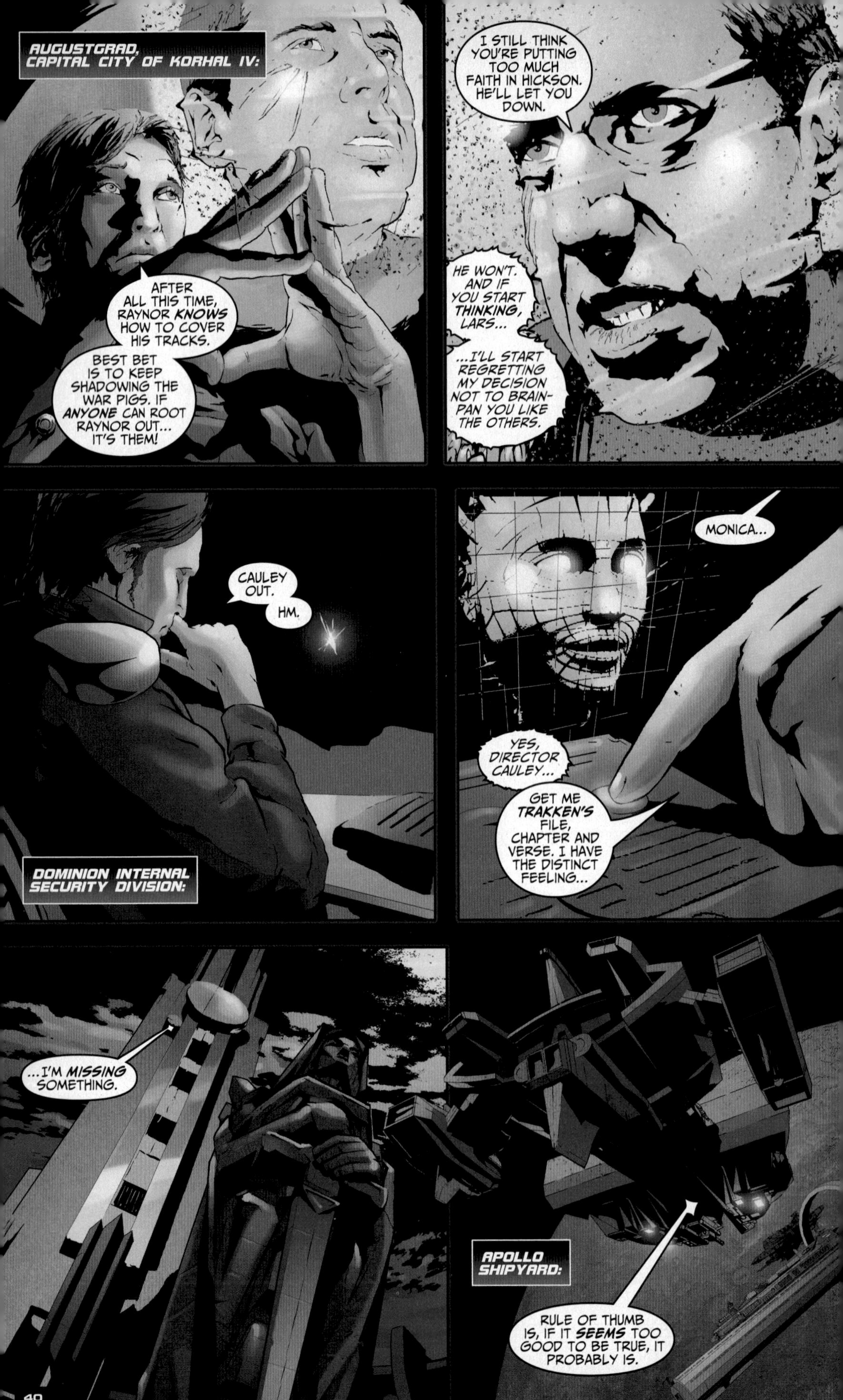
AUGUSTGRAD, CAPITAL CITY OF KORHAL IV:
AFTER ALL THIS TIME, RAYNOR KNOWS HOW TO COVER HIS TRACKS.
BEST BET IS TO KEEP SHADOWING THE WAR PIGS. IF ANYONE CAN ROOT RAYNOR OUT... IT'S THEM!
I STILL THINK YOU'RE PUTTING TOO MUCH FAITH IN HICKSON. HE'LL LET YOU DOWN.
HE WON'T. AND IF YOU START THINKING, LARS...
...I'LL START REGRETTING MY DECISION NOT TO BRAIN-PAN YOU LIKE THE OTHERS.
CAULEY OUT.
HM.
DOMINION INTERNAL SECURITY DIVISION:
MONICA...
YES, DIRECTOR CAULEY...
GET ME TRAKKEN'S FILE, CHAPTER AND VERSE. I HAVE THE DISTINCT FEELING...
...I'M MISSING SOMETHING.
APOLLO SHIPYARD:
RULE OF THUMB IS, IF IT SEEMS TOO GOOD TO BE TRUE, IT PROBABLY IS.

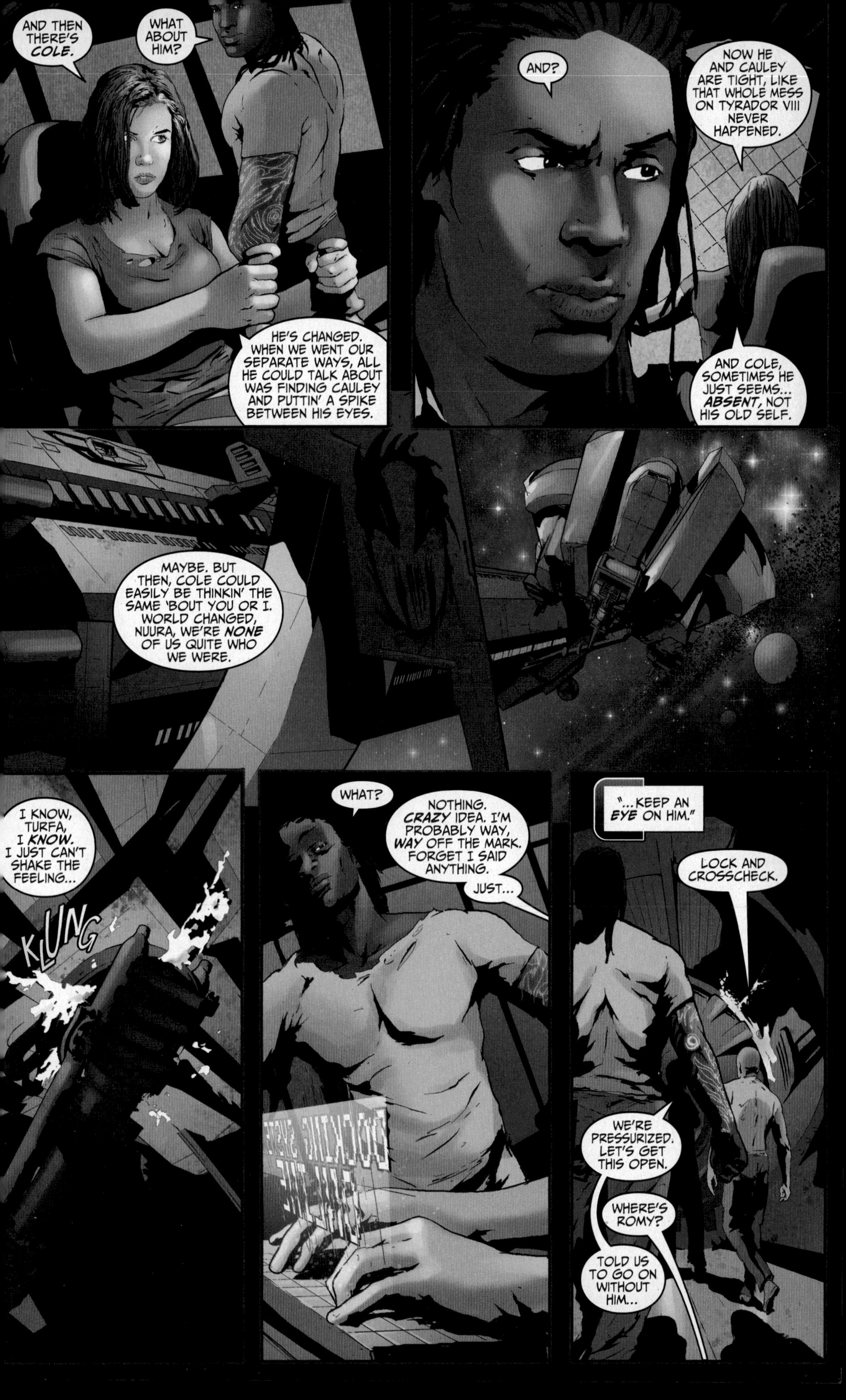
AND THEN THERE'S COLE.
WHAT ABOUT HIM?
HE'S CHANGED. WHEN WE WENT OUR SEPARATE WAYS, ALL HE COULD TALK ABOUT WAS FINDING CAULEY AND PUTTIN' A SPIKE BETWEEN HIS EYES.
AND?
NOW HE AND CAULEY ARE TIGHT, LIKE THAT WHOLE MESS ON TYRADOR VIII NEVER HAPPENED.
AND COLE, SOMETIMES HE JUST SEEMS... ABSENT, NOT HIS OLD SELF.
MAYBE. BUT THEN, COLE COULD EASILY BE THINKIN' THE SAME 'BOUT YOU OR I. WORLD CHANGED, NUURA, WE'RE NONE OF US QUITE WHO WE WERE.
I KNOW, TURFA, I KNOW. I JUST CAN'T SHAKE THE FEELING...
KLUNG
WHAT?
NOTHING. CRAZY IDEA. I'M PROBABLY WAY, WAY OFF THE MARK. FORGET I SAID ANYTHING.
JUST...
"...KEEP AN EYE ON HIM."
LOCK AND CROSSCHECK.
WE'RE PRESSURIZED. LET'S GET THIS OPEN.
WHERE'S ROMY?
TOLD US TO GO ON WITHOUT HIM...

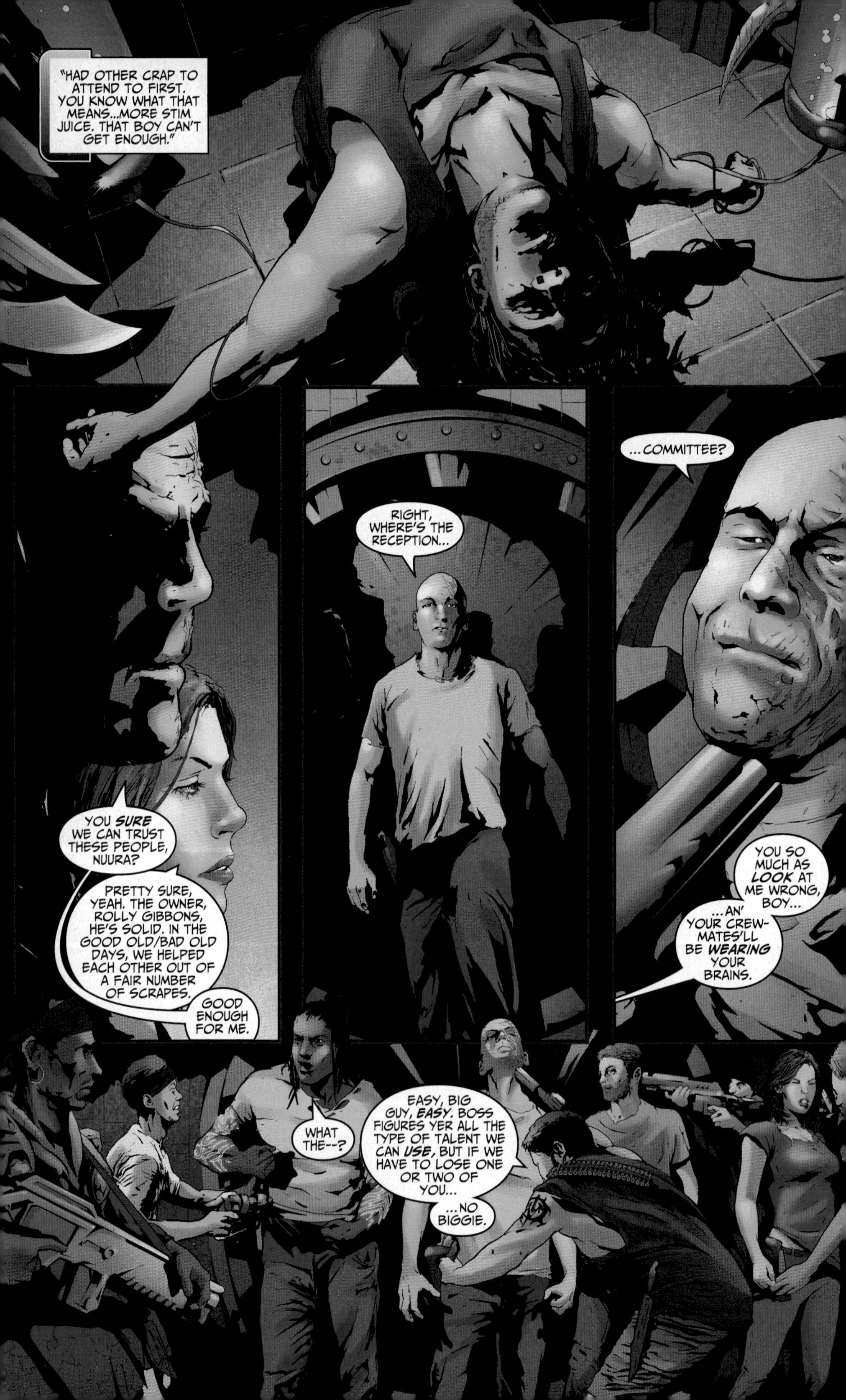
"HAD OTHER CRAP TO ATTEND TO FIRST. YOU KNOW WHAT THAT MEANS...MORE STIM JUICE. THAT BOY CAN'T GET ENOUGH."
YOU SURE WE CAN TRUST THESE PEOPLE, NUURA?
PRETTY SURE, YEAH. THE OWNER, ROLLY GIBBONS, HE'S SOLID. IN THE GOOD OLD/BAD OLD DAYS, WE HELPED EACH OTHER OUT OF A FAIR NUMBER OF SCRAPES.
GOOD ENOUGH FOR ME.
RIGHT, WHERE'S THE RECEPTION...
...COMMITTEE?
YOU SO MUCH AS LOOK AT ME WRONG, BOY...
...AN' YOUR CREW-MATES'LL BE WEARING YOUR BRAINS.
WHAT THE--?
EASY, BIG GUY, EASY. BOSS FIGURES YER ALL THE TYPE OF TALENT WE CAN USE, BUT IF WE HAVE TO LOSE ONE OR TWO OF YOU...
...NO BIGGIE.

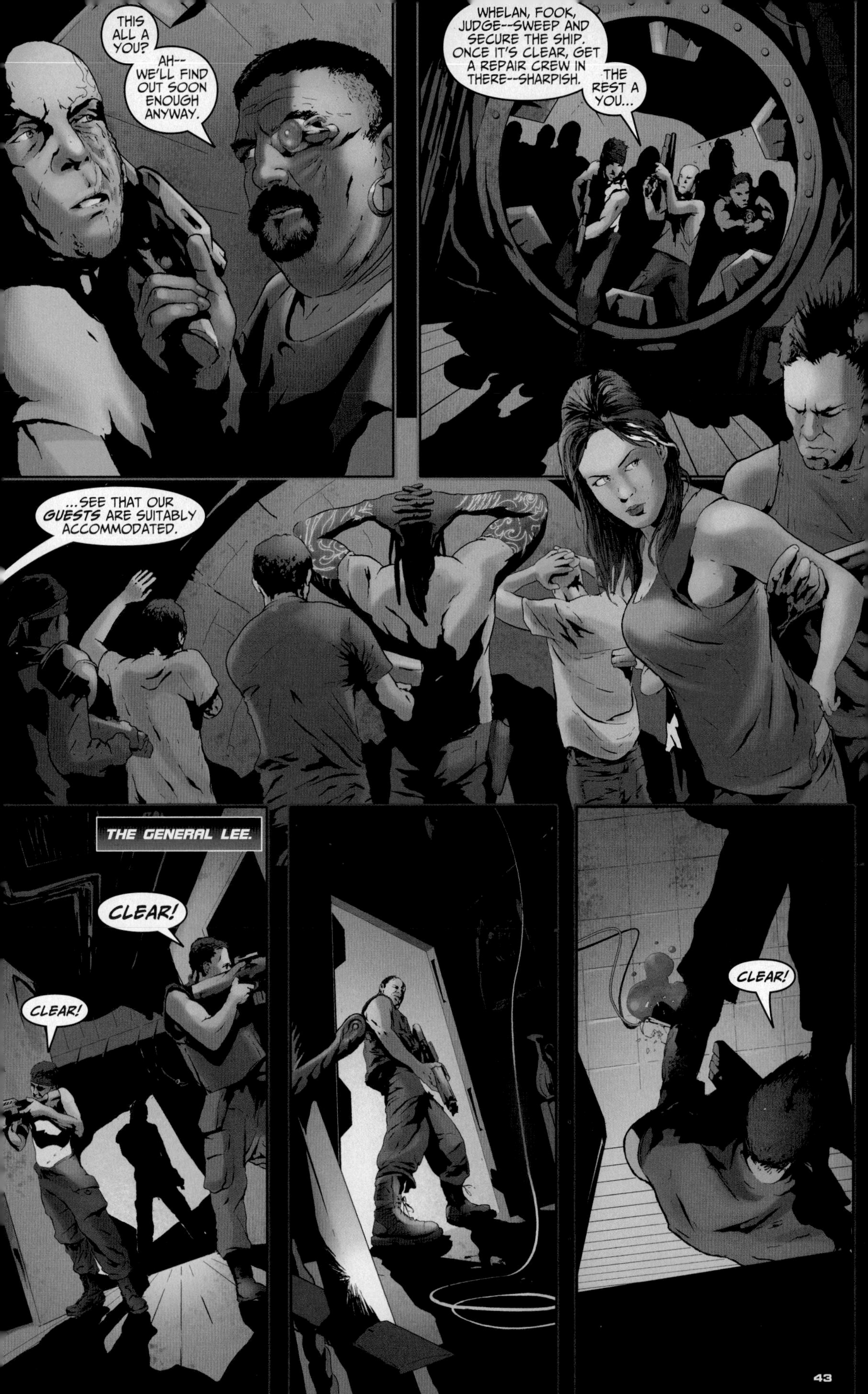
THIS ALL A YOU?
AH-- WE'LL FIND OUT SOON ENOUGH ANYWAY.
WHELAN, FOOK, JUDGE--SWEEP AND SECURE THE SHIP. ONCE IT'S CLEAR, GET A REPAIR CREW IN THERE--SHARPISH.
THE REST A YOU...
...SEE THAT OUR GUESTS ARE SUITABLY ACCOMMODATED.
THE GENERAL LEE.
CLEAR!
CLEAR!
CLEAR!

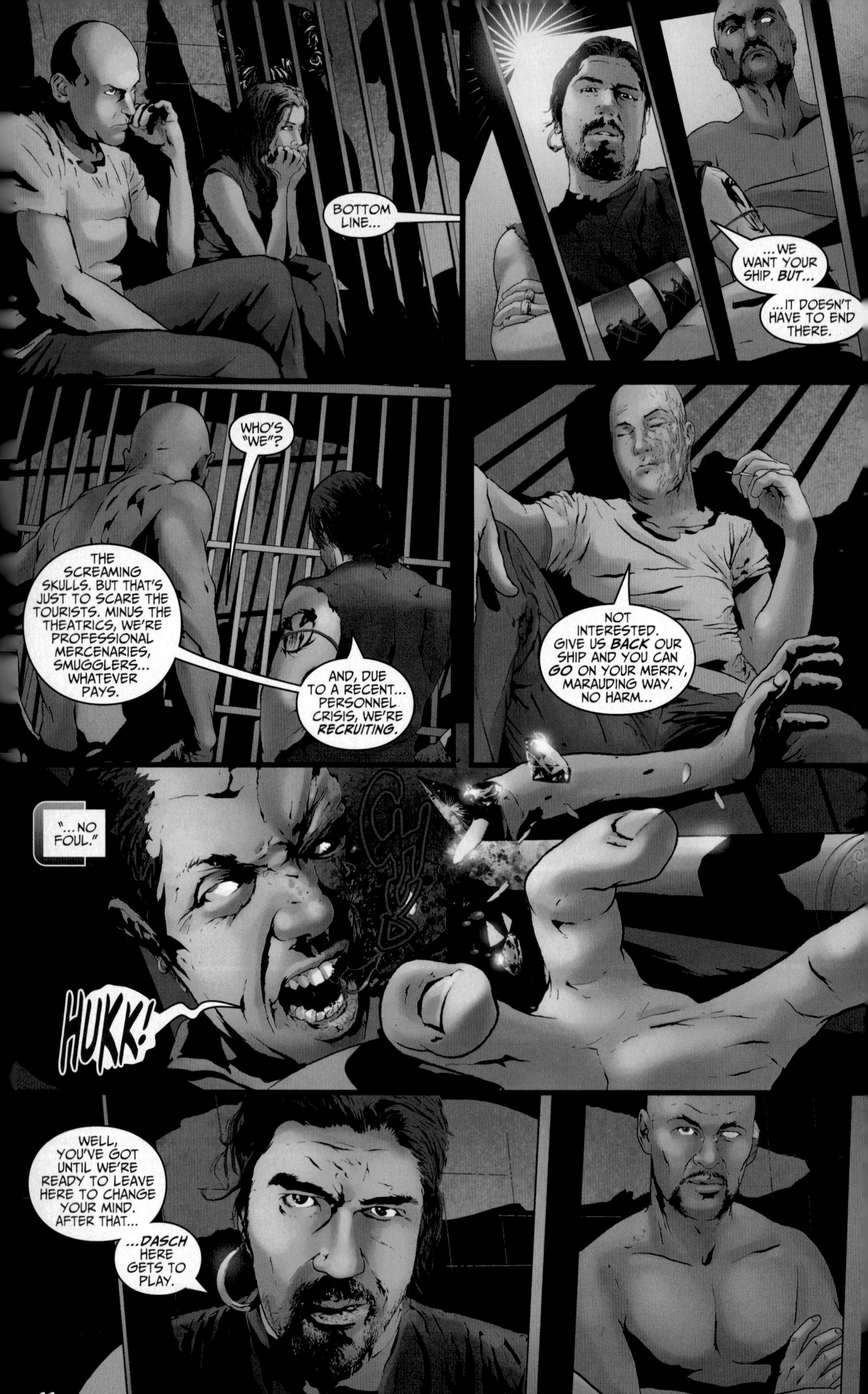
BOTTOM LINE...
...WE WANT YOUR SHIP. BUT...
...IT DOESN'T HAVE TO END THERE.
WHO'S "WE"?
THE SCREAMING SKULLS. BUT THAT'S JUST TO SCARE THE TOURISTS. MINUS THE THEATRICS, WE'RE PROFESSIONAL MERCENARIES, SMUGGLERS... WHATEVER PAYS.
AND, DUE TO A RECENT... PERSONNEL CRISIS, WE'RE RECRUITING.
NOT INTERESTED. GIVE US BACK OUR SHIP AND YOU CAN GO ON YOUR MERRY, MARAUDING WAY. NO HARM...
"...NO FOUL."
HUKK!
WELL, YOU'VE GOT UNTIL WE'RE READY TO LEAVE HERE TO CHANGE YOUR MIND. AFTER THAT...
...DASCH HERE GETS TO PLAY.

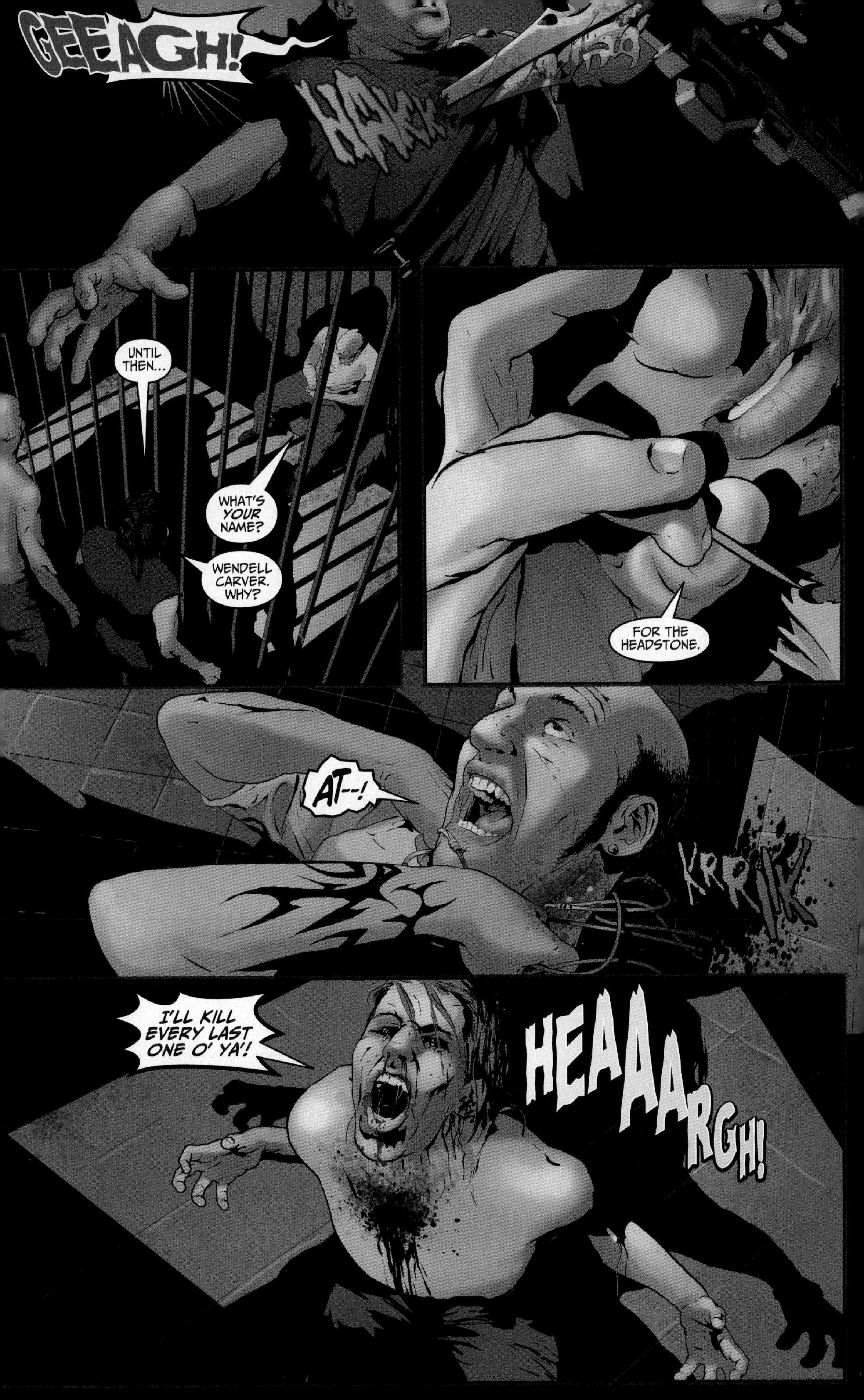
GEEAGH!
HAKK
UNTIL THEN...
WHAT'S YOUR NAME?
WENDELL CARVER. WHY?
FOR THE HEADSTONE.
AT--!
KRRIK
I'LL KILL EVERY LAST ONE O' YA'!
HEAAAARGH!

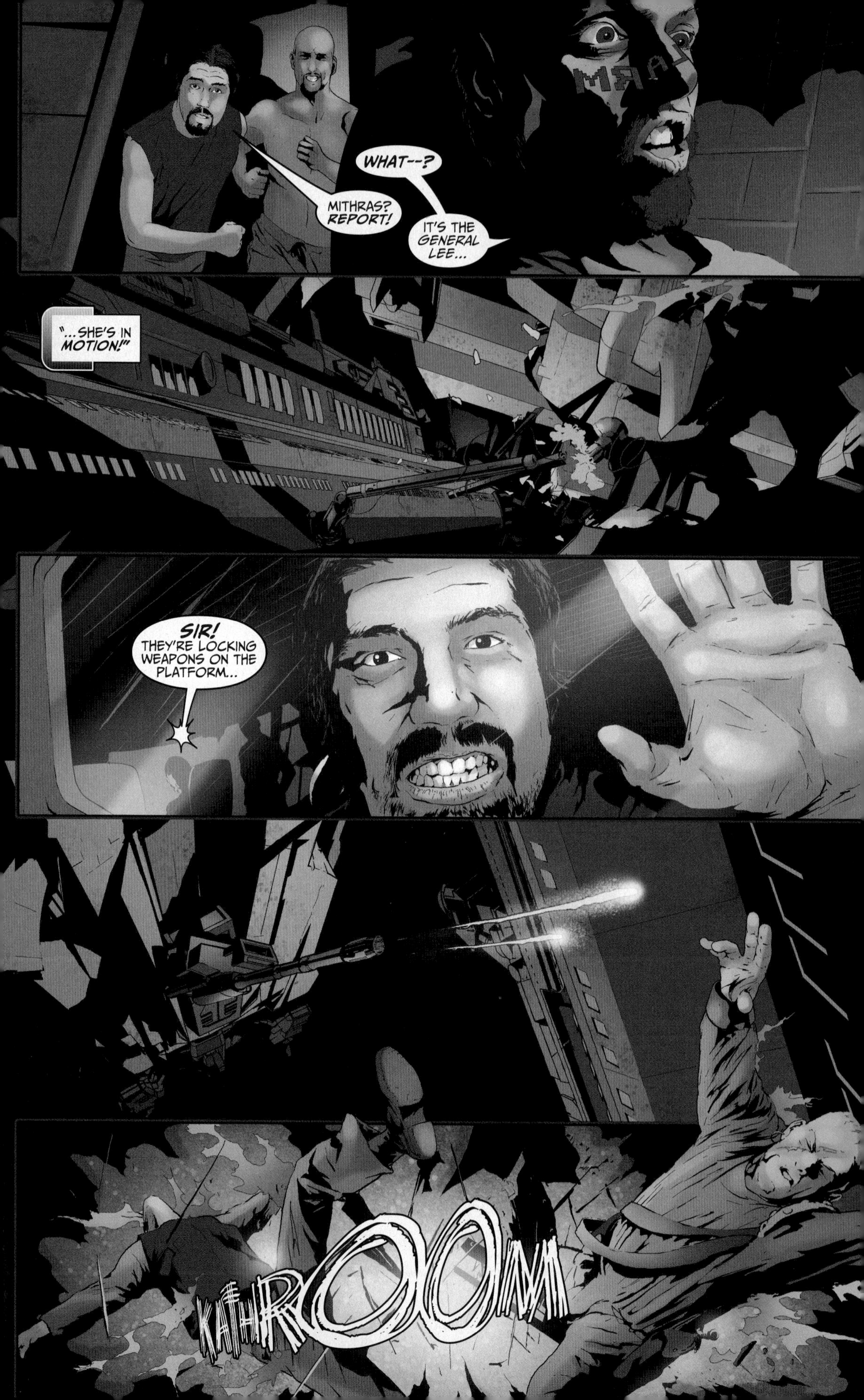
MITHRAS? REPORT!
WHAT--?
IT'S THE GENERAL LEE...
"...SHE'S IN MOTION!"
SIR! THEY'RE LOCKING WEAPONS ON THE PLATFORM...
KATHROOOM

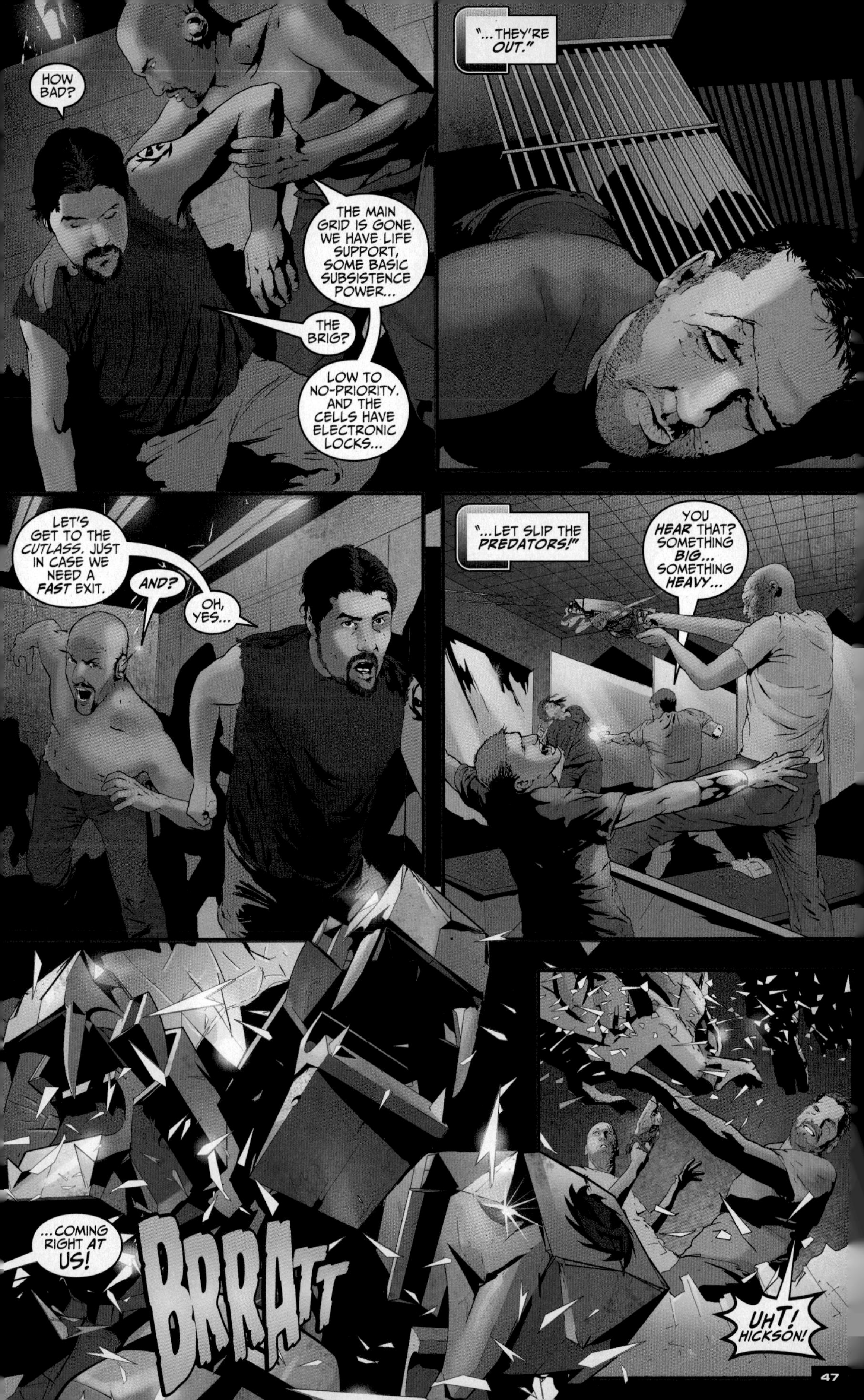
HOW BAD?
THE MAIN GRID IS GONE. WE HAVE LIFE SUPPORT, SOME BASIC SUBSISTENCE POWER...
THE BRIG?
LOW TO NO-PRIORITY. AND THE CELLS HAVE ELECTRONIC LOCKS...
"...THEY'RE *OUT*."
LET'S GET TO THE *CUTLASS*. JUST IN CASE WE NEED A *FAST* EXIT.
AND?
OH, YES...
"...LET SLIP THE *PREDATORS!*"
YOU *HEAR* THAT? SOMETHING *BIG*... SOMETHING *HEAVY*...
...COMING RIGHT *AT* US!
BRRATT
UHT! HICKSON!

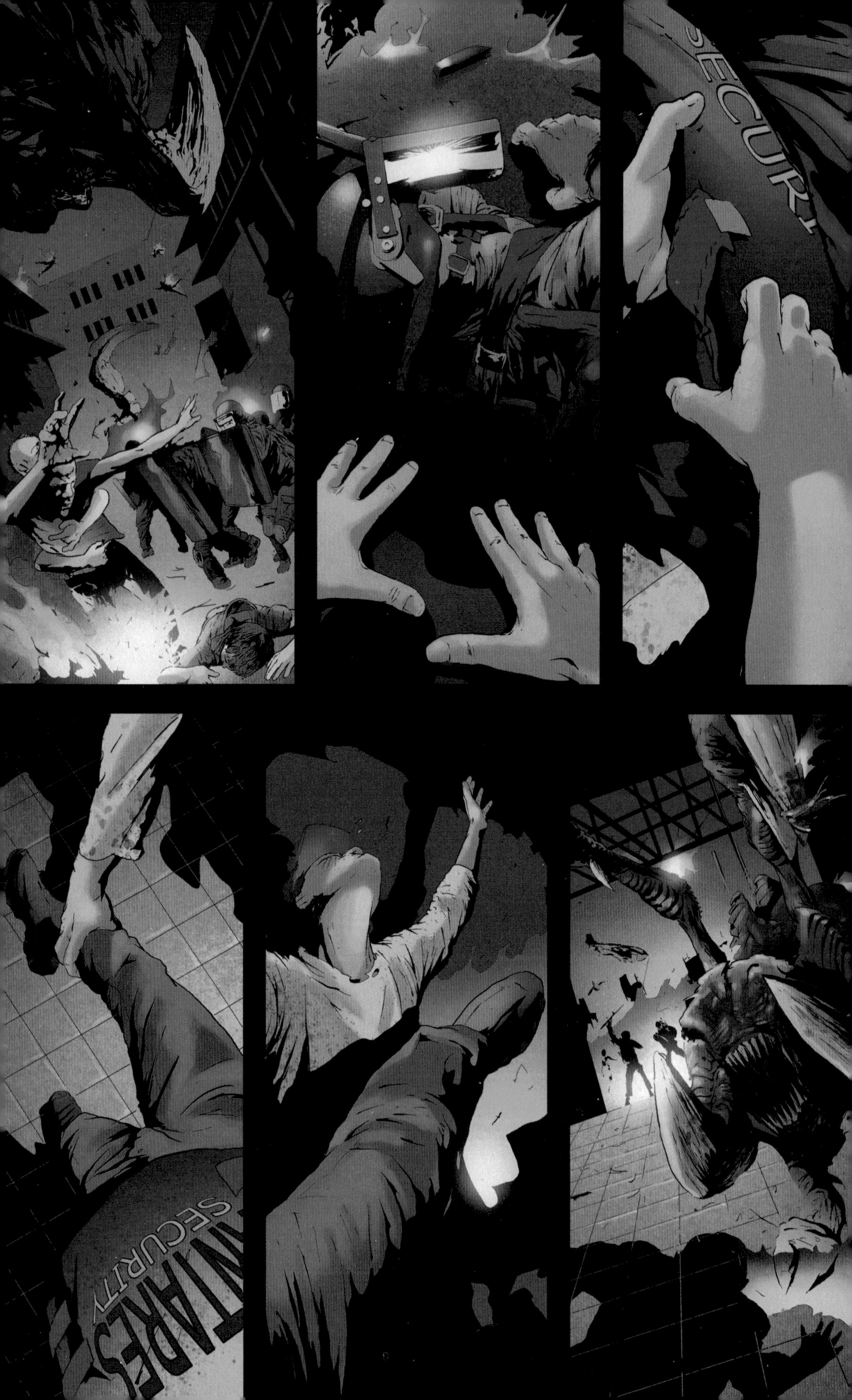
SECURITY

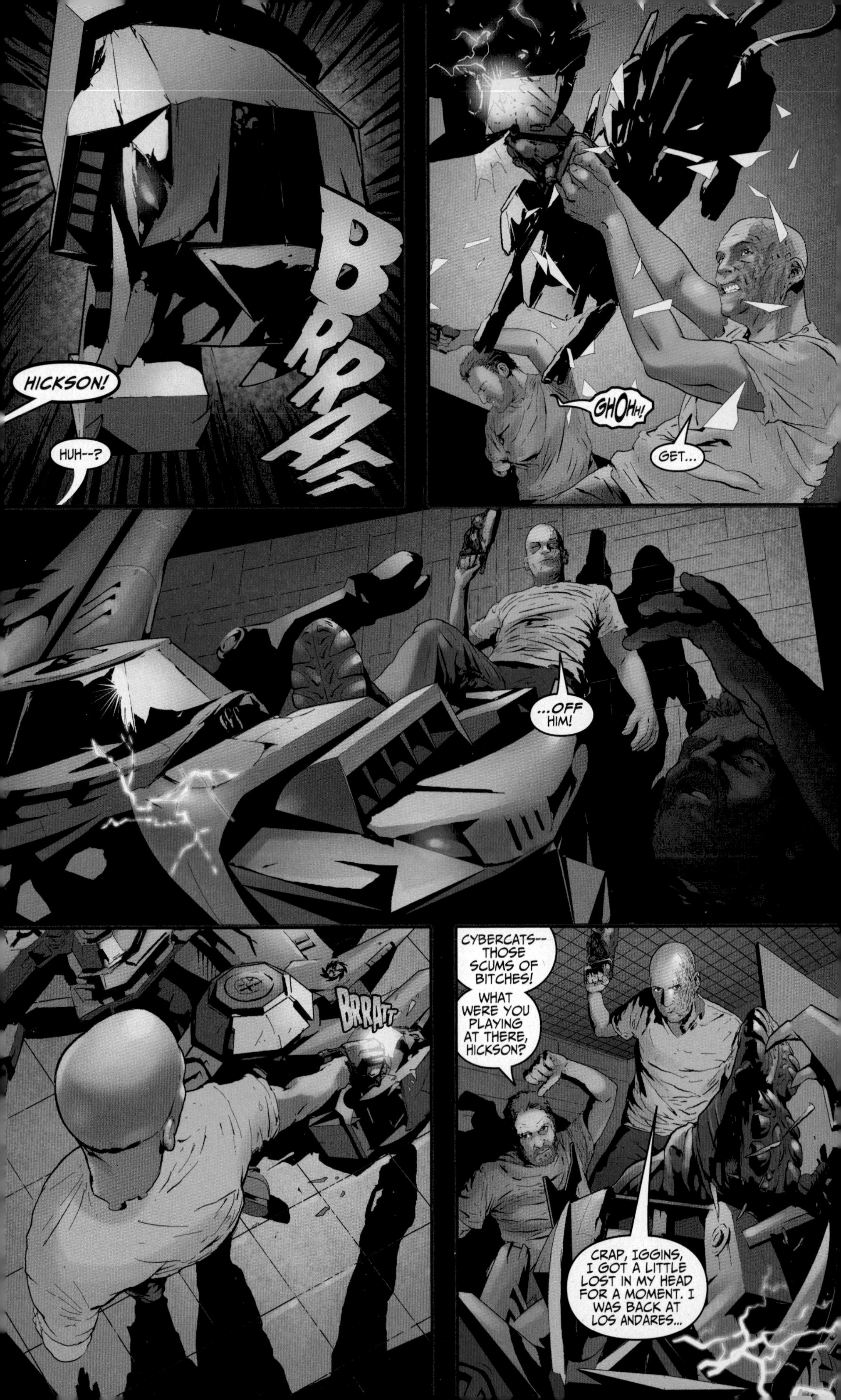
HICKSON!
HUH--?
BRRRATT
GHOHH!
GET...
...OFF HIM!
BRRATT
CYBERCATS-- THOSE SCUMS OF BITCHES!
WHAT WERE YOU PLAYING AT THERE, HICKSON?
CRAP, IGGINS, I GOT A LITTLE LOST IN MY HEAD FOR A MOMENT. I WAS BACK AT LOS ANDARES...

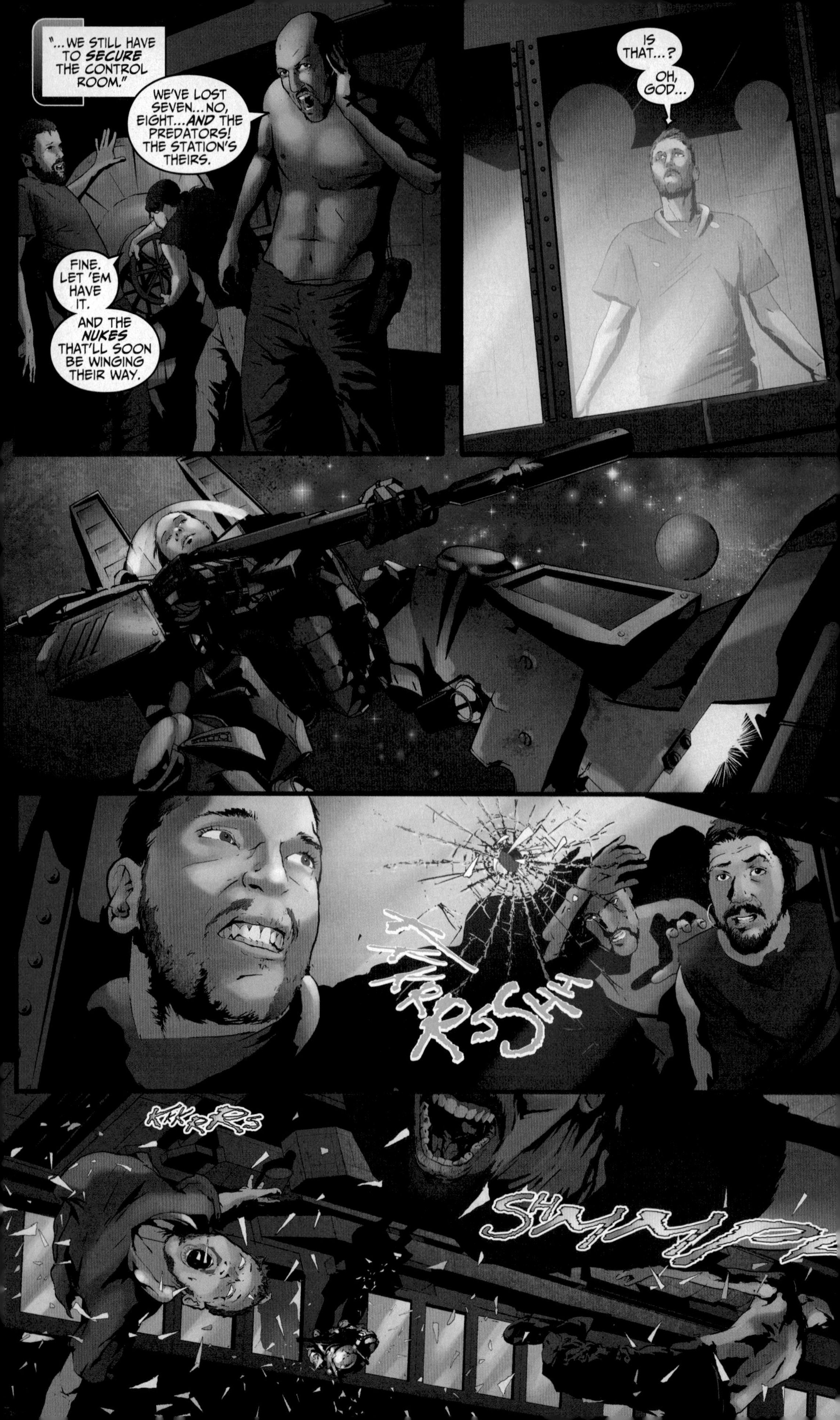
"...WE STILL HAVE TO SECURE THE CONTROL ROOM."
WE'VE LOST SEVEN...NO, EIGHT...AND THE PREDATORS! THE STATION'S THEIRS.
FINE. LET 'EM HAVE IT.
AND THE NUKES THAT'LL SOON BE WINGING THEIR WAY.
IS THAT...?
OH, GOD...
KRRSSH
SHMPF

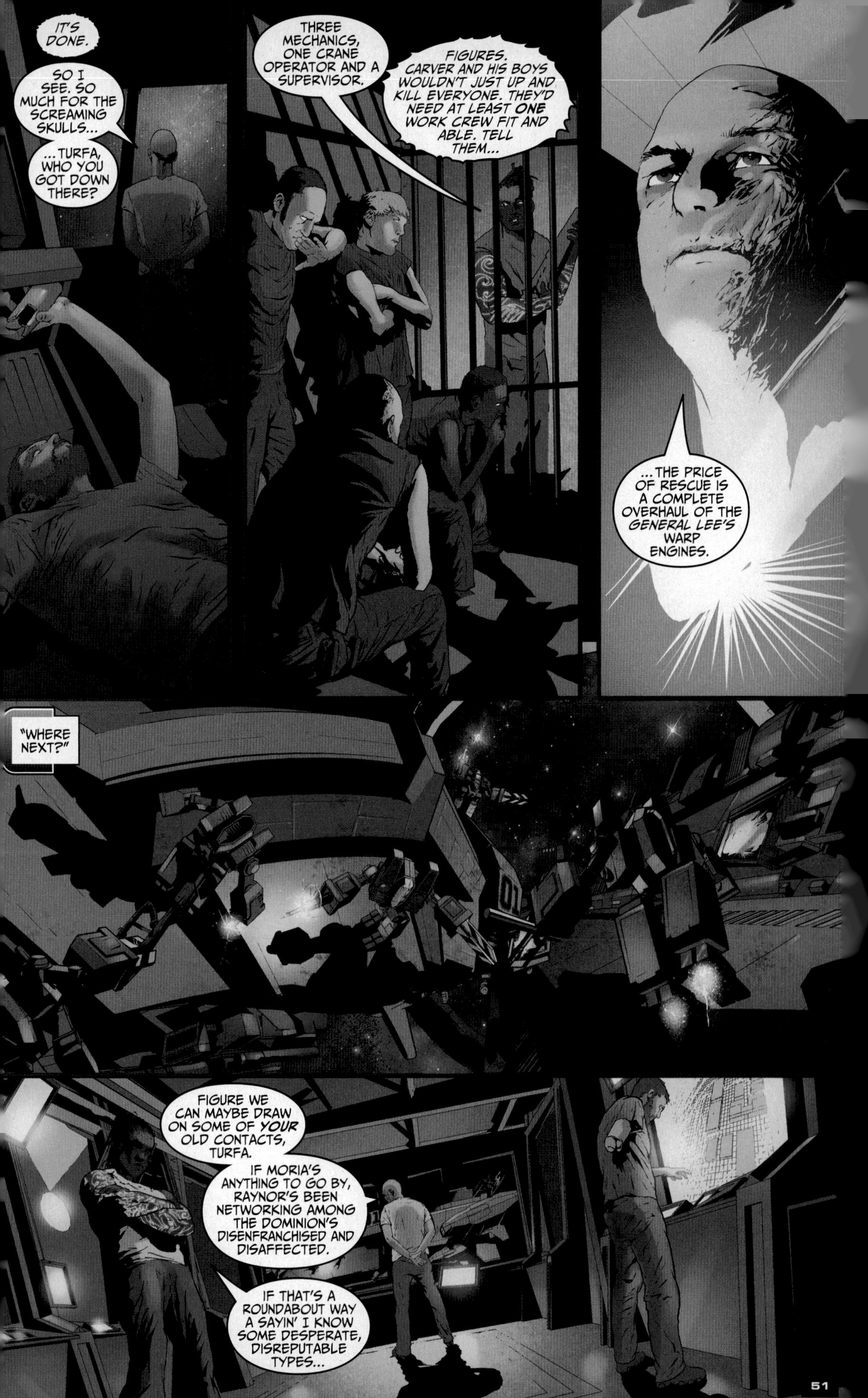
IT'S DONE.
SO I SEE. SO MUCH FOR THE SCREAMING SKULLS...
...TURFA, WHO YOU GOT DOWN THERE?
THREE MECHANICS, ONE CRANE OPERATOR AND A SUPERVISOR.
FIGURES. CARVER AND HIS BOYS WOULDN'T JUST UP AND KILL EVERYONE. THEY'D NEED AT LEAST ONE WORK CREW FIT AND ABLE. TELL THEM...
...THE PRICE OF RESCUE IS A COMPLETE OVERHAUL OF THE GENERAL LEE'S WARP ENGINES.
"WHERE NEXT?"
FIGURE WE CAN MAYBE DRAW ON SOME OF YOUR OLD CONTACTS, TURFA.
IF MORIA'S ANYTHING TO GO BY, RAYNOR'S BEEN NETWORKING AMONG THE DOMINION'S DISENFRANCHISED AND DISAFFECTED.
IF THAT'S A ROUNDABOUT WAY A SAYIN' I KNOW SOME DESPERATE, DISREPUTABLE TYPES...

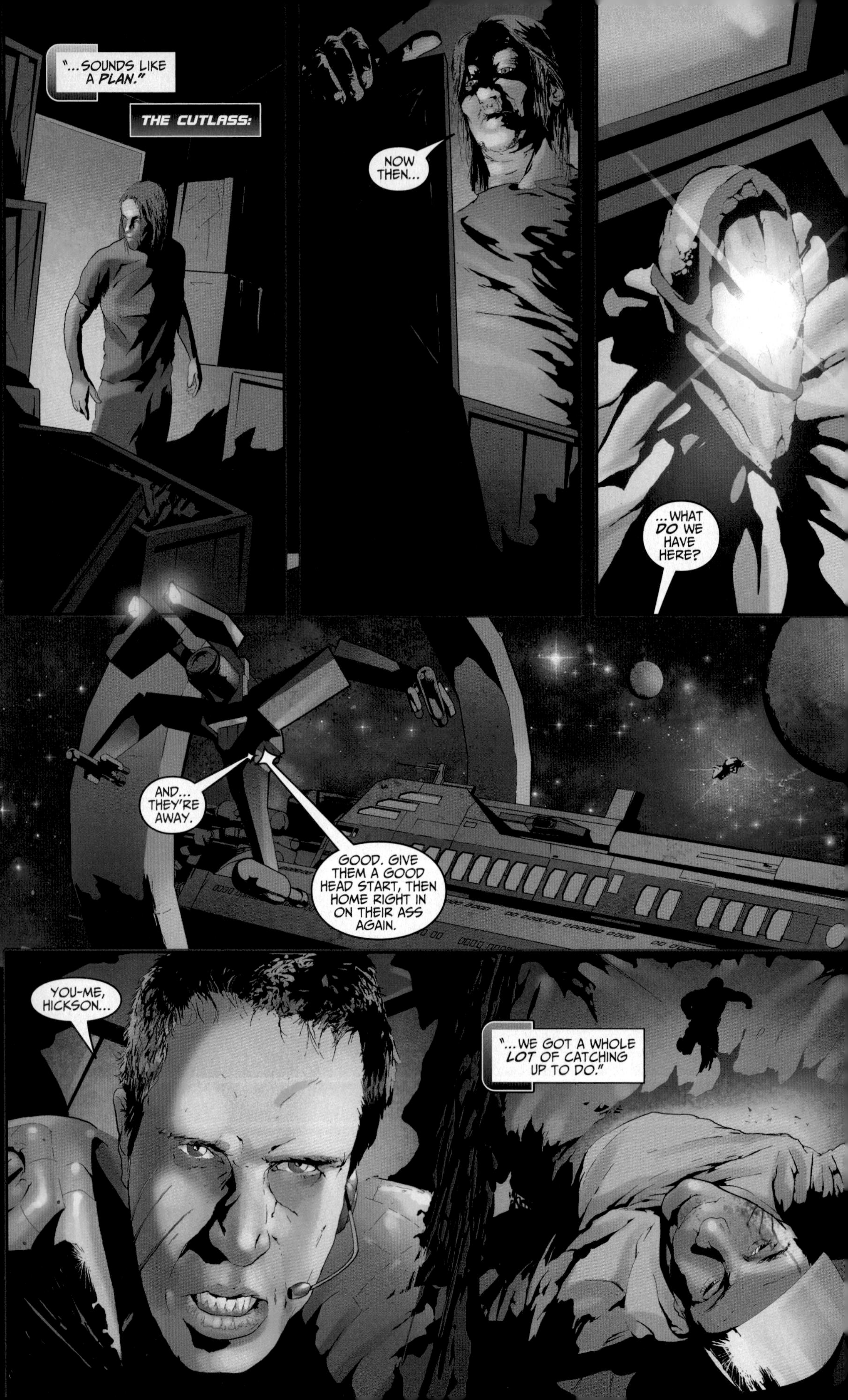
"...SOUNDS LIKE A PLAN."
THE CUTLASS:
NOW THEN...
...WHAT DO WE HAVE HERE?
AND... THEY'RE AWAY.
GOOD. GIVE THEM A GOOD HEAD START, THEN HOME RIGHT IN ON THEIR ASS AGAIN.
YOU-ME, HICKSON...
"...WE GOT A WHOLE LOT OF CATCHING UP TO DO."

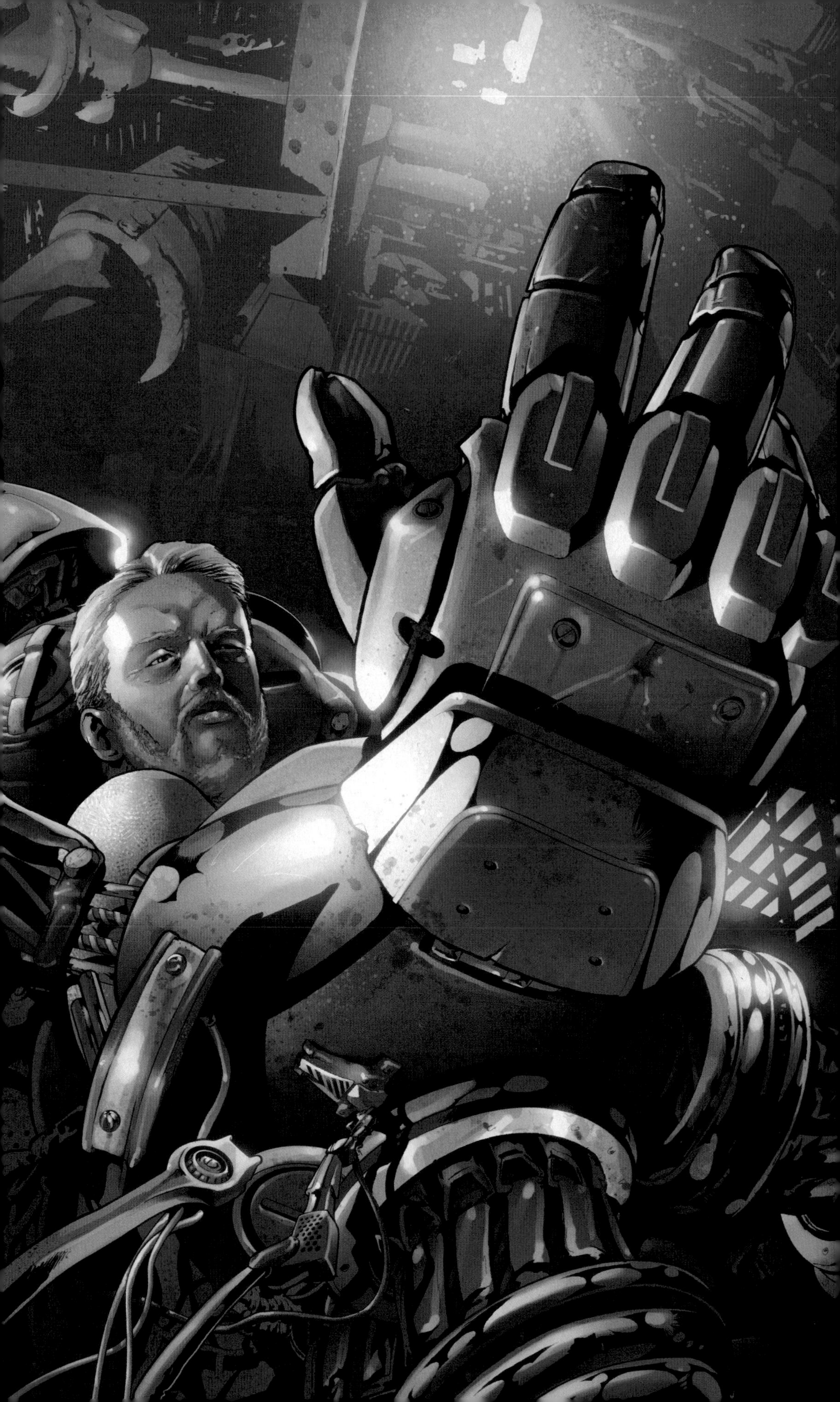

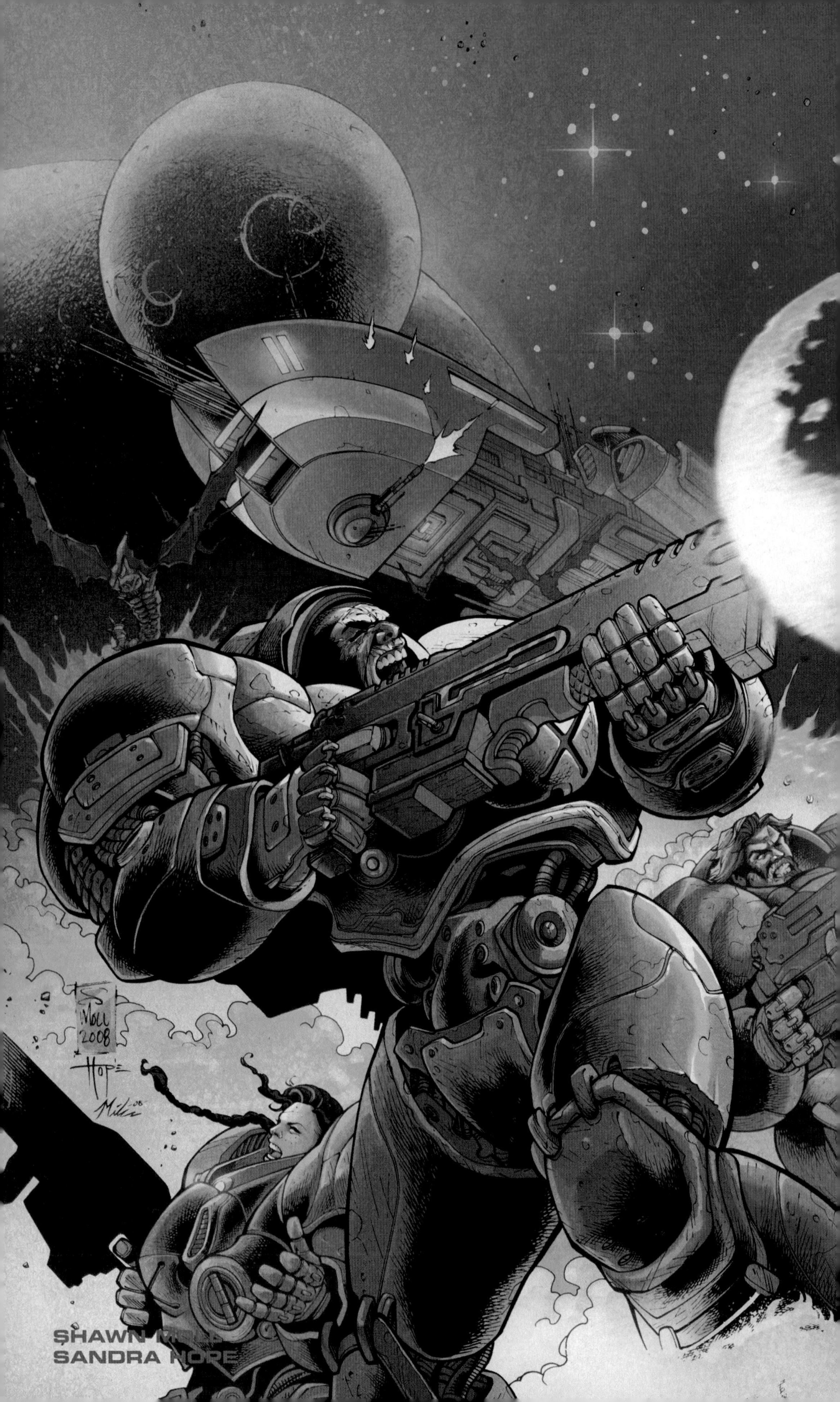
SHAWN MOLL
SANDRA HOPE

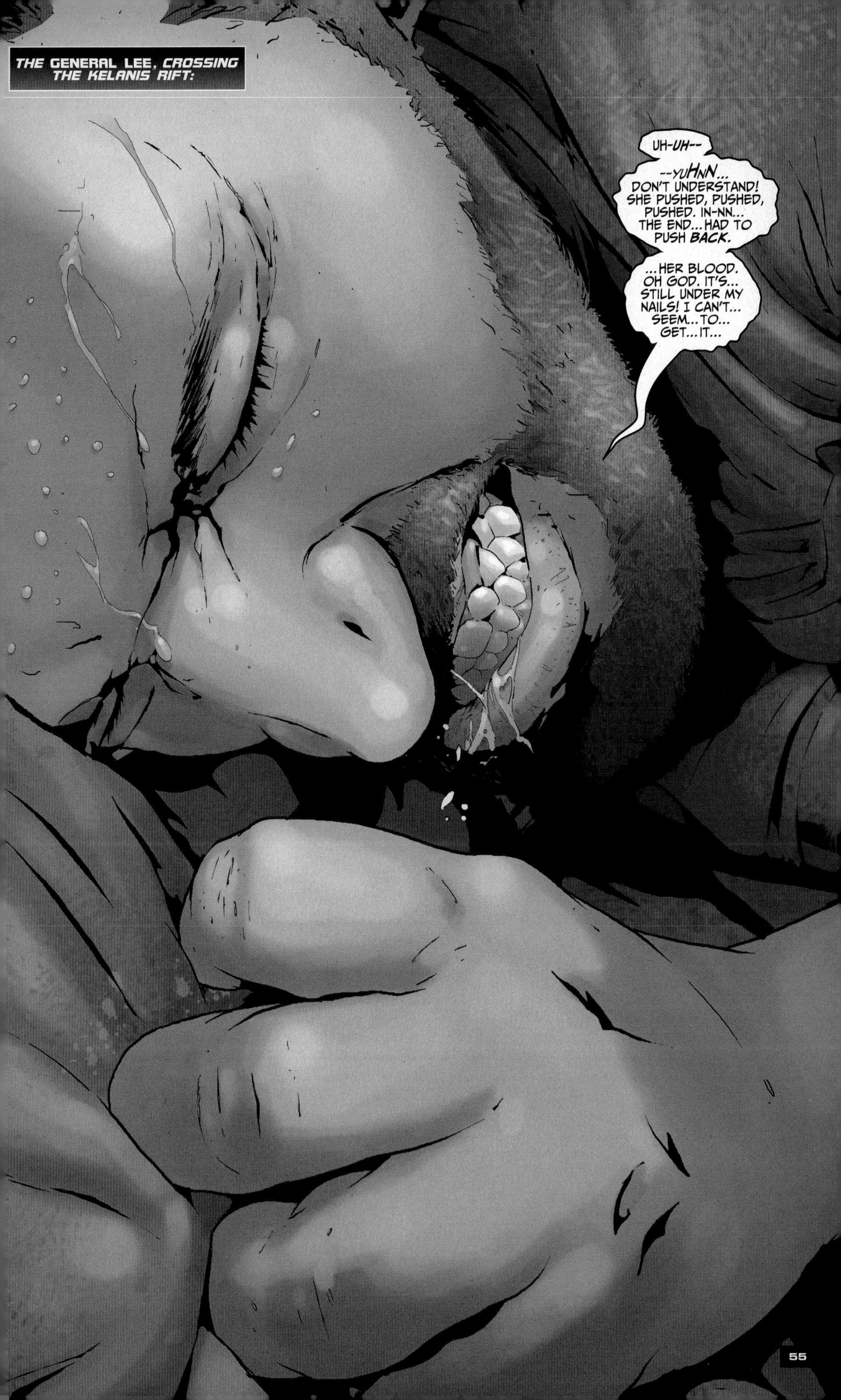
THE GENERAL LEE, CROSSING THE KELANIS RIFT:
UH-UH--
--YUHNN... DON'T UNDERSTAND! SHE PUSHED, PUSHED, PUSHED. IN-NN... THE END...HAD TO PUSH BACK.
...HER BLOOD. OH GOD. IT'S... STILL UNDER MY NAILS! I CAN'T... SEEM...TO... GET...IT...

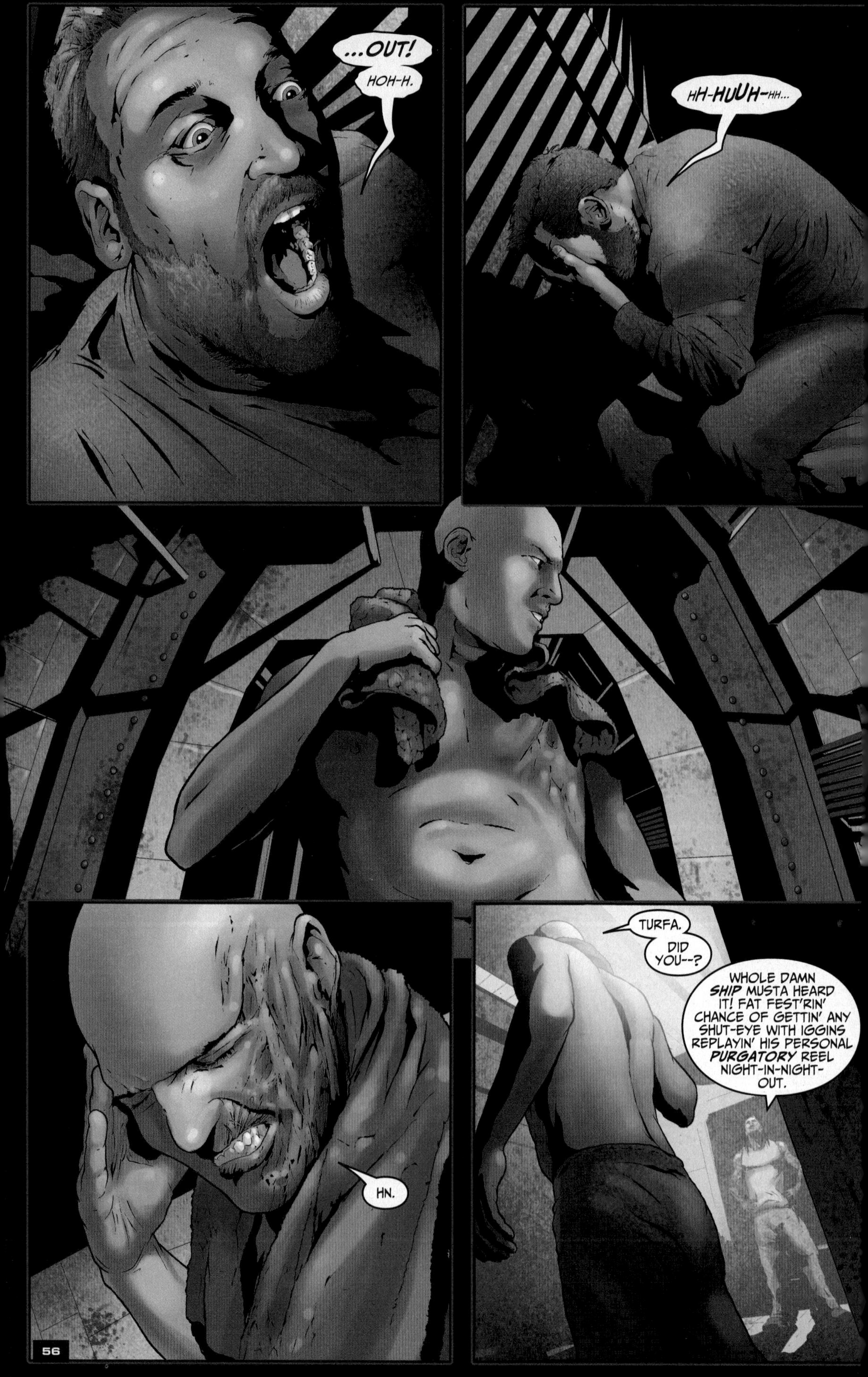

...OUT!
HOH-H.
HH-HUUH-HH...
HN.
TURFA.
DID YOU--?
WHOLE DAMN SHIP MUSTA HEARD IT! FAT FEST'RIN' CHANCE OF GETTIN' ANY SHUT-EYE WITH IGGINS REPLAYIN' HIS PERSONAL PURGATORY REEL NIGHT-IN-NIGHT-OUT.

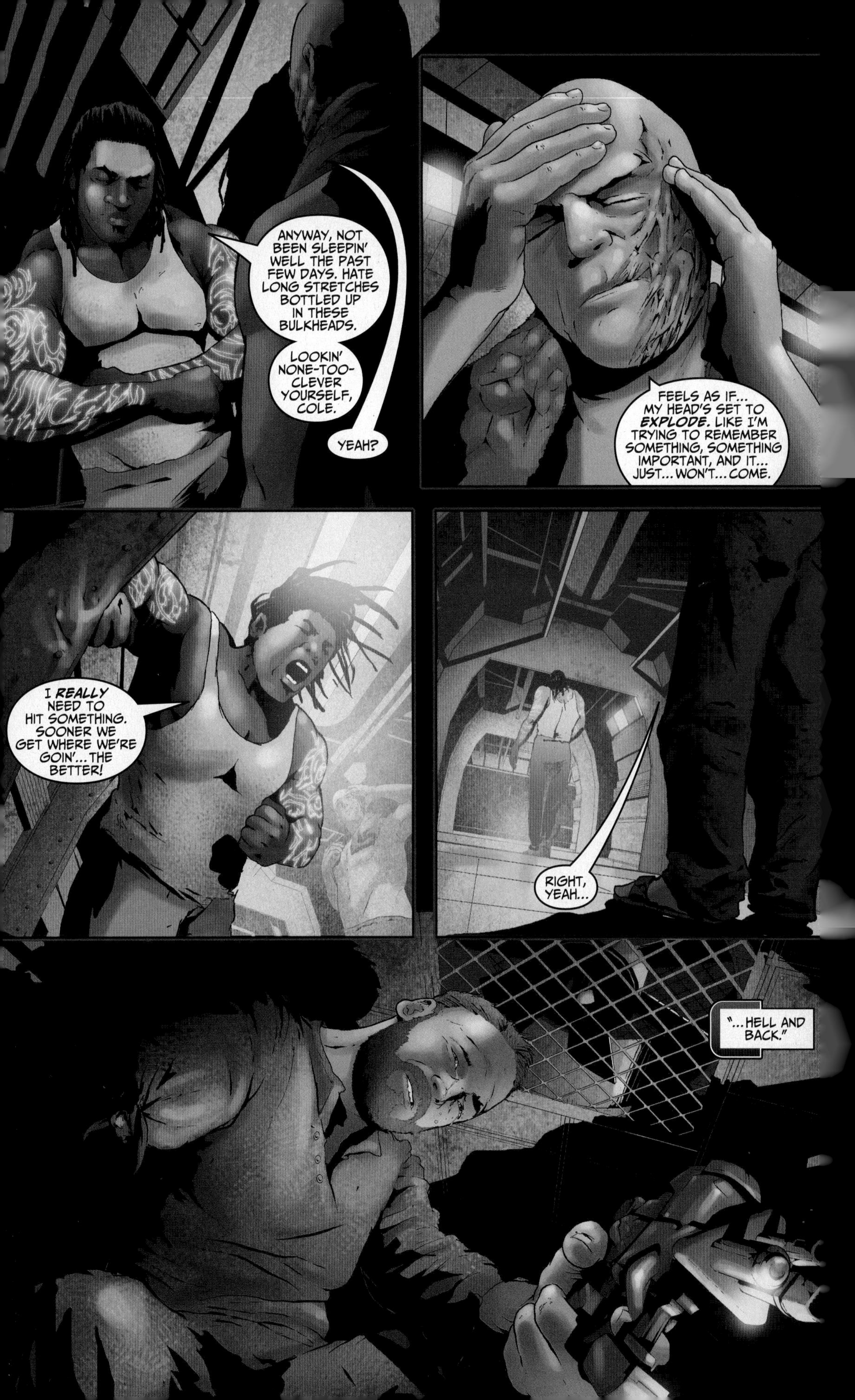
ANYWAY, NOT BEEN SLEEPIN' WELL THE PAST FEW DAYS. HATE LONG STRETCHES BOTTLED UP IN THESE BULKHEADS.
LOOKIN' NONE-TOO-CLEVER YOURSELF, COLE.
YEAH?
FEELS AS IF... MY HEAD'S SET TO ***EXPLODE.*** LIKE I'M TRYING TO REMEMBER SOMETHING, SOMETHING IMPORTANT, AND IT... JUST... WON'T... COME.
I ***REALLY*** NEED TO HIT SOMETHING. SOONER WE GET WHERE WE'RE GOIN'... THE BETTER!
RIGHT, YEAH...
"...HELL AND BACK."

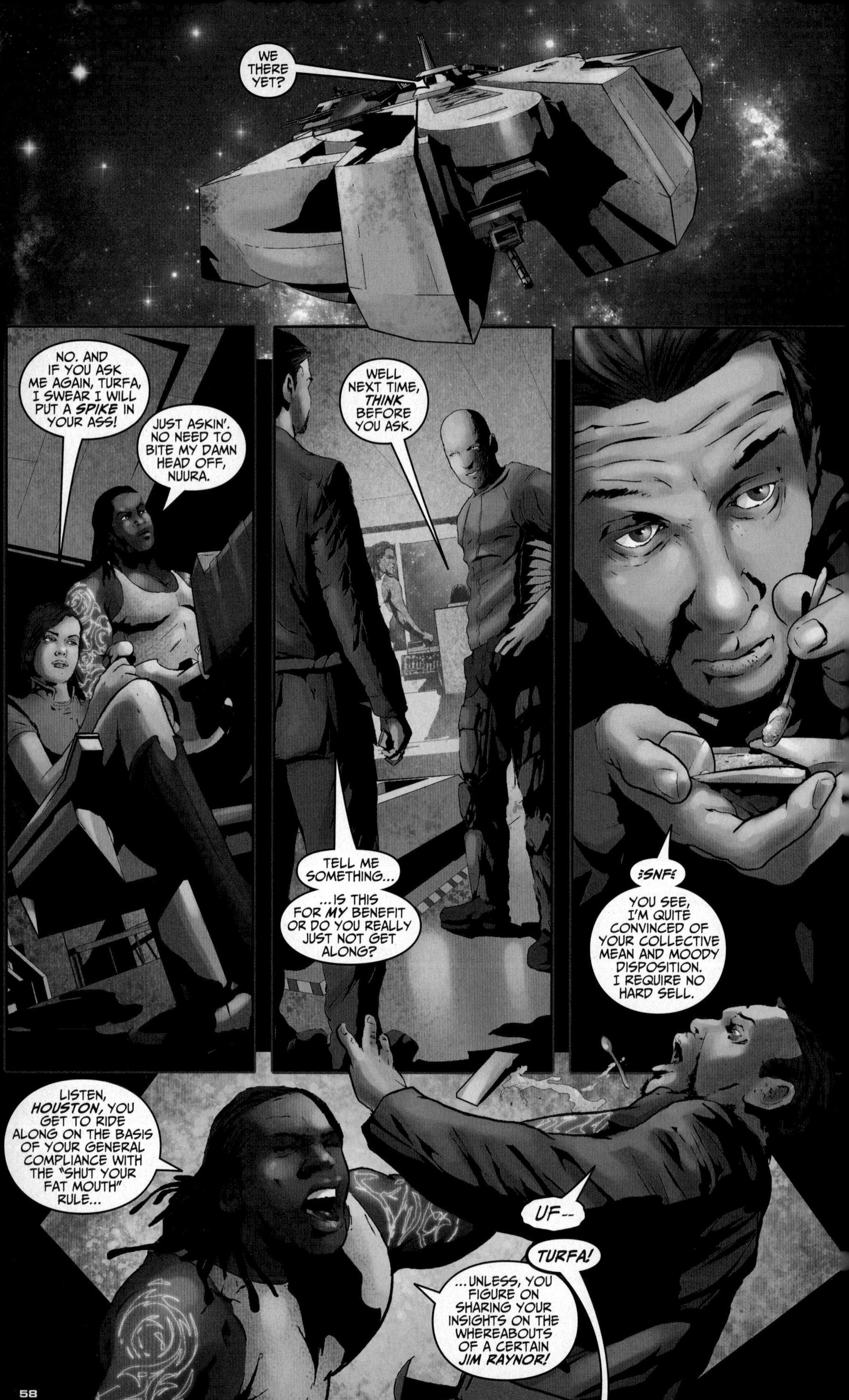
WE THERE YET?
NO. AND IF YOU ASK ME AGAIN, TURFA, I SWEAR I WILL PUT A *SPIKE* IN YOUR ASS!
JUST ASKIN'. NO NEED TO BITE MY DAMN HEAD OFF, NUURA.
WELL NEXT TIME, *THINK* BEFORE YOU ASK.
TELL ME SOMETHING...
...IS THIS FOR *MY* BENEFIT OR DO YOU REALLY JUST NOT GET ALONG?
SNF
YOU SEE, I'M QUITE CONVINCED OF YOUR COLLECTIVE MEAN AND MOODY DISPOSITION. I REQUIRE NO HARD SELL.
LISTEN, *HOUSTON*, YOU GET TO RIDE ALONG ON THE BASIS OF YOUR GENERAL COMPLIANCE WITH THE "SHUT YOUR FAT MOUTH" RULE...
UF--
TURFA!
...UNLESS, YOU FIGURE ON SHARING YOUR INSIGHTS ON THE WHEREABOUTS OF A CERTAIN *JIM RAYNOR*!

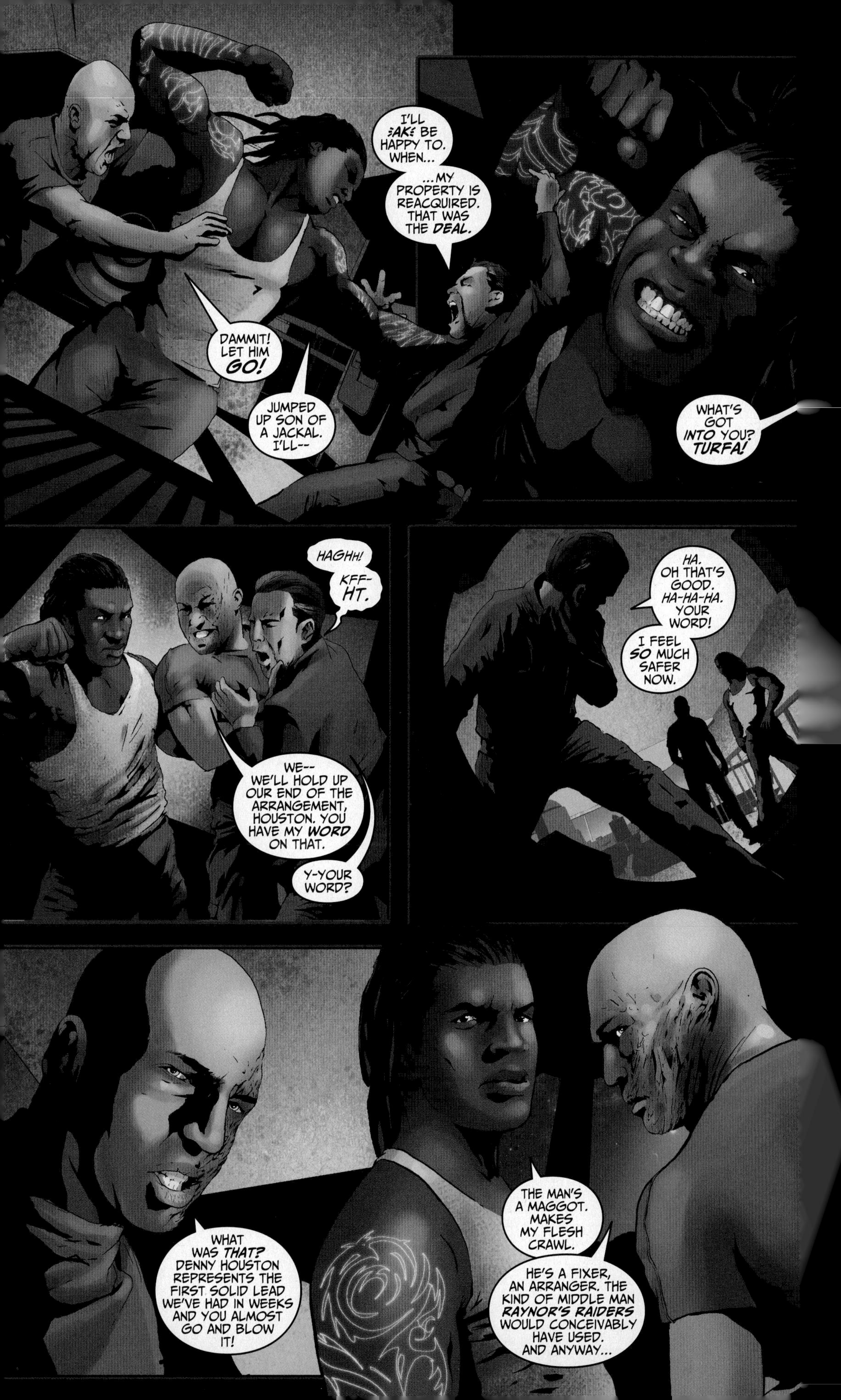

I'LL *AK* BE HAPPY TO. WHEN...
...MY PROPERTY IS REACQUIRED. THAT WAS THE DEAL.
DAMMIT! LET HIM GO!
JUMPED UP SON OF A JACKAL. I'LL--
WHAT'S GOT INTO YOU? TURFA!
HAGHH!
KFF-HT.
WE-- WE'LL HOLD UP OUR END OF THE ARRANGEMENT, HOUSTON. YOU HAVE MY WORD ON THAT.
Y-YOUR WORD?
HA. OH THAT'S GOOD. HA-HA-HA. YOUR WORD!
I FEEL SO MUCH SAFER NOW.
WHAT WAS THAT? DENNY HOUSTON REPRESENTS THE FIRST SOLID LEAD WE'VE HAD IN WEEKS AND YOU ALMOST GO AND BLOW IT!
THE MAN'S A MAGGOT. MAKES MY FLESH CRAWL.
HE'S A FIXER, AN ARRANGER. THE KIND OF MIDDLE MAN RAYNOR'S RAIDERS WOULD CONCEIVABLY HAVE USED. AND ANYWAY...

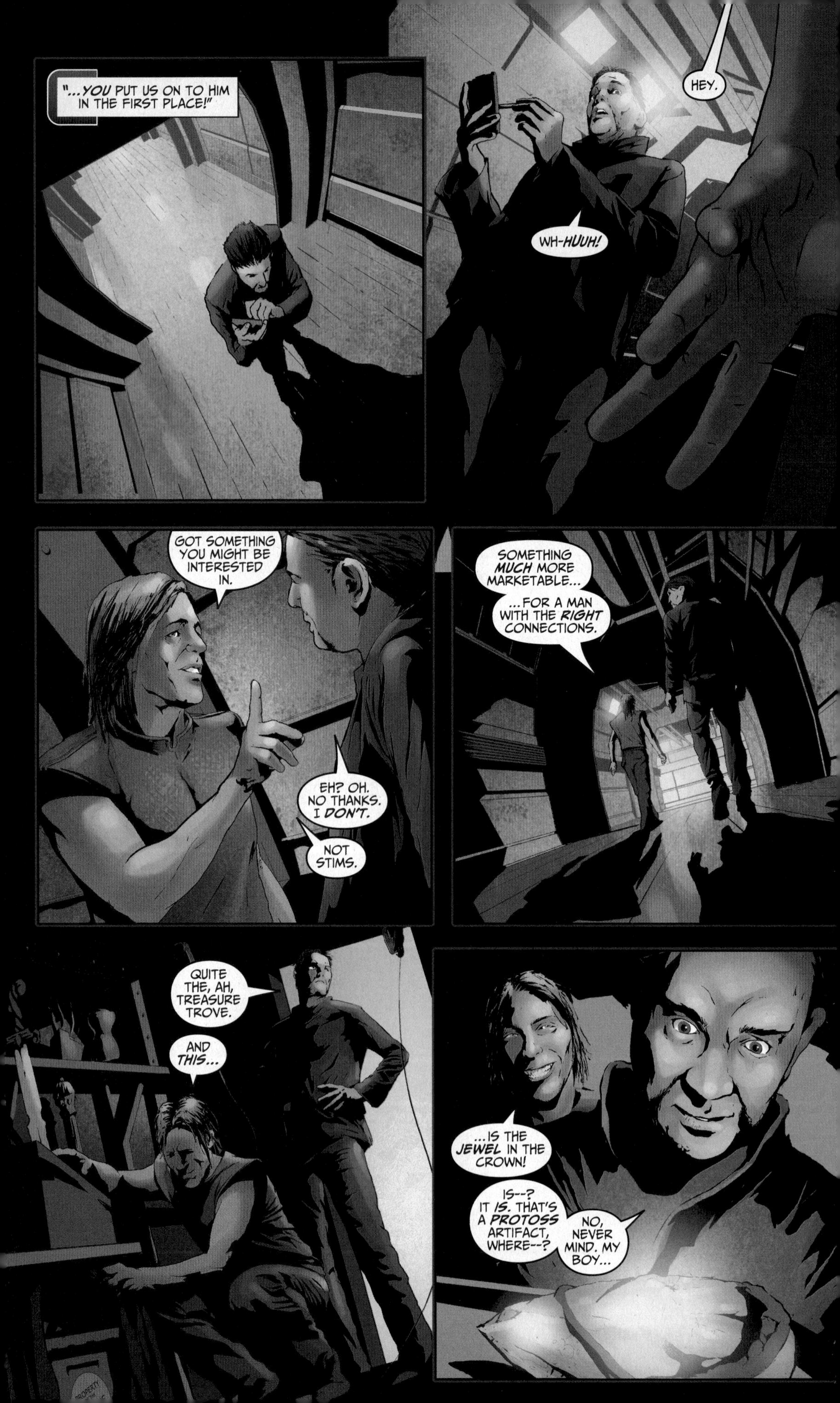
"...YOU PUT US ON TO HIM IN THE FIRST PLACE!"
HEY.
WH-HUUH!
GOT SOMETHING YOU MIGHT BE INTERESTED IN.
EH? OH. NO THANKS. I DON'T.
NOT STIMS.
SOMETHING MUCH MORE MARKETABLE...
...FOR A MAN WITH THE RIGHT CONNECTIONS.
QUITE THE, AH, TREASURE TROVE.
AND THIS...
...IS THE JEWEL IN THE CROWN!
IS--? IT IS. THAT'S A PROTOSS ARTIFACT, WHERE--?
NO, NEVER MIND. MY BOY...

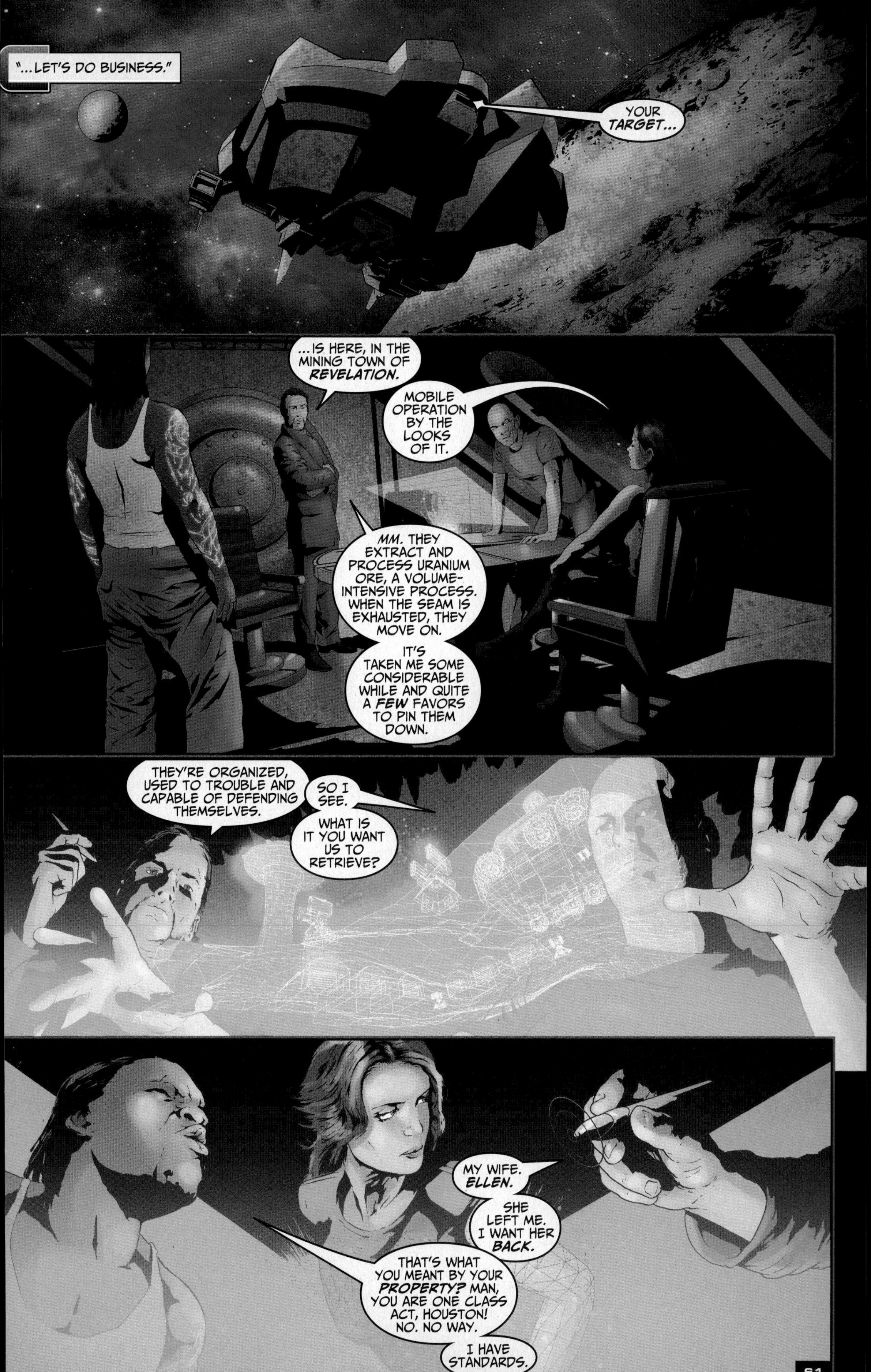
"...LET'S DO BUSINESS."
YOUR TARGET...
...IS HERE, IN THE MINING TOWN OF REVELATION.
MOBILE OPERATION BY THE LOOKS OF IT.
MM. THEY EXTRACT AND PROCESS URANIUM ORE, A VOLUME-INTENSIVE PROCESS. WHEN THE SEAM IS EXHAUSTED, THEY MOVE ON.
IT'S TAKEN ME SOME CONSIDERABLE WHILE AND QUITE A FEW FAVORS TO PIN THEM DOWN.
THEY'RE ORGANIZED, USED TO TROUBLE AND CAPABLE OF DEFENDING THEMSELVES.
SO I SEE.
WHAT IS IT YOU WANT US TO RETRIEVE?
MY WIFE. ELLEN.
SHE LEFT ME. I WANT HER BACK.
THAT'S WHAT YOU MEANT BY YOUR PROPERTY? MAN, YOU ARE ONE CLASS ACT, HOUSTON! NO. NO WAY.
I HAVE STANDARDS.

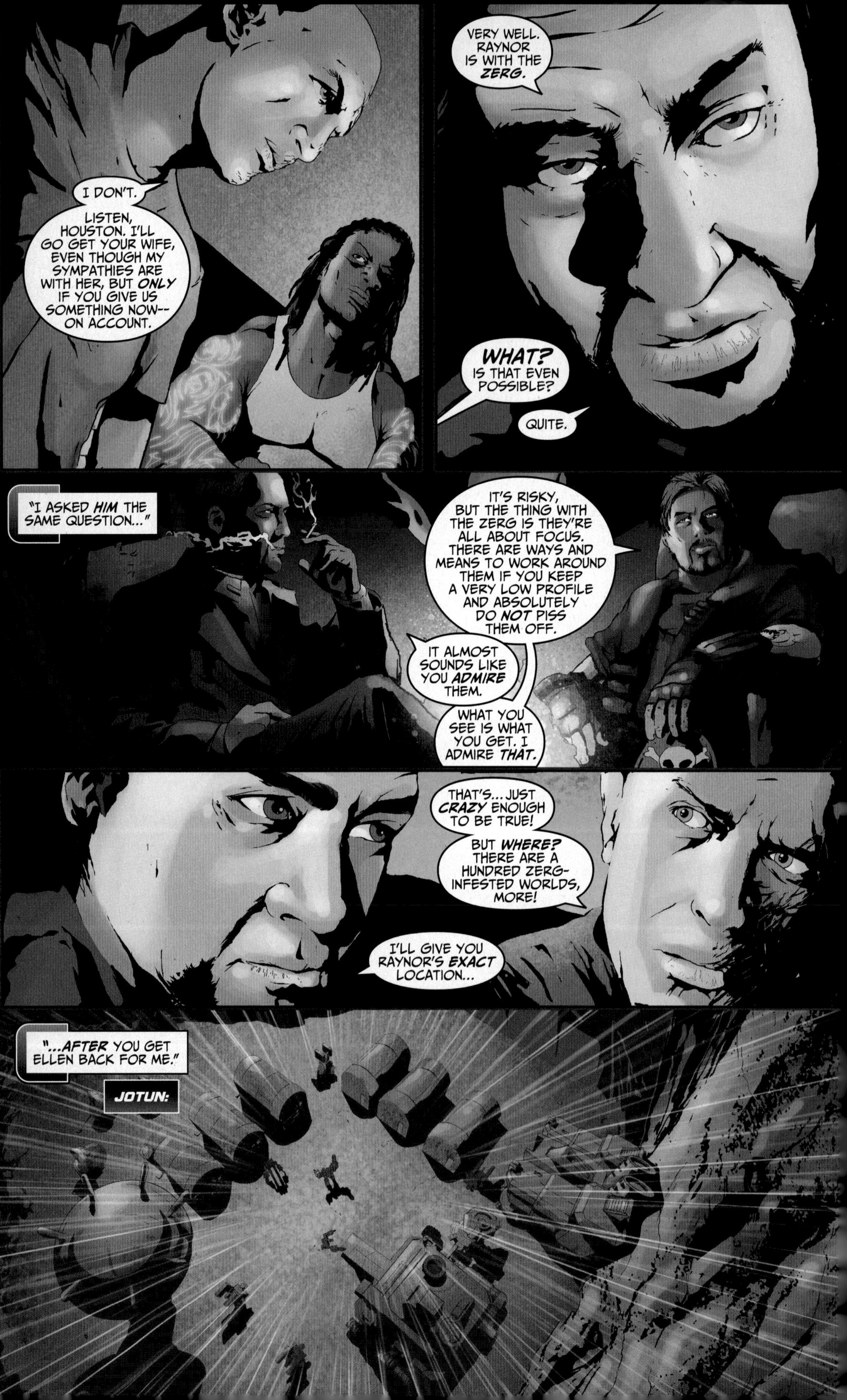
I DON'T.
LISTEN, HOUSTON. I'LL GO GET YOUR WIFE, EVEN THOUGH MY SYMPATHIES ARE WITH HER, BUT ONLY IF YOU GIVE US SOMETHING NOW-- ON ACCOUNT.
VERY WELL. RAYNOR IS WITH THE ZERG.
WHAT? IS THAT EVEN POSSIBLE?
QUITE.
"I ASKED HIM THE SAME QUESTION..."
IT'S RISKY, BUT THE THING WITH THE ZERG IS THEY'RE ALL ABOUT FOCUS. THERE ARE WAYS AND MEANS TO WORK AROUND THEM IF YOU KEEP A VERY LOW PROFILE AND ABSOLUTELY DO NOT PISS THEM OFF.
IT ALMOST SOUNDS LIKE YOU ADMIRE THEM.
WHAT YOU SEE IS WHAT YOU GET. I ADMIRE THAT.
THAT'S... JUST CRAZY ENOUGH TO BE TRUE!
BUT WHERE? THERE ARE A HUNDRED ZERG-INFESTED WORLDS, MORE!
I'LL GIVE YOU RAYNOR'S EXACT LOCATION...
"...AFTER YOU GET ELLEN BACK FOR ME."
JOTUN:

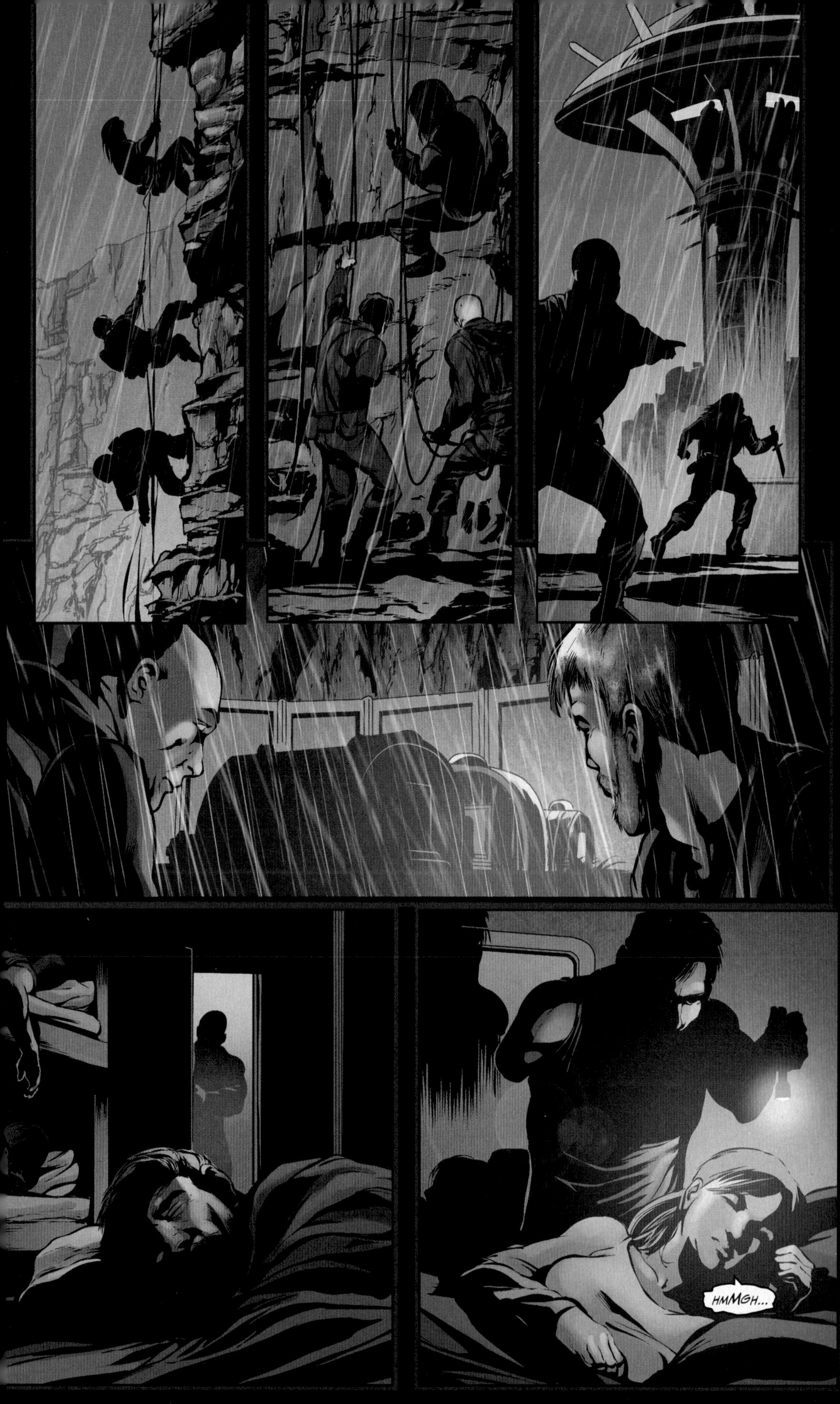
HMMGH...

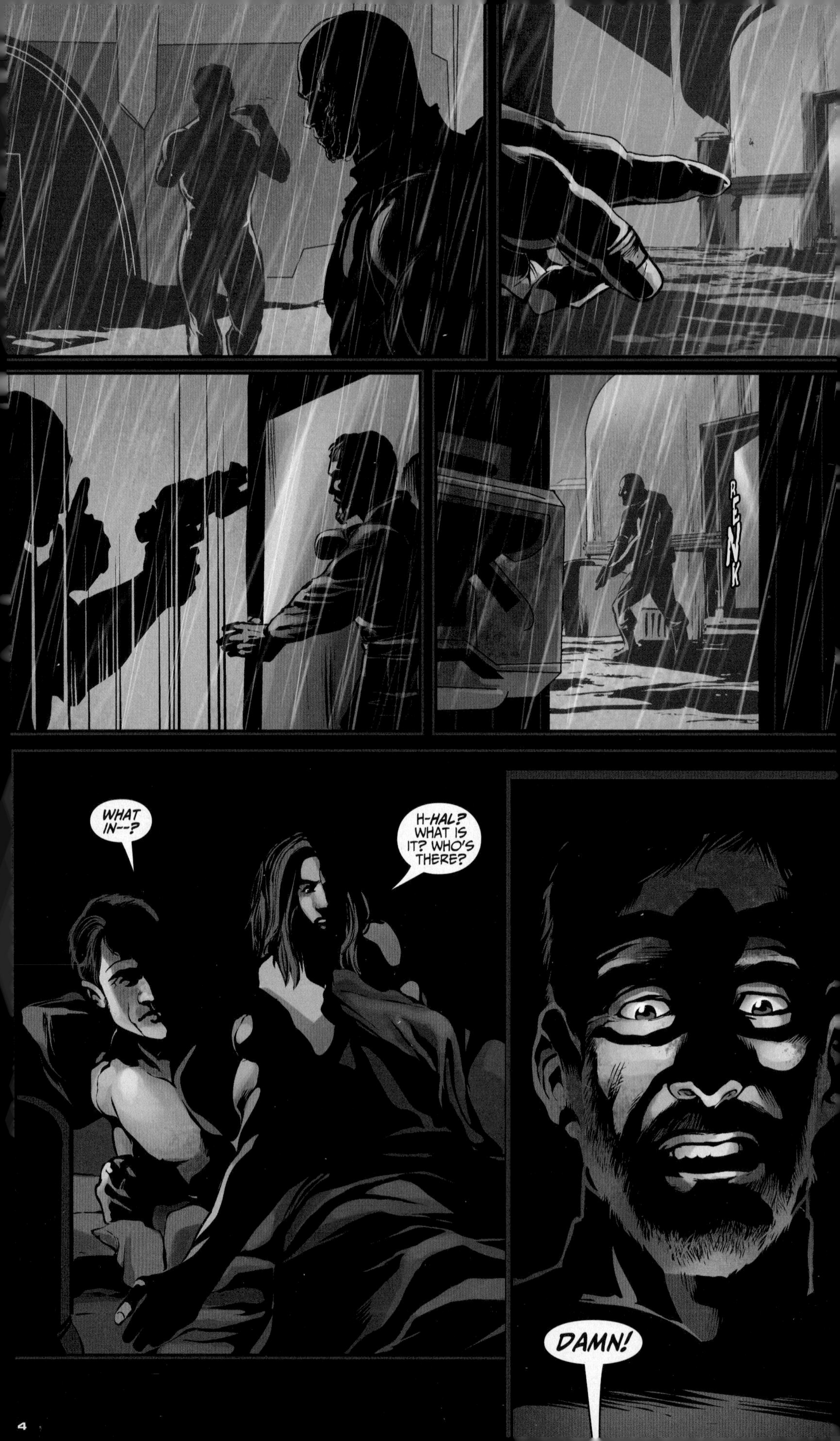

RENK
WHAT IN--?
H-HAL? WHAT IS IT? WHO'S THERE?
DAMN!

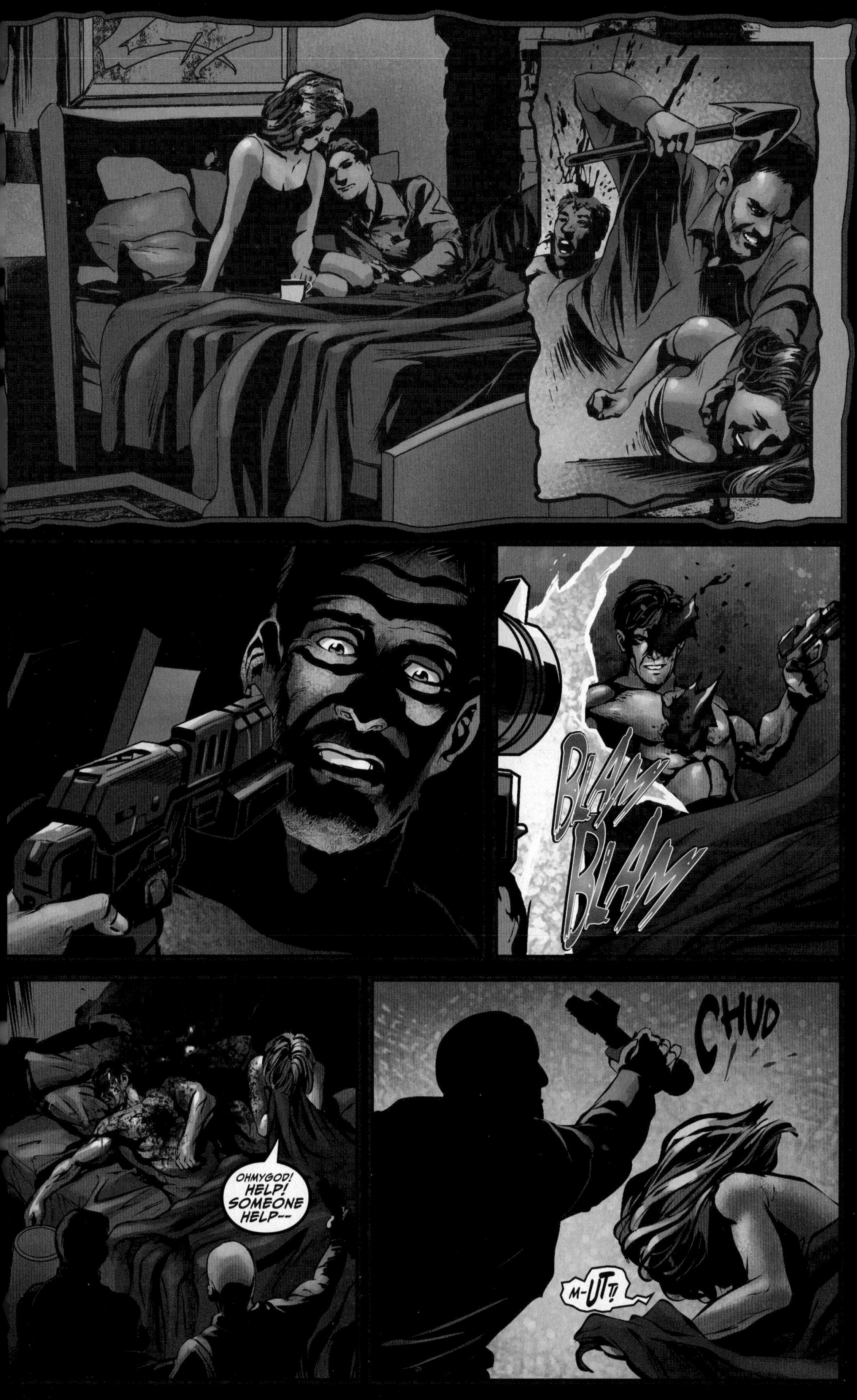
BLAM
BLAM
OHMYGOD! HELP! SOMEONE HELP--
CHUD
M-UT!!

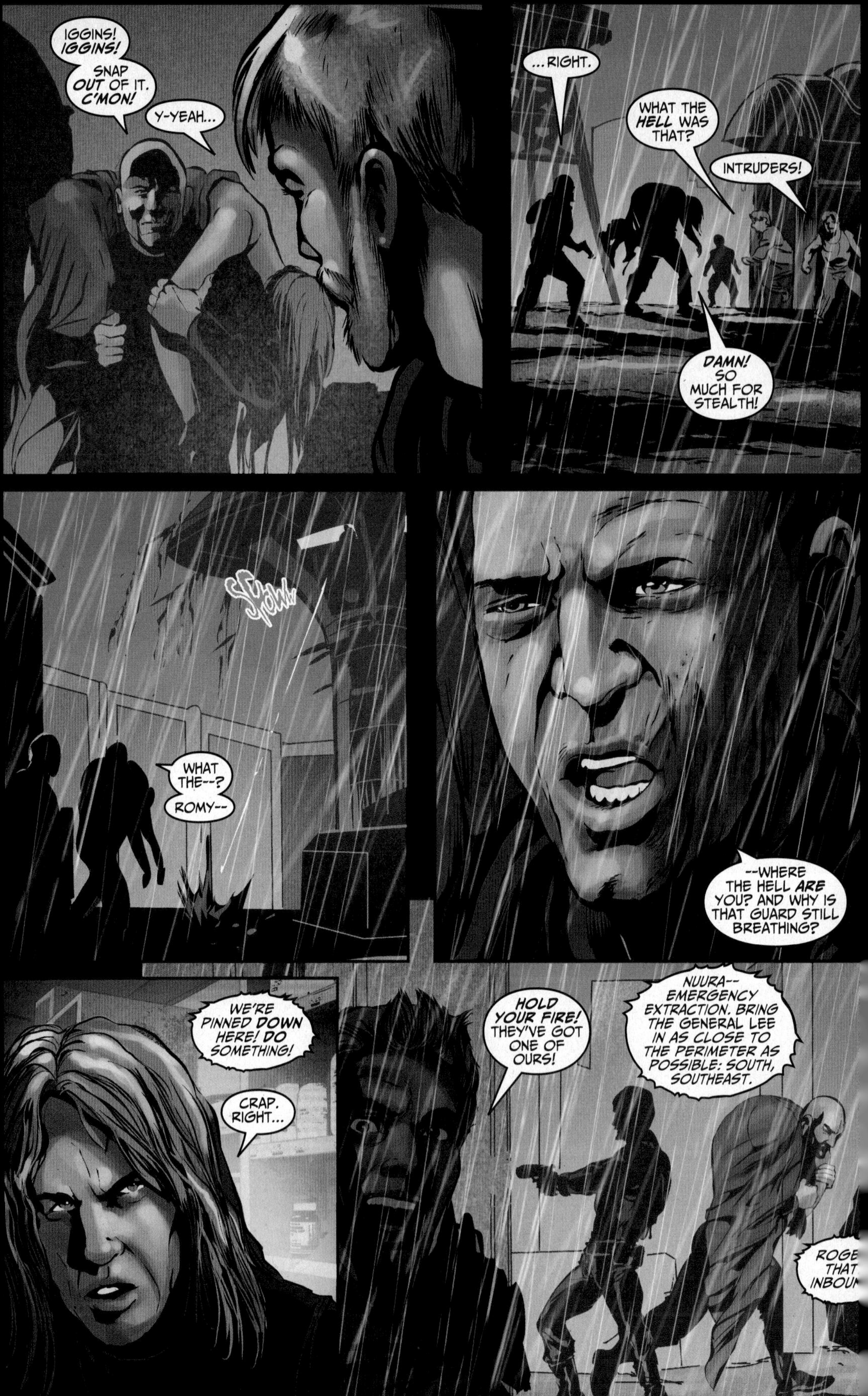
IGGINS! IGGINS!
SNAP OUT OF IT. C'MON!
Y-YEAH...
...RIGHT.
WHAT THE HELL WAS THAT?
INTRUDERS!
DAMN! SO MUCH FOR STEALTH!
WHAT THE--?
ROMY--
--WHERE THE HELL ARE YOU? AND WHY IS THAT GUARD STILL BREATHING?
WE'RE PINNED DOWN HERE! DO SOMETHING!
CRAP. RIGHT...
HOLD YOUR FIRE! THEY'VE GOT ONE OF OURS!
NUURA-- EMERGENCY EXTRACTION. BRING THE GENERAL LEE IN AS CLOSE TO THE PERIMETER AS POSSIBLE: SOUTH, SOUTHEAST.
ROGE
THAT
INBOUN

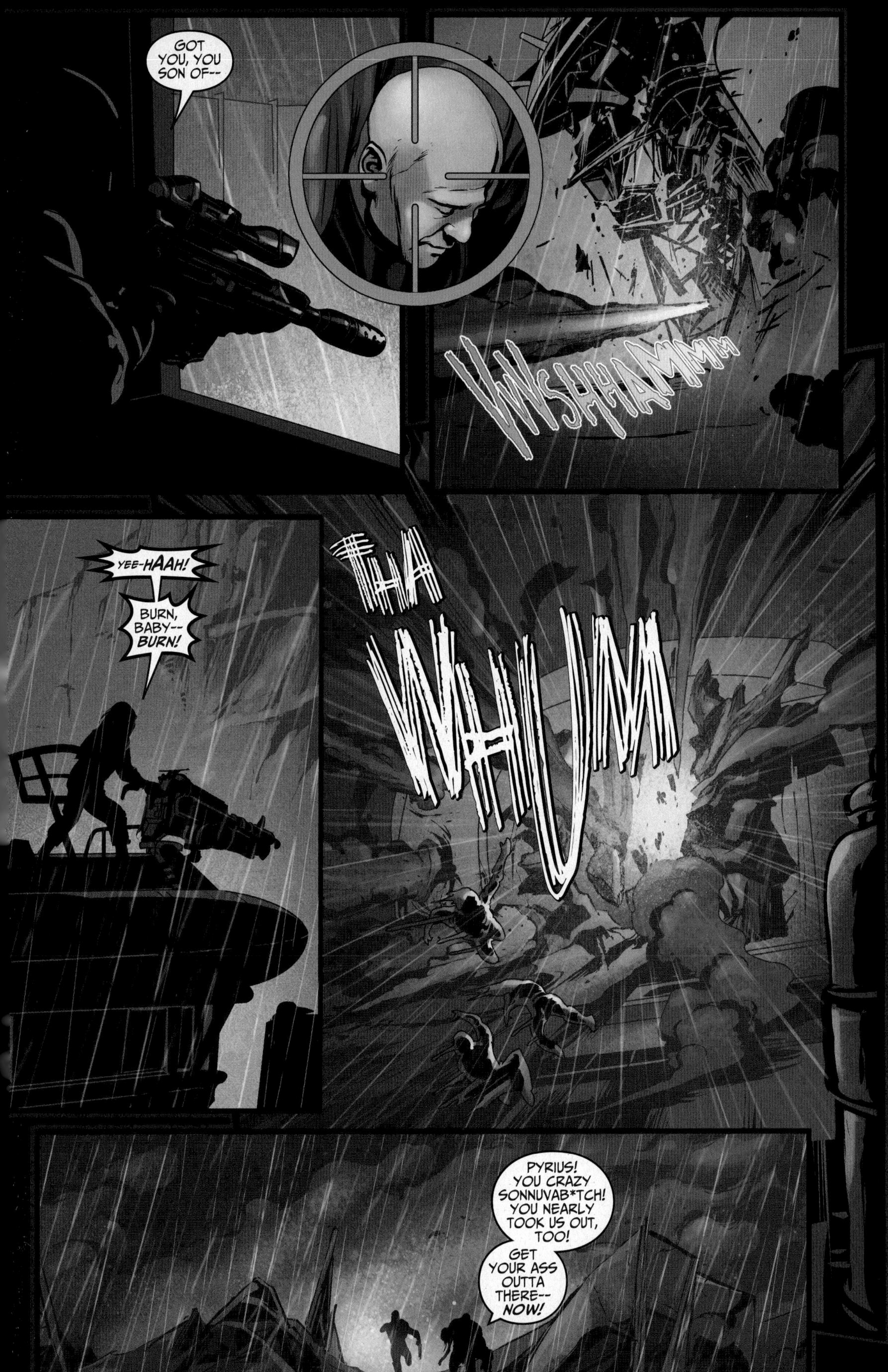
GOT YOU, YOU SON OF--
VVVSHHAMMMM
YEE-HAAH!
BURN, BABY-- BURN!
THA WHUMM
PYRIUS! YOU CRAZY SONNUVAB*TCH! YOU NEARLY TOOK US OUT, TOO!
GET YOUR ASS OUTTA THERE-- NOW!

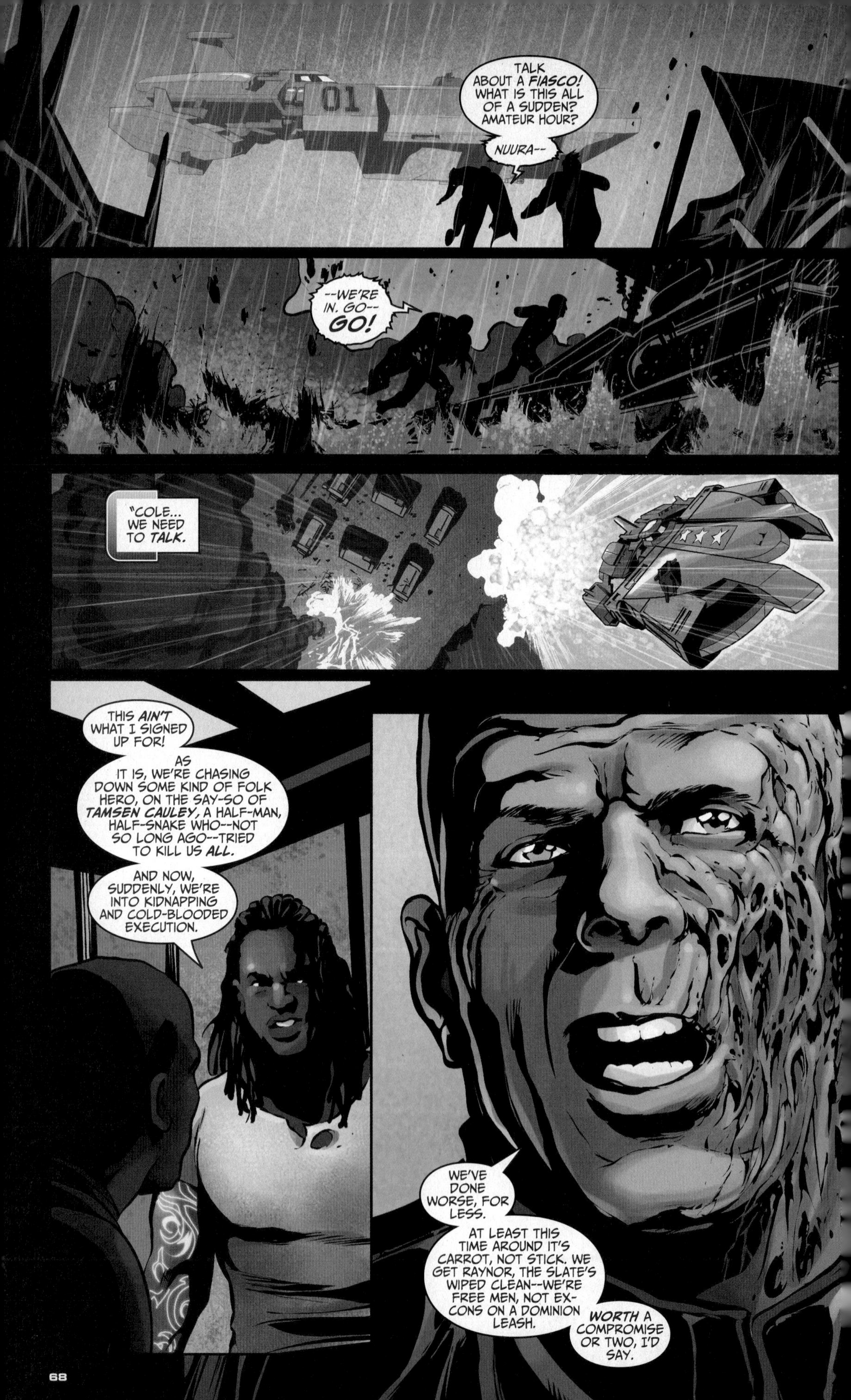
TALK ABOUT A *FIASCO!* WHAT IS THIS ALL OF A SUDDEN? AMATEUR HOUR?
NUURA--
--WE'RE IN. GO--*GO!*
"COLE... WE NEED TO *TALK.*
THIS *AIN'T* WHAT I SIGNED UP FOR!
AS IT IS, WE'RE CHASING DOWN SOME KIND OF FOLK HERO, ON THE SAY-SO OF *TAMSEN CAULEY,* A HALF-MAN, HALF-SNAKE WHO--NOT SO LONG AGO--TRIED TO KILL US *ALL.*
AND NOW, SUDDENLY, WE'RE INTO KIDNAPPING AND COLD-BLOODED EXECUTION.
WE'VE DONE WORSE, FOR LESS.
AT LEAST THIS TIME AROUND IT'S CARROT, NOT STICK. WE GET RAYNOR, THE SLATE'S WIPED CLEAN--WE'RE FREE MEN, NOT EX-CONS ON A DOMINION LEASH.
WORTH A COMPROMISE OR TWO, I'D SAY.

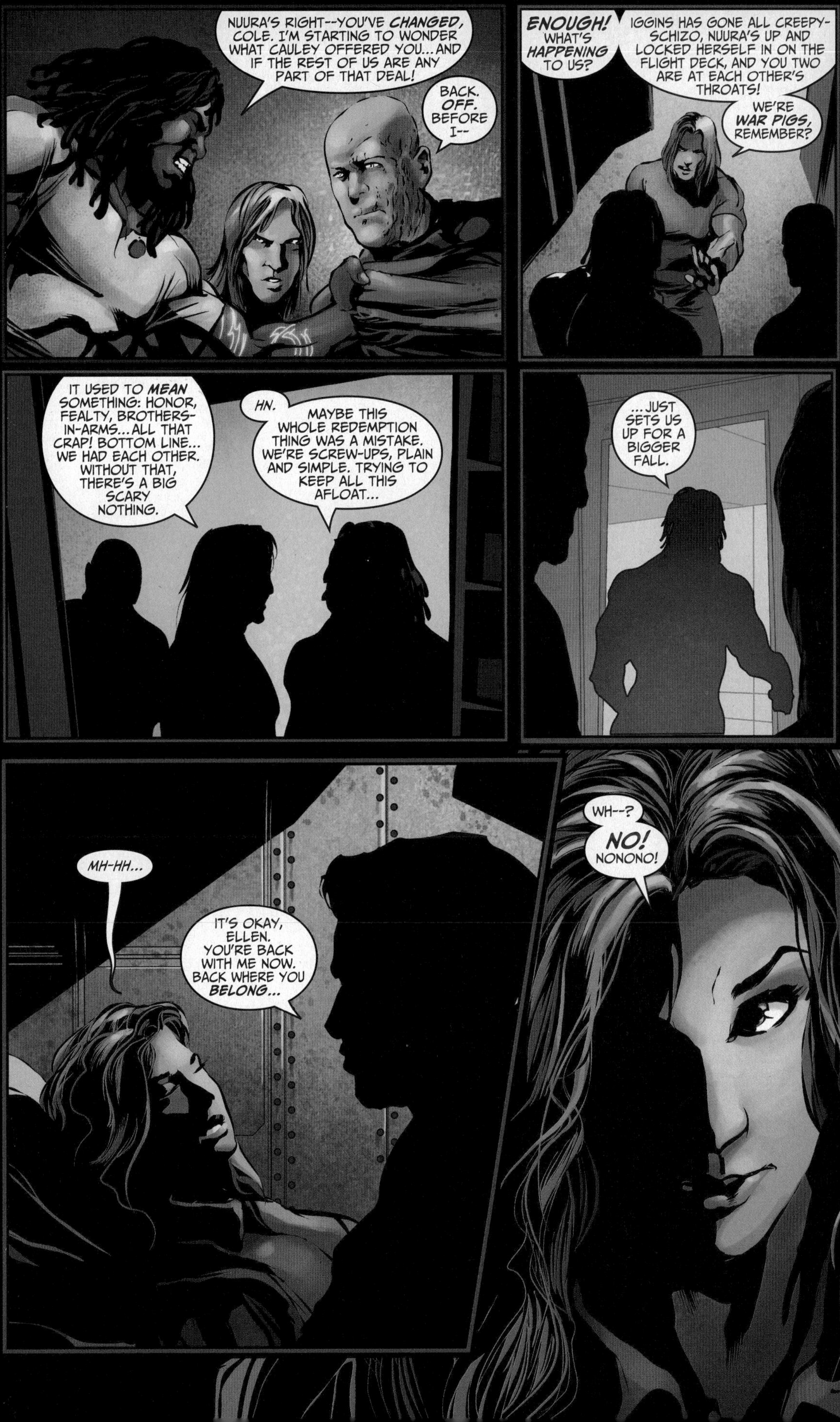
NUURA'S RIGHT--YOU'VE CHANGED, COLE. I'M STARTING TO WONDER WHAT CAULEY OFFERED YOU... AND IF THE REST OF US ARE ANY PART OF THAT DEAL!
BACK. OFF. BEFORE I--
ENOUGH! WHAT'S HAPPENING TO US?
IGGINS HAS GONE ALL CREEPY-SCHIZO, NUURA'S UP AND LOCKED HERSELF IN ON THE FLIGHT DECK, AND YOU TWO ARE AT EACH OTHER'S THROATS!
WE'RE WAR PIGS, REMEMBER?
IT USED TO MEAN SOMETHING: HONOR, FEALTY, BROTHERS-IN-ARMS... ALL THAT CRAP! BOTTOM LINE... WE HAD EACH OTHER. WITHOUT THAT, THERE'S A BIG SCARY NOTHING.
HN.
MAYBE THIS WHOLE REDEMPTION THING WAS A MISTAKE. WE'RE SCREW-UPS, PLAIN AND SIMPLE. TRYING TO KEEP ALL THIS AFLOAT...
...JUST SETS US UP FOR A BIGGER FALL.
MH-HH...
IT'S OKAY, ELLEN. YOU'RE BACK WITH ME NOW. BACK WHERE YOU BELONG...
WH--? NO! NONONO!

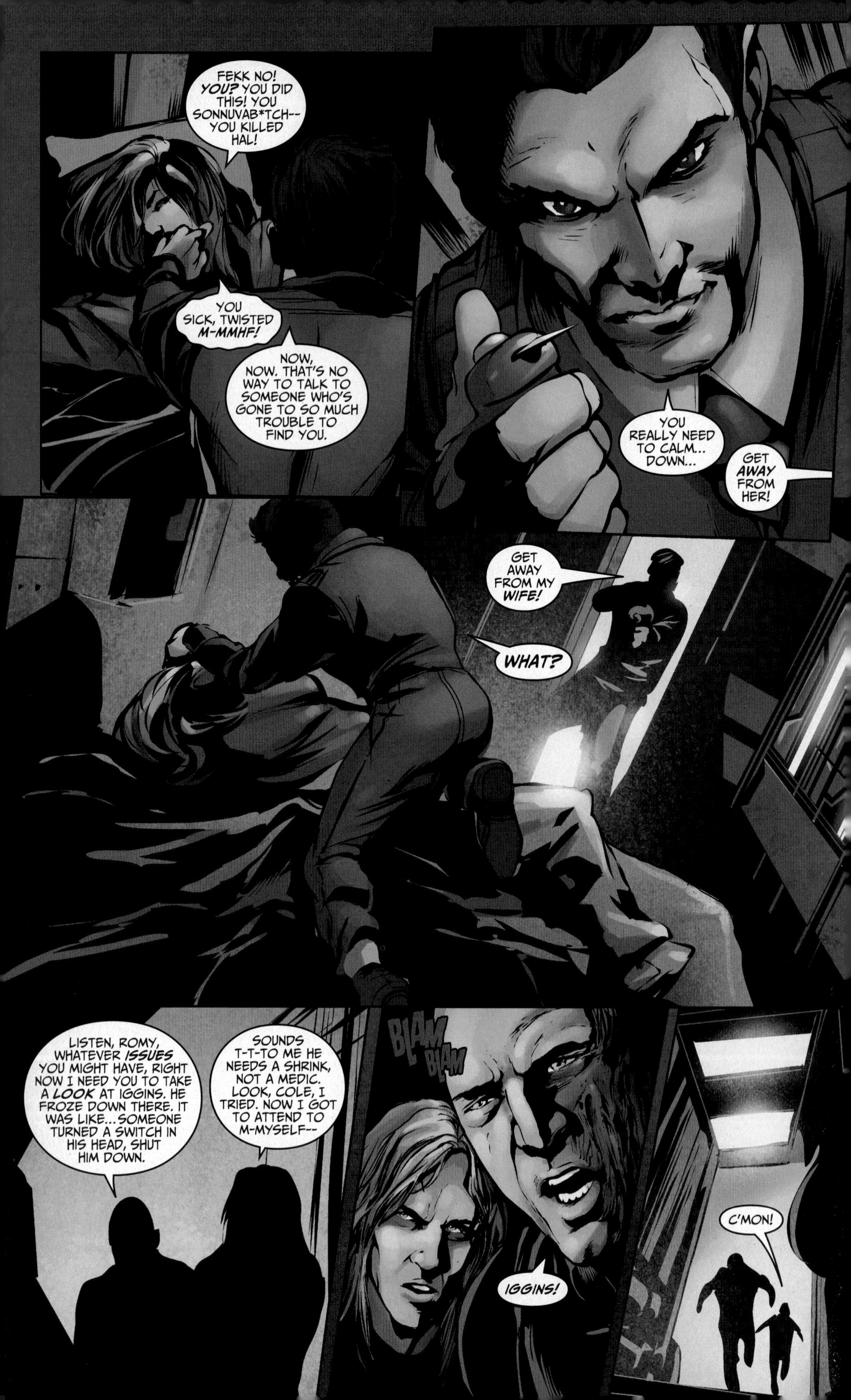

FEKK NO! YOU? YOU DID THIS! YOU SONNUVAB*TCH-- YOU KILLED HAL!
YOU SICK, TWISTED M-MMHF!
NOW, NOW. THAT'S NO WAY TO TALK TO SOMEONE WHO'S GONE TO SO MUCH TROUBLE TO FIND YOU.
YOU REALLY NEED TO CALM... DOWN...
GET AWAY FROM HER!
GET AWAY FROM MY WIFE!
WHAT?
LISTEN, ROMY, WHATEVER ISSUES YOU MIGHT HAVE, RIGHT NOW I NEED YOU TO TAKE A LOOK AT IGGINS. HE FROZE DOWN THERE. IT WAS LIKE... SOMEONE TURNED A SWITCH IN HIS HEAD, SHUT HIM DOWN.
SOUNDS T-T-TO ME HE NEEDS A SHRINK, NOT A MEDIC. LOOK, COLE, I TRIED. NOW I GOT TO ATTEND TO M-MYSELF--
BLAM BLAM
IGGINS!
C'MON!

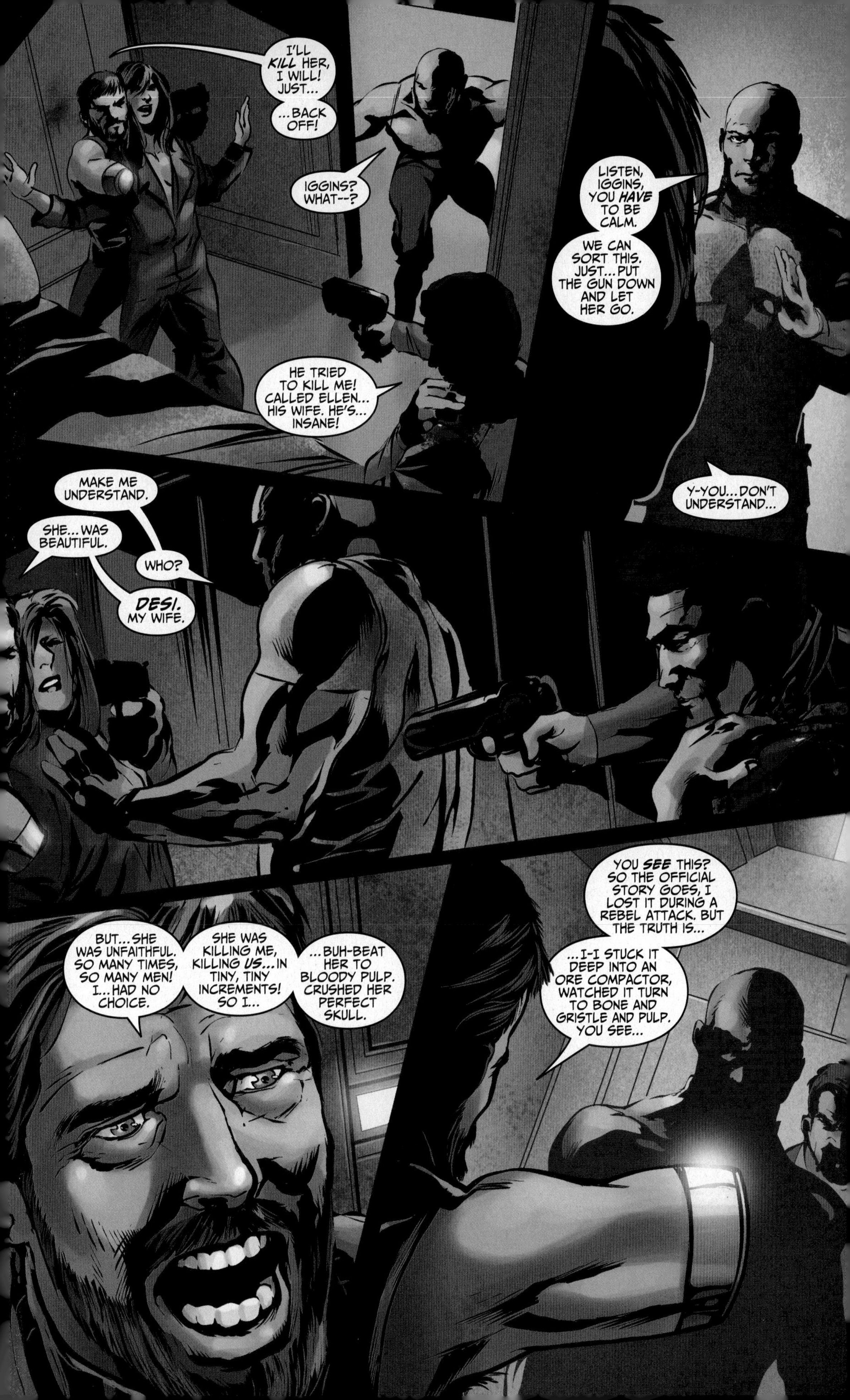
I'LL KILL HER, I WILL! JUST...
...BACK OFF!
IGGINS? WHAT--?
HE TRIED TO KILL ME! CALLED ELLEN... HIS WIFE. HE'S... INSANE!
LISTEN, IGGINS, YOU HAVE TO BE CALM.
WE CAN SORT THIS. JUST...PUT THE GUN DOWN AND LET HER GO.
Y-YOU...DON'T UNDERSTAND...
MAKE ME UNDERSTAND.
SHE...WAS BEAUTIFUL.
WHO?
DESI. MY WIFE.
BUT...SHE WAS UNFAITHFUL. SO MANY TIMES, SO MANY MEN! I...HAD NO CHOICE.
SHE WAS KILLING ME, KILLING US...IN TINY, TINY INCREMENTS! SO I...
...BUH-BEAT HER TO BLOODY PULP. CRUSHED HER PERFECT SKULL.
YOU SEE THIS? SO THE OFFICIAL STORY GOES, I LOST IT DURING A REBEL ATTACK. BUT THE TRUTH IS...
...I-I STUCK IT DEEP INTO AN ORE COMPACTOR, WATCHED IT TURN TO BONE AND GRISTLE AND PULP. YOU SEE...

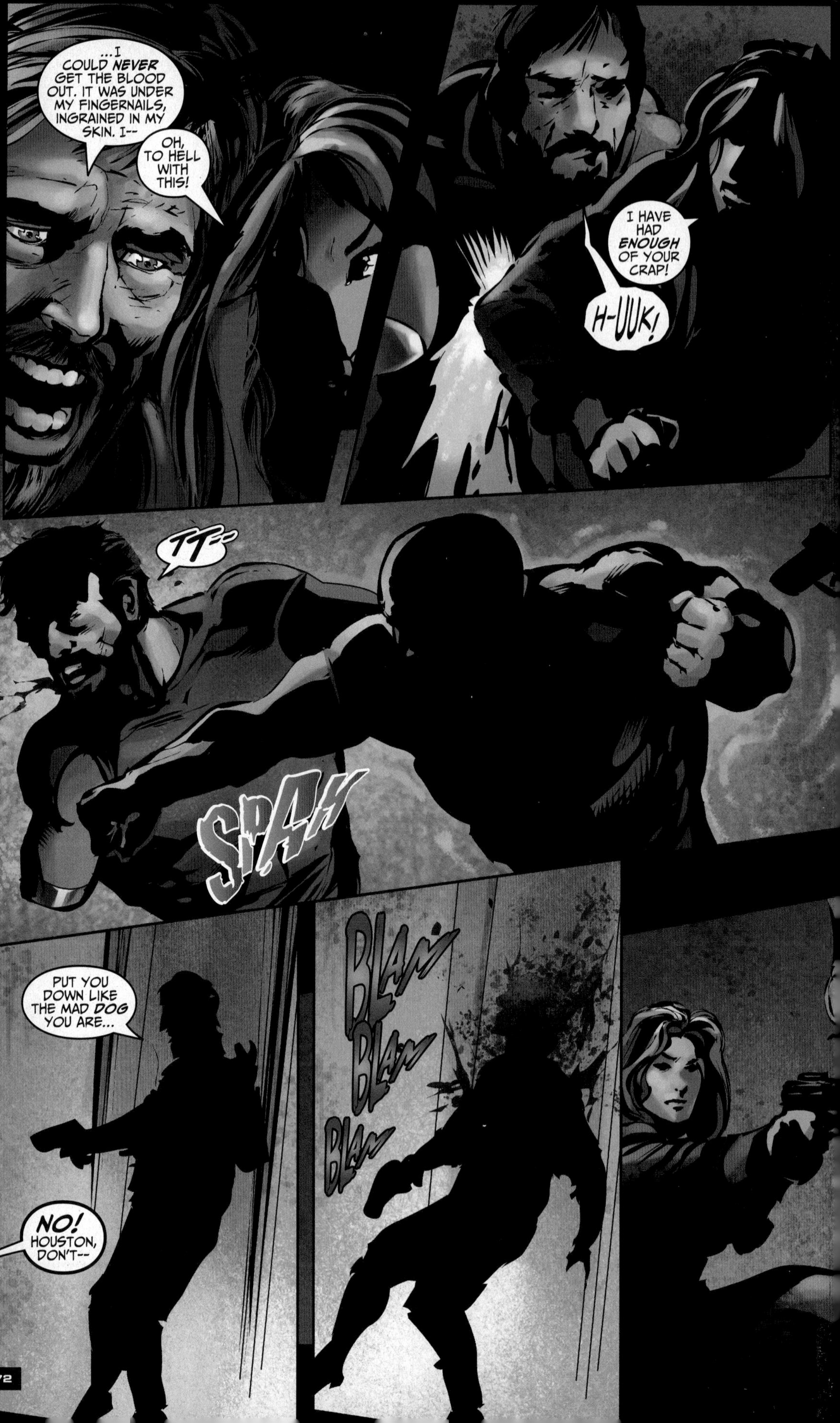
...I COULD NEVER GET THE BLOOD OUT. IT WAS UNDER MY FINGERNAILS, INGRAINED IN MY SKIN. I--
OH, TO HELL WITH THIS!
I HAVE HAD ENOUGH OF YOUR CRAP!
H-UUK!
TT--
SPAK
PUT YOU DOWN LIKE THE MAD DOG YOU ARE...
NO! HOUSTON, DON'T--
BLAM
BLAM
BLAM
BLAM

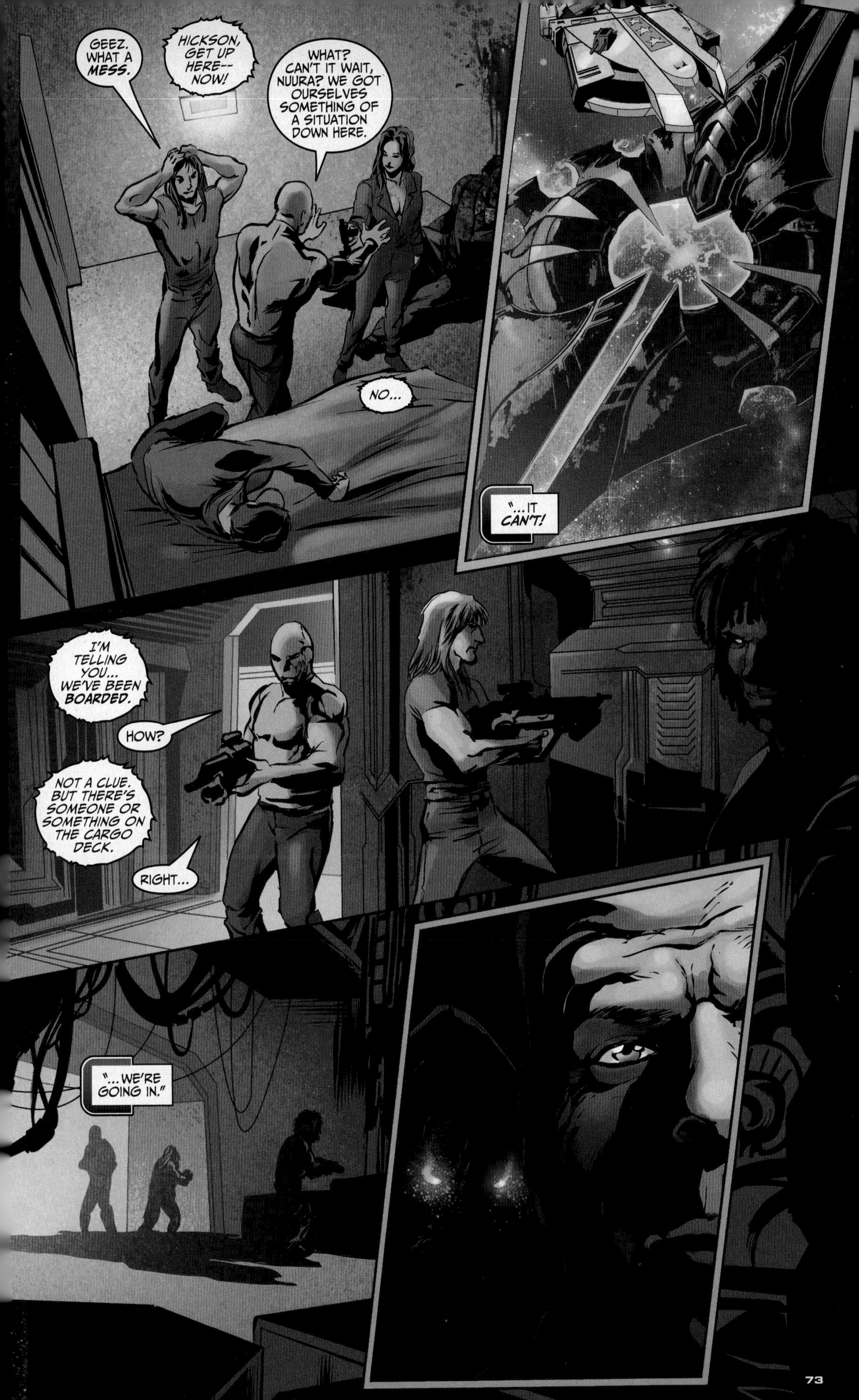
GEEZ. WHAT A MESS.
HICKSON, GET UP HERE-- NOW!
WHAT? CAN'T IT WAIT, NUURA? WE GOT OURSELVES SOMETHING OF A SITUATION DOWN HERE.
NO...
"...IT CAN'T!
I'M TELLING YOU... WE'VE BEEN BOARDED.
HOW?
NOT A CLUE. BUT THERE'S SOMEONE OR SOMETHING ON THE CARGO DECK.
RIGHT...
"...WE'RE GOING IN."

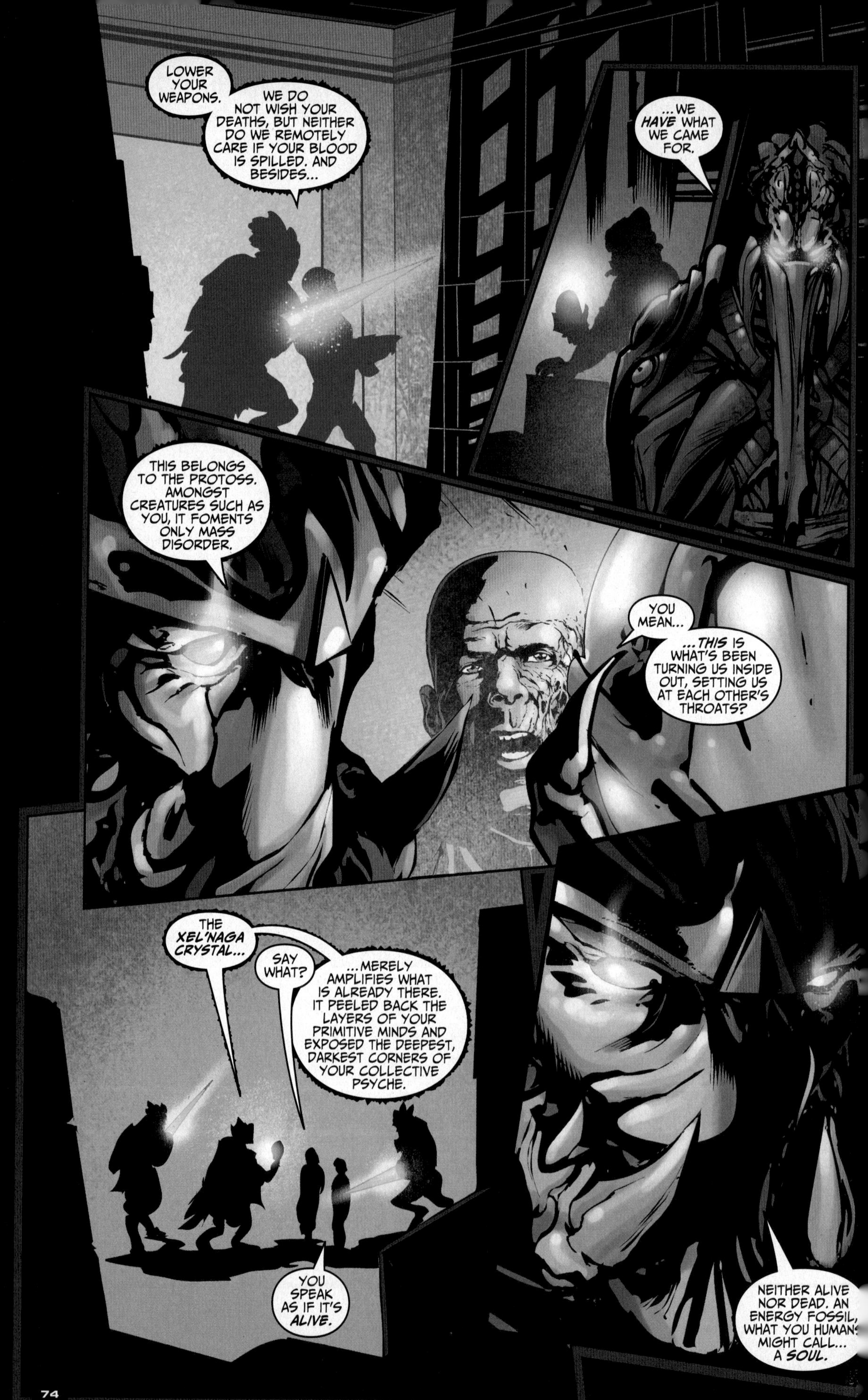
LOWER YOUR WEAPONS.
WE DO NOT WISH YOUR DEATHS, BUT NEITHER DO WE REMOTELY CARE IF YOUR BLOOD IS SPILLED. AND BESIDES...
...WE HAVE WHAT WE CAME FOR.
THIS BELONGS TO THE PROTOSS. AMONGST CREATURES SUCH AS YOU, IT FOMENTS ONLY MASS DISORDER.
YOU MEAN...
...THIS IS WHAT'S BEEN TURNING US INSIDE OUT, SETTING US AT EACH OTHER'S THROATS?
THE XEL'NAGA CRYSTAL...
SAY WHAT?
...MERELY AMPLIFIES WHAT IS ALREADY THERE. IT PEELED BACK THE LAYERS OF YOUR PRIMITIVE MINDS AND EXPOSED THE DEEPEST, DARKEST CORNERS OF YOUR COLLECTIVE PSYCHE.
YOU SPEAK AS IF IT'S ALIVE.
NEITHER ALIVE NOR DEAD. AN ENERGY FOSSIL, WHAT YOU HUMANS MIGHT CALL... A SOUL.

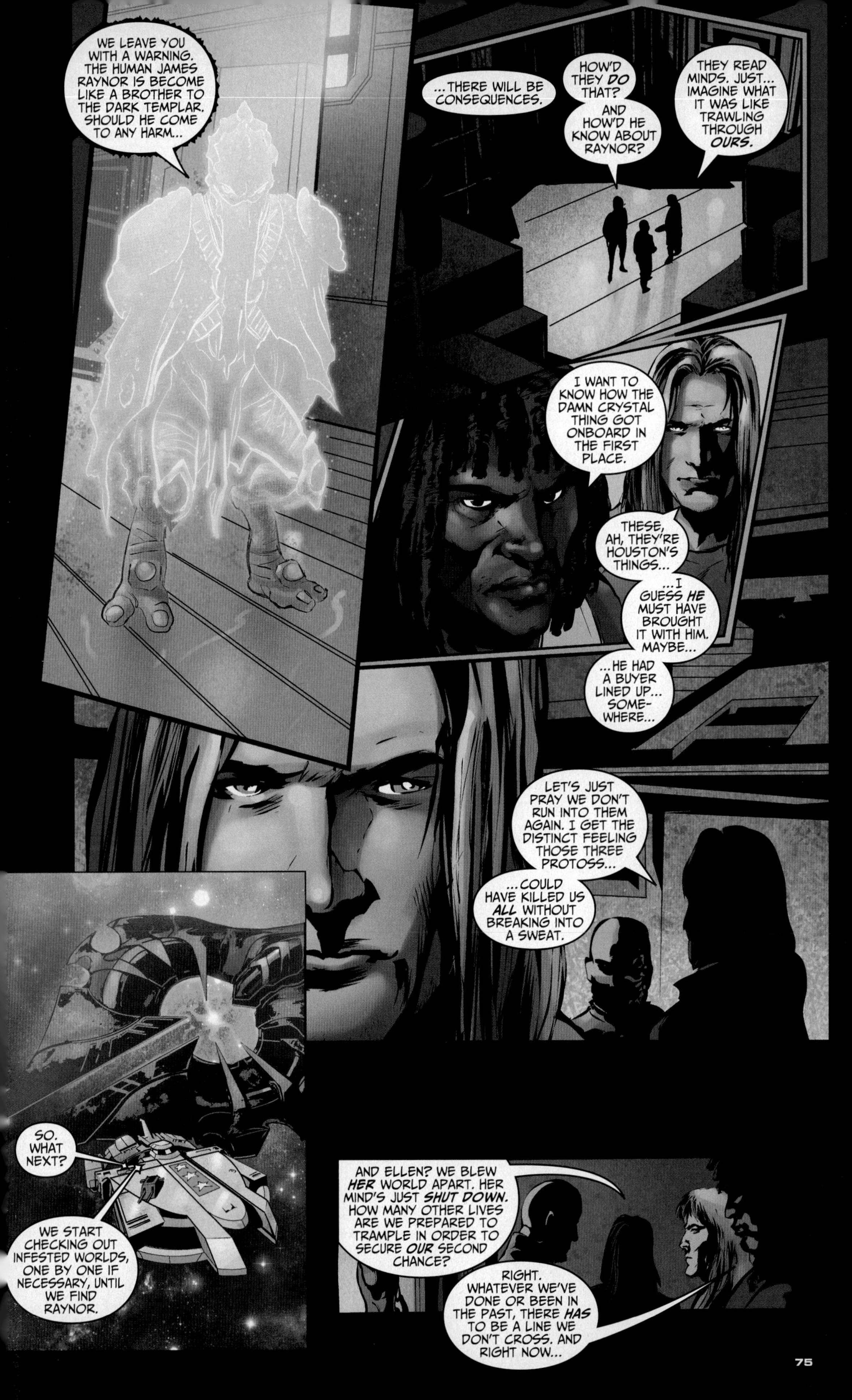
WE LEAVE YOU WITH A WARNING. THE HUMAN JAMES RAYNOR IS BECOME LIKE A BROTHER TO THE DARK TEMPLAR. SHOULD HE COME TO ANY HARM...
...THERE WILL BE CONSEQUENCES.
HOW'D THEY DO THAT?
AND HOW'D HE KNOW ABOUT RAYNOR?
THEY READ MINDS. JUST... IMAGINE WHAT IT WAS LIKE TRAWLING THROUGH OURS.
I WANT TO KNOW HOW THE DAMN CRYSTAL THING GOT ONBOARD IN THE FIRST PLACE.
THESE, AH, THEY'RE HOUSTON'S THINGS...
...I GUESS HE MUST HAVE BROUGHT IT WITH HIM. MAYBE...
...HE HAD A BUYER LINED UP... SOME-WHERE...
LET'S JUST PRAY WE DON'T RUN INTO THEM AGAIN. I GET THE DISTINCT FEELING THOSE THREE PROTOSS...
...COULD HAVE KILLED US ALL WITHOUT BREAKING INTO A SWEAT.
SO. WHAT NEXT?
WE START CHECKING OUT INFESTED WORLDS, ONE BY ONE IF NECESSARY, UNTIL WE FIND RAYNOR.
AND ELLEN? WE BLEW HER WORLD APART. HER MIND'S JUST SHUT DOWN. HOW MANY OTHER LIVES ARE WE PREPARED TO TRAMPLE IN ORDER TO SECURE OUR SECOND CHANCE?
RIGHT. WHATEVER WE'VE DONE OR BEEN IN THE PAST, THERE HAS TO BE A LINE WE DON'T CROSS. AND RIGHT NOW...

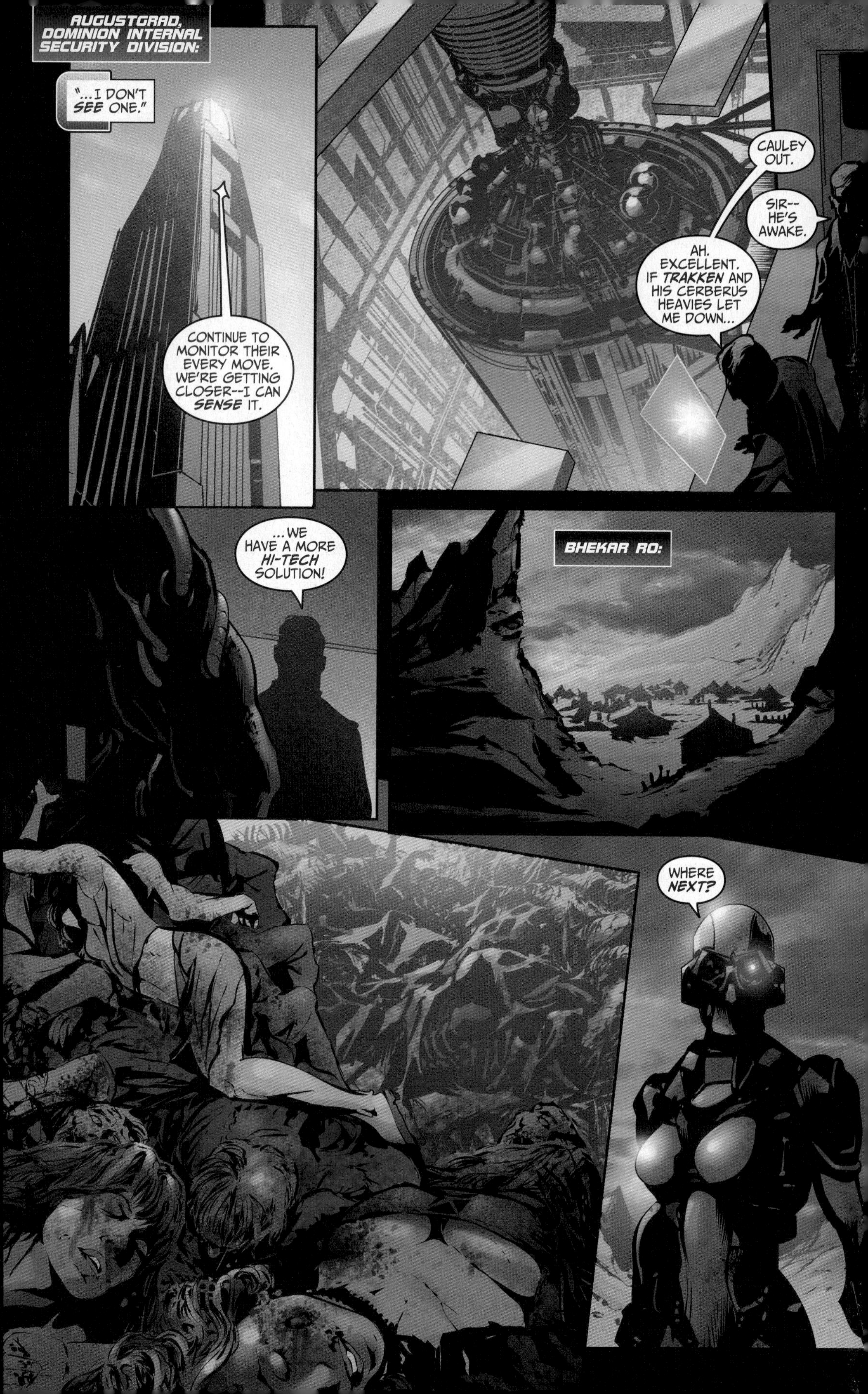
AUGUSTGRAD, DOMINION INTERNAL SECURITY DIVISION:
"...I DON'T SEE ONE."
CONTINUE TO MONITOR THEIR EVERY MOVE. WE'RE GETTING CLOSER--I CAN SENSE IT.
CAULEY OUT.
SIR--HE'S AWAKE.
AH. EXCELLENT. IF TRAKKEN AND HIS CERBERUS HEAVIES LET ME DOWN...
...WE HAVE A MORE HI-TECH SOLUTION!
BHEKAR RO:
WHERE NEXT?

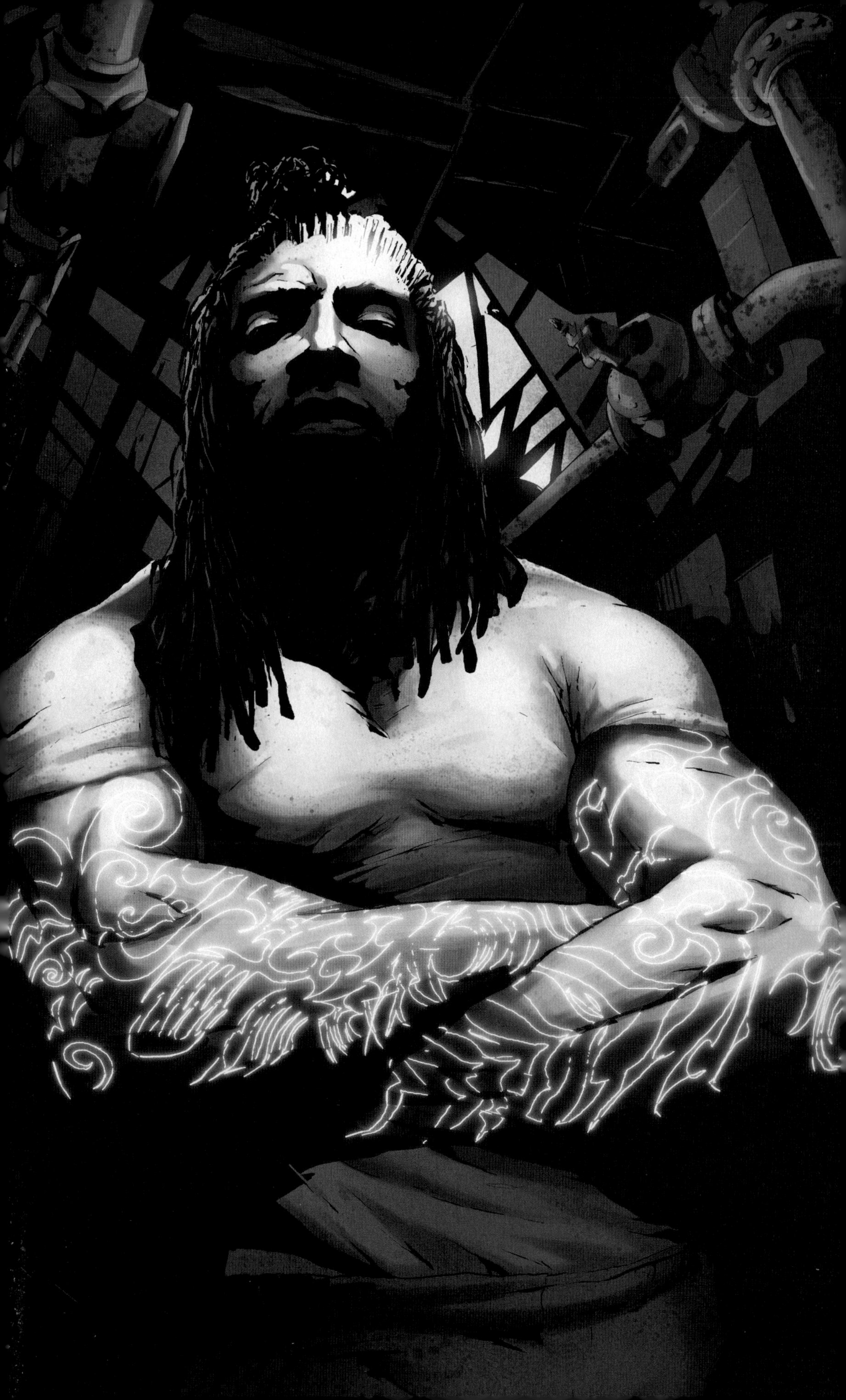

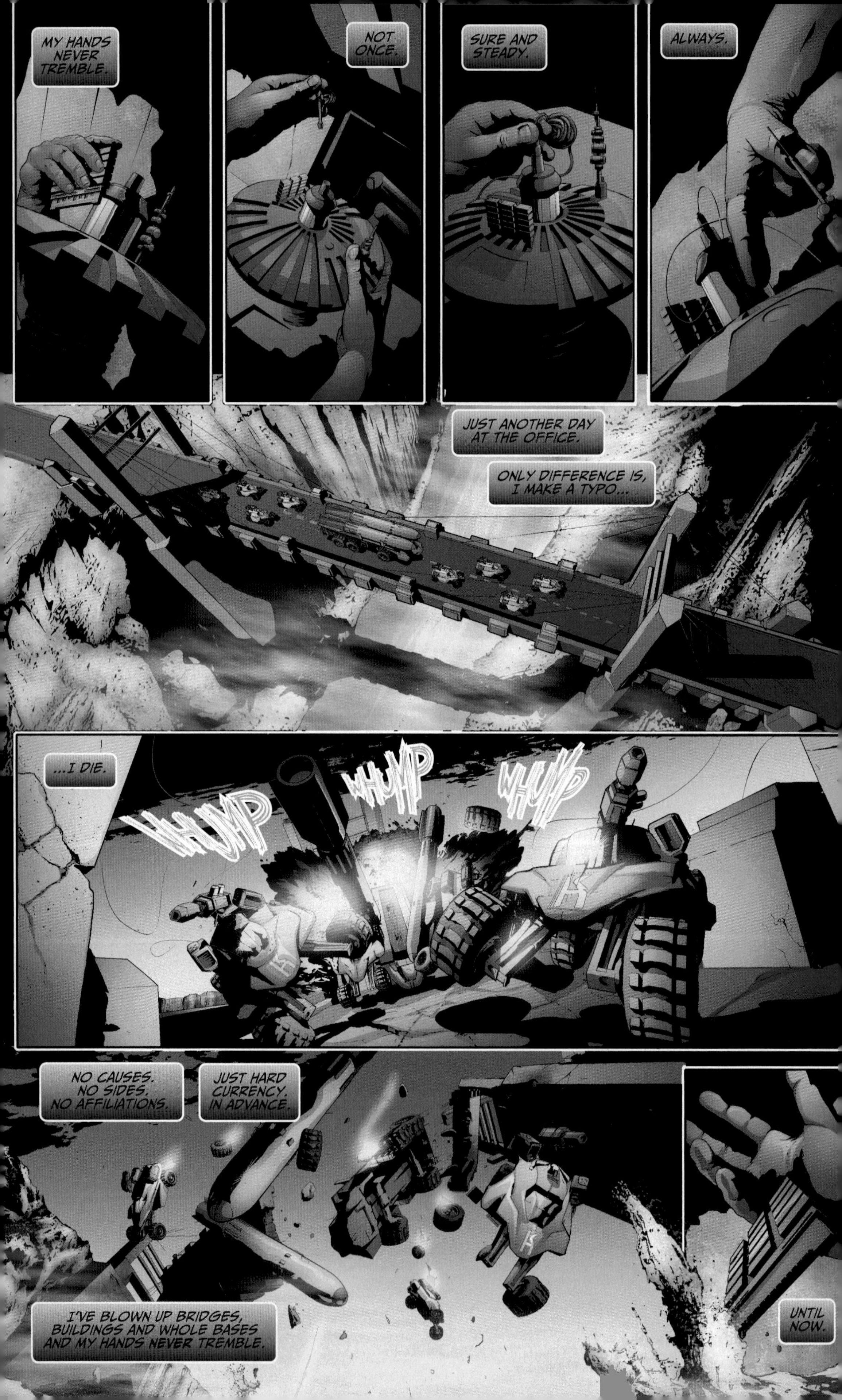

MY HANDS NEVER TREMBLE.
NOT ONCE.
SURE AND STEADY.
ALWAYS.
JUST ANOTHER DAY AT THE OFFICE.
ONLY DIFFERENCE IS, I MAKE A TYPO...
...I DIE.
WHUMP
WHUMP
WHUMP
NO CAUSES. NO SIDES. NO AFFILIATIONS.
JUST HARD CURRENCY. IN ADVANCE.
I'VE BLOWN UP BRIDGES, BUILDINGS AND WHOLE BASES AND MY HANDS NEVER TREMBLE.
UNTIL NOW.

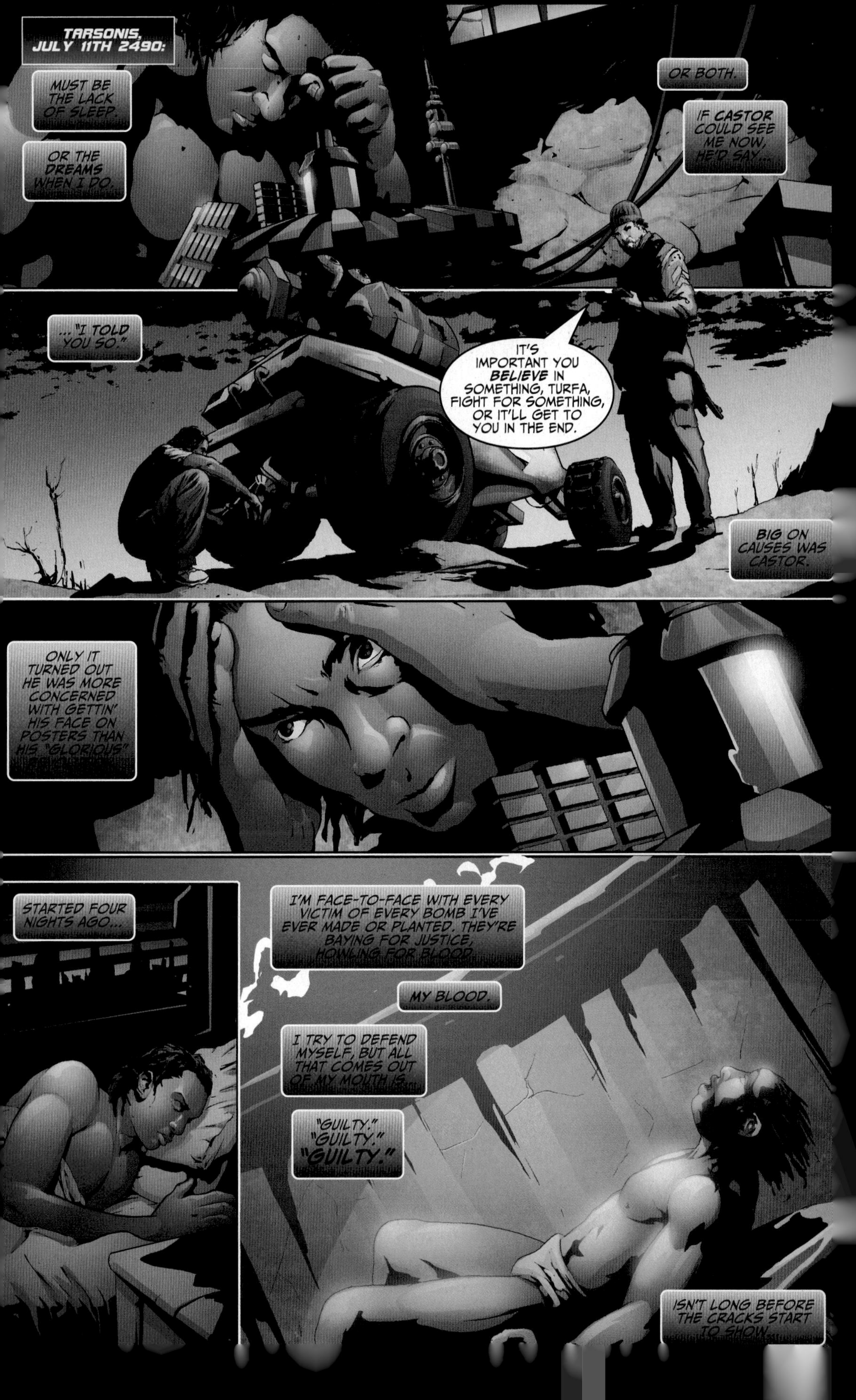
TARSONIS, JULY 11TH 2490:
MUST BE THE LACK OF SLEEP.
OR THE DREAMS WHEN I DO.
OR BOTH.
IF CASTOR COULD SEE ME NOW, HE'D SAY...
..."I TOLD YOU SO."
IT'S IMPORTANT YOU BELIEVE IN SOMETHING, TURFA, FIGHT FOR SOMETHING, OR IT'LL GET TO YOU IN THE END.
BIG ON CAUSES WAS CASTOR.
ONLY IT TURNED OUT HE WAS MORE CONCERNED WITH GETTIN' HIS FACE ON POSTERS THAN HIS "GLORIOUS"
STARTED FOUR NIGHTS AGO...
I'M FACE-TO-FACE WITH EVERY VICTIM OF EVERY BOMB I'VE EVER MADE OR PLANTED. THEY'RE BAYING FOR JUSTICE, HOWLING FOR BLOOD.
MY BLOOD.
I TRY TO DEFEND MYSELF, BUT ALL THAT COMES OUT OF MY MOUTH IS...
"GUILTY." "GUILTY." "GUILTY."
ISN'T LONG BEFORE THE CRACKS START TO SHOW...

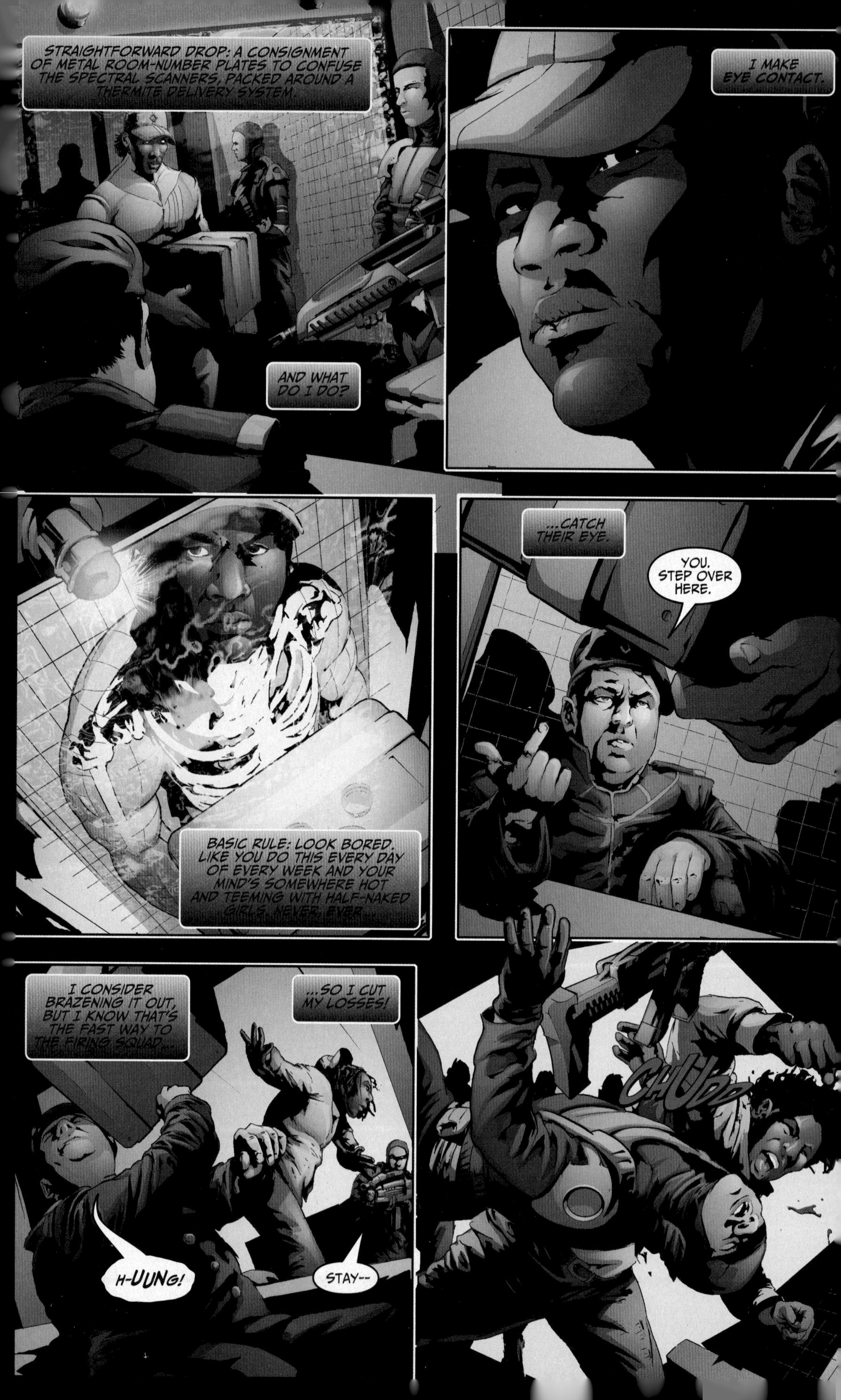
STRAIGHTFORWARD DROP: A CONSIGNMENT OF METAL ROOM-NUMBER PLATES TO CONFUSE THE SPECTRAL SCANNERS, PACKED AROUND A THERMITE DELIVERY SYSTEM.
AND WHAT DO I DO?
I MAKE EYE CONTACT.
BASIC RULE: LOOK BORED. LIKE YOU DO THIS EVERY DAY OF EVERY WEEK AND YOUR MIND'S SOMEWHERE HOT AND TEEMING WITH HALF-NAKED GIRLS. NEVER, EVER...
...CATCH THEIR EYE.
YOU. STEP OVER HERE.
I CONSIDER BRAZENING IT OUT, BUT I KNOW THAT'S THE FAST WAY TO THE FIRING SQUAD...
...SO I CUT MY LOSSES!
H-UUNG!
STAY--
CHUDD

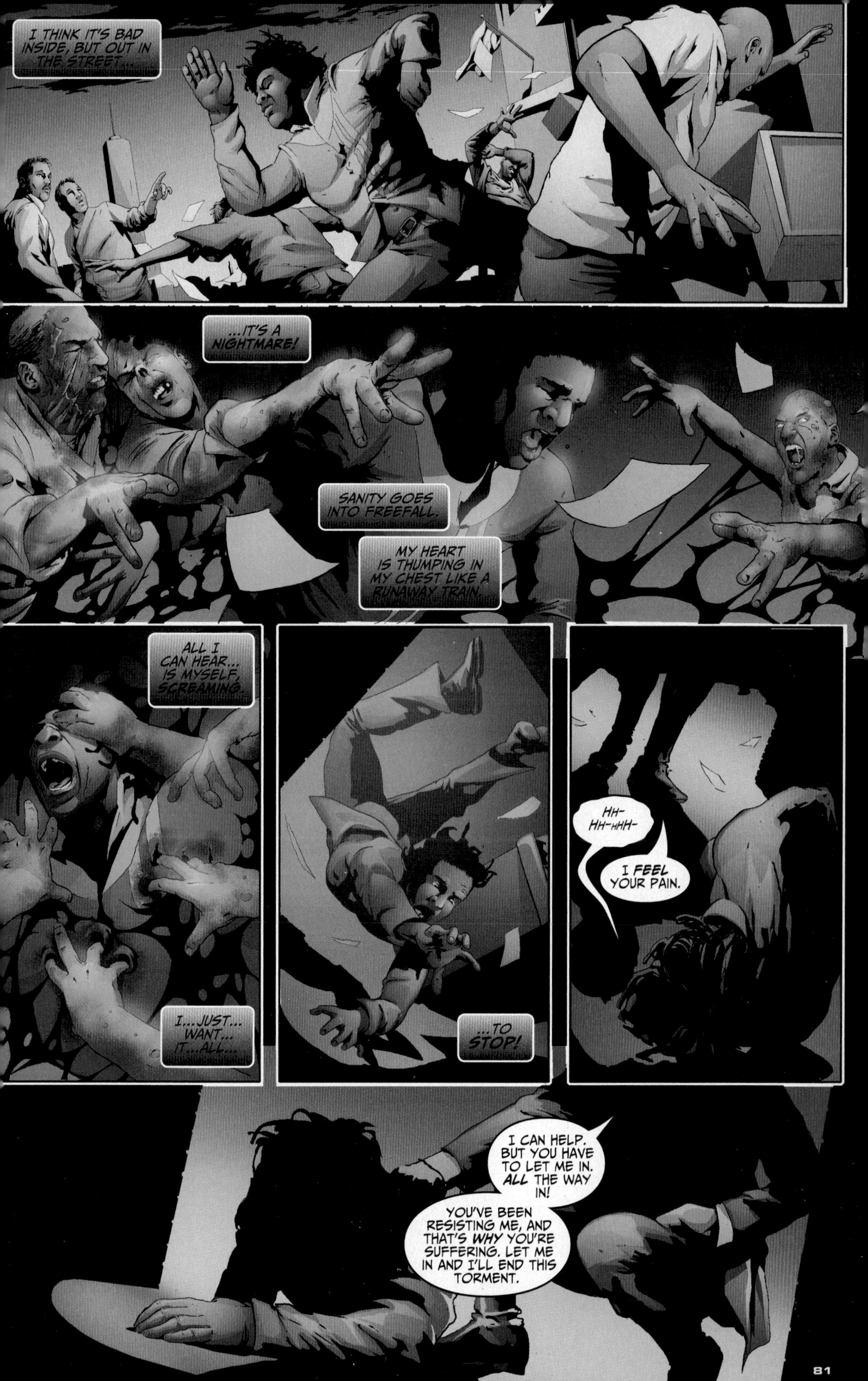
I THINK IT'S BAD INSIDE, BUT OUT IN THE STREET...
...IT'S A NIGHTMARE!
SANITY GOES INTO FREEFALL.
MY HEART IS THUMPING IN MY CHEST LIKE A RUNAWAY TRAIN.
ALL I CAN HEAR... IS MYSELF, SCREAMING.
I...JUST... WANT... IT...ALL...
...TO STOP!
HH- HH-HHH-
I FEEL YOUR PAIN.
I CAN HELP. BUT YOU HAVE TO LET ME IN. ALL THE WAY IN!
YOU'VE BEEN RESISTING ME, AND THAT'S WHY YOU'RE SUFFERING. LET ME IN AND I'LL END THIS TORMENT.

Y-YOU. I *KNOW* YOU.

BECAUSE WE'VE BEEN TOGETHER NOW FOR FOUR DAYS... OH YES, AND NIGHTS. ALL I WANT IS A FEW NAMES, A LOCATION OR TWO, AND I'LL BE GONE.

I'M JUST LIKE YOU, TURFA, TALENT-FOR-HIRE MAKING A LIVING ANY WAY I CAN. *DON'T* FIGHT ME...

YOU'VE... BEEN... IN... MY... HEAD!

TURFA? WHAT ARE YOU DOING, TURFA?

WHY... AREN'T YOU BROKEN? CRYING FOR OBLIVION? *WHY?*

YOU... *VIOLATED* ME. YOU TURNED MY LIFE INTO A LIVING HELL, AND FOR WHAT? INFORMATION? I'M NOT BROKEN...

...I'M MAD AS HELL!

I DON'T RUSH. HE TAKES LONG MINUTES TO DIE.

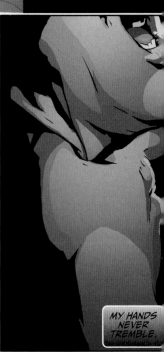

MY HANDS NEVER TREMBLE.

I FIND OUT LATER I GOT ME AN ABOVE AVERAGE PSI-INDEX OF MY OWN, BUT-- ULTIMATELY--THE POWERS-THAT-BE CHOOSE BRAWN OVER BRAIN.

IT'S WHY I WAS ABLE TO RESIST THE TELEPATH'S PROBES, WHY I WAS ABLE TO FIGHT BACK, BUT STILL...

...IT LEAVES SCARS, ONES THAT WILL NEVER GO AWAY. EVER.

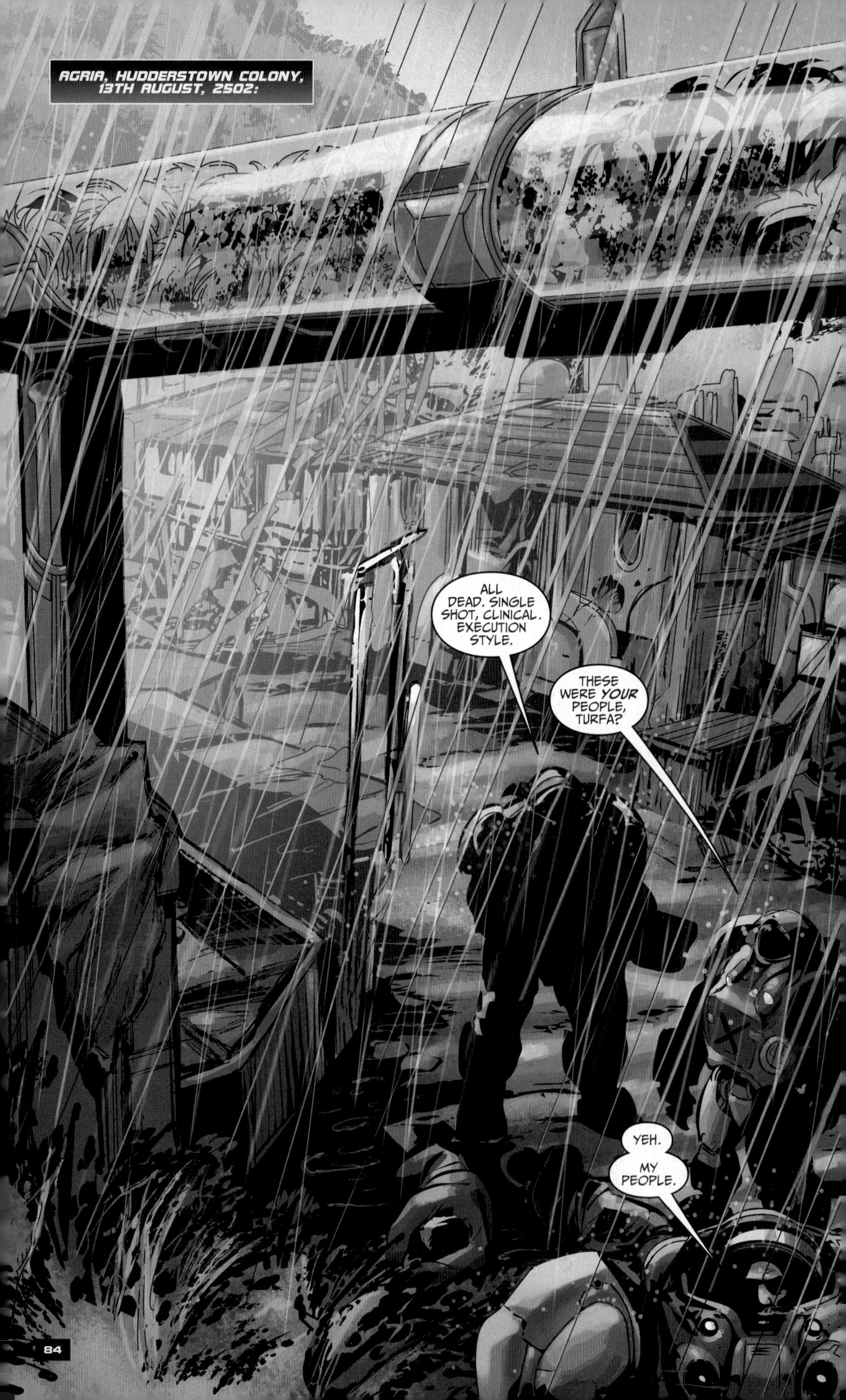
AGRIA, HUDDERSTOWN COLONY, 13TH AUGUST, 2502:
ALL DEAD. SINGLE SHOT, CLINICAL. EXECUTION STYLE.
THESE WERE YOUR PEOPLE, TURFA?
YEH.
MY PEOPLE.

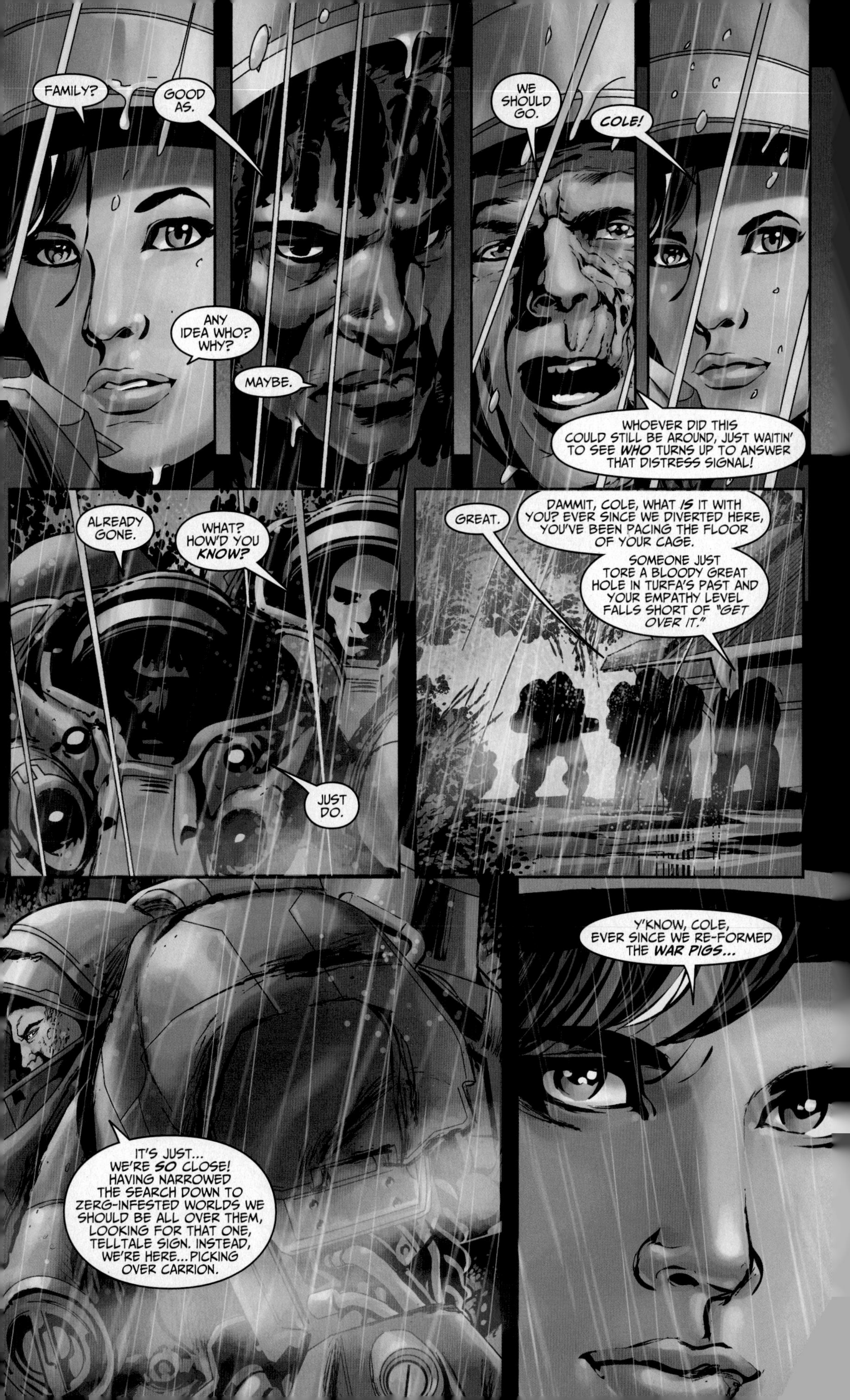
FAMILY?
GOOD AS.
ANY IDEA WHO? WHY?
MAYBE.
WE SHOULD GO.
COLE!
WHOEVER DID THIS COULD STILL BE AROUND, JUST WAITIN' TO SEE WHO TURNS UP TO ANSWER THAT DISTRESS SIGNAL!
ALREADY GONE.
WHAT? HOW'D YOU KNOW?
JUST DO.
GREAT.
DAMMIT, COLE, WHAT IS IT WITH YOU? EVER SINCE WE DIVERTED HERE, YOU'VE BEEN PACING THE FLOOR OF YOUR CAGE.
SOMEONE JUST TORE A BLOODY GREAT HOLE IN TURFA'S PAST AND YOUR EMPATHY LEVEL FALLS SHORT OF "GET OVER IT."
IT'S JUST... WE'RE SO CLOSE! HAVING NARROWED THE SEARCH DOWN TO ZERG-INFESTED WORLDS WE SHOULD BE ALL OVER THEM, LOOKING FOR THAT ONE, TELLTALE SIGN. INSTEAD, WE'RE HERE...PICKING OVER CARRION.
Y'KNOW, COLE, EVER SINCE WE RE-FORMED THE WAR PIGS...

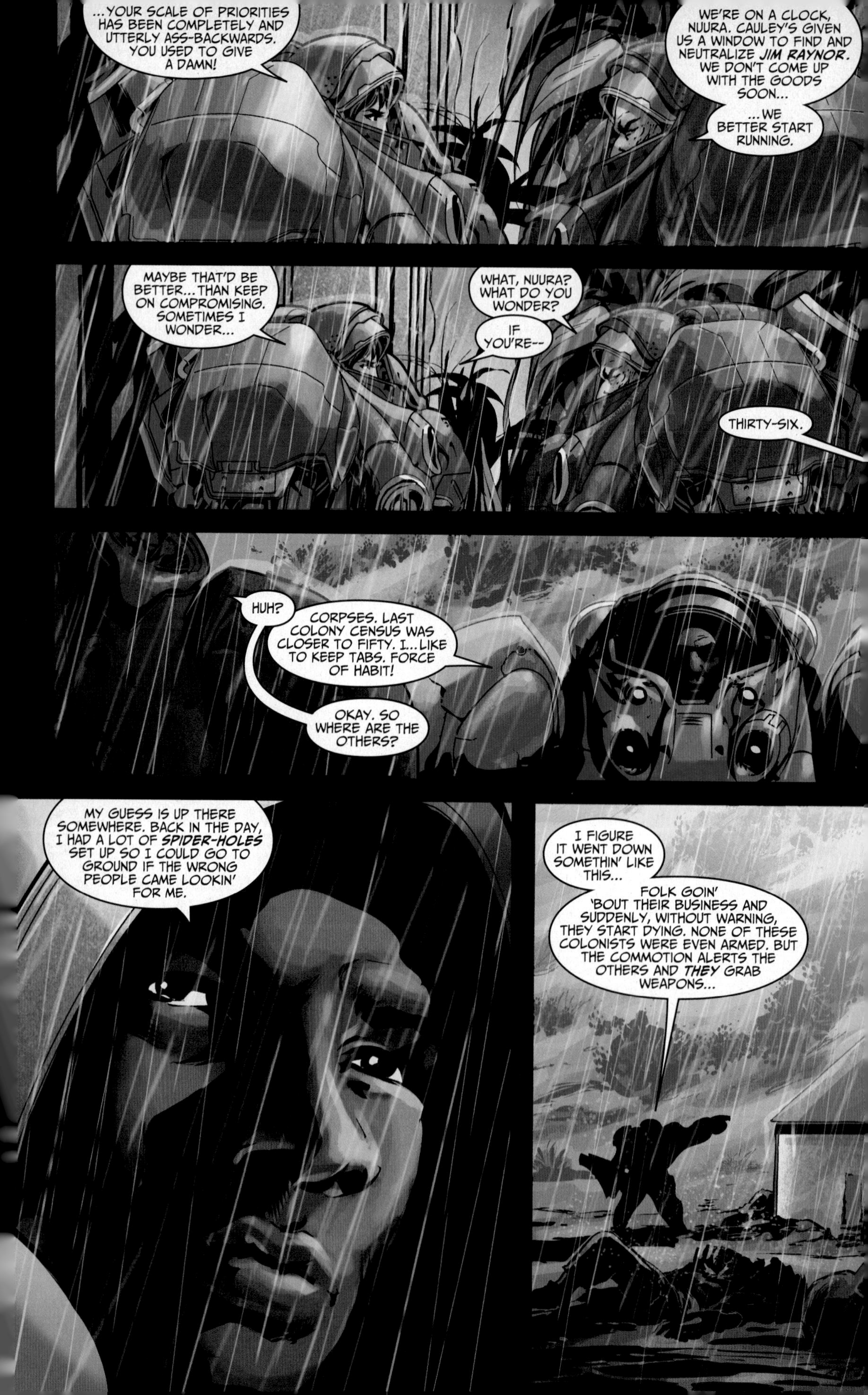
...YOUR SCALE OF PRIORITIES HAS BEEN COMPLETELY AND UTTERLY ASS-BACKWARDS. YOU USED TO GIVE A DAMN!
WE'RE ON A CLOCK, NUURA. CAULEY'S GIVEN US A WINDOW TO FIND AND NEUTRALIZE JIM RAYNOR. WE DON'T COME UP WITH THE GOODS SOON...
...WE BETTER START RUNNING.
MAYBE THAT'D BE BETTER... THAN KEEP ON COMPROMISING. SOMETIMES I WONDER...
WHAT, NUURA? WHAT DO YOU WONDER?
IF YOU'RE--
THIRTY-SIX.
HUH?
CORPSES. LAST COLONY CENSUS WAS CLOSER TO FIFTY. I...LIKE TO KEEP TABS. FORCE OF HABIT!
OKAY. SO WHERE ARE THE OTHERS?
MY GUESS IS UP THERE SOMEWHERE. BACK IN THE DAY, I HAD A LOT OF SPIDER-HOLES SET UP SO I COULD GO TO GROUND IF THE WRONG PEOPLE CAME LOOKIN' FOR ME.
I FIGURE IT WENT DOWN SOMETHIN' LIKE THIS...
FOLK GOIN' 'BOUT THEIR BUSINESS AND SUDDENLY, WITHOUT WARNING, THEY START DYING. NONE OF THESE COLONISTS WERE EVEN ARMED. BUT THE COMMOTION ALERTS THE OTHERS AND THEY GRAB WEAPONS...

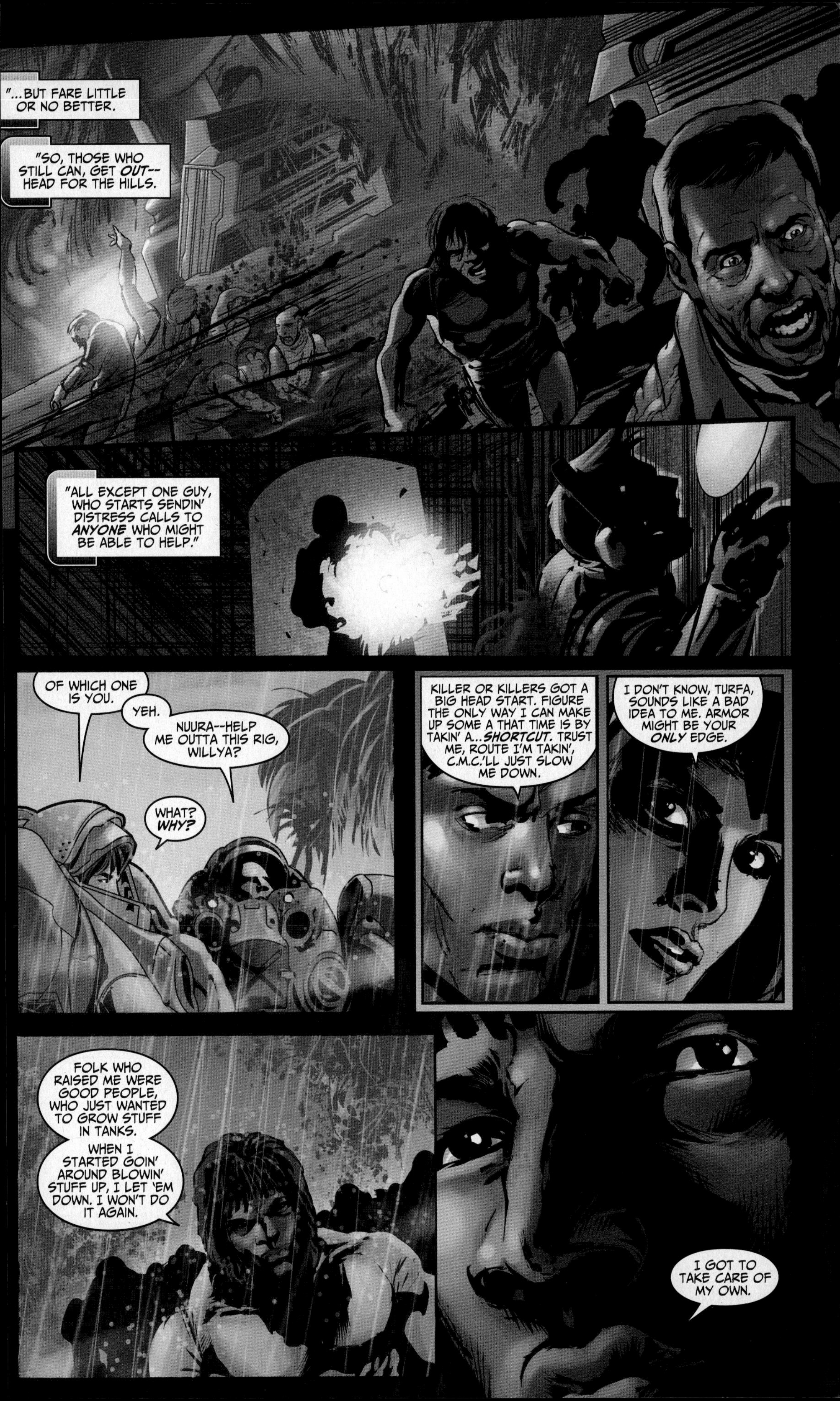
"...BUT FARE LITTLE OR NO BETTER.
"SO, THOSE WHO STILL CAN, GET *OUT*-- HEAD FOR THE HILLS.
"ALL EXCEPT ONE GUY, WHO STARTS SENDIN' DISTRESS CALLS TO *ANYONE* WHO MIGHT BE ABLE TO HELP."
OF WHICH ONE IS YOU.
YEH.
NUURA--HELP ME OUTTA THIS RIG, WILLYA?
WHAT? *WHY?*
KILLER OR KILLERS GOT A BIG HEAD START. FIGURE THE ONLY WAY I CAN MAKE UP SOME A THAT TIME IS BY TAKIN' A...*SHORTCUT*. TRUST ME, ROUTE I'M TAKIN', C.M.C.'LL JUST SLOW ME DOWN.
I DON'T KNOW, TURFA, SOUNDS LIKE A BAD IDEA TO ME. ARMOR MIGHT BE YOUR *ONLY* EDGE.
FOLK WHO RAISED ME WERE GOOD PEOPLE, WHO JUST WANTED TO GROW STUFF IN TANKS.
WHEN I STARTED GOIN' AROUND BLOWIN' STUFF UP, I LET 'EM DOWN. I WON'T DO IT AGAIN.
I GOT TO TAKE CARE OF MY OWN.

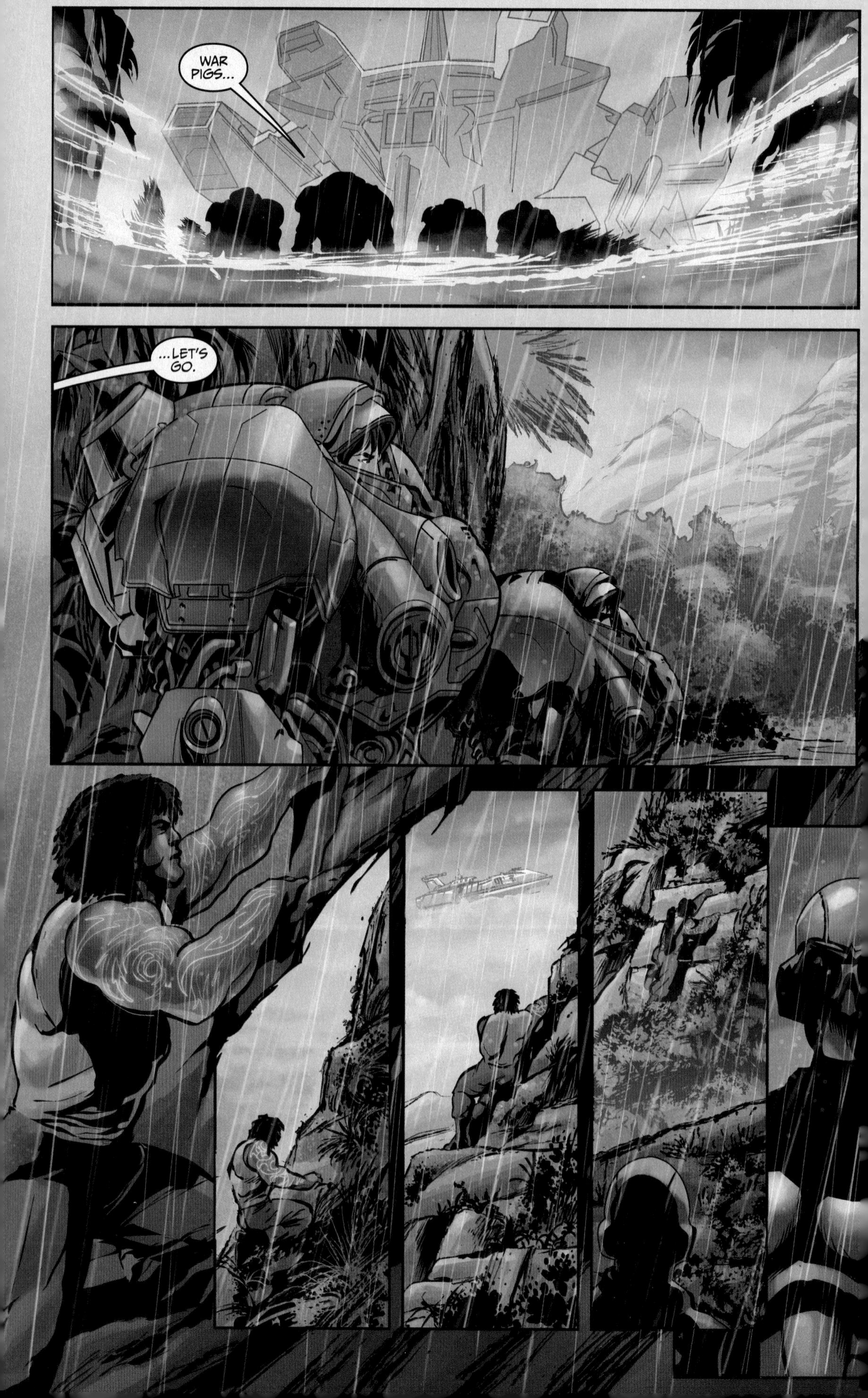
WAR PIGS...
...LET'S GO.

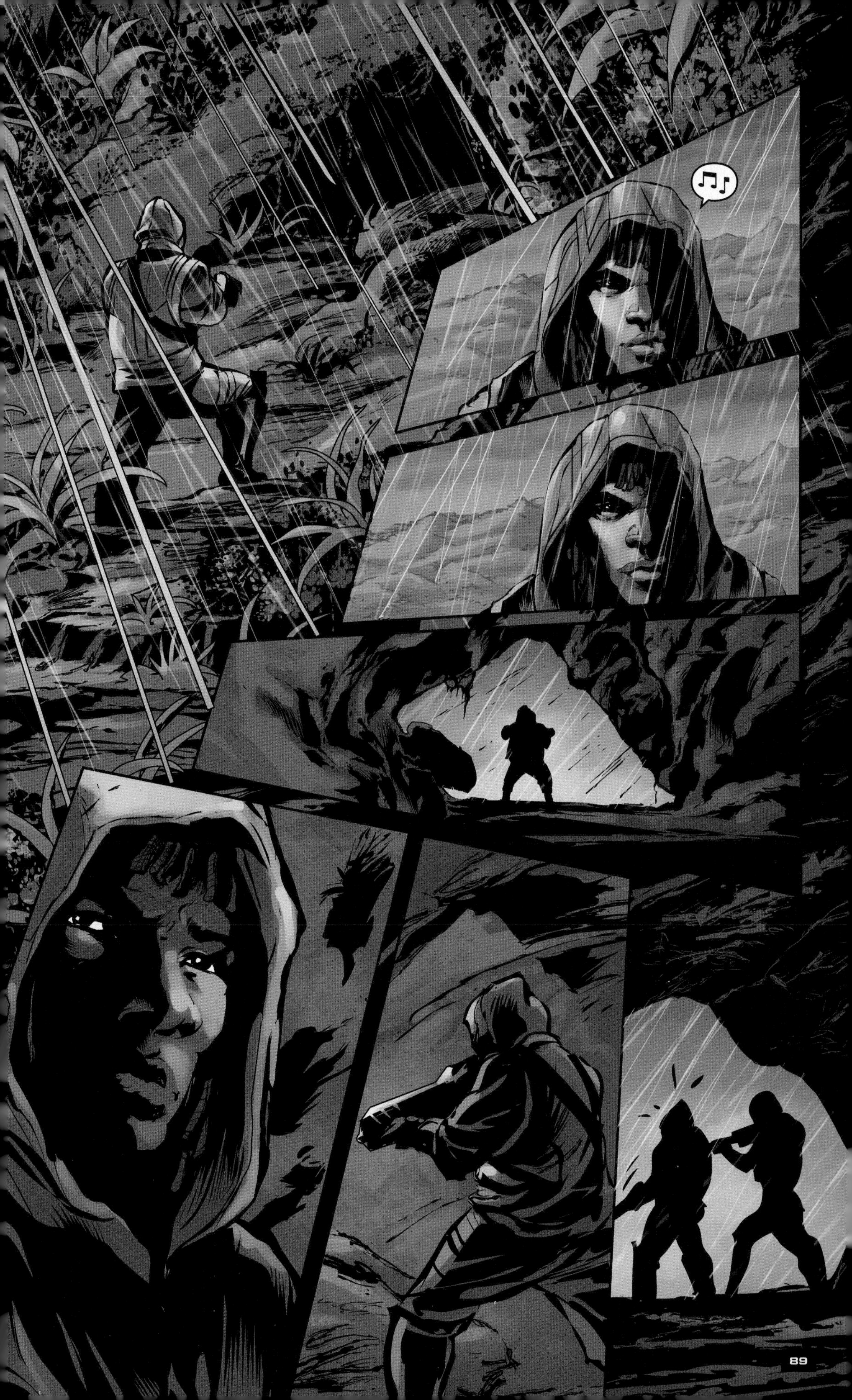

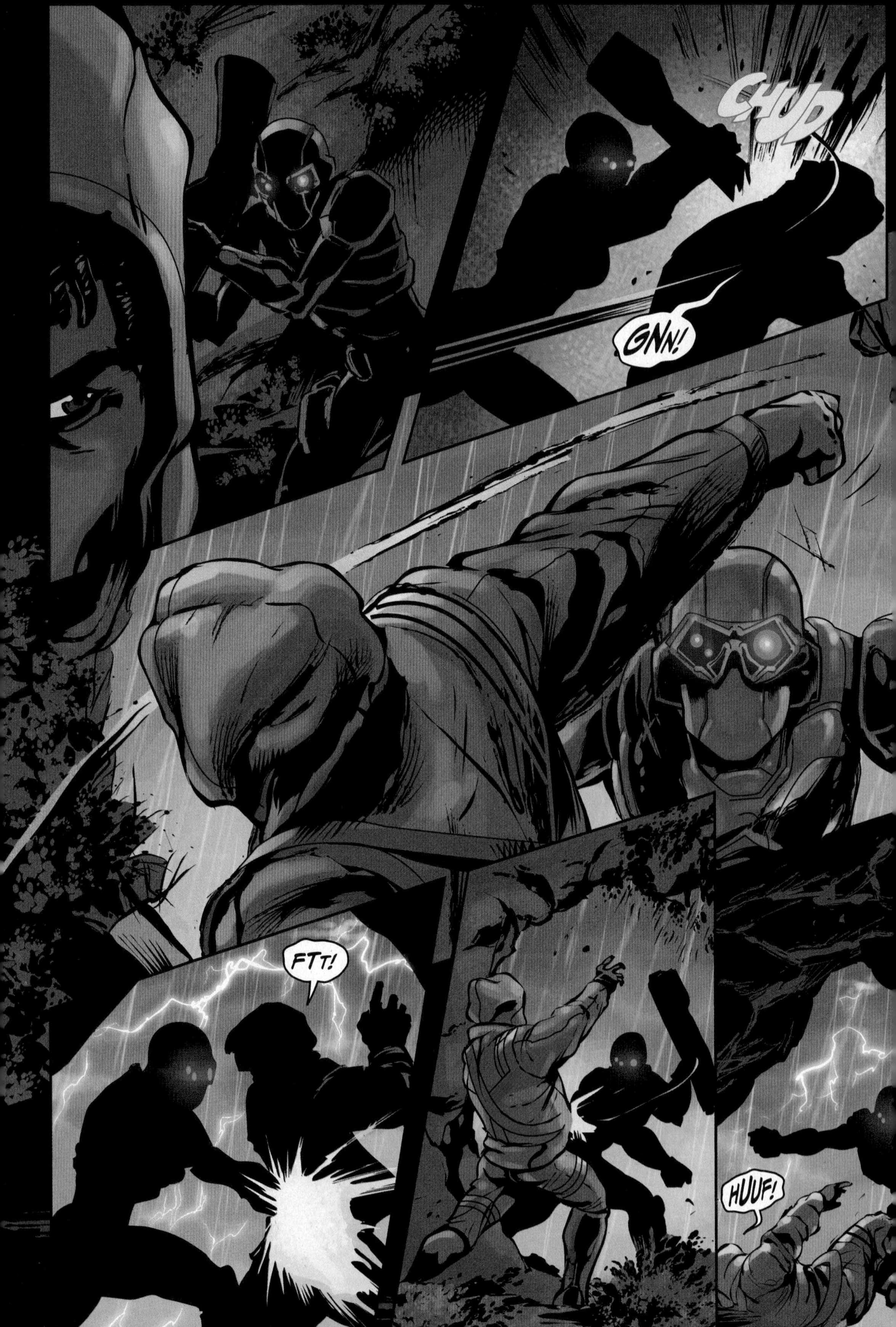
CHUD
GNN!
FTT!
HUUF!

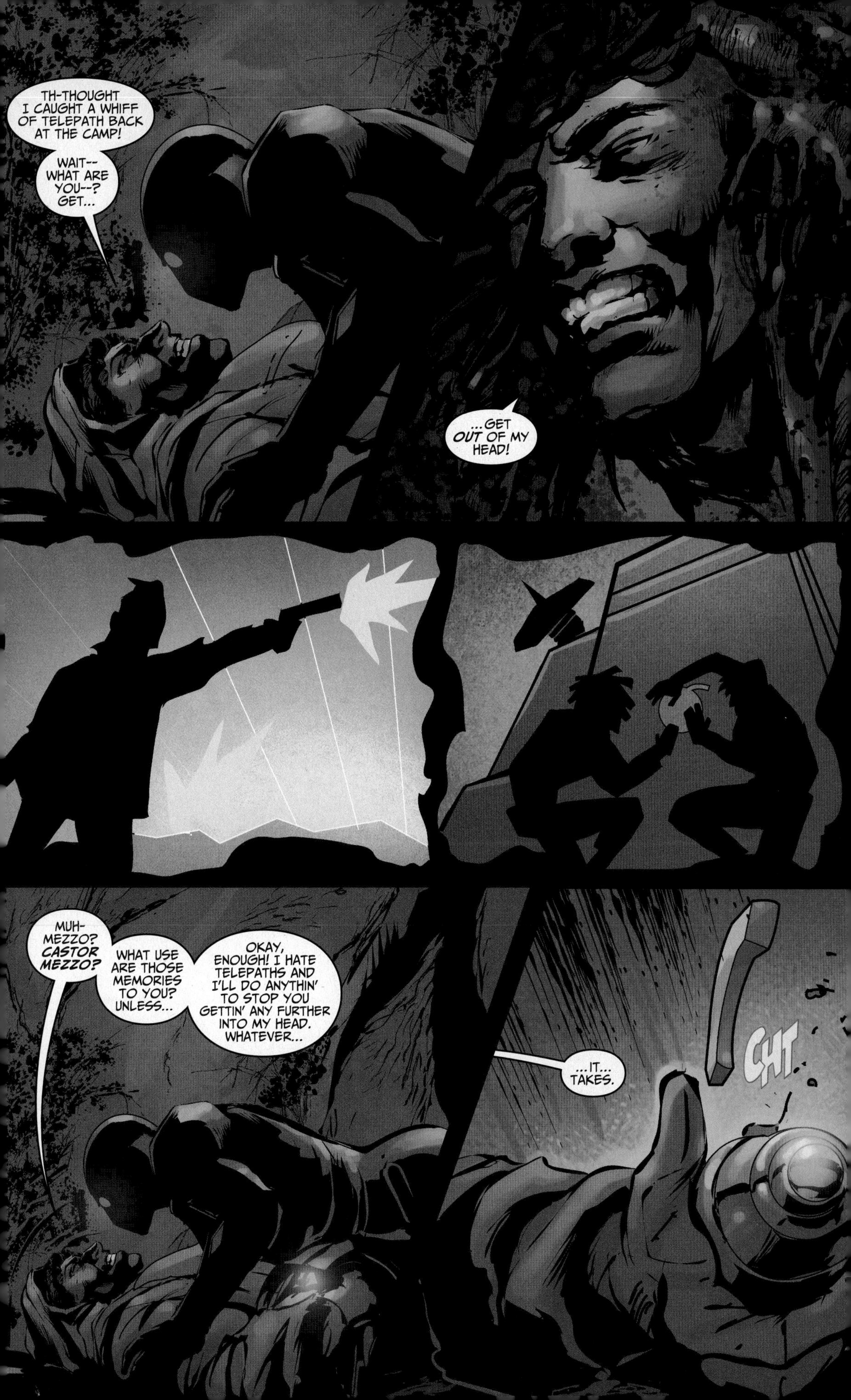
TH-THOUGHT I CAUGHT A WHIFF OF TELEPATH BACK AT THE CAMP!
WAIT-- WHAT ARE YOU--? GET...
...GET *OUT* OF MY HEAD!
MUH-MEZZO? *CASTOR MEZZO?*
WHAT USE ARE THOSE MEMORIES TO YOU? UNLESS...
OKAY, ENOUGH! I HATE TELEPATHS AND I'LL DO ANYTHIN' TO STOP YOU GETTIN' ANY FURTHER INTO MY HEAD. WHATEVER...
...IT... TAKES.
CHT

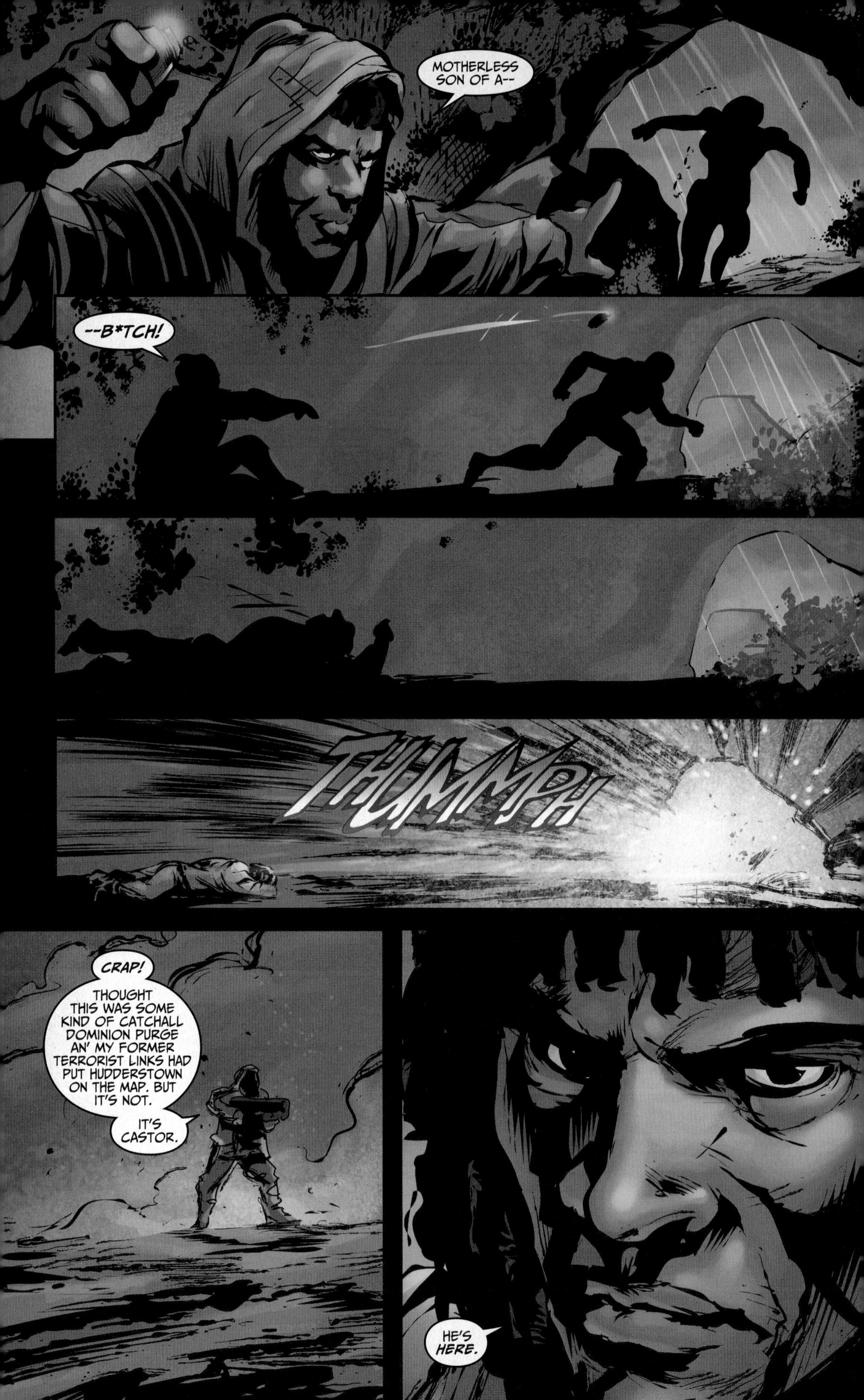
MOTHERLESS SON OF A--
--B*TCH!
THUMMPH
CRAP!
THOUGHT THIS WAS SOME KIND OF CATCHALL DOMINION PURGE AN' MY FORMER TERRORIST LINKS HAD PUT HUDDERSTOWN ON THE MAP. BUT IT'S NOT.
IT'S CASTOR.
HE'S HERE.

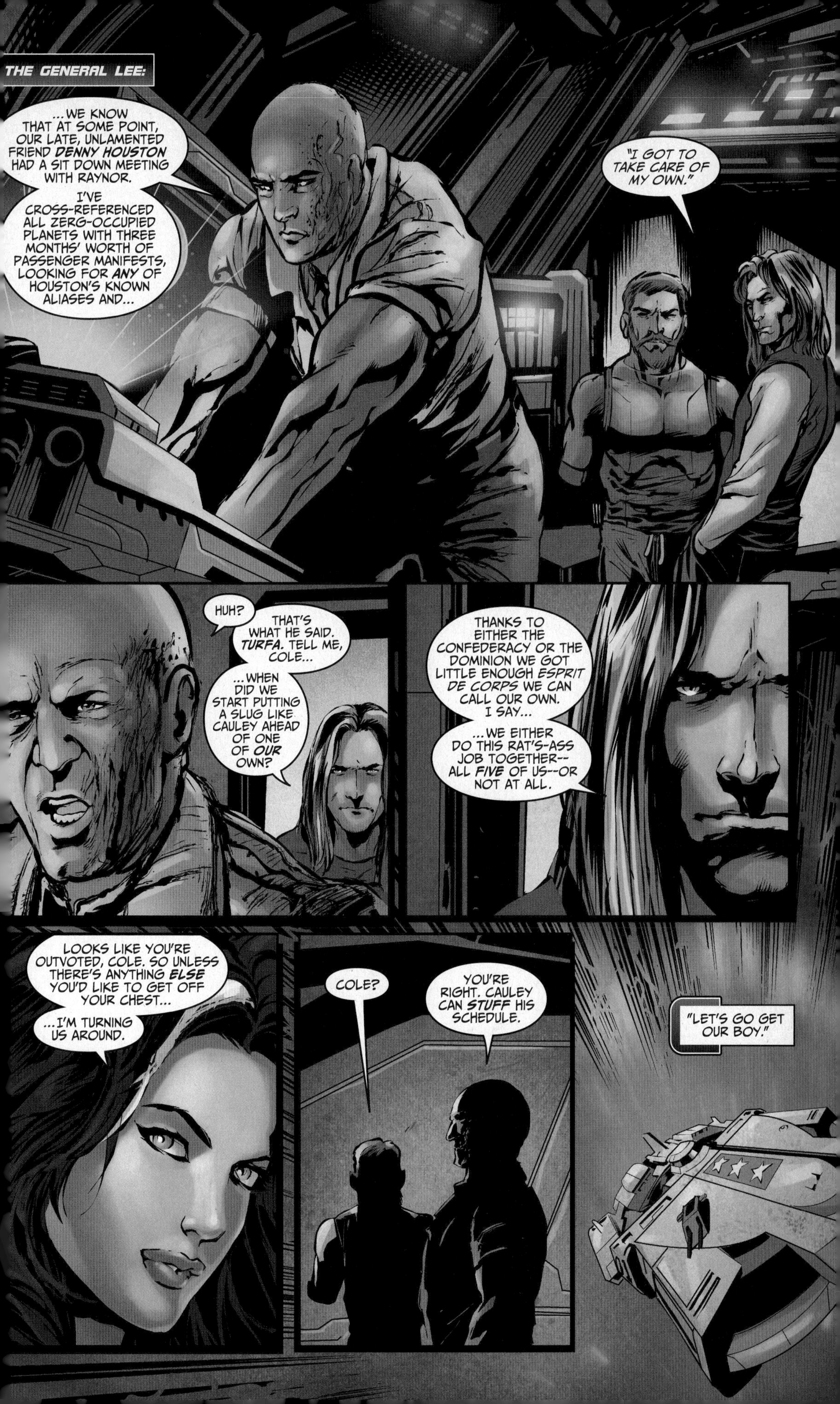
THE GENERAL LEE:
...WE KNOW THAT AT SOME POINT, OUR LATE, UNLAMENTED FRIEND DENNY HOUSTON HAD A SIT DOWN MEETING WITH RAYNOR.
I'VE CROSS-REFERENCED ALL ZERG-OCCUPIED PLANETS WITH THREE MONTHS' WORTH OF PASSENGER MANIFESTS, LOOKING FOR ANY OF HOUSTON'S KNOWN ALIASES AND...
"I GOT TO TAKE CARE OF MY OWN."
HUH?
THAT'S WHAT HE SAID. TURFA. TELL ME, COLE...
...WHEN DID WE START PUTTING A SLUG LIKE CAULEY AHEAD OF ONE OF OUR OWN?
THANKS TO EITHER THE CONFEDERACY OR THE DOMINION WE GOT LITTLE ENOUGH ESPRIT DE CORPS WE CAN CALL OUR OWN. I SAY...
...WE EITHER DO THIS RAT'S-ASS JOB TOGETHER--ALL FIVE OF US--OR NOT AT ALL.
LOOKS LIKE YOU'RE OUTVOTED, COLE. SO UNLESS THERE'S ANYTHING ELSE YOU'D LIKE TO GET OFF YOUR CHEST...
...I'M TURNING US AROUND.
COLE?
YOU'RE RIGHT. CAULEY CAN STUFF HIS SCHEDULE.
"LET'S GO GET OUR BOY."

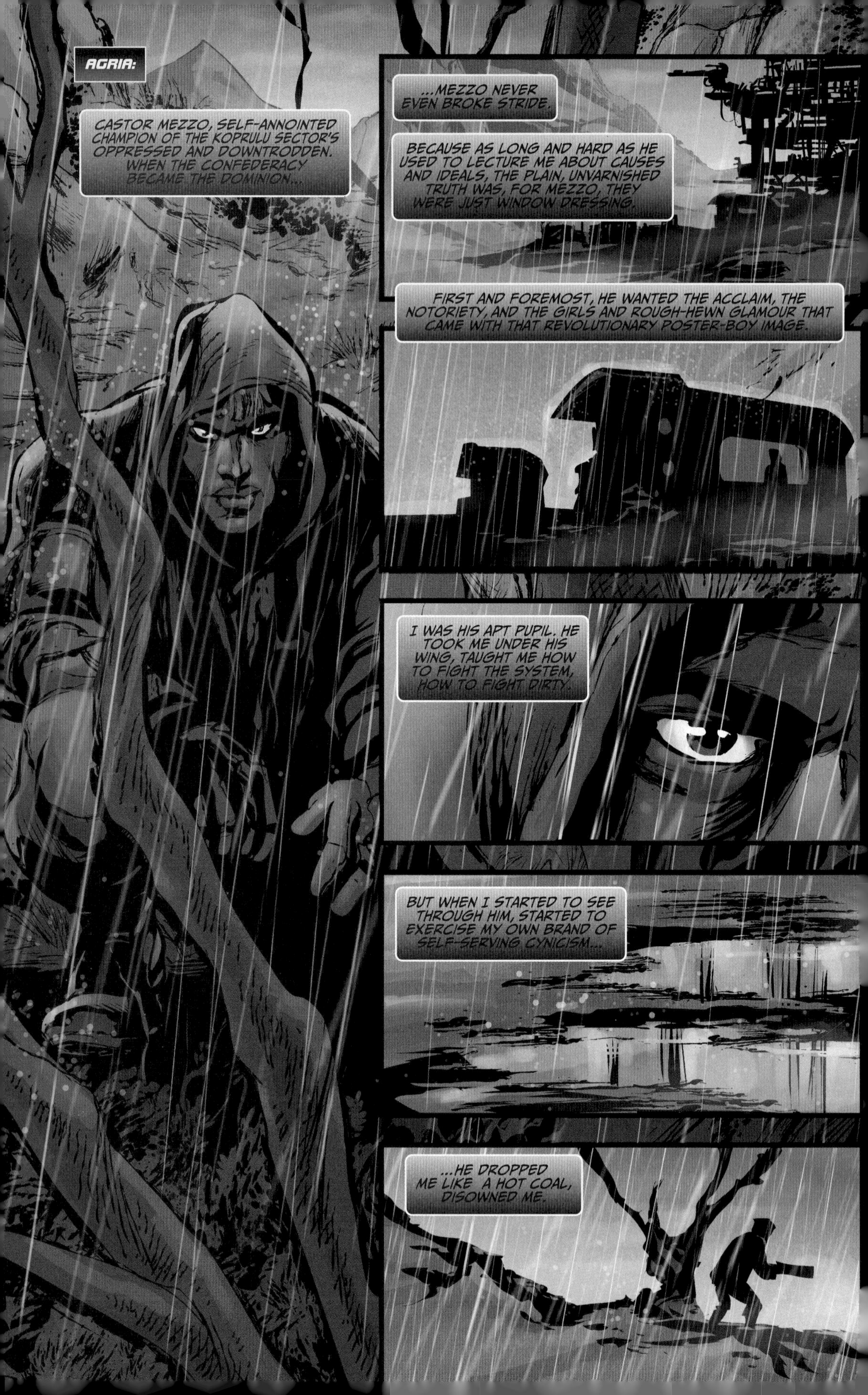
AGRIA:
CASTOR MEZZO, SELF-ANNOINTED CHAMPION OF THE KOPRULU SECTOR'S OPPRESSED AND DOWNTRODDEN. WHEN THE CONFEDERACY BECAME THE DOMINION...
...MEZZO NEVER EVEN BROKE STRIDE.
BECAUSE AS LONG AND HARD AS HE USED TO LECTURE ME ABOUT CAUSES AND IDEALS, THE PLAIN, UNVARNISHED TRUTH WAS, FOR MEZZO, THEY WERE JUST WINDOW DRESSING.
FIRST AND FOREMOST, HE WANTED THE ACCLAIM, THE NOTORIETY, AND THE GIRLS AND ROUGH-HEWN GLAMOUR THAT CAME WITH THAT REVOLUTIONARY POSTER-BOY IMAGE.
I WAS HIS APT PUPIL. HE TOOK ME UNDER HIS WING, TAUGHT ME HOW TO FIGHT THE SYSTEM, HOW TO FIGHT DIRTY.
BUT WHEN I STARTED TO SEE THROUGH HIM, STARTED TO EXERCISE MY OWN BRAND OF SELF-SERVING CYNICISM...
...HE DROPPED ME LIKE A HOT COAL, DISOWNED ME.

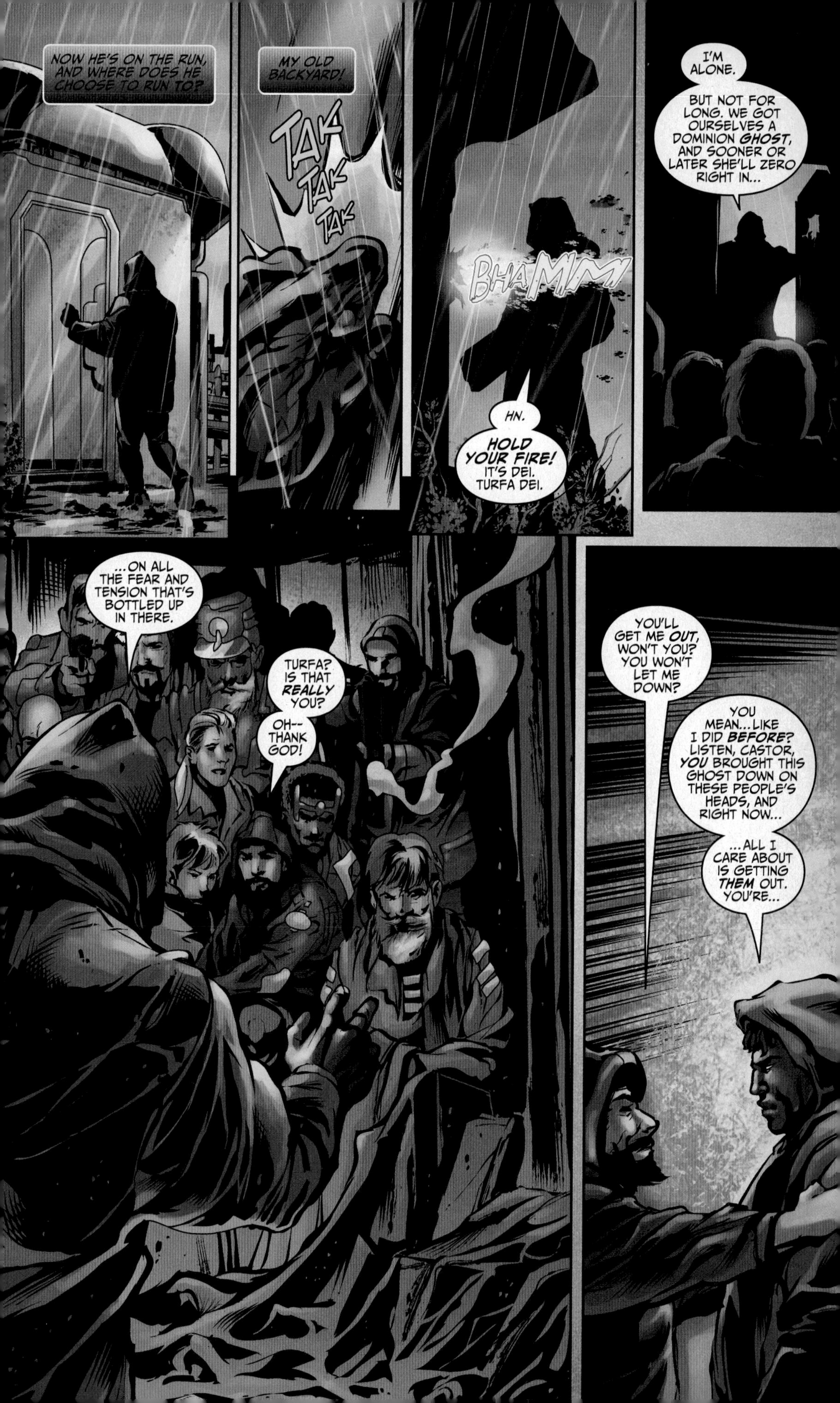

NOW HE'S ON THE RUN, AND WHERE DOES HE CHOOSE TO RUN TO?
MY OLD BACKYARD!
TAK TAK TAK
BHAMM
HN.
HOLD YOUR FIRE! IT'S DEI. TURFA DEI.
I'M ALONE.
BUT NOT FOR LONG. WE GOT OURSELVES A DOMINION GHOST, AND SOONER OR LATER SHE'LL ZERO RIGHT IN...
...ON ALL THE FEAR AND TENSION THAT'S BOTTLED UP IN THERE.
TURFA? IS THAT REALLY YOU?
OH-- THANK GOD!
YOU'LL GET ME OUT, WON'T YOU? YOU WON'T LET ME DOWN?
YOU MEAN...LIKE I DID BEFORE? LISTEN, CASTOR, YOU BROUGHT THIS GHOST DOWN ON THESE PEOPLE'S HEADS, AND RIGHT NOW...
...ALL I CARE ABOUT IS GETTING THEM OUT. YOU'RE...

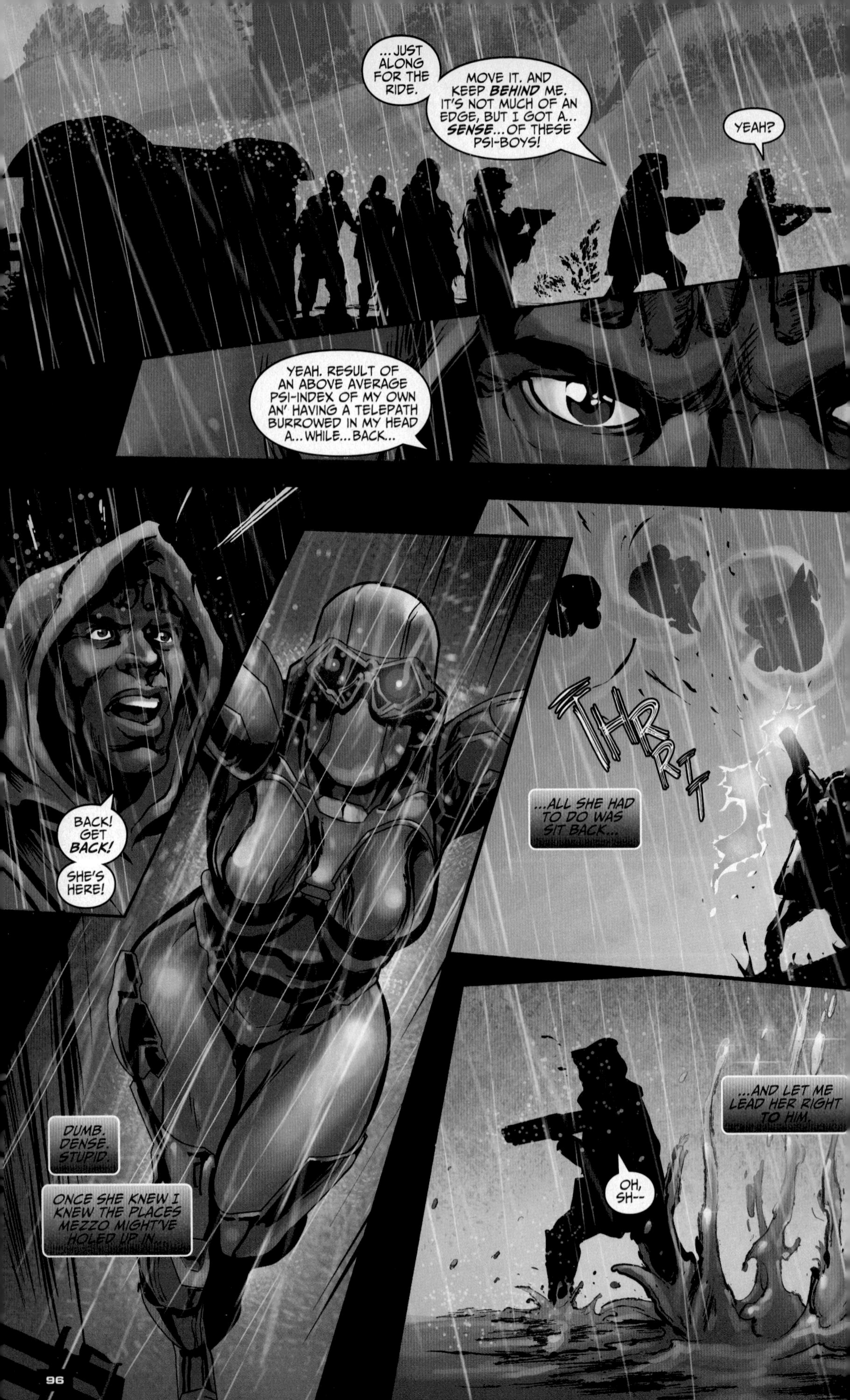

...JUST ALONG FOR THE RIDE.
MOVE IT. AND KEEP BEHIND ME. IT'S NOT MUCH OF AN EDGE, BUT I GOT A... SENSE...OF THESE PSI-BOYS!
YEAH?
YEAH. RESULT OF AN ABOVE AVERAGE PSI-INDEX OF MY OWN AN' HAVING A TELEPATH BURROWED IN MY HEAD A...WHILE...BACK...
BACK! GET BACK!
SHE'S HERE!
THRRIT
...ALL SHE HAD TO DO WAS SIT BACK...
DUMB. DENSE. STUPID.
ONCE SHE KNEW I KNEW THE PLACES MEZZO MIGHT'VE HOLED UP IN...
...AND LET ME LEAD HER RIGHT TO HIM.
OH, SH--

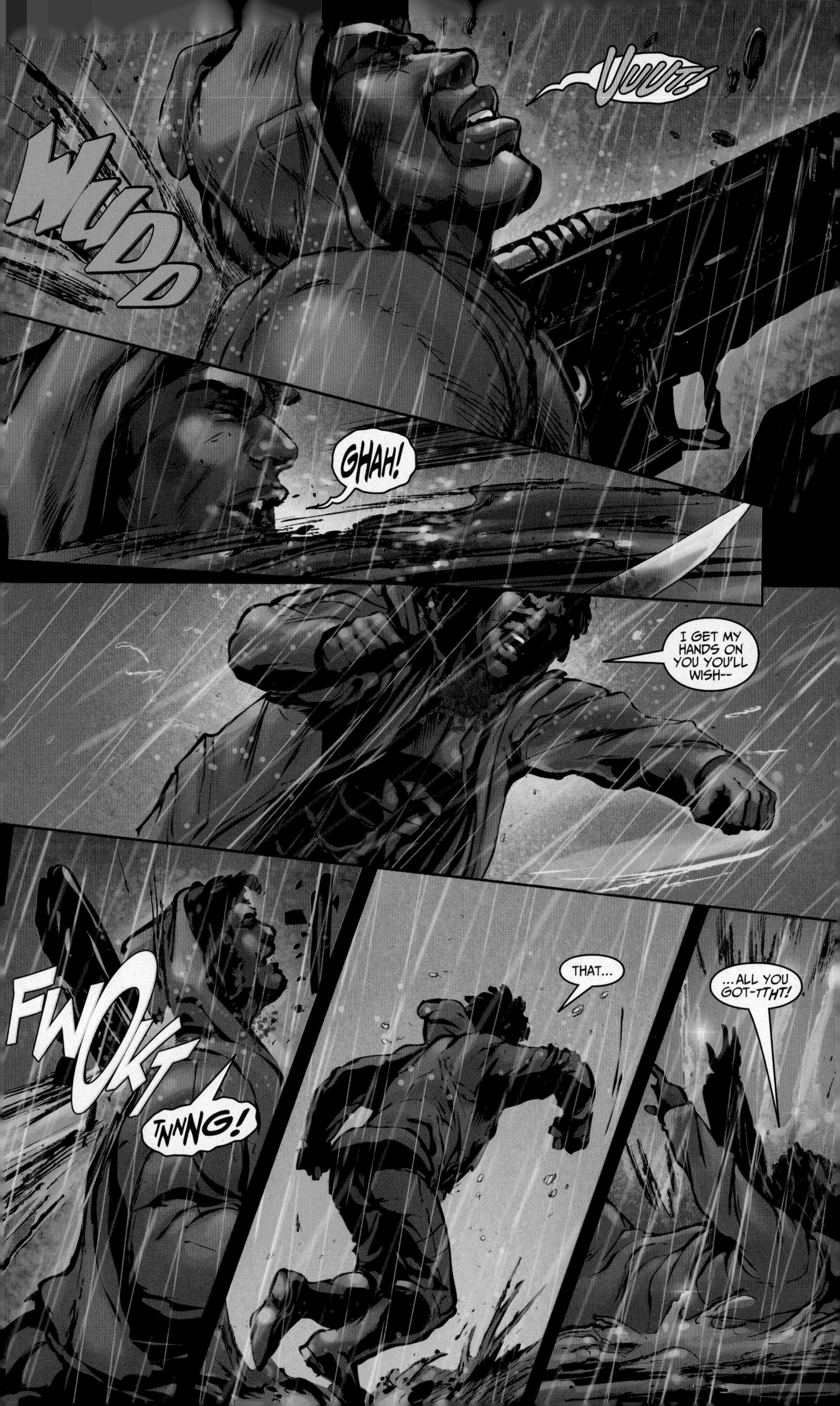
WUDD
VUUUT!
GHAH!
I GET MY HANDS ON YOU YOU'LL WISH--
FWOKT
TNNNG!
THAT...
...ALL YOU GOT-TTHT!

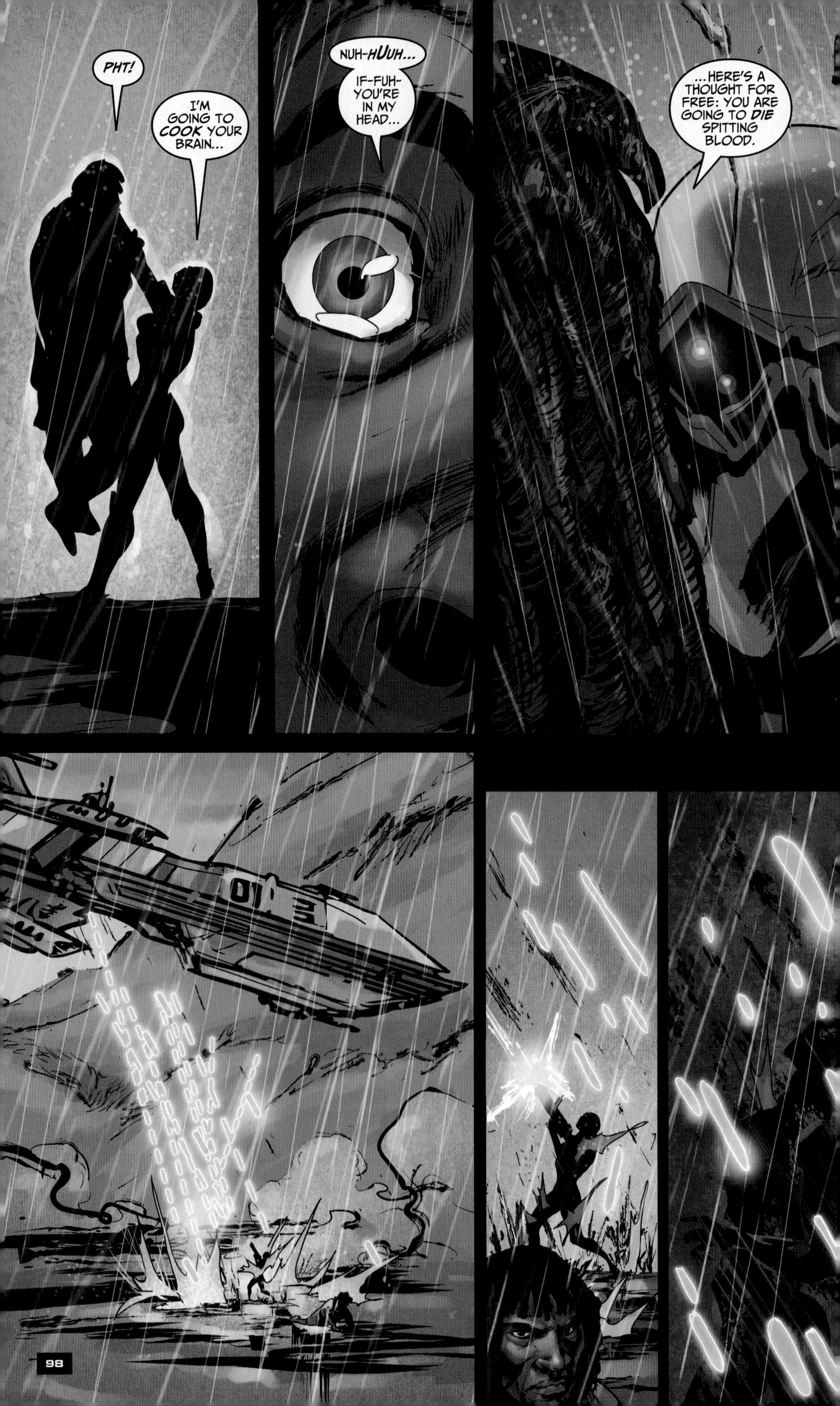
PHT!
I'M GOING TO COOK YOUR BRAIN...
NUH-HUUH...
IF-FUH-YOU'RE IN MY HEAD...
...HERE'S A THOUGHT FOR FREE: YOU ARE GOING TO DIE SPITTING BLOOD.

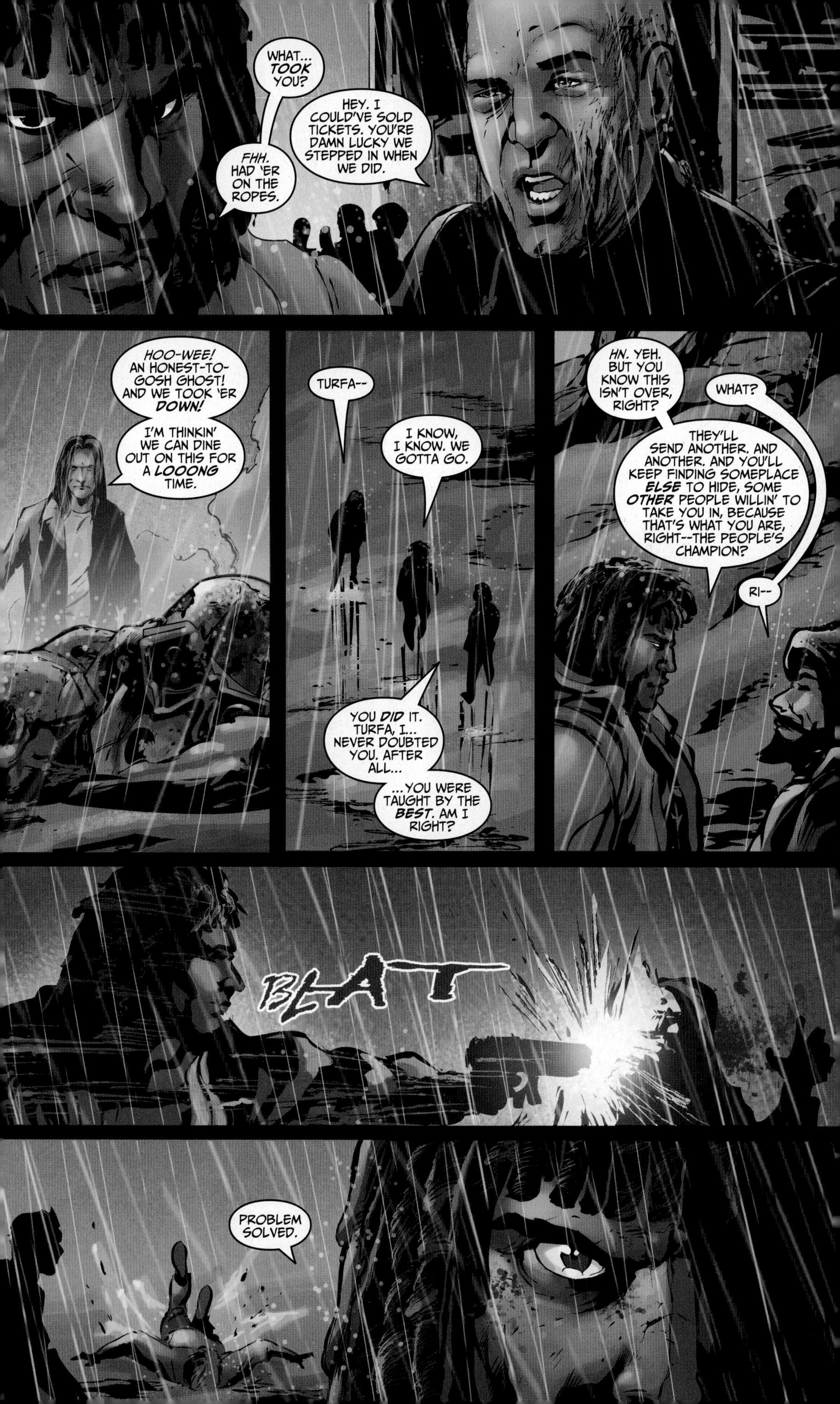
WHAT... TOOK YOU?
FHH. HAD 'ER ON THE ROPES.
HEY. I COULD'VE SOLD TICKETS. YOU'RE DAMN LUCKY WE STEPPED IN WHEN WE DID.
HOO-WEE! AN HONEST-TO-GOSH GHOST! AND WE TOOK 'ER DOWN!
I'M THINKIN' WE CAN DINE OUT ON THIS FOR A LOOONG TIME.
TURFA--
I KNOW, I KNOW. WE GOTTA GO.
YOU DID IT. TURFA, I... NEVER DOUBTED YOU. AFTER ALL...
...YOU WERE TAUGHT BY THE BEST. AM I RIGHT?
HN. YEH. BUT YOU KNOW THIS ISN'T OVER, RIGHT?
WHAT?
THEY'LL SEND ANOTHER. AND ANOTHER. AND YOU'LL KEEP FINDING SOMEPLACE ELSE TO HIDE, SOME OTHER PEOPLE WILLIN' TO TAKE YOU IN, BECAUSE THAT'S WHAT YOU ARE, RIGHT--THE PEOPLE'S CHAMPION?
RI--
BLAT
PROBLEM SOLVED.

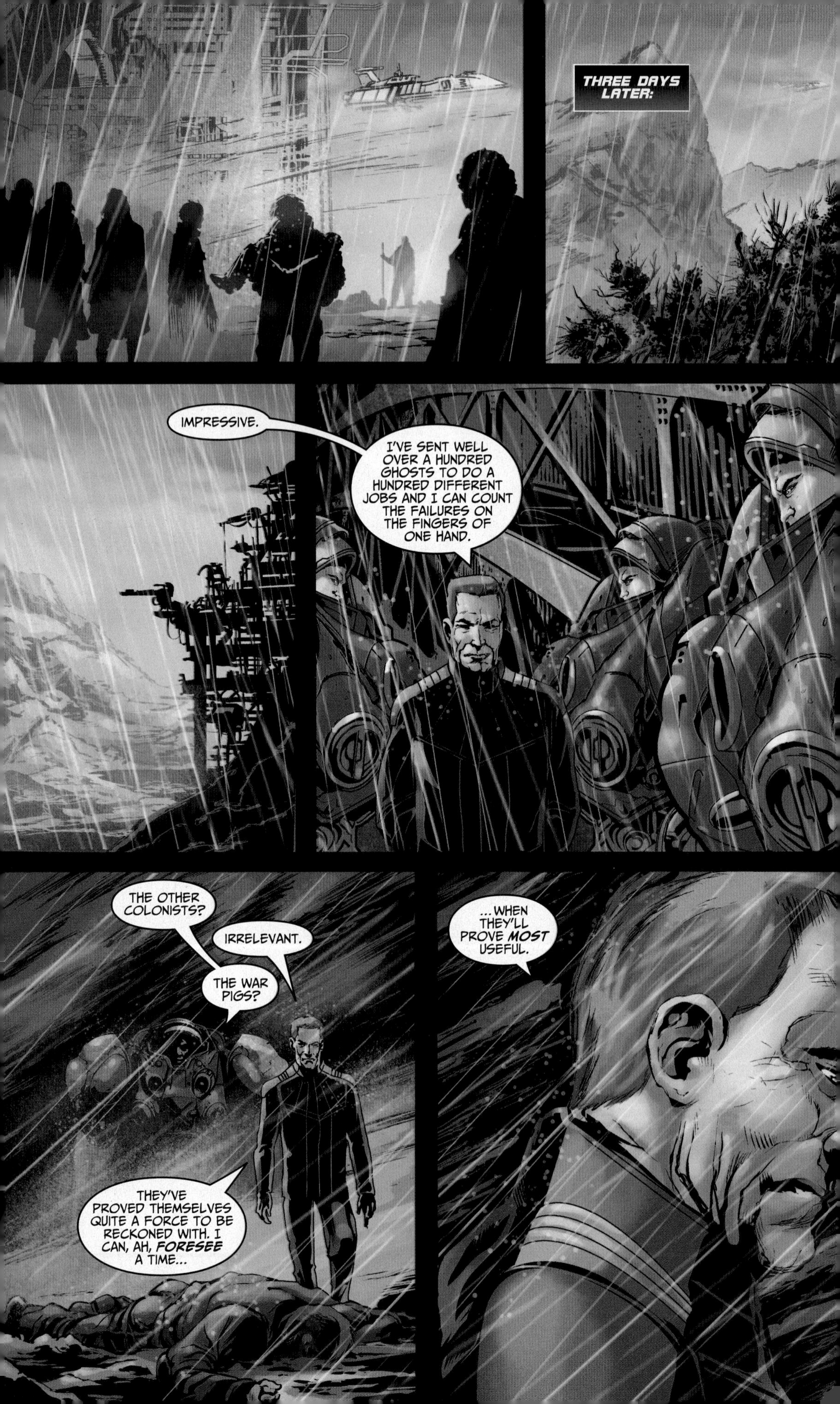
THREE DAYS LATER:
IMPRESSIVE.
I'VE SENT WELL OVER A HUNDRED GHOSTS TO DO A HUNDRED DIFFERENT JOBS AND I CAN COUNT THE FAILURES ON THE FINGERS OF ONE HAND.
THE OTHER COLONISTS?
IRRELEVANT.
THE WAR PIGS?
THEY'VE PROVED THEMSELVES QUITE A FORCE TO BE RECKONED WITH. I CAN, AH, *FORESEE* A TIME...
...WHEN THEY'LL PROVE *MOST* USEFUL.

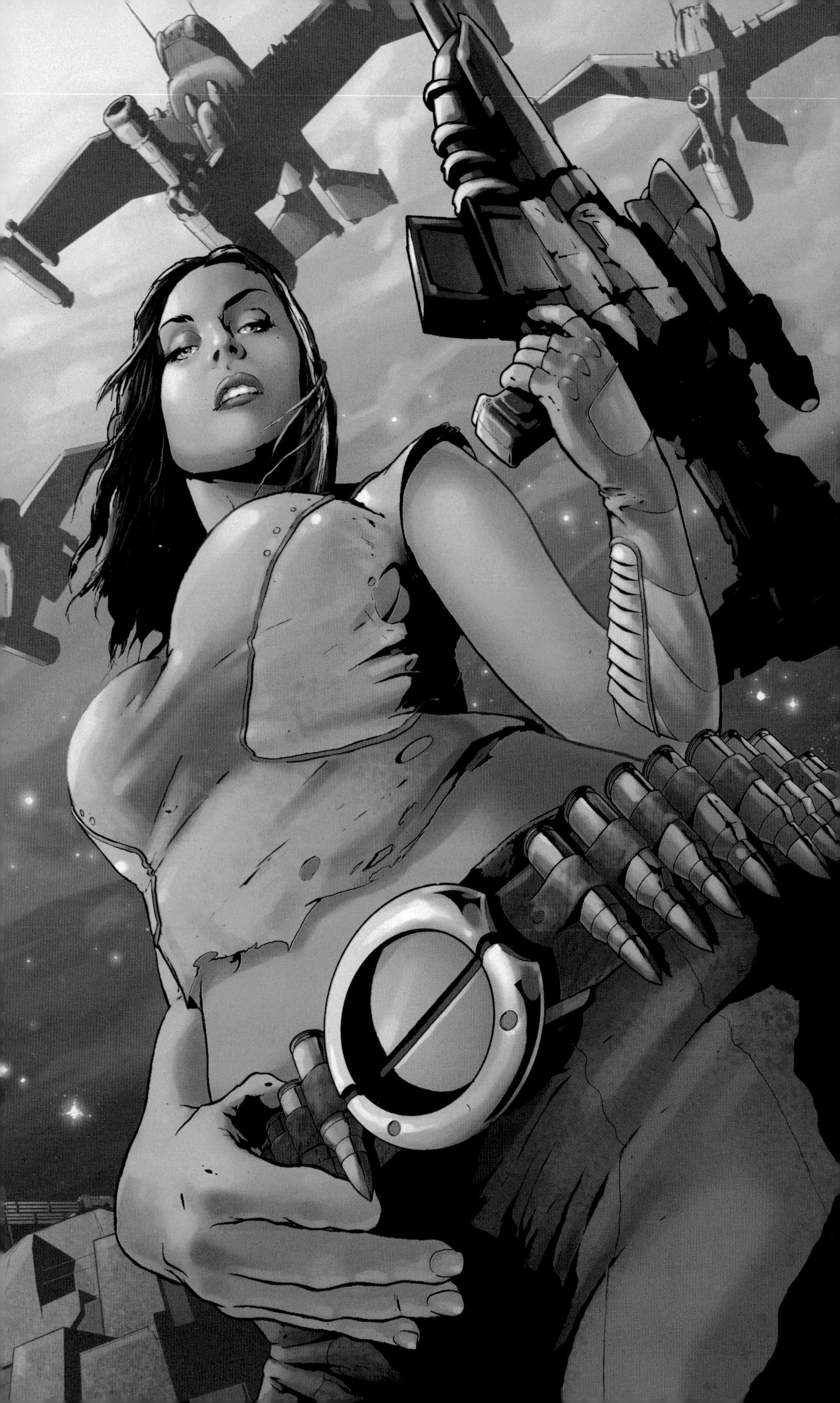

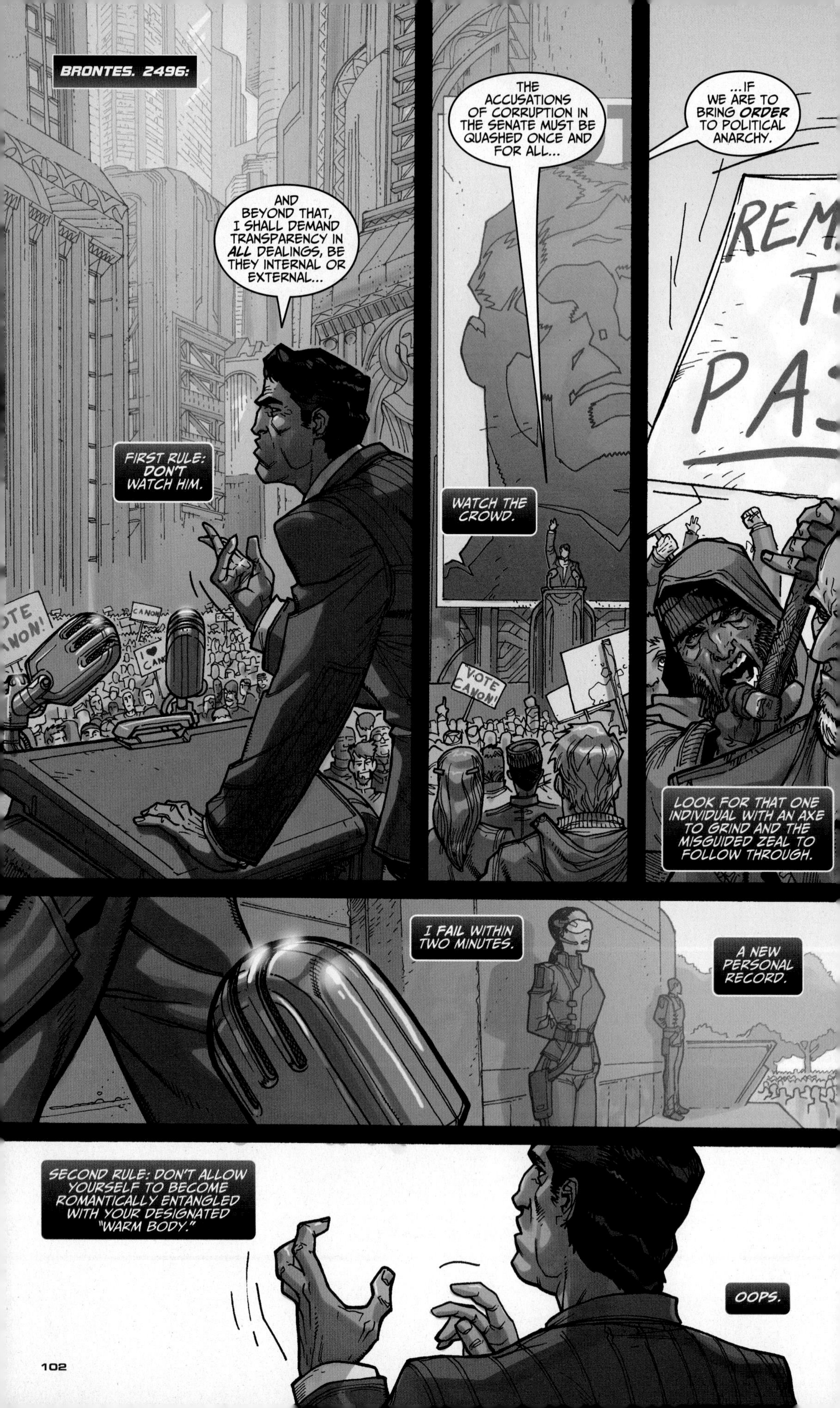

BRONTES. 2496:
AND BEYOND THAT, I SHALL DEMAND TRANSPARENCY IN ALL DEALINGS, BE THEY INTERNAL OR EXTERNAL...
FIRST RULE: DON'T WATCH HIM.
VOTE CANON!
CANON
I ♥ CANON
THE ACCUSATIONS OF CORRUPTION IN THE SENATE MUST BE QUASHED ONCE AND FOR ALL...
WATCH THE CROWD.
VOTE CANON!
...IF WE ARE TO BRING ORDER TO POLITICAL ANARCHY.
LOOK FOR THAT ONE INDIVIDUAL WITH AN AXE TO GRIND AND THE MISGUIDED ZEAL TO FOLLOW THROUGH.
I FAIL WITHIN TWO MINUTES.
A NEW PERSONAL RECORD.
SECOND RULE: DON'T ALLOW YOURSELF TO BECOME ROMANTICALLY ENTANGLED WITH YOUR DESIGNATED "WARM BODY."
OOPS.

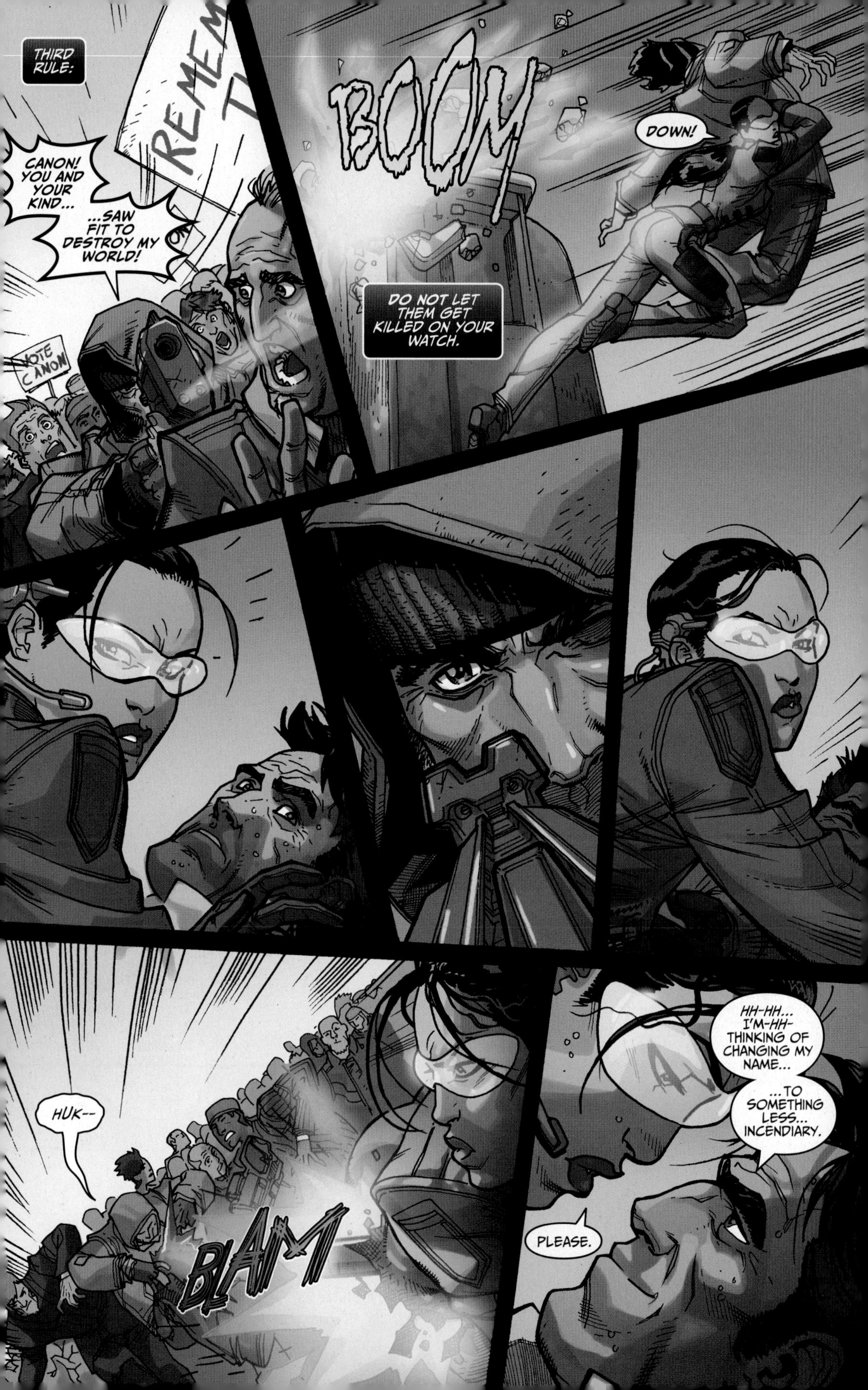
THIRD RULE:
REMEM
VOTE CANON
CANON! YOU AND YOUR KIND...
...SAW FIT TO DESTROY MY WORLD!
BOOM
DOWN!
DO NOT LET THEM GET KILLED ON YOUR WATCH.
HUK--
BLAM
HH-HH... I'M-HH- THINKING OF CHANGING MY NAME...
...TO SOMETHING LESS... INCENDIARY.
PLEASE.

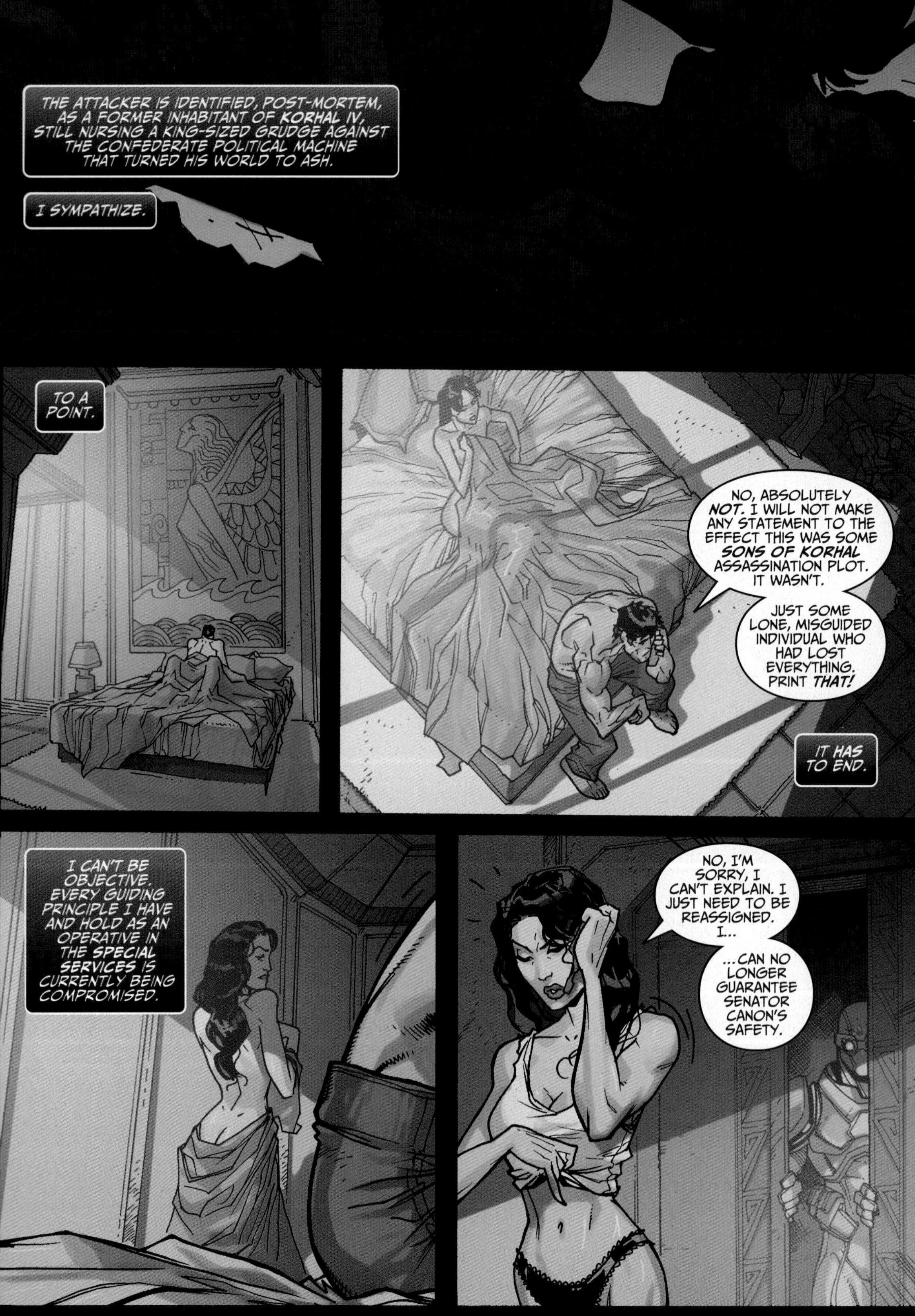
THE ATTACKER IS IDENTIFIED, POST-MORTEM, AS A FORMER INHABITANT OF KORHAL IV, STILL NURSING A KING-SIZED GRUDGE AGAINST THE CONFEDERATE POLITICAL MACHINE THAT TURNED HIS WORLD TO ASH.
I SYMPATHIZE.
TO A POINT.
NO, ABSOLUTELY NOT. I WILL NOT MAKE ANY STATEMENT TO THE EFFECT THIS WAS SOME SONS OF KORHAL ASSASSINATION PLOT. IT WASN'T.
JUST SOME LONE, MISGUIDED INDIVIDUAL WHO HAD LOST EVERYTHING. PRINT THAT!
IT HAS TO END.
I CAN'T BE OBJECTIVE. EVERY GUIDING PRINCIPLE I HAVE AND HOLD AS AN OPERATIVE IN THE SPECIAL SERVICES IS CURRENTLY BEING COMPROMISED.
NO, I'M SORRY, I CAN'T EXPLAIN. I JUST NEED TO BE REASSIGNED. I...
...CAN NO LONGER GUARANTEE SENATOR CANON'S SAFETY.

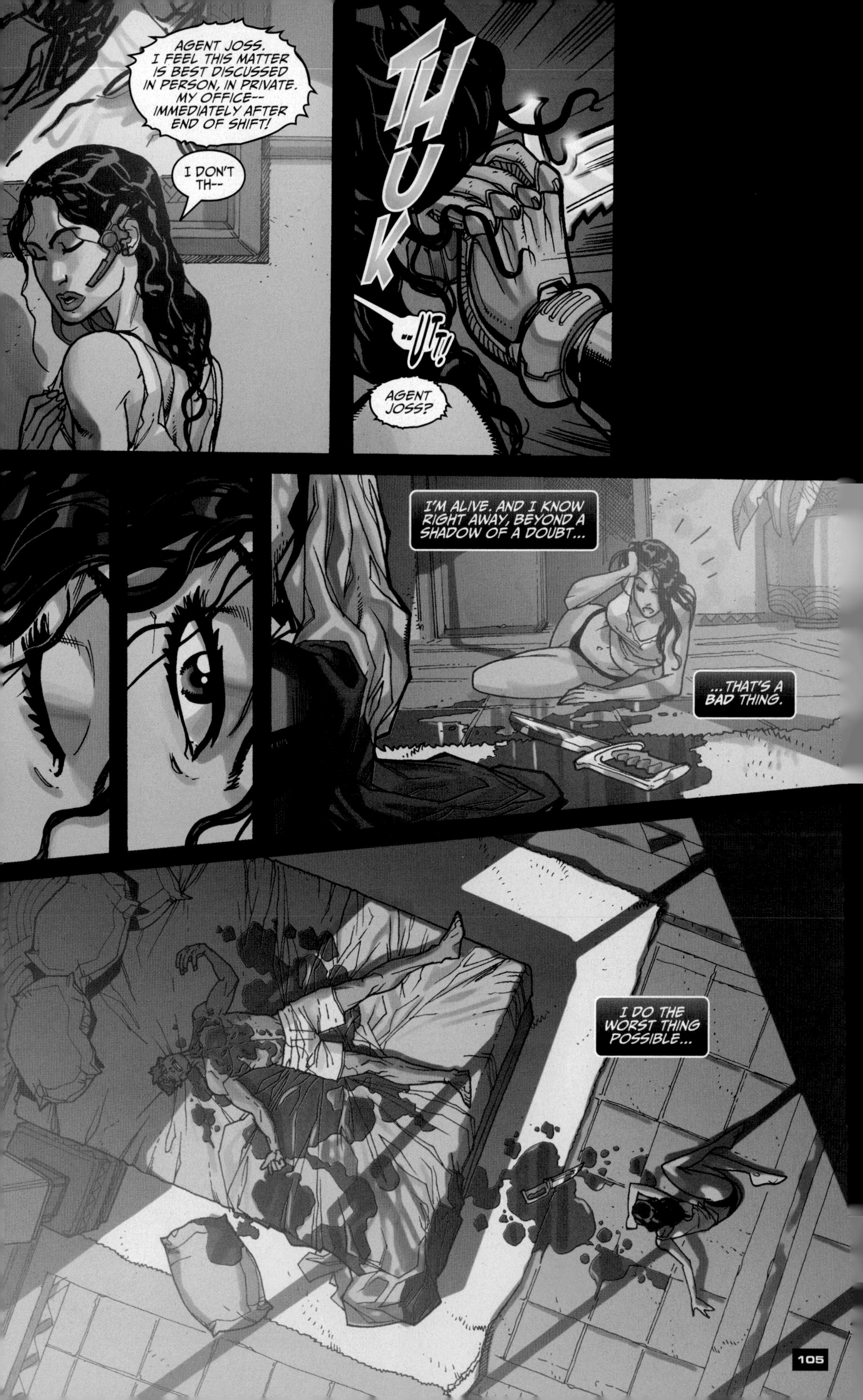
AGENT JOSS. I FEEL THIS MATTER IS BEST DISCUSSED IN PERSON, IN PRIVATE. MY OFFICE-- IMMEDIATELY AFTER END OF SHIFT!
I DON'T TH--
THUK
--UT!
AGENT JOSS?
I'M ALIVE. AND I KNOW RIGHT AWAY, BEYOND A SHADOW OF A DOUBT...
...THAT'S A BAD THING.
I DO THE WORST THING POSSIBLE...

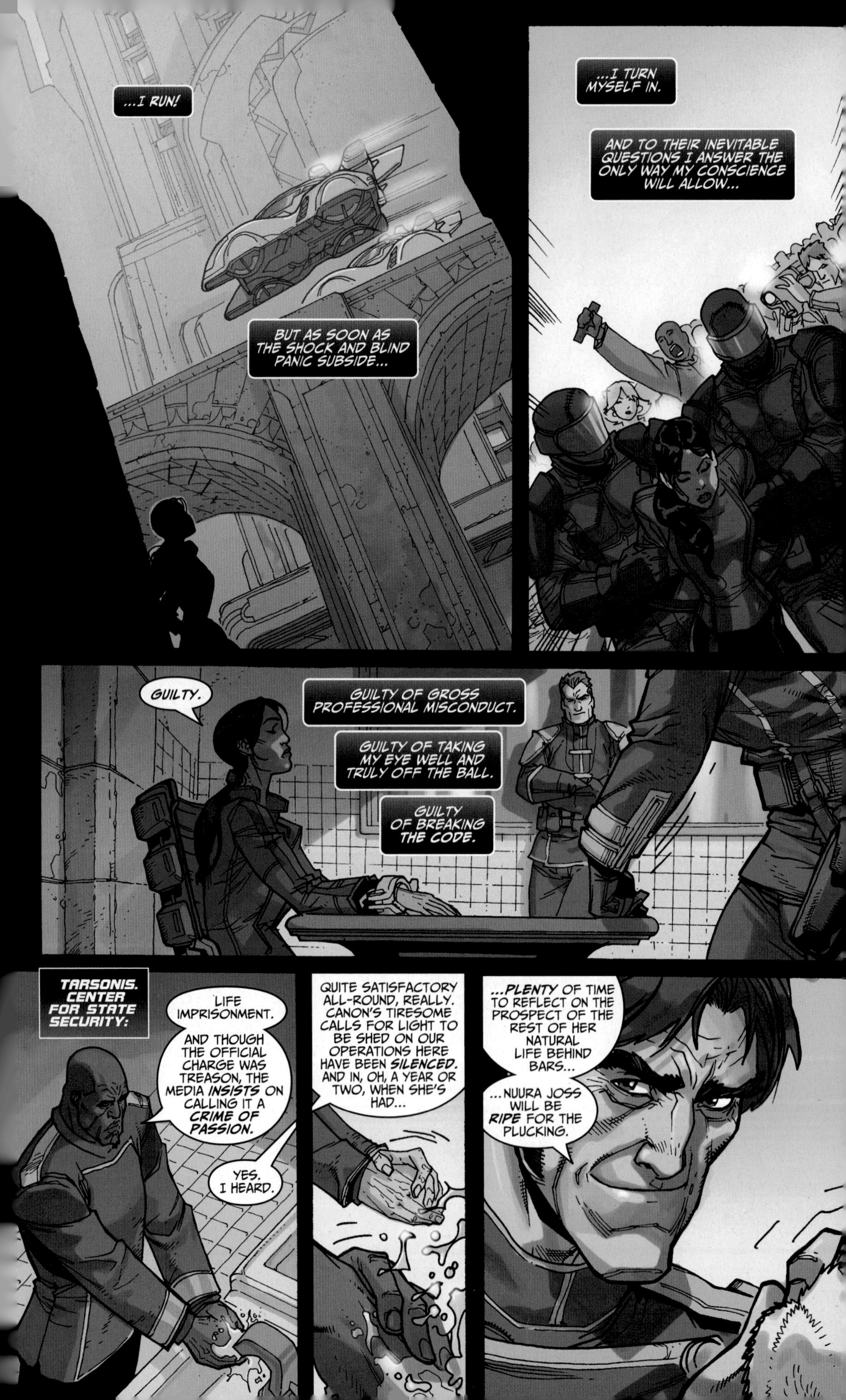
...I RUN!
BUT AS SOON AS THE SHOCK AND BLIND PANIC SUBSIDE...
...I TURN MYSELF IN.
AND TO THEIR INEVITABLE QUESTIONS I ANSWER THE ONLY WAY MY CONSCIENCE WILL ALLOW...
GUILTY.
GUILTY OF GROSS PROFESSIONAL MISCONDUCT.
GUILTY OF TAKING MY EYE WELL AND TRULY OFF THE BALL.
GUILTY OF BREAKING THE CODE.
TARSONIS. CENTER FOR STATE SECURITY:
LIFE IMPRISONMENT.
AND THOUGH THE OFFICIAL CHARGE WAS TREASON, THE MEDIA INSISTS ON CALLING IT A CRIME OF PASSION.
YES. I HEARD.
QUITE SATISFACTORY ALL-ROUND, REALLY. CANON'S TIRESOME CALLS FOR LIGHT TO BE SHED ON OUR OPERATIONS HERE HAVE BEEN SILENCED. AND IN, OH, A YEAR OR TWO, WHEN SHE'S HAD...
...PLENTY OF TIME TO REFLECT ON THE PROSPECT OF THE REST OF HER NATURAL LIFE BEHIND BARS...
...NUURA JOSS WILL BE RIPE FOR THE PLUCKING.

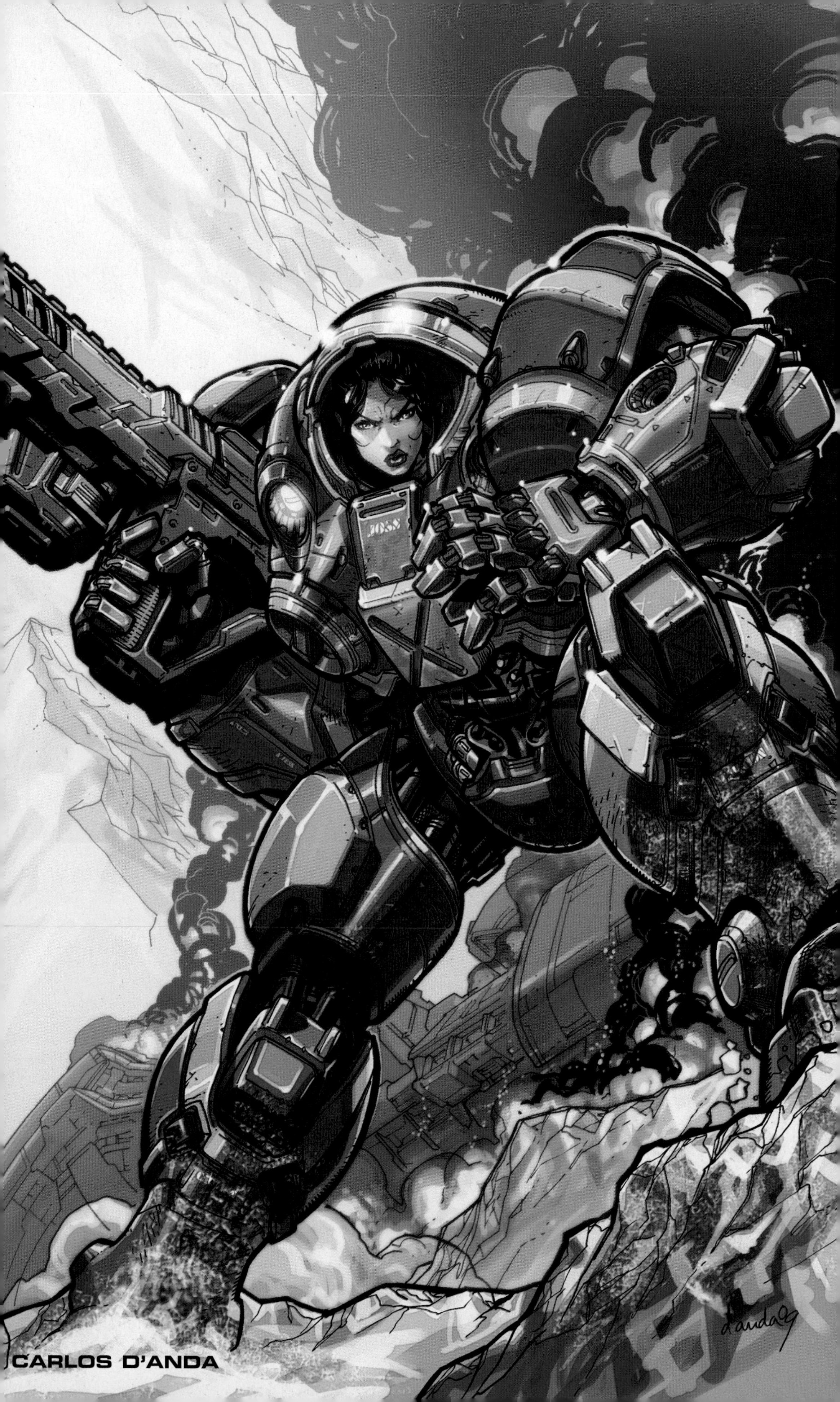
d'anda 09

CARLOS D'ANDA

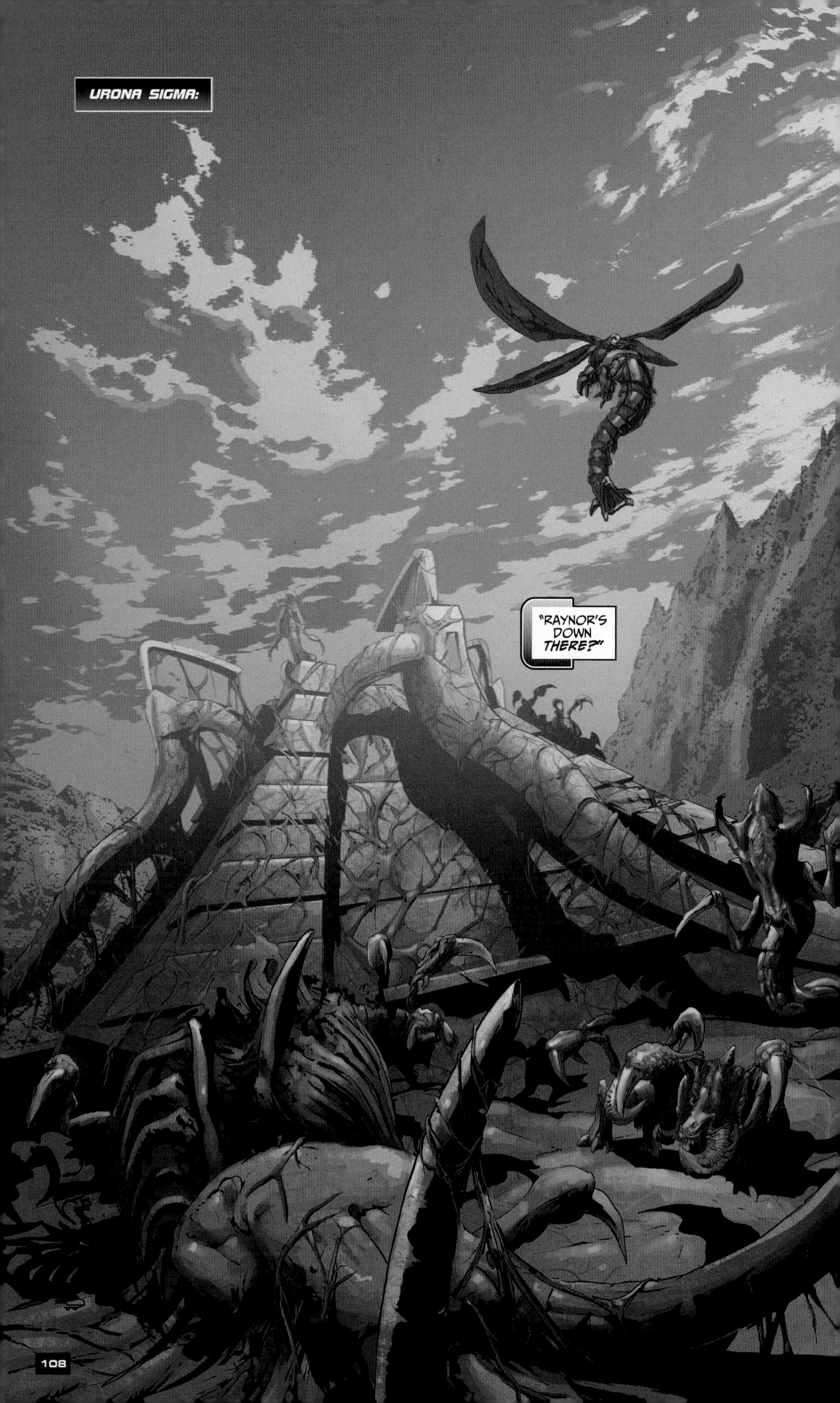
URONA SIGMA:
"RAYNOR'S DOWN THERE?"

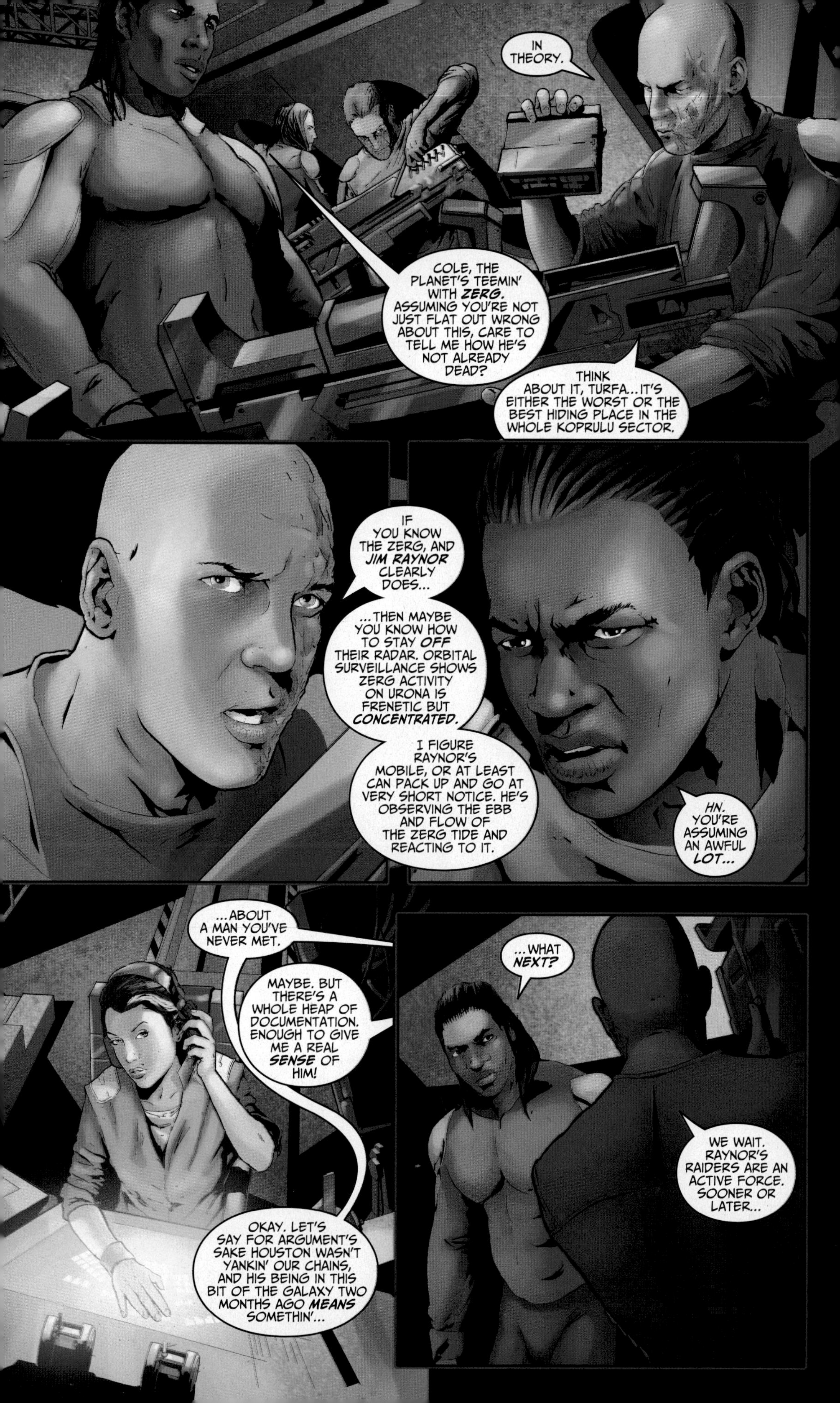
IN THEORY.
COLE, THE PLANET'S TEEMIN' WITH ZERG. ASSUMING YOU'RE NOT JUST FLAT OUT WRONG ABOUT THIS, CARE TO TELL ME HOW HE'S NOT ALREADY DEAD?
THINK ABOUT IT, TURFA...IT'S EITHER THE WORST OR THE BEST HIDING PLACE IN THE WHOLE KOPRULU SECTOR.
IF YOU KNOW THE ZERG, AND JIM RAYNOR CLEARLY DOES...
...THEN MAYBE YOU KNOW HOW TO STAY OFF THEIR RADAR. ORBITAL SURVEILLANCE SHOWS ZERG ACTIVITY ON URONA IS FRENETIC BUT CONCENTRATED.
I FIGURE RAYNOR'S MOBILE, OR AT LEAST CAN PACK UP AND GO AT VERY SHORT NOTICE. HE'S OBSERVING THE EBB AND FLOW OF THE ZERG TIDE AND REACTING TO IT.
HN. YOU'RE ASSUMING AN AWFUL LOT...
...ABOUT A MAN YOU'VE NEVER MET.
MAYBE. BUT THERE'S A WHOLE HEAP OF DOCUMENTATION. ENOUGH TO GIVE ME A REAL SENSE OF HIM!
OKAY. LET'S SAY FOR ARGUMENT'S SAKE HOUSTON WASN'T YANKIN' OUR CHAINS, AND HIS BEING IN THIS BIT OF THE GALAXY TWO MONTHS AGO MEANS SOMETHIN'...
...WHAT NEXT?
WE WAIT. RAYNOR'S RAIDERS ARE AN ACTIVE FORCE. SOONER OR LATER...

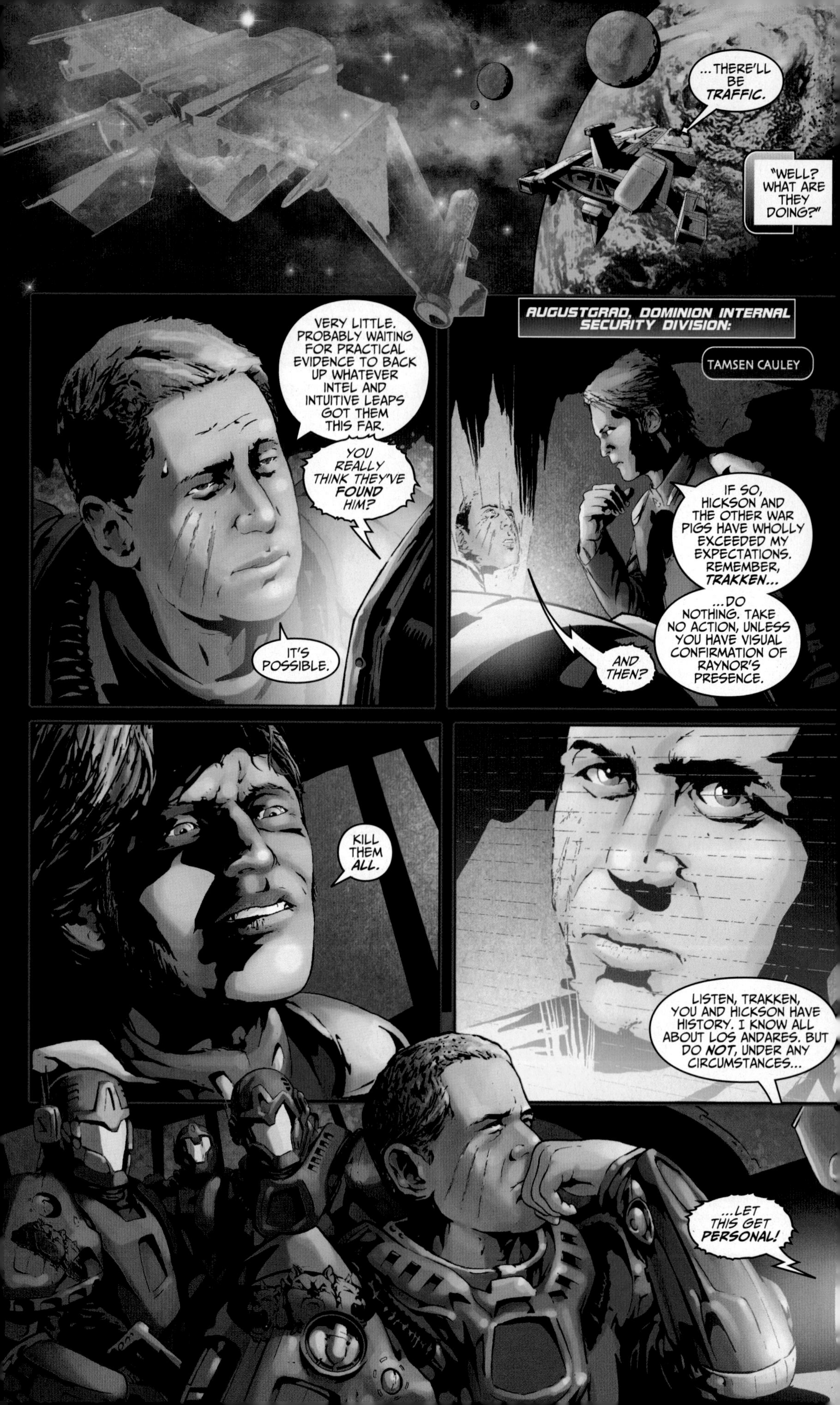
...THERE'LL BE TRAFFIC.
"WELL? WHAT ARE THEY DOING?"
VERY LITTLE. PROBABLY WAITING FOR PRACTICAL EVIDENCE TO BACK UP WHATEVER INTEL AND INTUITIVE LEAPS GOT THEM THIS FAR.
YOU REALLY THINK THEY'VE FOUND HIM?
IT'S POSSIBLE.
AUGUSTGRAD, DOMINION INTERNAL SECURITY DIVISION:
TAMSEN CAULEY
IF SO, HICKSON AND THE OTHER WAR PIGS HAVE WHOLLY EXCEEDED MY EXPECTATIONS. REMEMBER, TRAKKEN...
...DO NOTHING. TAKE NO ACTION, UNLESS YOU HAVE VISUAL CONFIRMATION OF RAYNOR'S PRESENCE.
AND THEN?
KILL THEM ALL.
LISTEN, TRAKKEN, YOU AND HICKSON HAVE HISTORY. I KNOW ALL ABOUT LOS ANDARES. BUT DO NOT, UNDER ANY CIRCUMSTANCES...
...LET THIS GET PERSONAL!

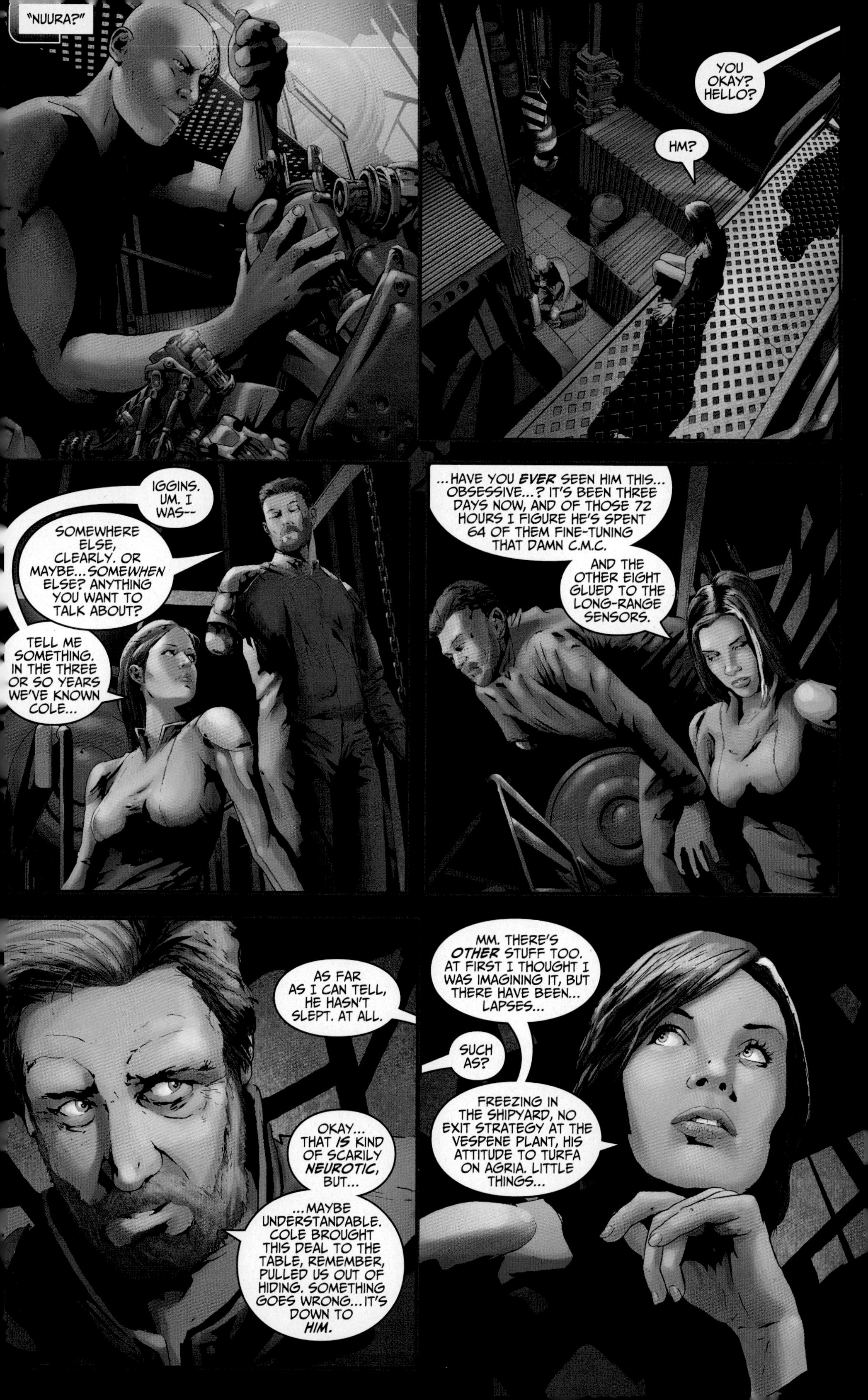
"NUURA?"
YOU OKAY? HELLO?
HM?
IGGINS. UM. I WAS--
SOMEWHERE ELSE, CLEARLY. OR MAYBE... SOMEWHEN ELSE? ANYTHING YOU WANT TO TALK ABOUT?
TELL ME SOMETHING. IN THE THREE OR SO YEARS WE'VE KNOWN COLE...
...HAVE YOU EVER SEEN HIM THIS... OBSESSIVE...? IT'S BEEN THREE DAYS NOW, AND OF THOSE 72 HOURS I FIGURE HE'S SPENT 64 OF THEM FINE-TUNING THAT DAMN C.M.C.
AND THE OTHER EIGHT GLUED TO THE LONG-RANGE SENSORS.
AS FAR AS I CAN TELL, HE HASN'T SLEPT. AT ALL.
OKAY... THAT IS KIND OF SCARILY NEUROTIC, BUT...
...MAYBE UNDERSTANDABLE. COLE BROUGHT THIS DEAL TO THE TABLE, REMEMBER, PULLED US OUT OF HIDING. SOMETHING GOES WRONG... IT'S DOWN TO HIM.
MM. THERE'S OTHER STUFF TOO. AT FIRST I THOUGHT I WAS IMAGINING IT, BUT THERE HAVE BEEN... LAPSES...
SUCH AS?
FREEZING IN THE SHIPYARD, NO EXIT STRATEGY AT THE VESPENE PLANT, HIS ATTITUDE TO TURFA ON AGRIA. LITTLE THINGS...

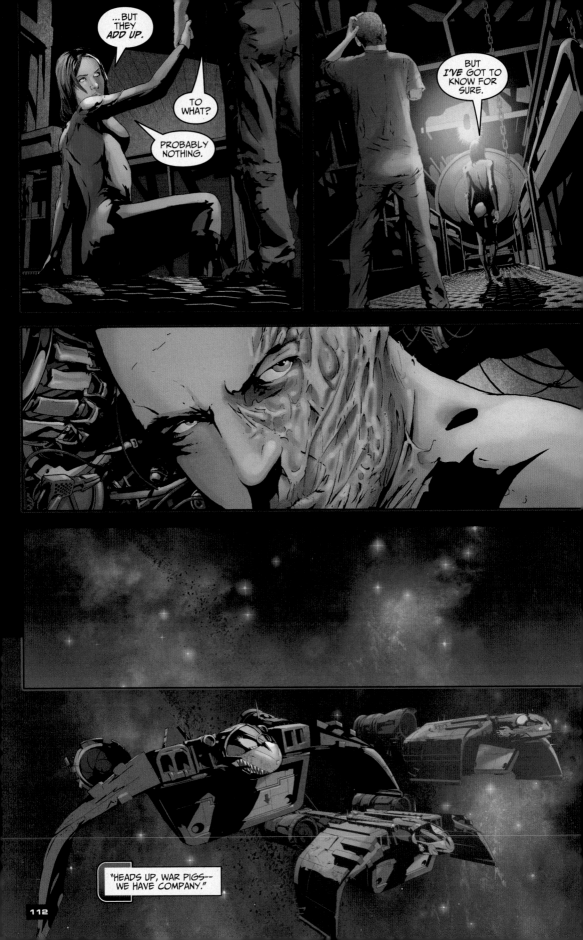

...BUT THEY *ADD UP.*

TO WHAT?

PROBABLY NOTHING.

BUT *I'VE GOT TO* KNOW FOR SURE.

"HEADS UP, WAR PIGS—— WE HAVE COMPANY."

112

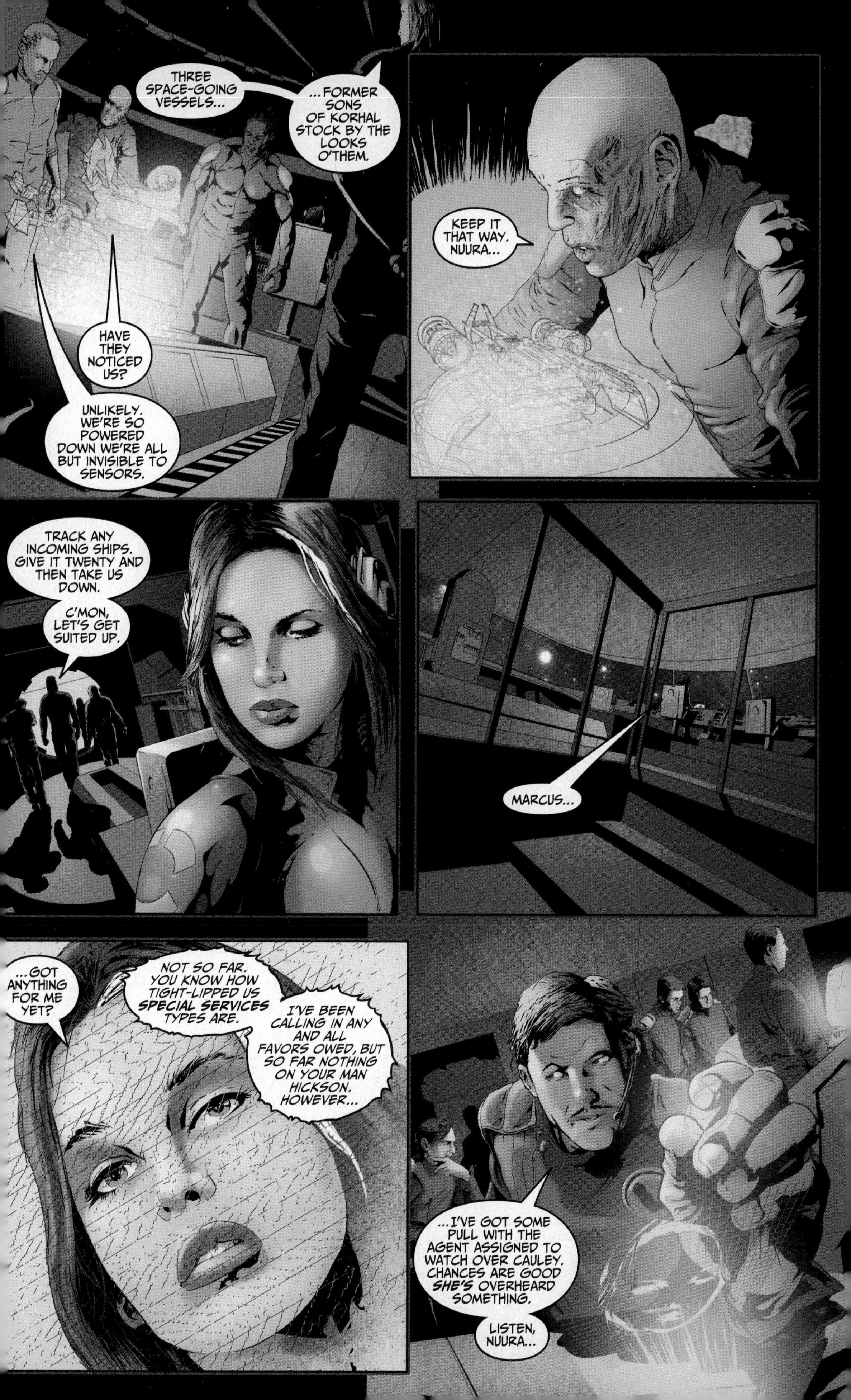
THREE SPACE-GOING VESSELS...
...FORMER SONS OF KORHAL STOCK BY THE LOOKS O'THEM.
HAVE THEY NOTICED US?
UNLIKELY. WE'RE SO POWERED DOWN WE'RE ALL BUT INVISIBLE TO SENSORS.
KEEP IT THAT WAY. NUURA...
TRACK ANY INCOMING SHIPS. GIVE IT TWENTY AND THEN TAKE US DOWN.
C'MON, LET'S GET SUITED UP.
MARCUS...
...GOT ANYTHING FOR ME YET?
NOT SO FAR. YOU KNOW HOW TIGHT-LIPPED US SPECIAL SERVICES TYPES ARE.
I'VE BEEN CALLING IN ANY AND ALL FAVORS OWED, BUT SO FAR NOTHING ON YOUR MAN HICKSON. HOWEVER...
...I'VE GOT SOME PULL WITH THE AGENT ASSIGNED TO WATCH OVER CAULEY. CHANCES ARE GOOD SHE'S OVERHEARD SOMETHING.
LISTEN, NUURA...

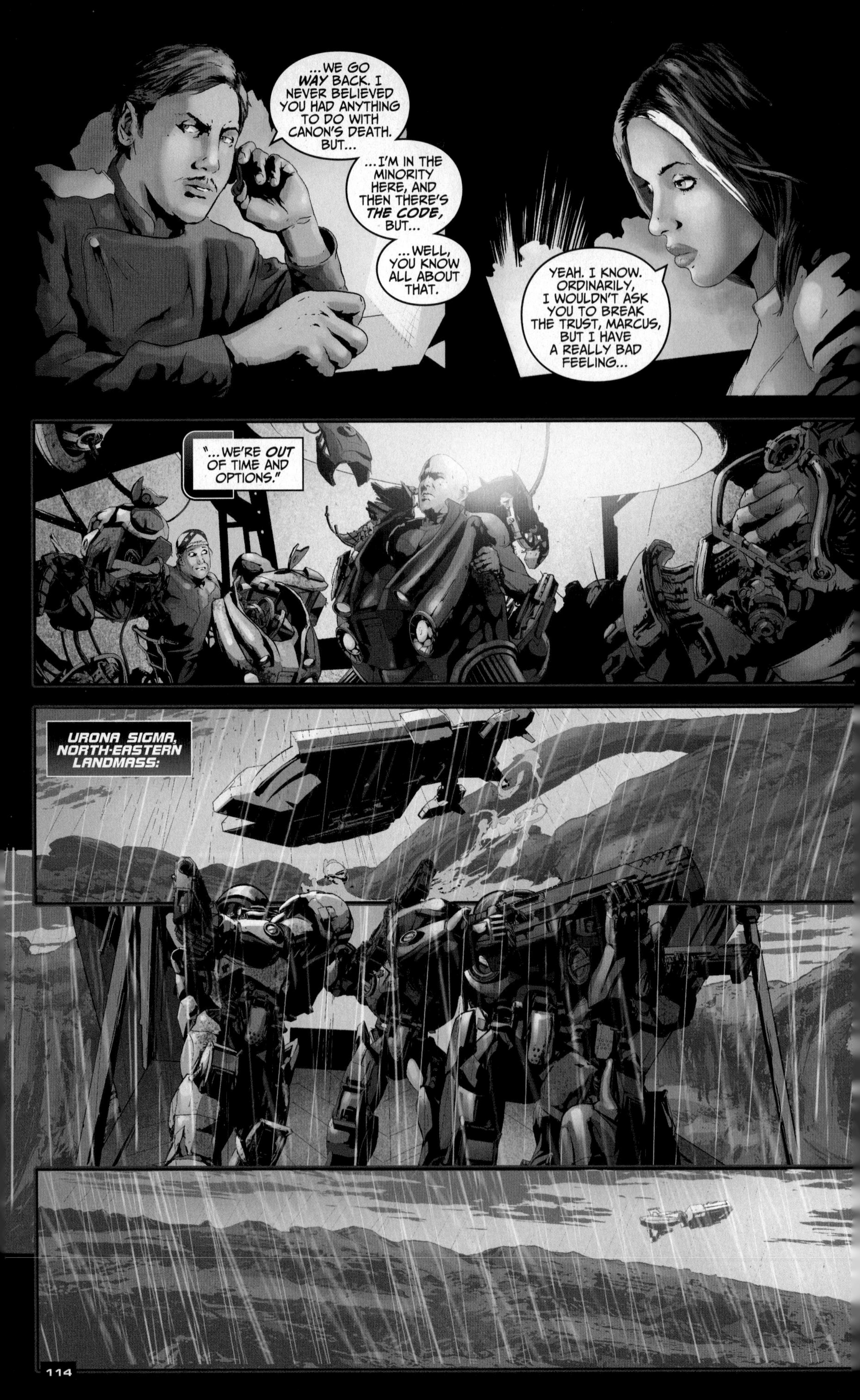
...WE GO WAY BACK. I NEVER BELIEVED YOU HAD ANYTHING TO DO WITH CANON'S DEATH. BUT...
...I'M IN THE MINORITY HERE, AND THEN THERE'S THE CODE, BUT...
...WELL, YOU KNOW ALL ABOUT THAT.
YEAH. I KNOW. ORDINARILY, I WOULDN'T ASK YOU TO BREAK THE TRUST, MARCUS, BUT I HAVE A REALLY BAD FEELING...
"...WE'RE OUT OF TIME AND OPTIONS."
URONA SIGMA, NORTH-EASTERN LANDMASS:

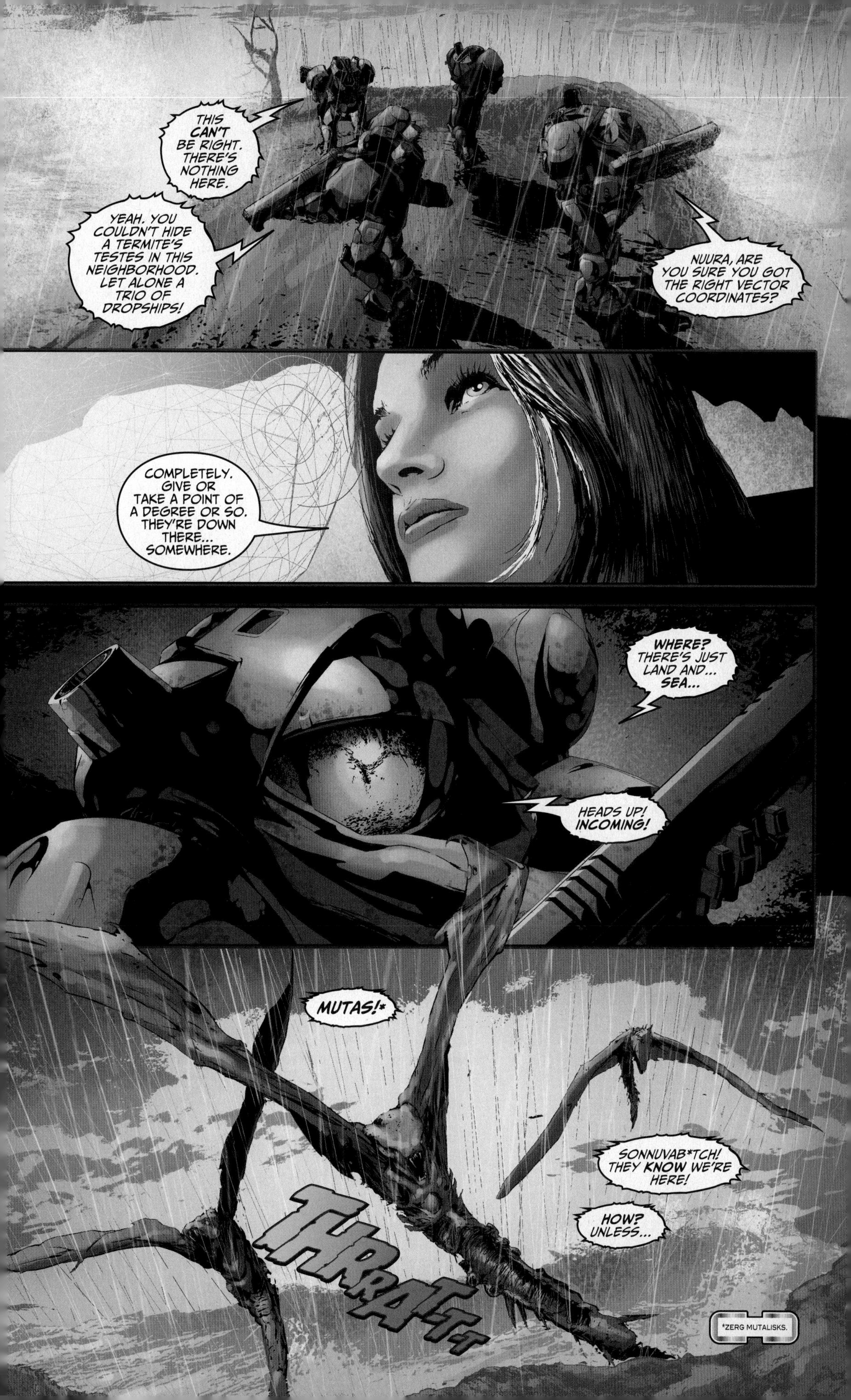
THIS CAN'T BE RIGHT. THERE'S NOTHING HERE.
YEAH. YOU COULDN'T HIDE A TERMITE'S TESTES IN THIS NEIGHBORHOOD. LET ALONE A TRIO OF DROPSHIPS!
NUURA, ARE YOU SURE YOU GOT THE RIGHT VECTOR COORDINATES?
COMPLETELY. GIVE OR TAKE A POINT OF A DEGREE OR SO. THEY'RE DOWN THERE... SOMEWHERE.
WHERE? THERE'S JUST LAND AND... SEA...
HEADS UP! INCOMING!
MUTAS!*
SONNUVAB*TCH! THEY KNOW WE'RE HERE!
HOW? UNLESS...
THRRAT-T-T
*ZERG MUTALISKS.

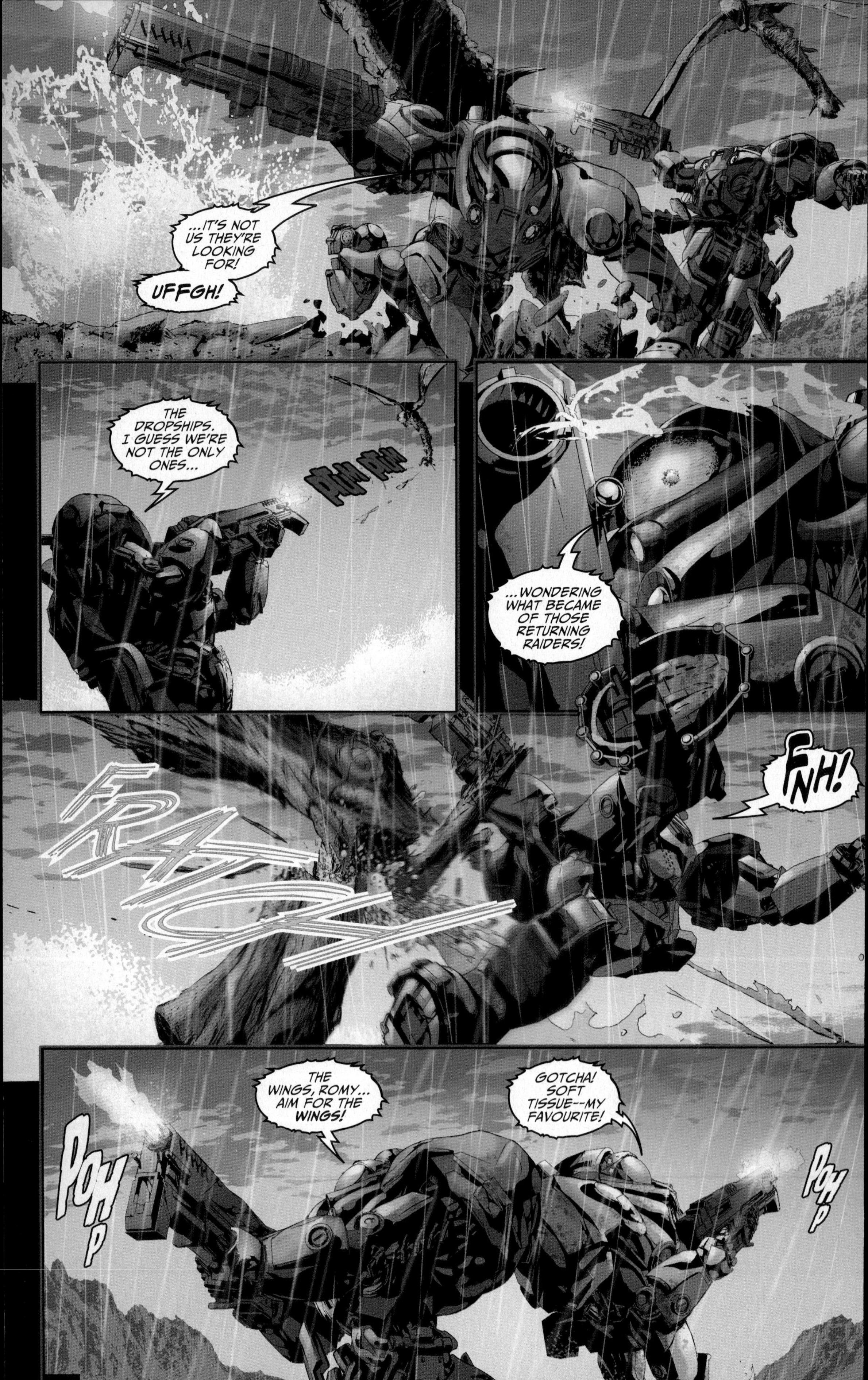
...IT'S NOT US THEY'RE LOOKING FOR!
UFFGH!
THE DROPSHIPS. I GUESS WE'RE NOT THE ONLY ONES...
...WONDERING WHAT BECAME OF THOSE RETURNING RAIDERS!
FRATCH
FNH!
THE WINGS, ROMY... AIM FOR THE WINGS!
GOTCHA! SOFT TISSUE--MY FAVOURITE!
POHP
POHP

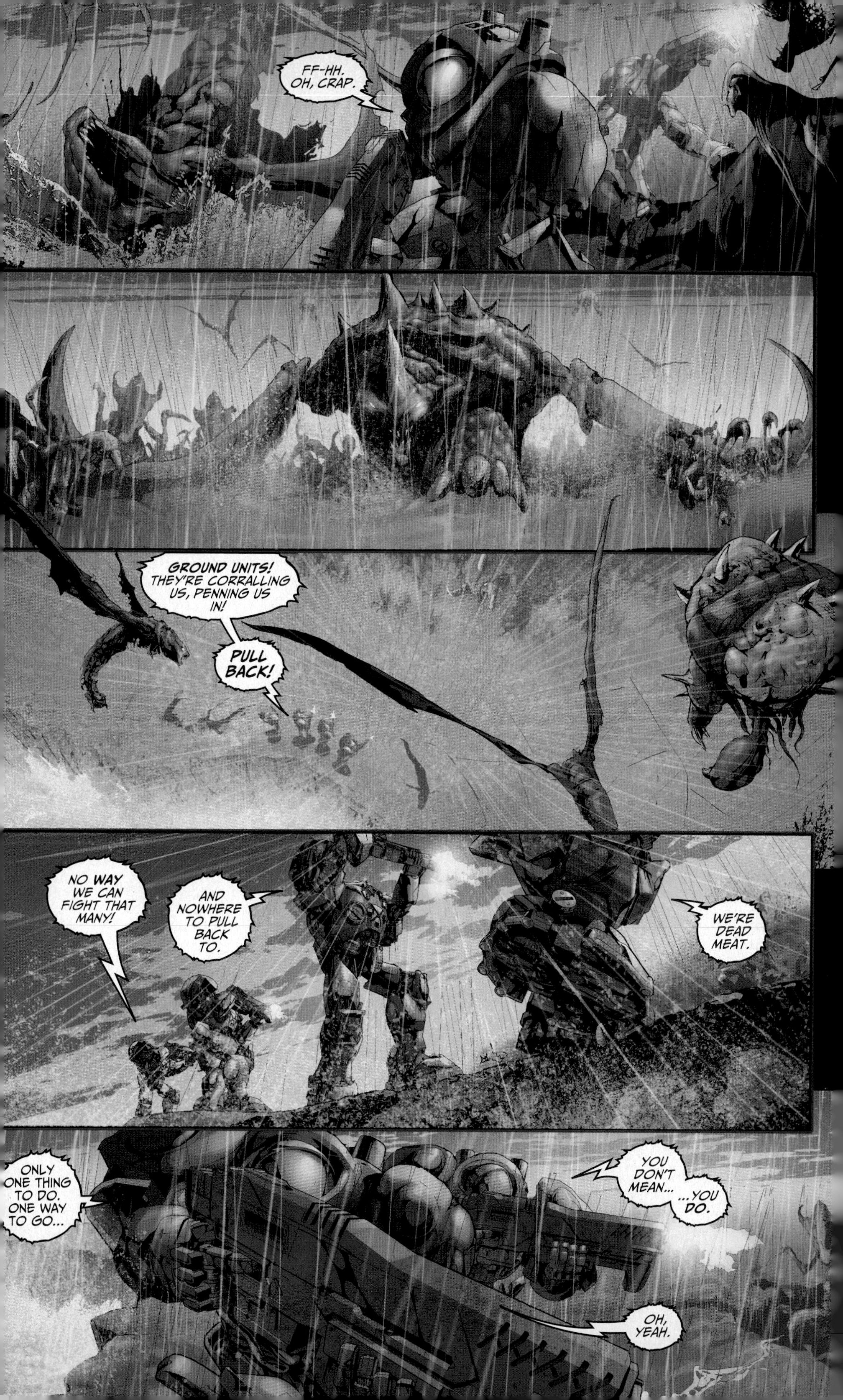
FF-HH. OH, CRAP.
GROUND UNITS! THEY'RE CORRALLING US, PENNING US IN!
PULL BACK!
NO WAY WE CAN FIGHT THAT MANY!
AND NOWHERE TO PULL BACK TO.
WE'RE DEAD MEAT.
ONLY ONE THING TO DO. ONE WAY TO GO...
YOU DON'T MEAN...
...YOU DO.
OH, YEAH.

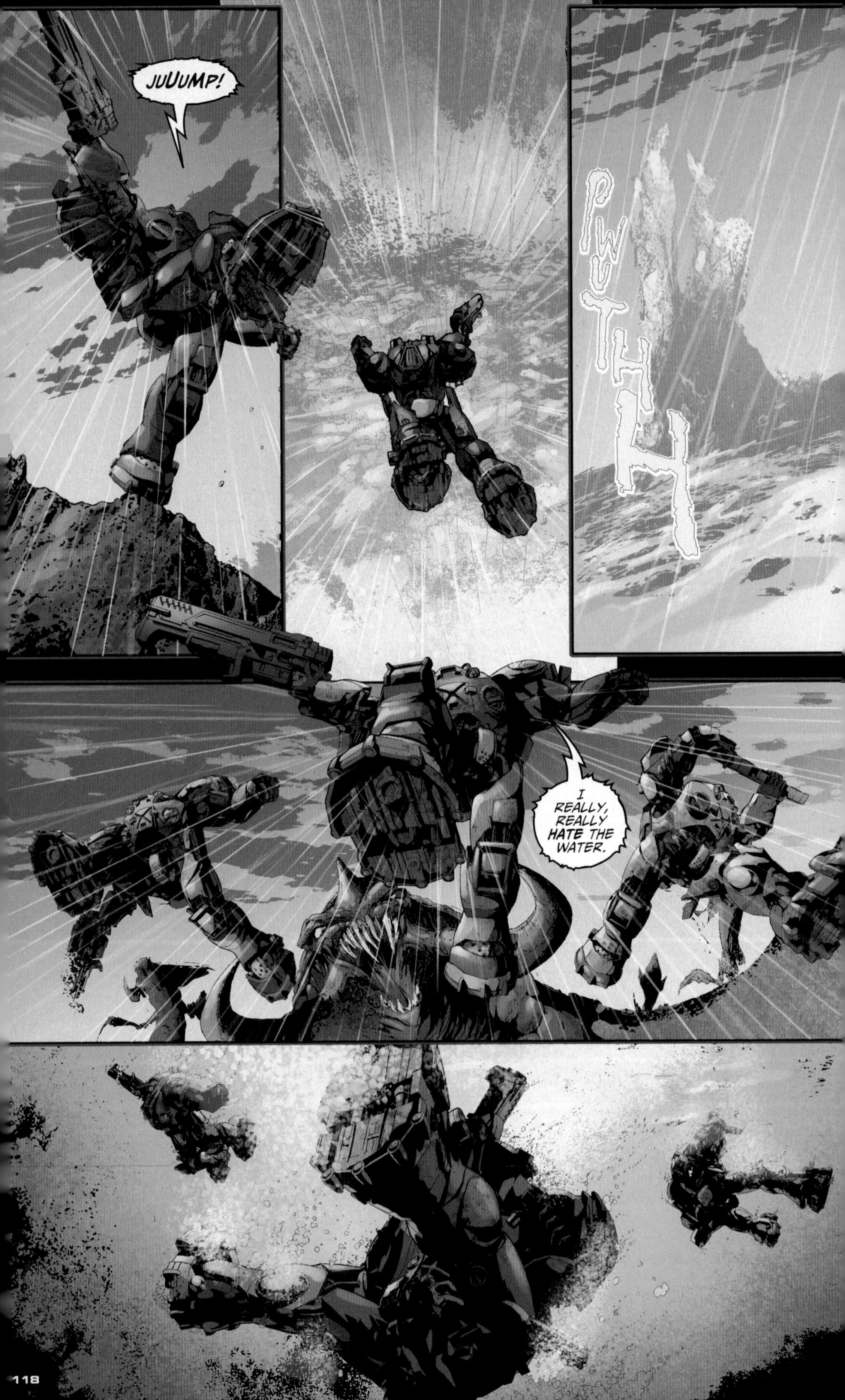
JUUUMP!
PWUTHH
I REALLY, REALLY HATE THE WATER.

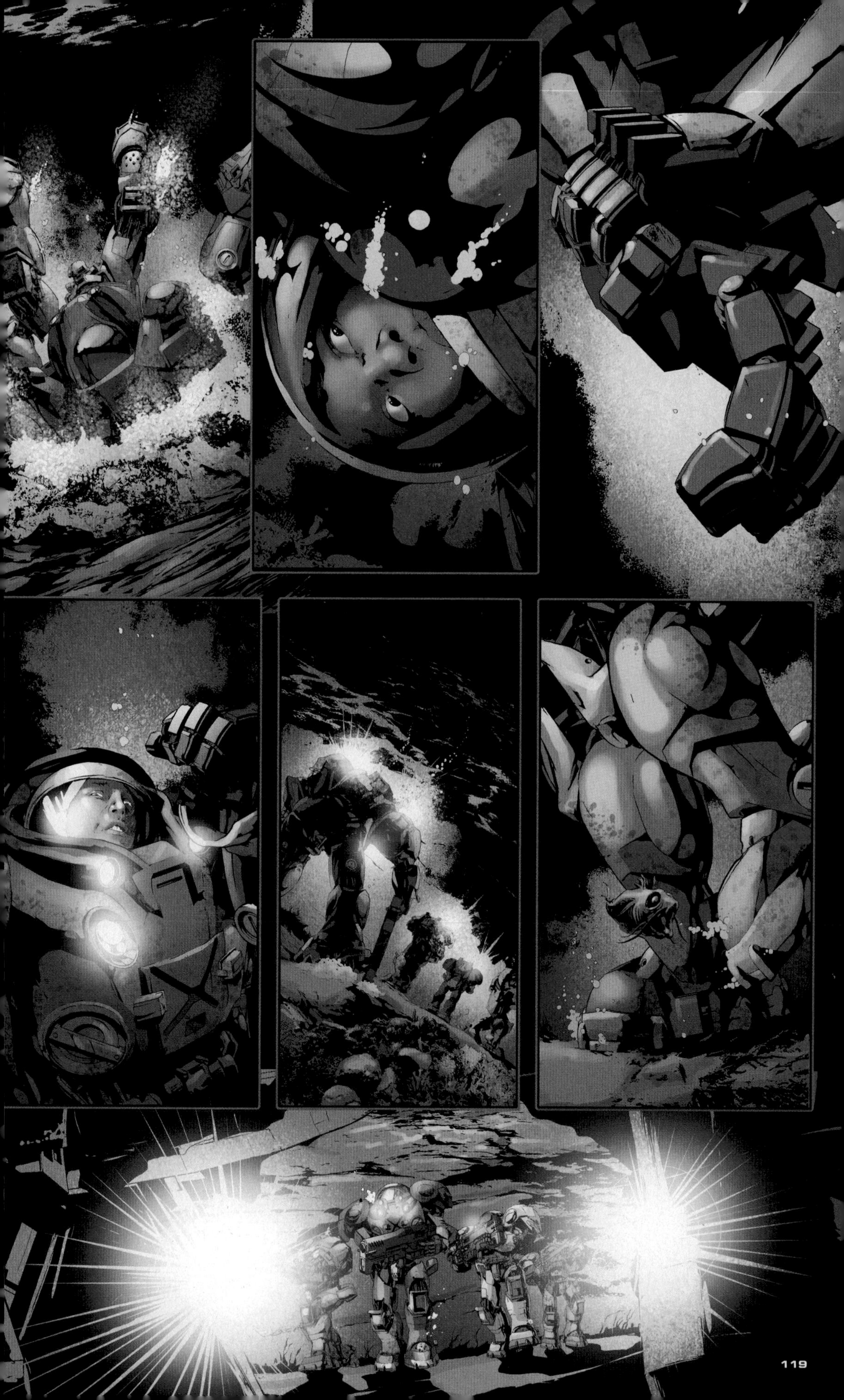

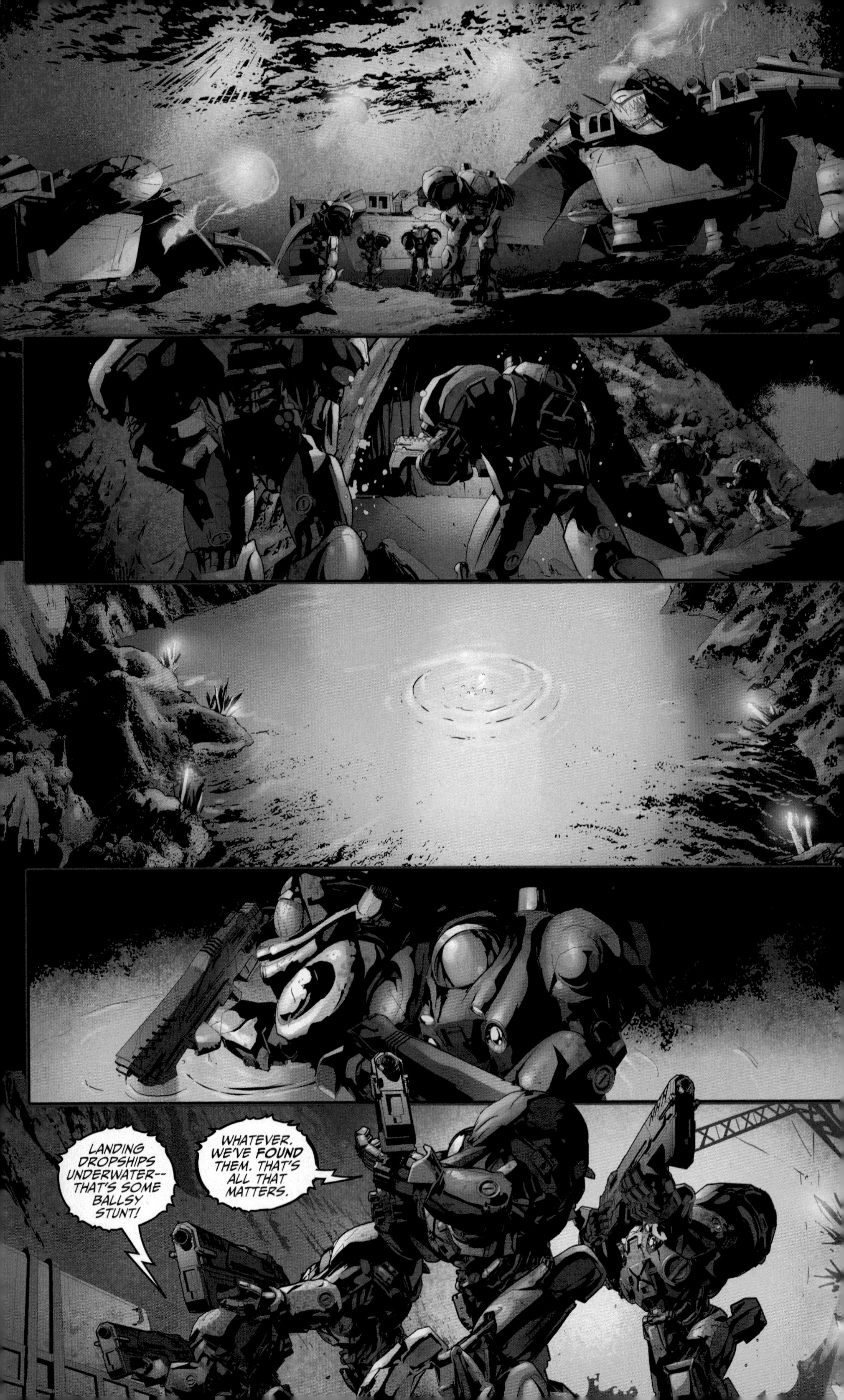
LANDING DROPSHIPS UNDERWATER-- THAT'S SOME BALLSY STUNT!
WHATEVER. WE'VE FOUND THEM. THAT'S ALL THAT MATTERS.

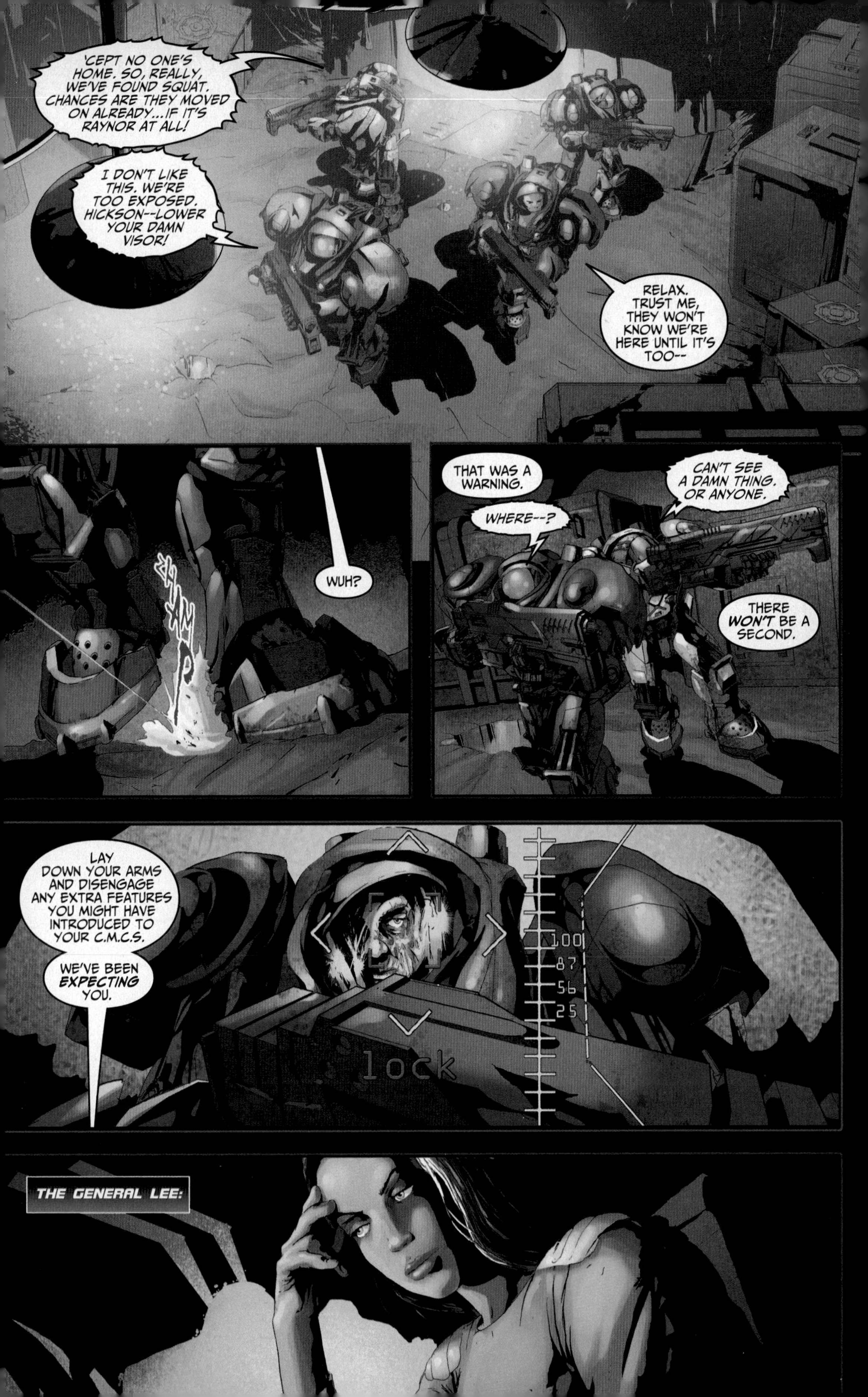
'CEPT NO ONE'S HOME. SO, REALLY, WE'VE FOUND SQUAT. CHANCES ARE THEY MOVED ON ALREADY...IF IT'S RAYNOR AT ALL!
I DON'T LIKE THIS. WE'RE TOO EXPOSED. HICKSON--LOWER YOUR DAMN VISOR!
RELAX. TRUST ME, THEY WON'T KNOW WE'RE HERE UNTIL IT'S TOO--
ZHHMP
WUH?
THAT WAS A WARNING.
WHERE--?
CAN'T SEE A DAMN THING. OR ANYONE.
THERE *WON'T* BE A SECOND.
LAY DOWN YOUR ARMS AND DISENGAGE ANY EXTRA FEATURES YOU MIGHT HAVE INTRODUCED TO YOUR C.M.C.S.
WE'VE BEEN *EXPECTING* YOU.
100
87
56
25
lock
THE GENERAL LEE:

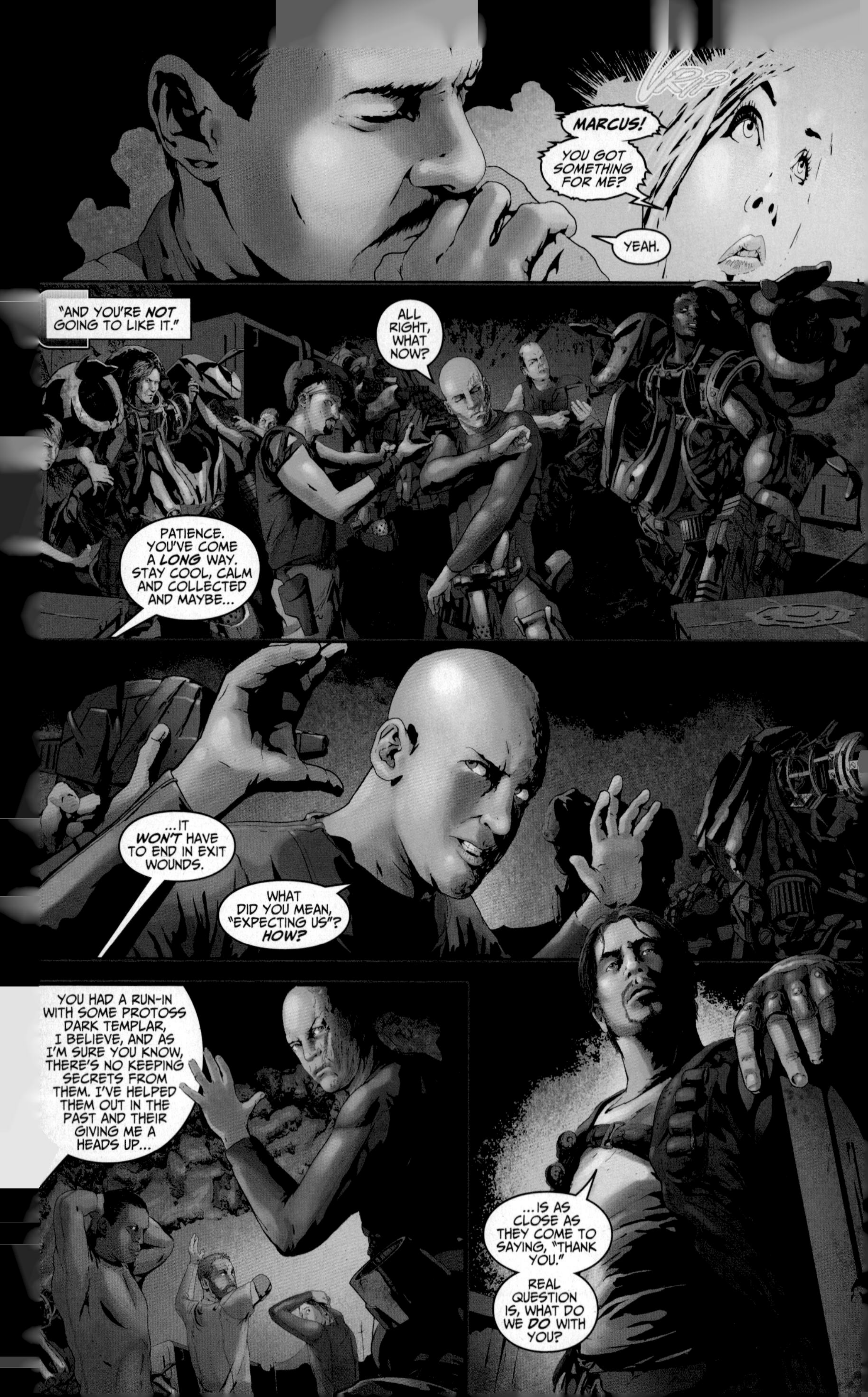
VRIP
MARCUS!
YOU GOT SOMETHING FOR ME?
YEAH.
"AND YOU'RE NOT GOING TO LIKE IT."
ALL RIGHT, WHAT NOW?
PATIENCE. YOU'VE COME A LONG WAY. STAY COOL, CALM AND COLLECTED AND MAYBE...
...IT WON'T HAVE TO END IN EXIT WOUNDS.
WHAT DID YOU MEAN, "EXPECTING US"? HOW?
YOU HAD A RUN-IN WITH SOME PROTOSS DARK TEMPLAR, I BELIEVE, AND AS I'M SURE YOU KNOW, THERE'S NO KEEPING SECRETS FROM THEM. I'VE HELPED THEM OUT IN THE PAST AND THEIR GIVING ME A HEADS UP...
...IS AS CLOSE AS THEY COME TO SAYING, "THANK YOU."
REAL QUESTION IS, WHAT DO WE DO WITH YOU?

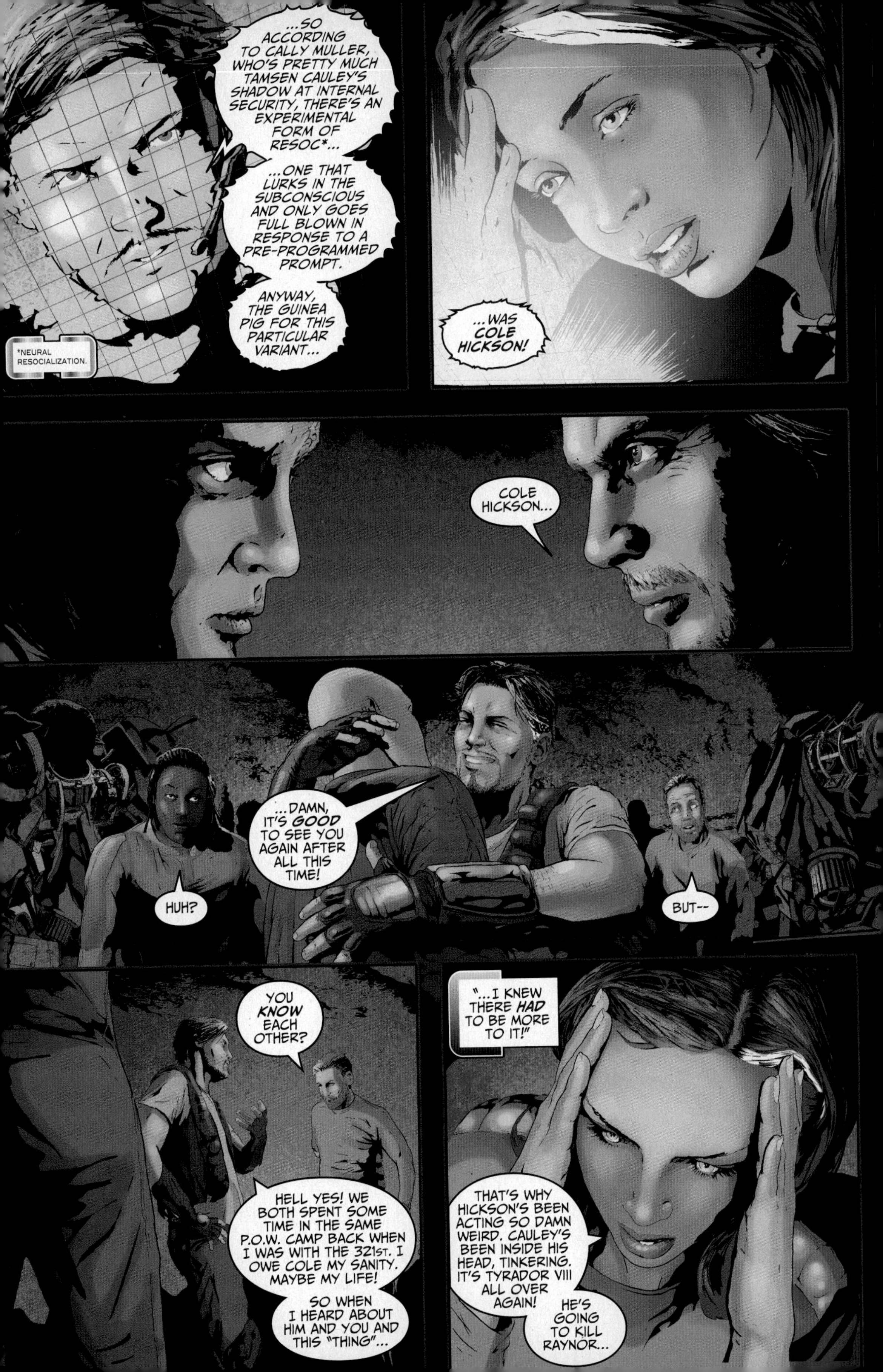
...SO ACCORDING TO CALLY MULLER, WHO'S PRETTY MUCH TAMSEN CAULEY'S SHADOW AT INTERNAL SECURITY, THERE'S AN EXPERIMENTAL FORM OF RESOC*...
...ONE THAT LURKS IN THE SUBCONSCIOUS AND ONLY GOES FULL BLOWN IN RESPONSE TO A PRE-PROGRAMMED PROMPT.
ANYWAY, THE GUINEA PIG FOR THIS PARTICULAR VARIANT...
*NEURAL RESOCIALIZATION.
...WAS COLE HICKSON!
COLE HICKSON...
...DAMN, IT'S GOOD TO SEE YOU AGAIN AFTER ALL THIS TIME!
HUH?
BUT--
YOU KNOW EACH OTHER?
HELL YES! WE BOTH SPENT SOME TIME IN THE SAME P.O.W. CAMP BACK WHEN I WAS WITH THE 321ST. I OWE COLE MY SANITY. MAYBE MY LIFE!
SO WHEN I HEARD ABOUT HIM AND YOU AND THIS "THING"...
"...I KNEW THERE HAD TO BE MORE TO IT!"
THAT'S WHY HICKSON'S BEEN ACTING SO DAMN WEIRD. CAULEY'S BEEN INSIDE HIS HEAD, TINKERING. IT'S TYRADOR VIII ALL OVER AGAIN!
HE'S GOING TO KILL RAYNOR...

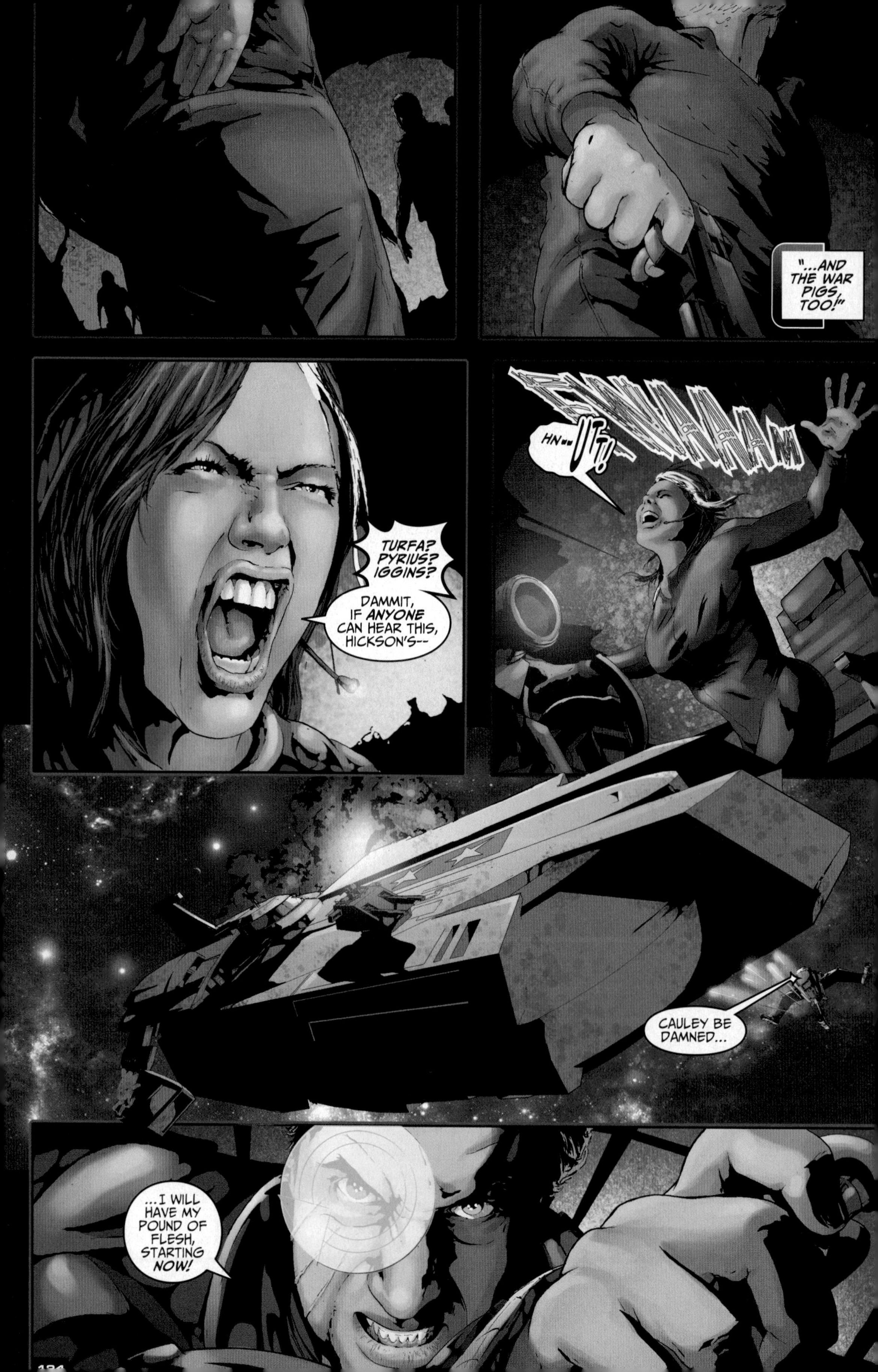
"...AND THE WAR PIGS, TOO!"
TURFA? PYRIUS? IGGINS?
DAMMIT, IF ANYONE CAN HEAR THIS, HICKSON'S--
HN--UTT!
CAULEY BE DAMNED...
...I WILL HAVE MY POUND OF FLESH, STARTING NOW!

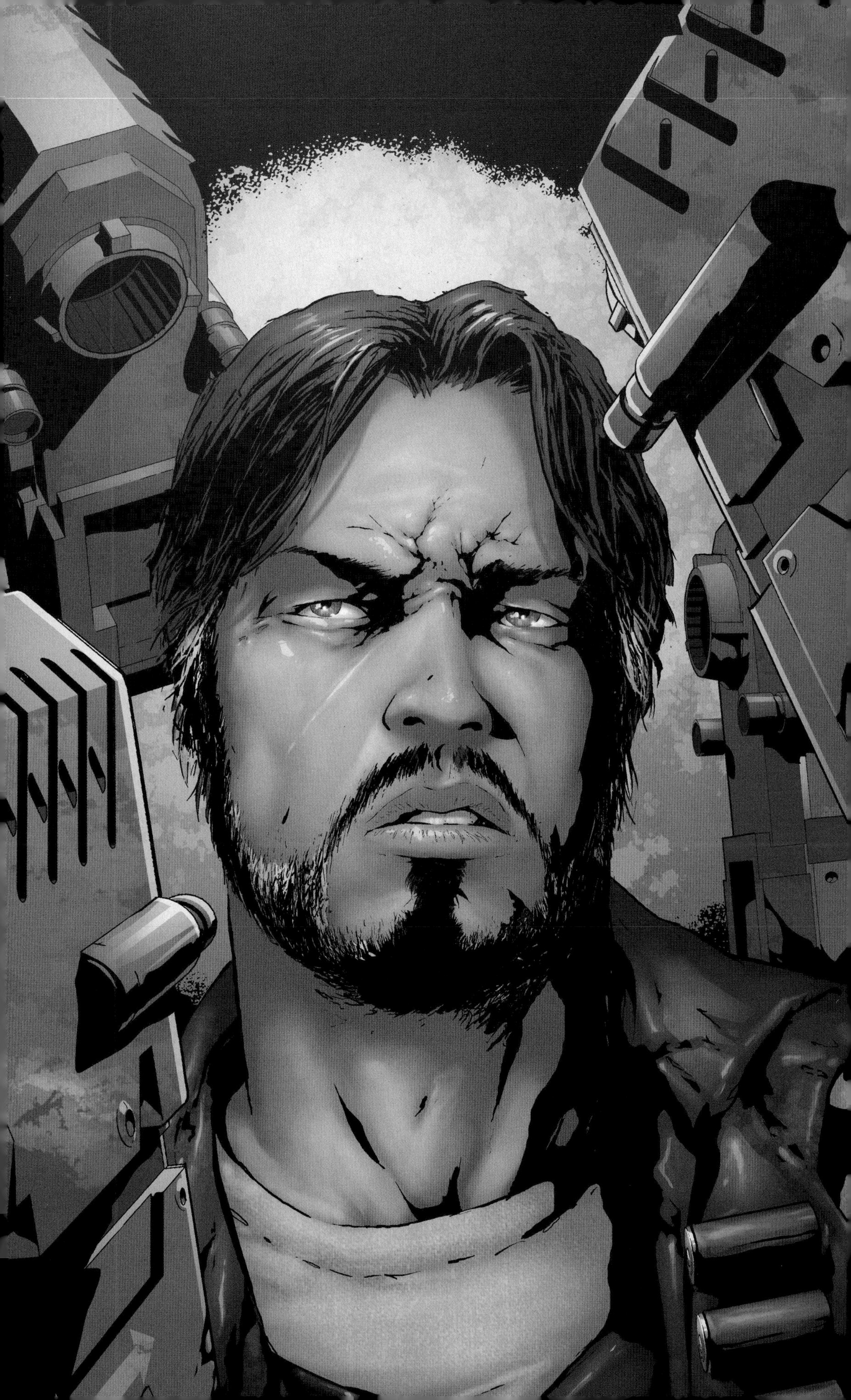

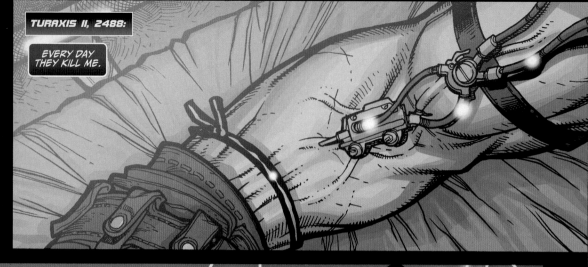

EVERY DAY THEY KILL ME.

THEN THEY BRING ME BACK.

CAN'T TELL IF IT'S TORTURE OR AN EXPERIMENT.

EITHER WAY...

...IT PUSHES BODY... AND MIND... WAY PAST ANYTHING LIKE NORMAL!

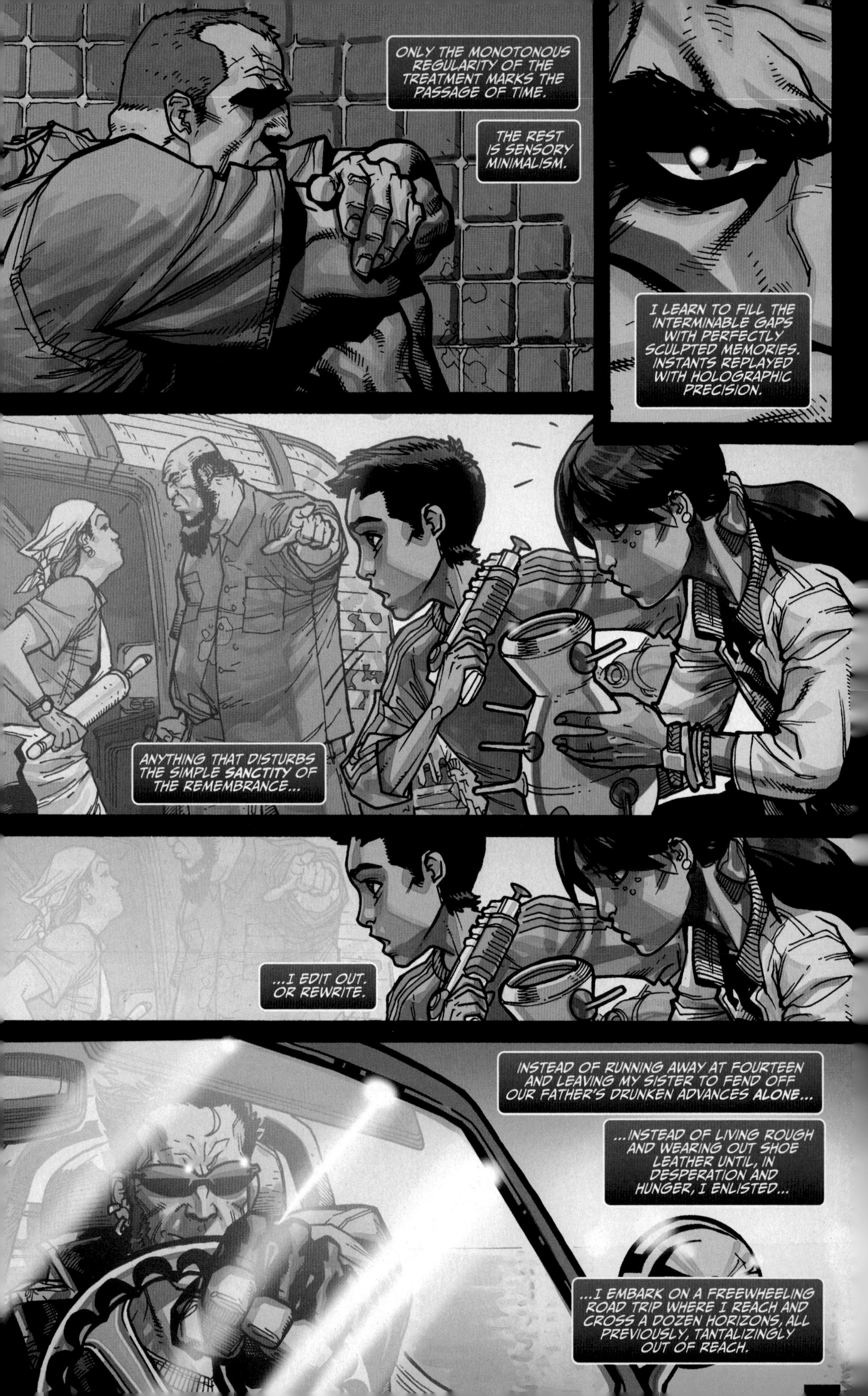
ONLY THE MONOTONOUS REGULARITY OF THE TREATMENT MARKS THE PASSAGE OF TIME.
THE REST IS SENSORY MINIMALISM.
I LEARN TO FILL THE INTERMINABLE GAPS WITH PERFECTLY SCULPTED MEMORIES. INSTANTS REPLAYED WITH HOLOGRAPHIC PRECISION.
ANYTHING THAT DISTURBS THE SIMPLE SANCTITY OF THE REMEMBRANCE...
...I EDIT OUT. OR REWRITE.
INSTEAD OF RUNNING AWAY AT FOURTEEN AND LEAVING MY SISTER TO FEND OFF OUR FATHER'S DRUNKEN ADVANCES ALONE...
...INSTEAD OF LIVING ROUGH AND WEARING OUT SHOE LEATHER UNTIL, IN DESPERATION AND HUNGER, I ENLISTED...
...I EMBARK ON A FREEWHEELING ROAD TRIP WHERE I REACH AND CROSS A DOZEN HORIZONS, ALL PREVIOUSLY, TANTALIZINGLY OUT OF REACH.

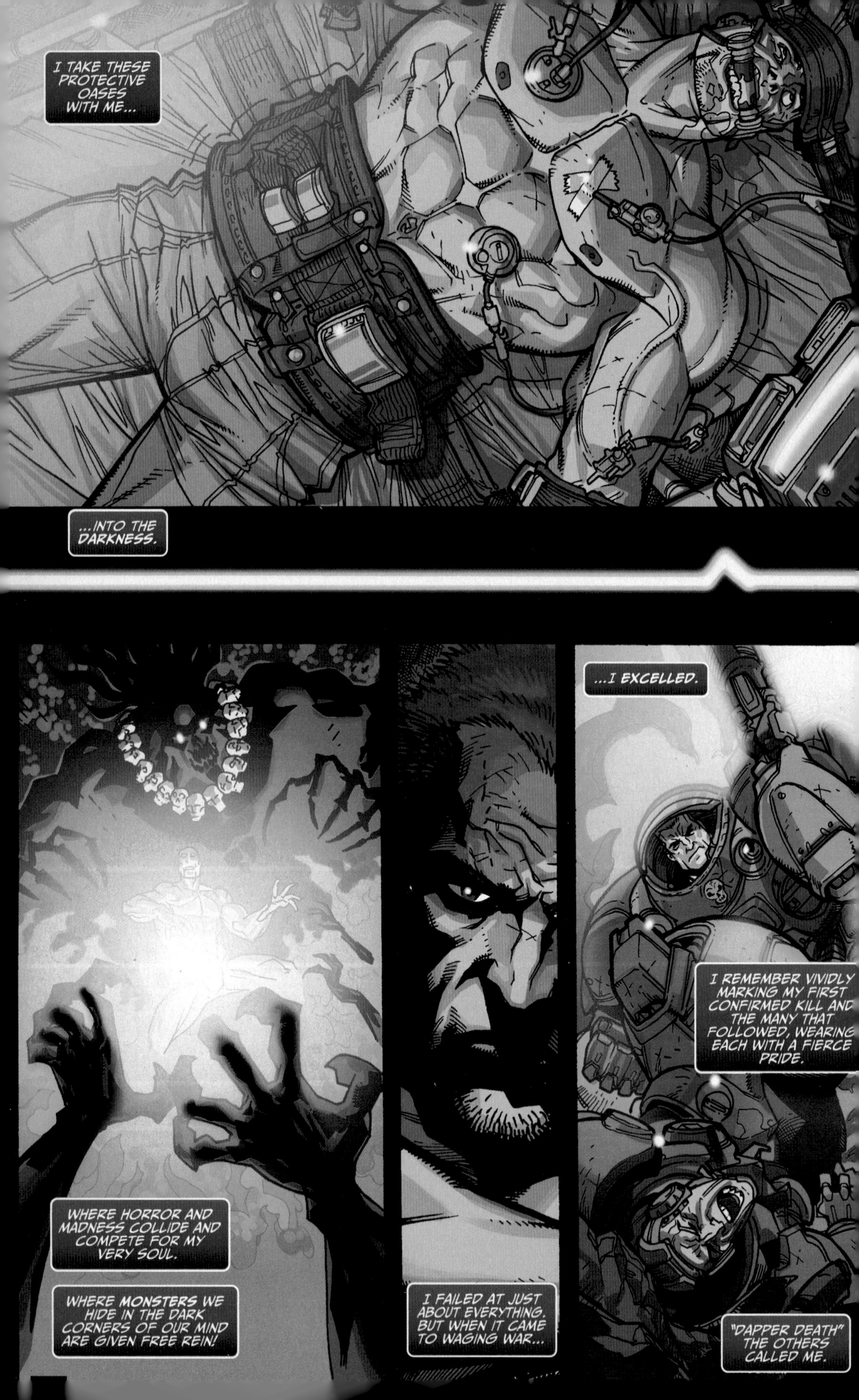
I TAKE THESE PROTECTIVE OASES WITH ME...
...INTO THE DARKNESS.
WHERE HORROR AND MADNESS COLLIDE AND COMPETE FOR MY VERY SOUL.
WHERE MONSTERS WE HIDE IN THE DARK CORNERS OF OUR MIND ARE GIVEN FREE REIN!
I FAILED AT JUST ABOUT EVERYTHING. BUT WHEN IT CAME TO WAGING WAR...
...I EXCELLED.
I REMEMBER VIVIDLY MARKING MY FIRST CONFIRMED KILL AND THE MANY THAT FOLLOWED, WEARING EACH WITH A FIERCE PRIDE.
"DAPPER DEATH" THE OTHERS CALLED ME.

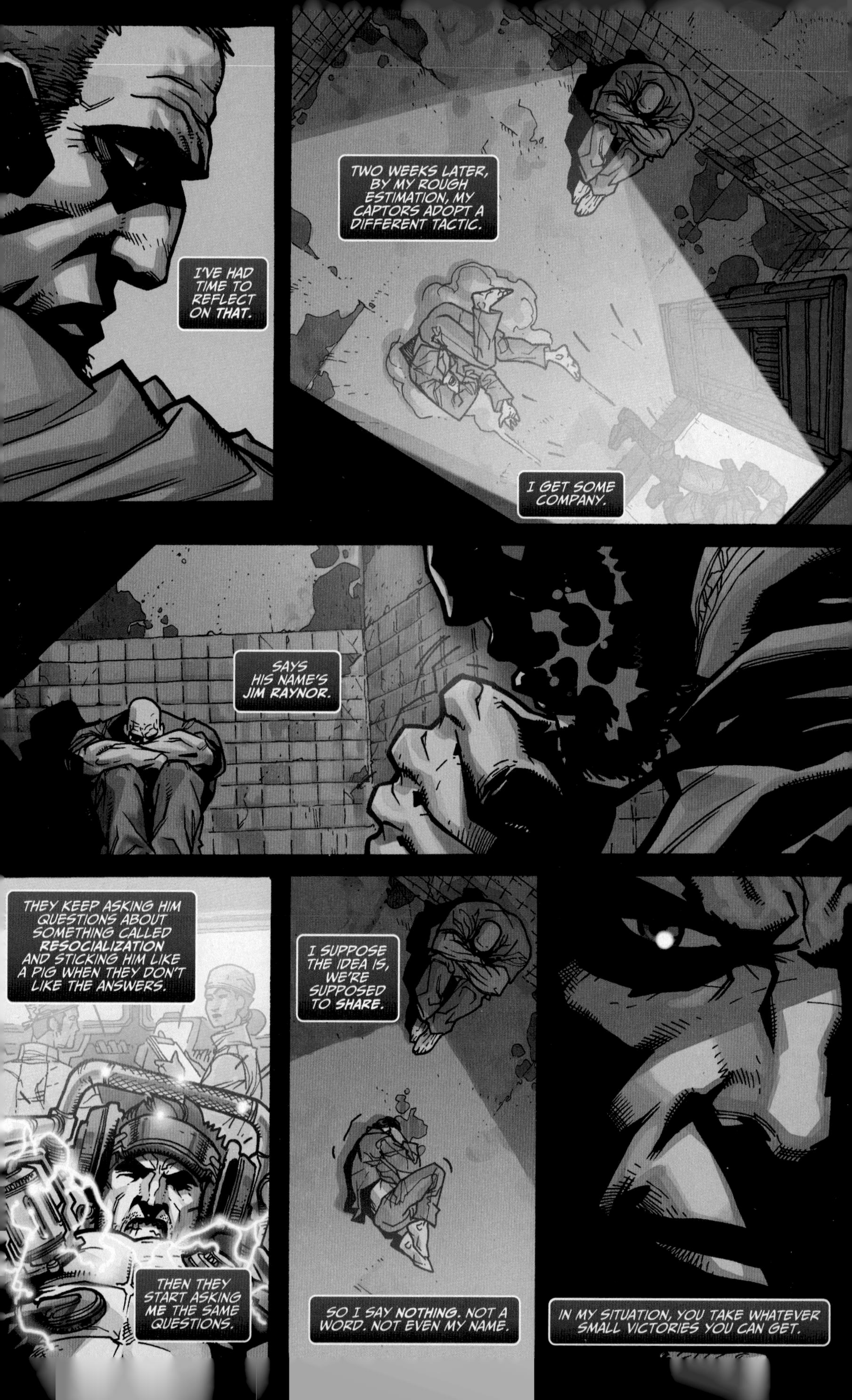

I'VE HAD TIME TO REFLECT ON THAT.
TWO WEEKS LATER, BY MY ROUGH ESTIMATION, MY CAPTORS ADOPT A DIFFERENT TACTIC.
I GET SOME COMPANY.
SAYS HIS NAME'S JIM RAYNOR.
THEY KEEP ASKING HIM QUESTIONS ABOUT SOMETHING CALLED RESOCIALIZATION AND STICKING HIM LIKE A PIG WHEN THEY DON'T LIKE THE ANSWERS.
THEN THEY START ASKING ME THE SAME QUESTIONS.
I SUPPOSE THE IDEA IS, WE'RE SUPPOSED TO SHARE.
SO I SAY NOTHING. NOT A WORD. NOT EVEN MY NAME.
IN MY SITUATION, YOU TAKE WHATEVER SMALL VICTORIES YOU CAN GET.

ANYWAY, RAYNOR TALKS ENOUGH FOR THE BOTH OF US.

...SEE, MY DAD, HE DIDN'T EXACTLY TEACH ME RIGHT AND WRONG, MORE WHERE TO DRAW THE LINE. IT WAS A KIND OF *IN-THE-TRENCHES* PHILOSOPHY, ADAPTABLE...

AT FIRST I PHASE HIM OUT, DISLOCATE, TAKING REFUGE IN ONE OF MY MANY MENTAL SPIDER HOLES.

BUT EVENTUALLY, MAYBE BY OSMOSIS, I START TO GET THE SENSE OF A GOOD MAN, A DECENT MAN, KNEE-DEEP IN EVENTS HE'S ONLY NOW BEGINNING TO GRASP.

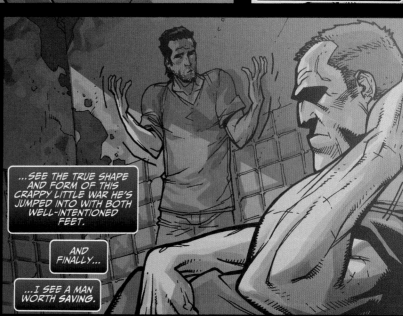

...SEE THE TRUE SHAPE AND FORM OF THIS CRAPPY LITTLE WAR HE'S JUMPED INTO WITH BOTH WELL-INTENTIONED FEET.

AND FINALLY...

I SEE HIM SLOWLY DISCERN THE LIES HE'S BEEN TOLD...

...I SEE A MAN WORTH SAVING.

PLAIN TRUTH IS, THE GUILD WARS ONLY SERVED TO CHISEL THE ROUGH EDGES OFF MY LATENT SOCIOPATHIC TENDENCIES.

BUT IN JAMES RAYNOR I SEE HOPE...AND SOME SMALL MEASURE OF PERSONAL SALVATION.

IF I CAN TEACH HIM, SHOW HIM HOW TO RESIST, HOW *NOT* TO LET THEM BREAK HIM...

...MAYBE, JUST MAYBE, I'M NOT A COMPLETELY LOST CAUSE!

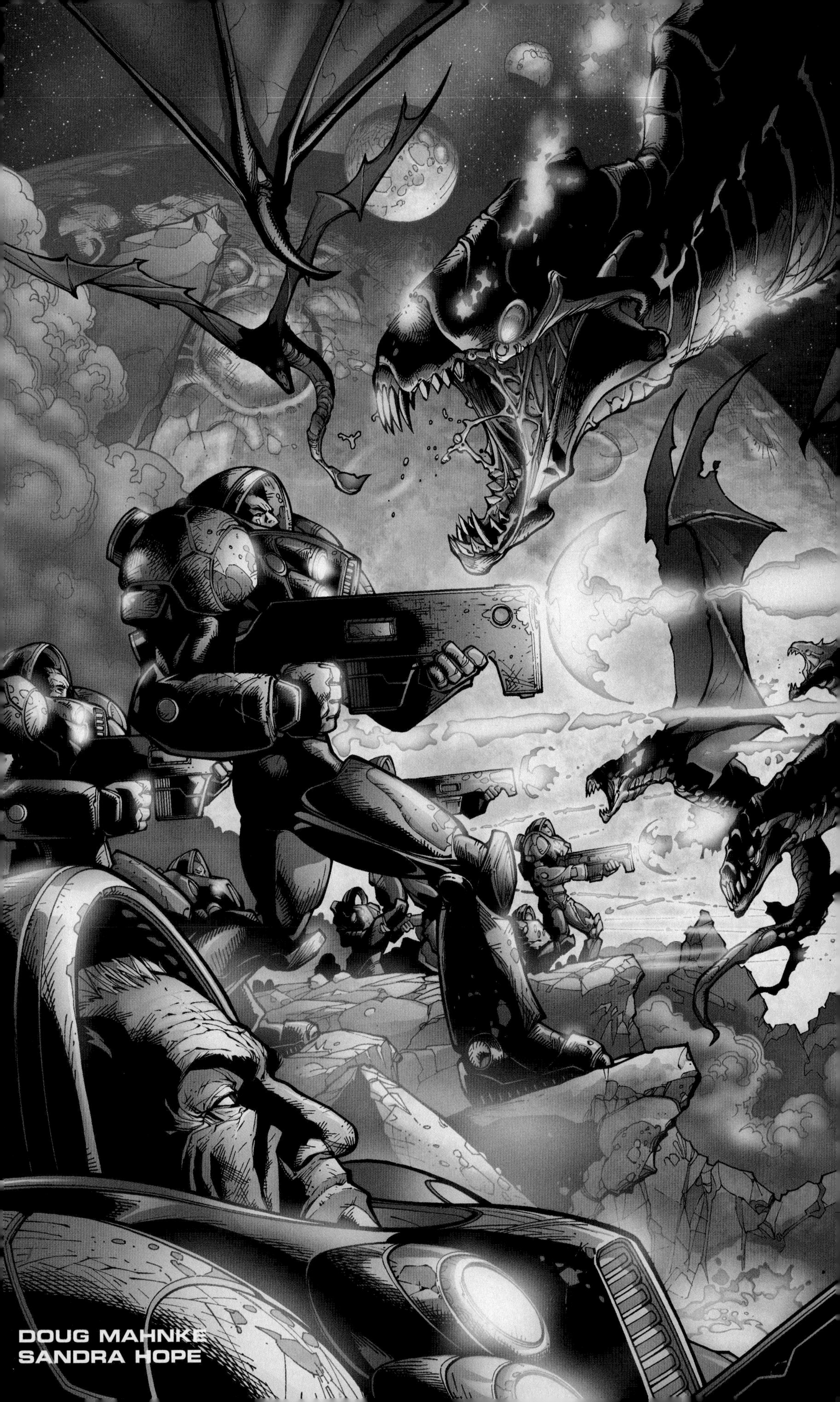
DOUG MAHNKE
SANDRA HOPE

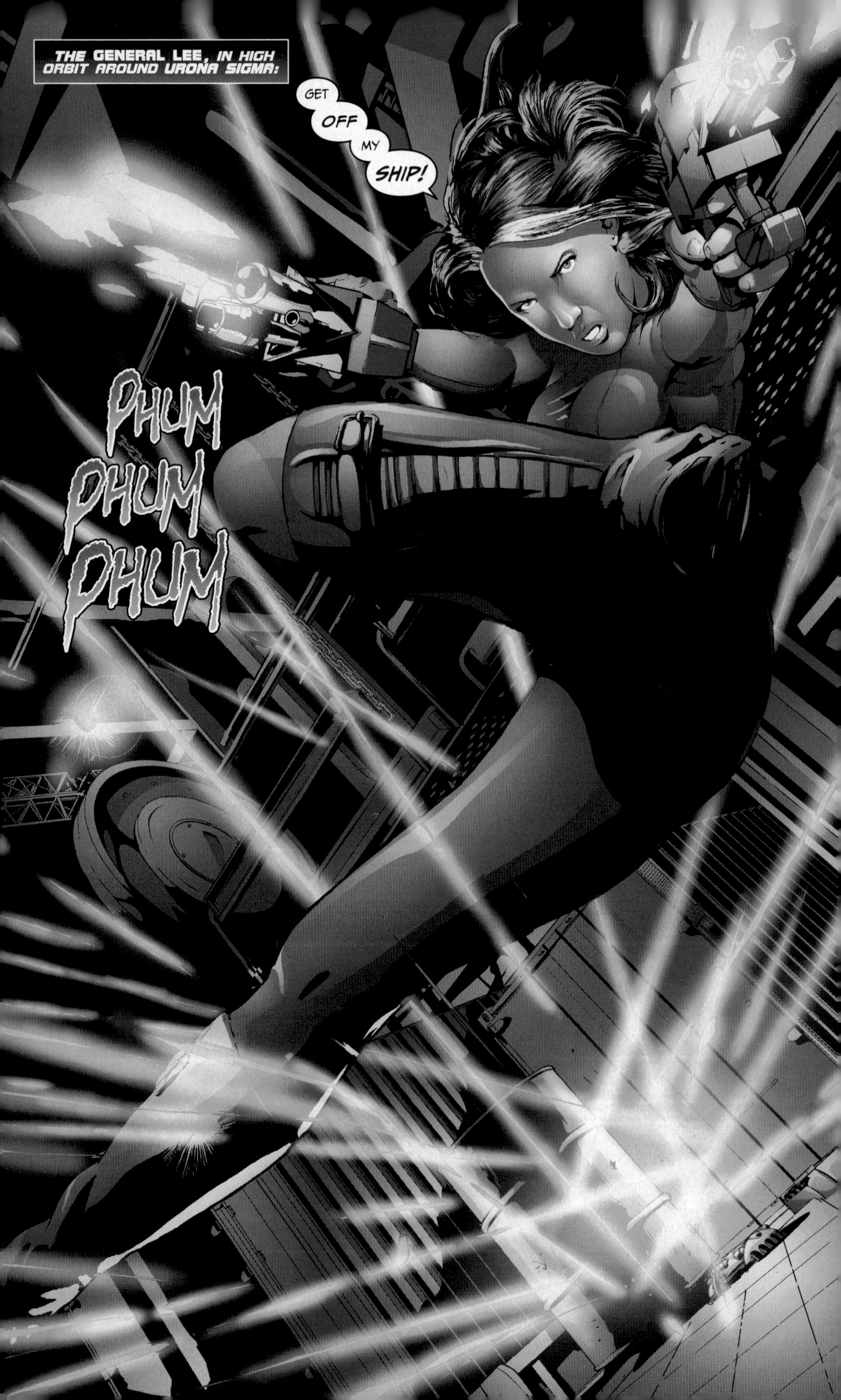
THE GENERAL LEE, IN HIGH ORBIT AROUND URONA SIGMA:
GET OFF MY SHIP!
PHUM PHUM PHUM

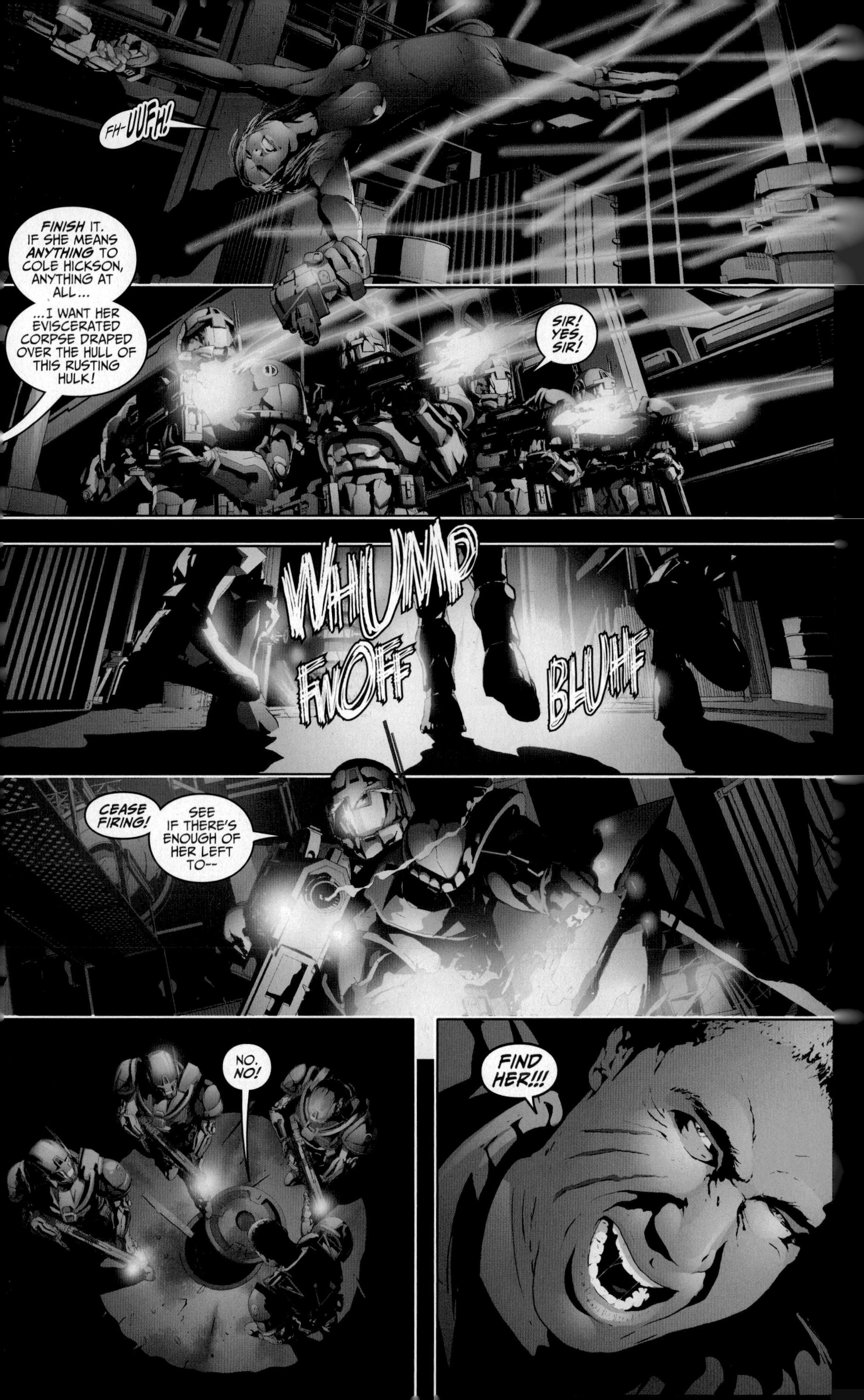
FH-UUFH!
FINISH IT. IF SHE MEANS ANYTHING TO COLE HICKSON, ANYTHING AT ALL...
...I WANT HER EVISCERATED CORPSE DRAPED OVER THE HULL OF THIS RUSTING HULK!
SIR! YES, SIR!
WHUMP
FWOFF
BLUHF
CEASE FIRING!
SEE IF THERE'S ENOUGH OF HER LEFT TO--
NO. NO!
FIND HER!!!

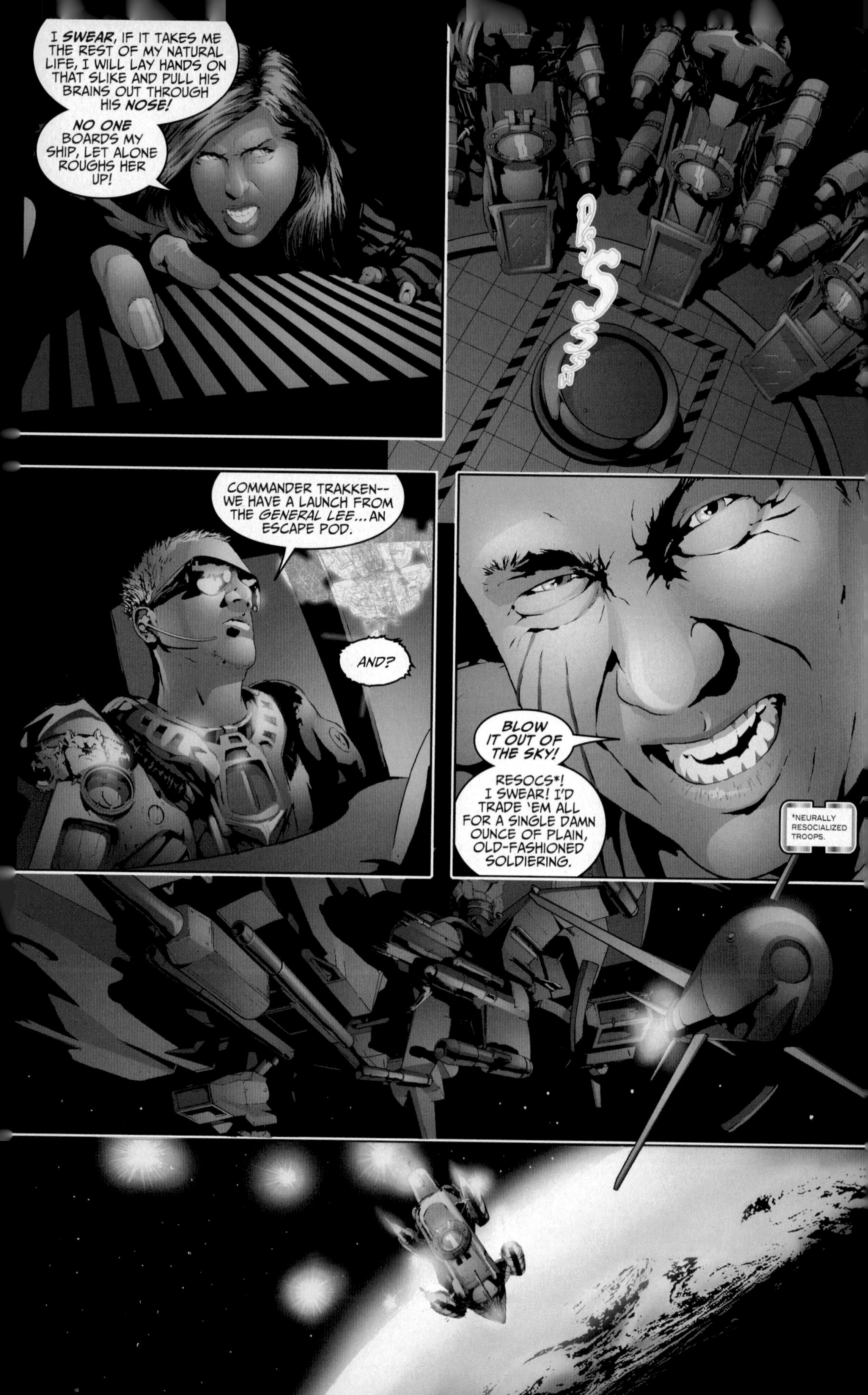
I SWEAR, IF IT TAKES ME THE REST OF MY NATURAL LIFE, I WILL LAY HANDS ON THAT SLIKE AND PULL HIS BRAINS OUT THROUGH HIS NOSE!
NO ONE BOARDS MY SHIP, LET ALONE ROUGHS HER UP!
COMMANDER TRAKKEN-- WE HAVE A LAUNCH FROM THE GENERAL LEE... AN ESCAPE POD.
AND?
BLOW IT OUT OF THE SKY!
RESOCS*! I SWEAR! I'D TRADE 'EM ALL FOR A SINGLE DAMN OUNCE OF PLAIN, OLD-FASHIONED SOLDIERING.
*NEURALLY RESOCIALIZED TROOPS.

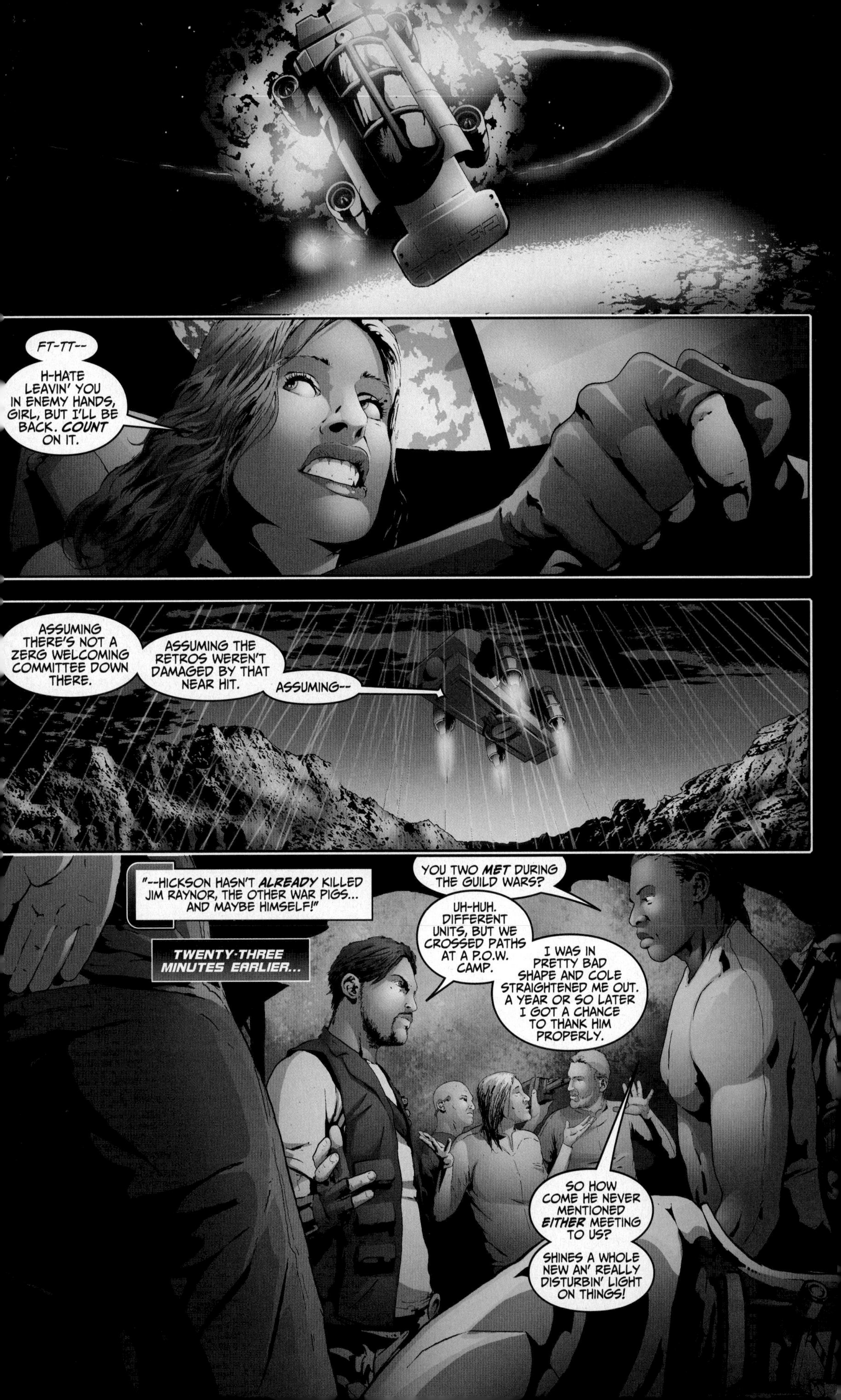
FT-TT--
H-HATE LEAVIN' YOU IN ENEMY HANDS, GIRL, BUT I'LL BE BACK. COUNT ON IT.
ASSUMING THERE'S NOT A ZERG WELCOMING COMMITTEE DOWN THERE.
ASSUMING THE RETROS WEREN'T DAMAGED BY THAT NEAR HIT.
ASSUMING--
"--HICKSON HASN'T ALREADY KILLED JIM RAYNOR, THE OTHER WAR PIGS... AND MAYBE HIMSELF!"
TWENTY-THREE MINUTES EARLIER...
YOU TWO MET DURING THE GUILD WARS?
UH-HUH. DIFFERENT UNITS, BUT WE CROSSED PATHS AT A P.O.W. CAMP.
I WAS IN PRETTY BAD SHAPE AND COLE STRAIGHTENED ME OUT. A YEAR OR SO LATER I GOT A CHANCE TO THANK HIM PROPERLY.
SO HOW COME HE NEVER MENTIONED EITHER MEETING TO US?
SHINES A WHOLE NEW AN' REALLY DISTURBIN' LIGHT ON THINGS!

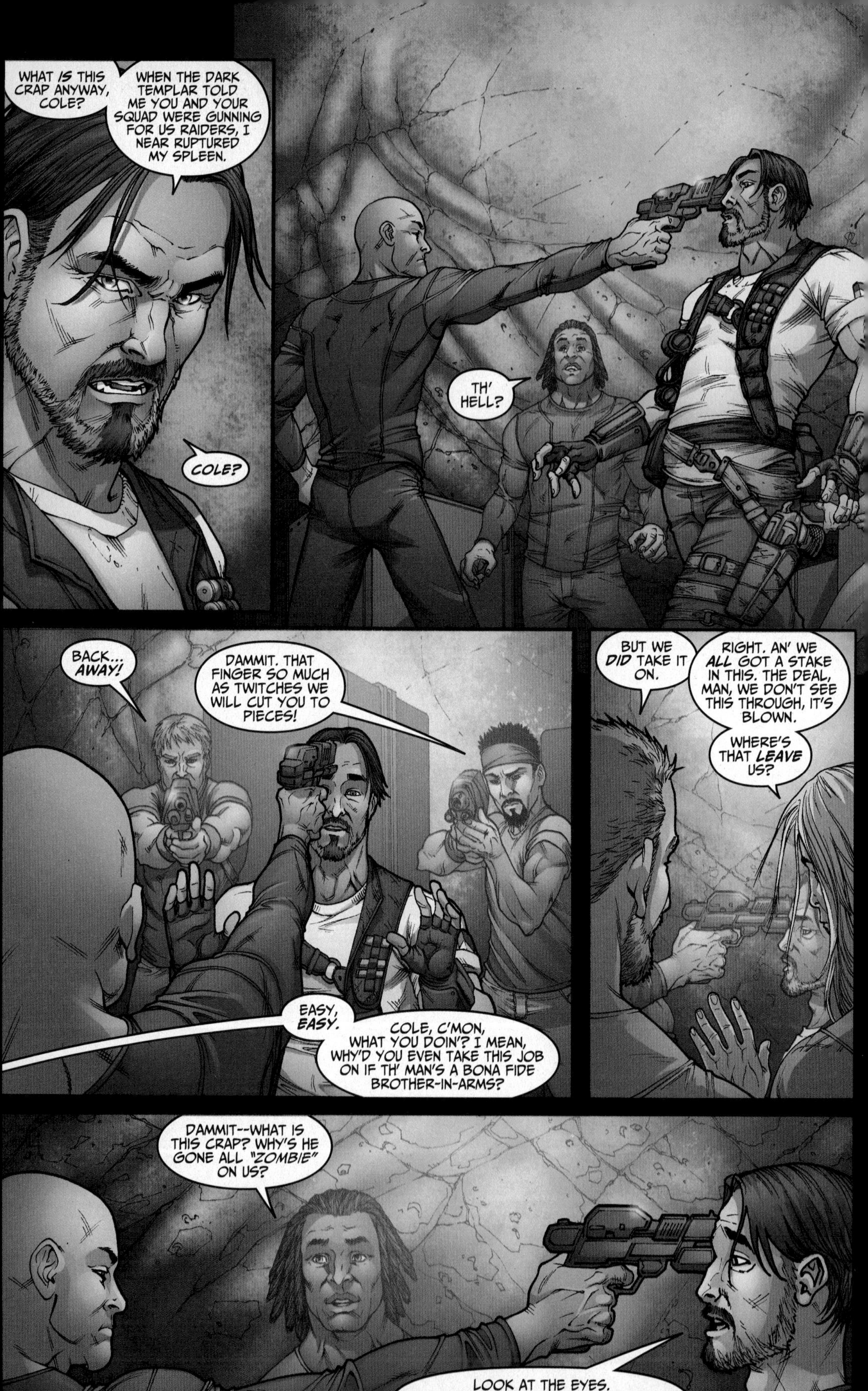

WHAT *IS* THIS CRAP ANYWAY, COLE?
WHEN THE DARK TEMPLAR TOLD ME YOU AND YOUR SQUAD WERE GUNNING FOR US RAIDERS, I NEAR RUPTURED MY SPLEEN.
COLE?
TH' HELL?
BACK... *AWAY!*
DAMMIT. THAT FINGER SO MUCH AS TWITCHES WE WILL CUT YOU TO PIECES!
EASY, *EASY.*
COLE, C'MON, WHAT YOU DOIN'? I MEAN, WHY'D YOU EVEN TAKE THIS JOB ON IF TH' MAN'S A BONA FIDE BROTHER-IN-ARMS?
BUT WE *DID* TAKE IT ON.
RIGHT. AN' WE *ALL* GOT A STAKE IN THIS. THE DEAL, MAN, WE DON'T SEE THIS THROUGH, IT'S BLOWN.
WHERE'S THAT *LEAVE* US?
DAMMIT--WHAT IS THIS CRAP? WHY'S HE GONE ALL "*ZOMBIE*" ON US?
LOOK AT THE EYES. RESOC FOR SURE, MAYBE SOME SNEAKY "*SLEEPER*" VARIANT THE DOMINION EGGHEADS DREAMED UP.

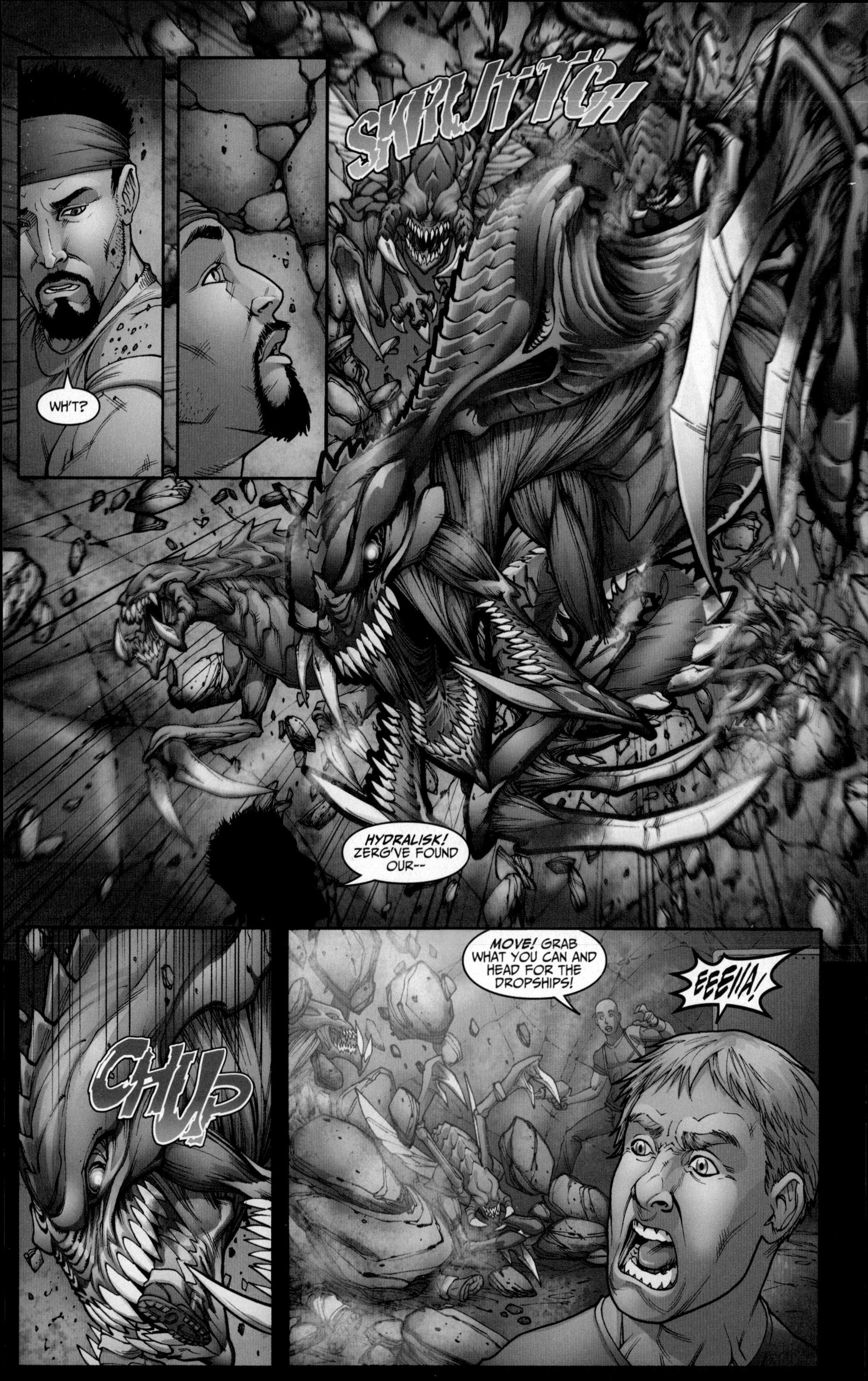
SKRUUTTCH
WH'T?
HYDRALISK! ZERG'VE FOUND OUR--
CHUP
MOVE! GRAB WHAT YOU CAN AND HEAD FOR THE DROPSHIPS!
EEEIIA!

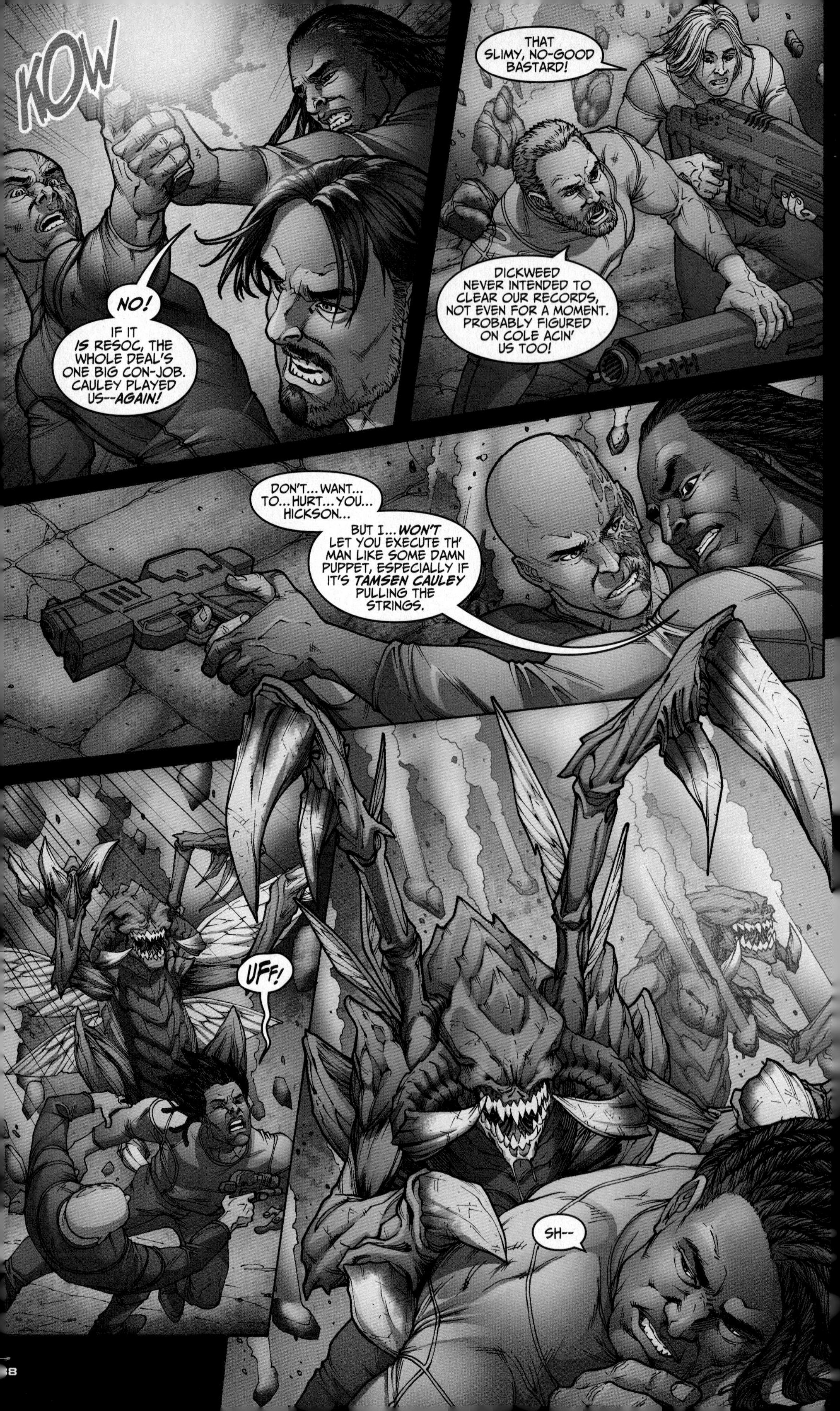
KOW
NO!
IF IT *IS* RESOC, THE WHOLE DEAL'S ONE BIG CON-JOB. CAULEY PLAYED US--*AGAIN!*
THAT SLIMY, NO-GOOD BASTARD!
DICKWEED NEVER INTENDED TO CLEAR OUR RECORDS, NOT EVEN FOR A MOMENT. PROBABLY FIGURED ON COLE ACIN' US TOO!
DON'T...WANT... TO...HURT...YOU... HICKSON...
BUT I...*WON'T* LET YOU EXECUTE TH' MAN LIKE SOME DAMN PUPPET, ESPECIALLY IF IT'S *TAMSEN CAULEY* PULLING THE STRINGS.
UFF!
SH--

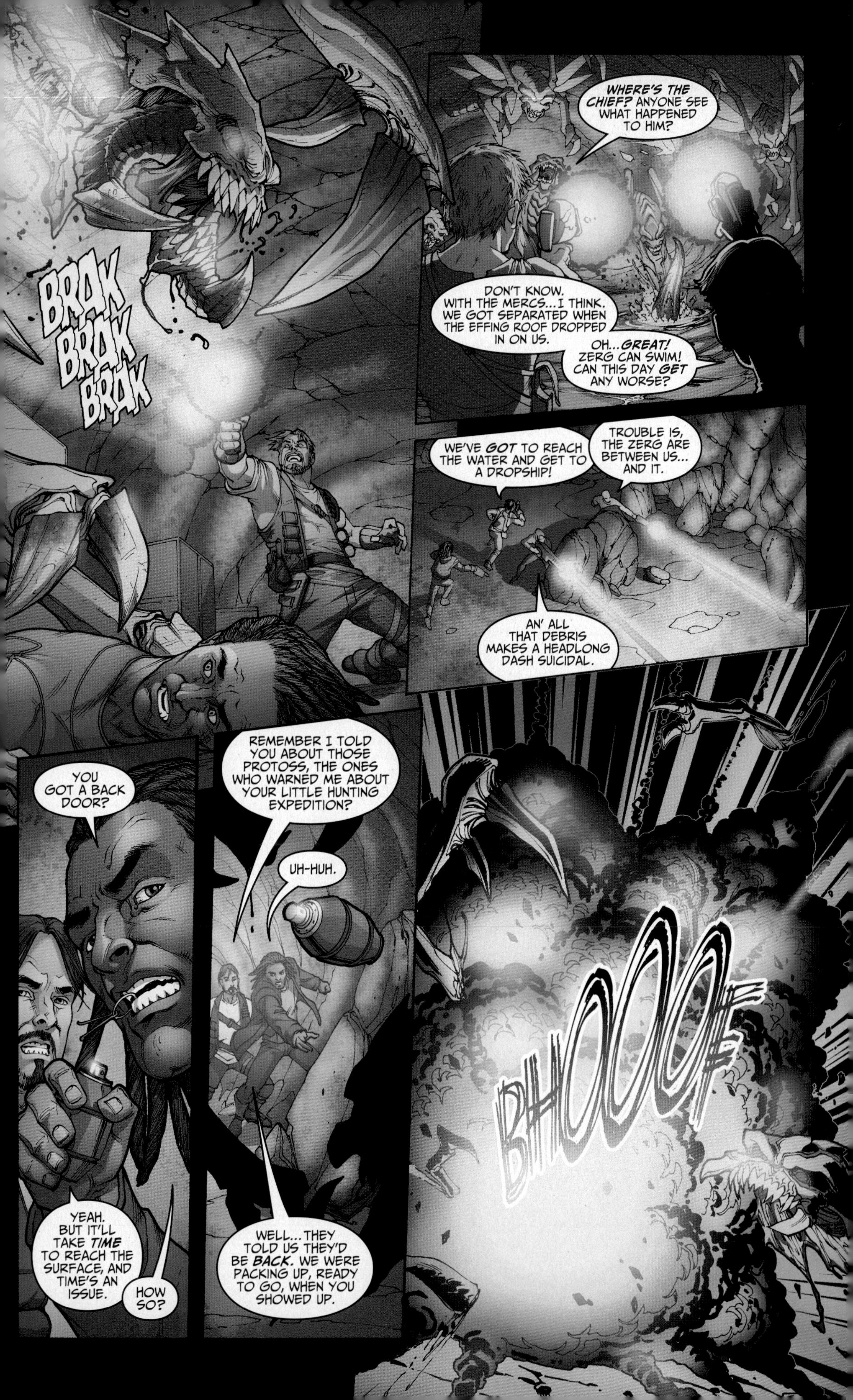
BRAK BRAK BRAK
WHERE'S THE CHIEF? ANYONE SEE WHAT HAPPENED TO HIM?
DON'T KNOW. WITH THE MERCS...I THINK. WE GOT SEPARATED WHEN THE EFFING ROOF DROPPED IN ON US.
OH...GREAT! ZERG CAN SWIM! CAN THIS DAY GET ANY WORSE?
WE'VE GOT TO REACH THE WATER AND GET TO A DROPSHIP!
TROUBLE IS, THE ZERG ARE BETWEEN US... AND IT.
AN' ALL THAT DEBRIS MAKES A HEADLONG DASH SUICIDAL.
YOU GOT A BACK DOOR?
YEAH. BUT IT'LL TAKE TIME TO REACH THE SURFACE, AND TIME'S AN ISSUE.
HOW SO?
REMEMBER I TOLD YOU ABOUT THOSE PROTOSS, THE ONES WHO WARNED ME ABOUT YOUR LITTLE HUNTING EXPEDITION?
UH-HUH.
WELL...THEY TOLD US THEY'D BE BACK. WE WERE PACKING UP, READY TO GO, WHEN YOU SHOWED UP.
BHOOOF

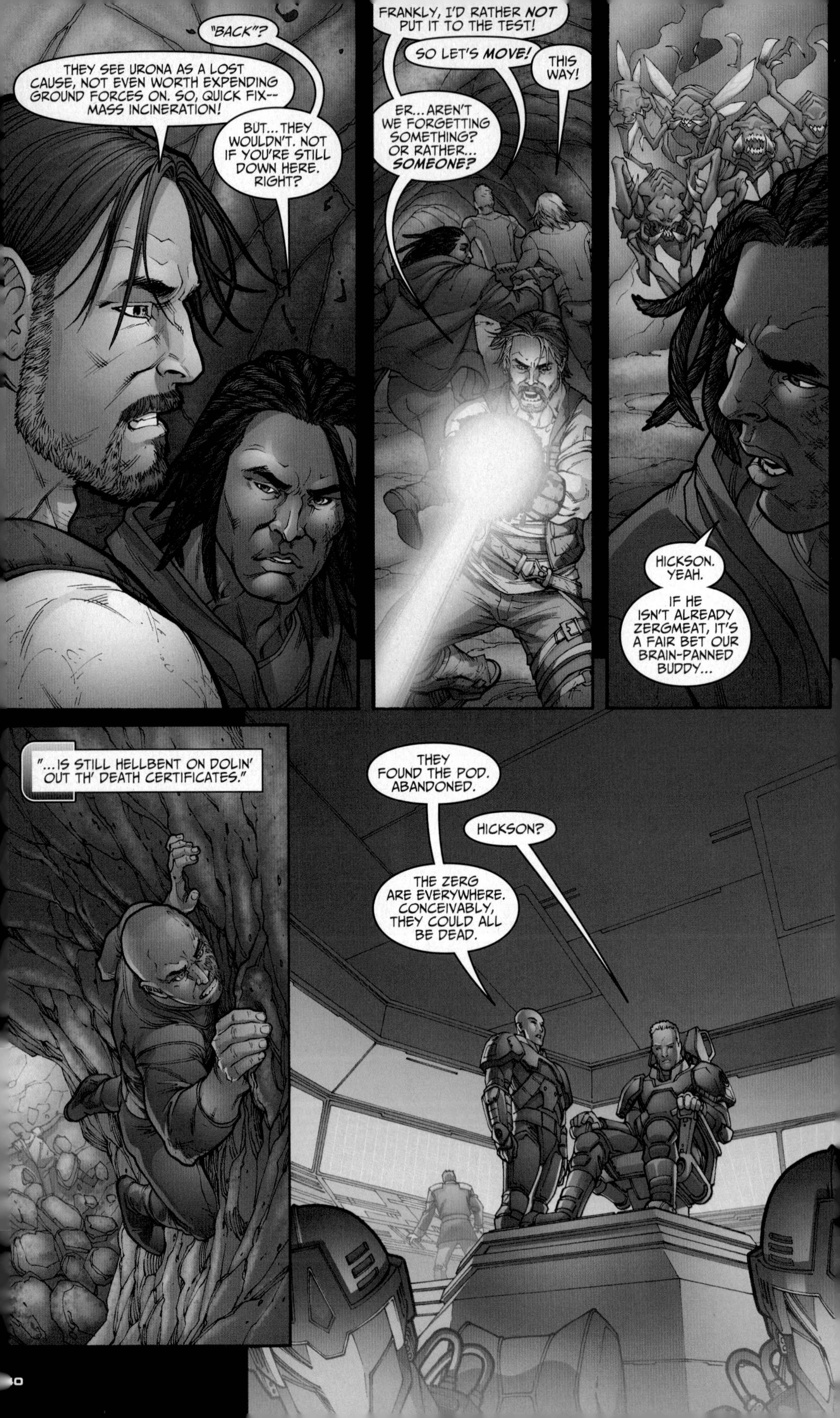
"BACK"?
THEY SEE URONA AS A LOST CAUSE, NOT EVEN WORTH EXPENDING GROUND FORCES ON. SO, QUICK FIX--MASS INCINERATION!
BUT...THEY WOULDN'T. NOT IF YOU'RE STILL DOWN HERE. RIGHT?
FRANKLY, I'D RATHER NOT PUT IT TO THE TEST!
SO LET'S MOVE!
THIS WAY!
ER...AREN'T WE FORGETTING SOMETHING? OR RATHER... SOMEONE?
HICKSON. YEAH.
IF HE ISN'T ALREADY ZERGMEAT, IT'S A FAIR BET OUR BRAIN-PANNED BUDDY...
"...IS STILL HELLBENT ON DOLIN' OUT TH' DEATH CERTIFICATES."
THEY FOUND THE POD. ABANDONED.
HICKSON?
THE ZERG ARE EVERYWHERE. CONCEIVABLY, THEY COULD ALL BE DEAD.

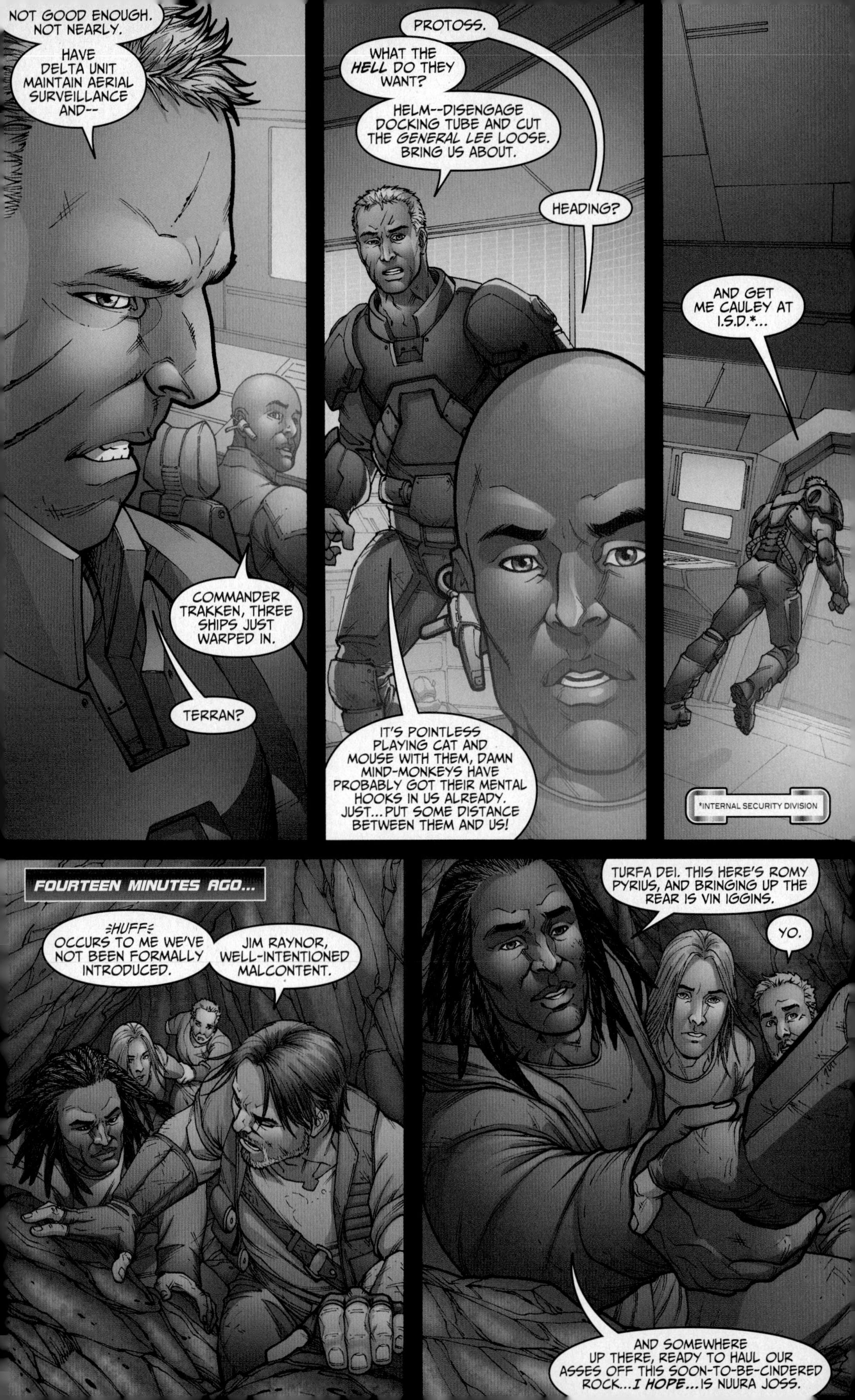
NOT GOOD ENOUGH. NOT NEARLY.
HAVE DELTA UNIT MAINTAIN AERIAL SURVEILLANCE AND--
COMMANDER TRAKKEN, THREE SHIPS JUST WARPED IN.
TERRAN?
PROTOSS.
WHAT THE HELL DO THEY WANT?
HELM--DISENGAGE DOCKING TUBE AND CUT THE GENERAL LEE LOOSE. BRING US ABOUT.
HEADING?
IT'S POINTLESS PLAYING CAT AND MOUSE WITH THEM, DAMN MIND-MONKEYS HAVE PROBABLY GOT THEIR MENTAL HOOKS IN US ALREADY. JUST...PUT SOME DISTANCE BETWEEN THEM AND US!
AND GET ME CAULEY AT I.S.D.*...
*INTERNAL SECURITY DIVISION
FOURTEEN MINUTES AGO...
HUFF
OCCURS TO ME WE'VE NOT BEEN FORMALLY INTRODUCED.
JIM RAYNOR, WELL-INTENTIONED MALCONTENT.
TURFA DEI. THIS HERE'S ROMY PYRIUS, AND BRINGING UP THE REAR IS VIN IGGINS.
YO.
AND SOMEWHERE UP THERE, READY TO HAUL OUR ASSES OFF THIS SOON-TO-BE-CINDERED ROCK...I HOPE...IS NUURA JOSS.

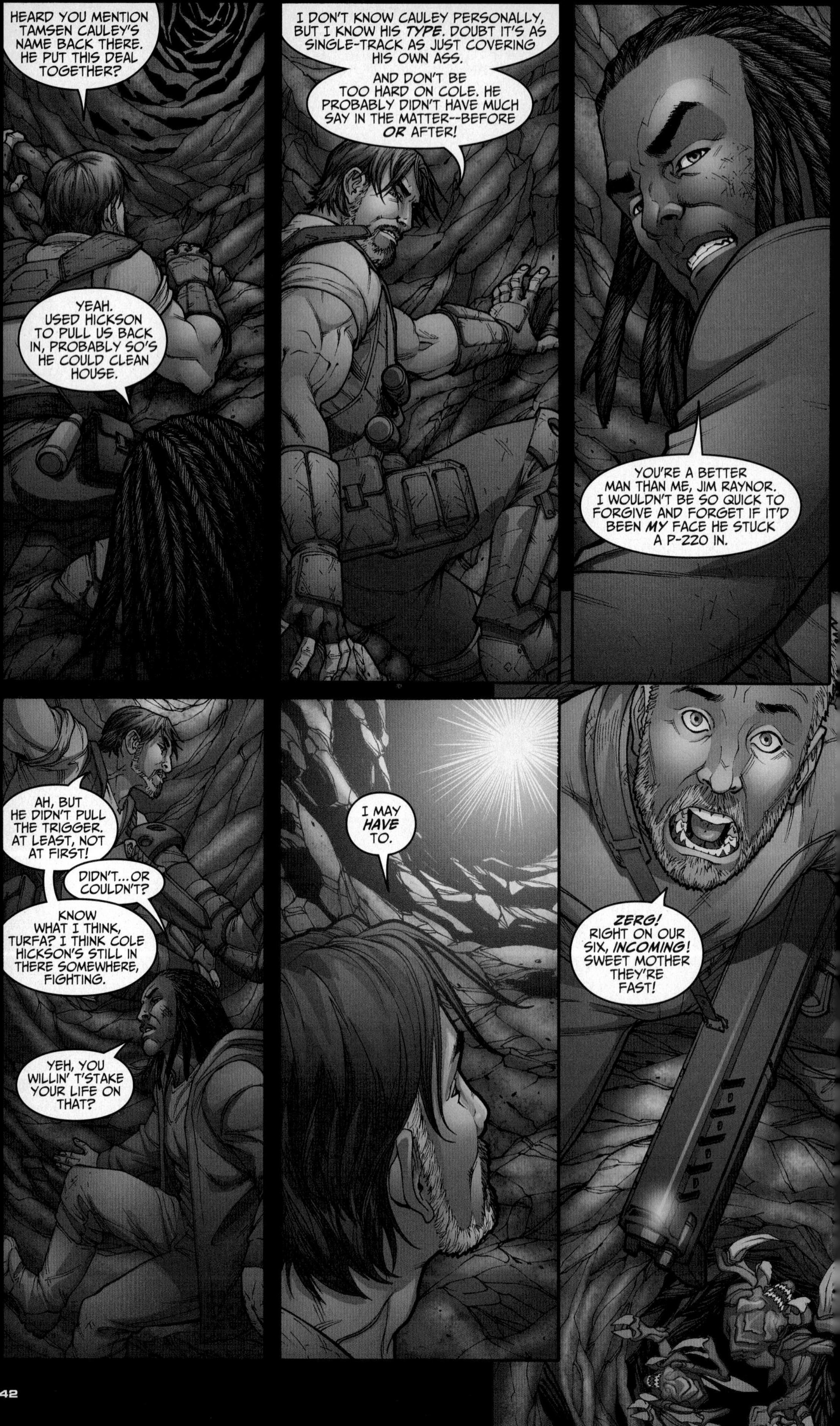
HEARD YOU MENTION TAMSEN CAULEY'S NAME BACK THERE. HE PUT THIS DEAL TOGETHER?
YEAH. USED HICKSON TO PULL US BACK IN, PROBABLY SO'S HE COULD CLEAN HOUSE.
I DON'T KNOW CAULEY PERSONALLY, BUT I KNOW HIS *TYPE*. DOUBT IT'S AS SINGLE-TRACK AS JUST COVERING HIS OWN ASS.
AND DON'T BE TOO HARD ON COLE. HE PROBABLY DIDN'T HAVE MUCH SAY IN THE MATTER--BEFORE *OR* AFTER!
YOU'RE A BETTER MAN THAN ME, JIM RAYNOR. I WOULDN'T BE SO QUICK TO FORGIVE AND FORGET IF IT'D BEEN *MY* FACE HE STUCK A P-220 IN.
AH, BUT HE DIDN'T PULL THE TRIGGER. AT LEAST, NOT AT FIRST!
DIDN'T...OR COULDN'T?
KNOW WHAT I THINK, TURFA? I THINK COLE HICKSON'S STILL IN THERE SOMEWHERE, FIGHTING.
YEH, YOU WILLIN' T'STAKE YOUR LIFE ON THAT?
I MAY *HAVE* TO.
ZERG! RIGHT ON OUR SIX, *INCOMING!* SWEET MOTHER THEY'RE FAST!

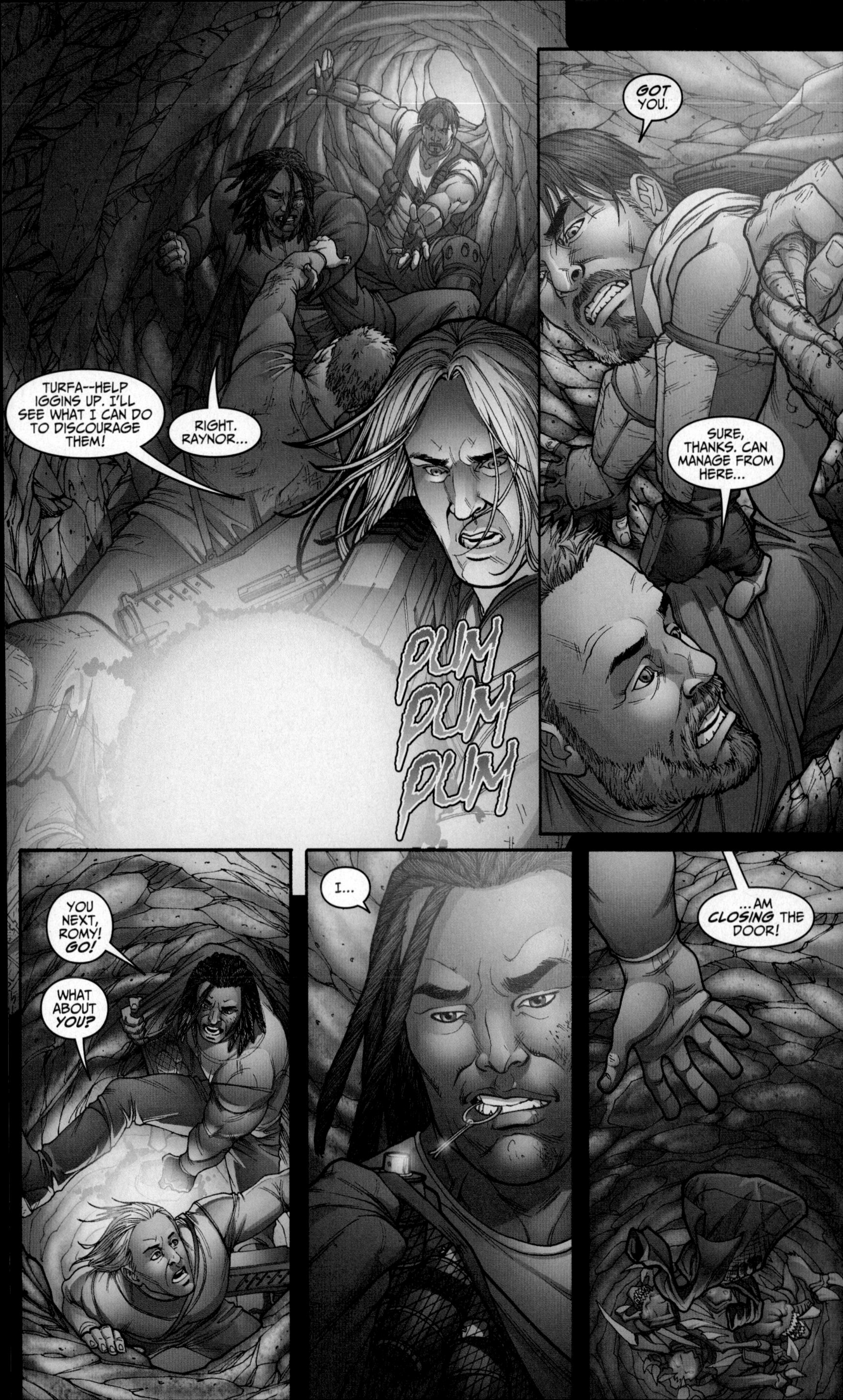

TURFA--HELP IGGINS UP. I'LL SEE WHAT I CAN DO TO DISCOURAGE THEM!
RIGHT. RAYNOR...
DUM DUM DUM
GOT YOU.
SURE, THANKS. CAN MANAGE FROM HERE...
YOU NEXT, ROMY! GO!
WHAT ABOUT YOU?
I...
...AM CLOSING THE DOOR!

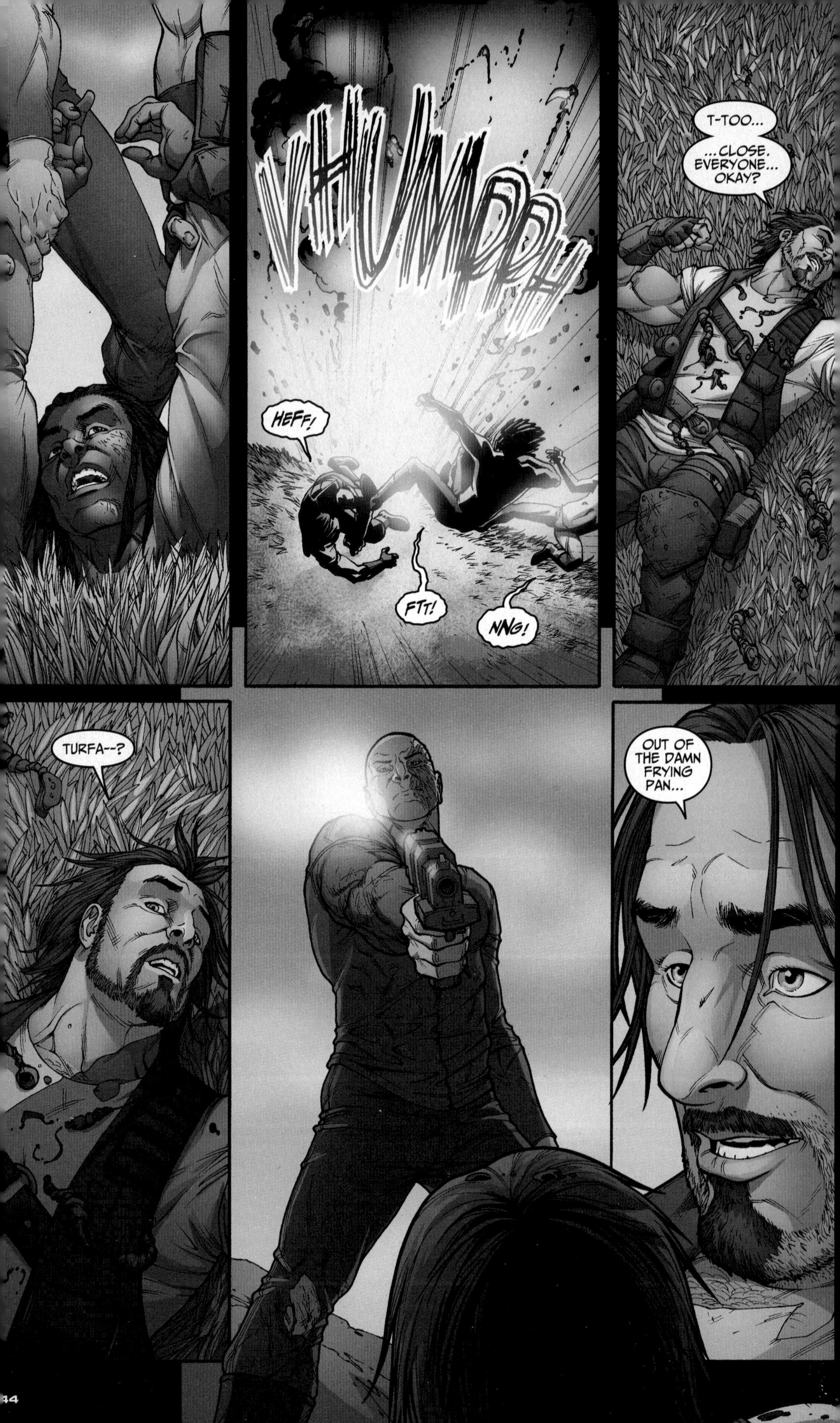

VHUMPPH
HEFF!
FTT!
NNG!
T-TOO...
...CLOSE. EVERYONE... OKAY?
TURFA--?
OUT OF THE DAMN FRYING PAN...

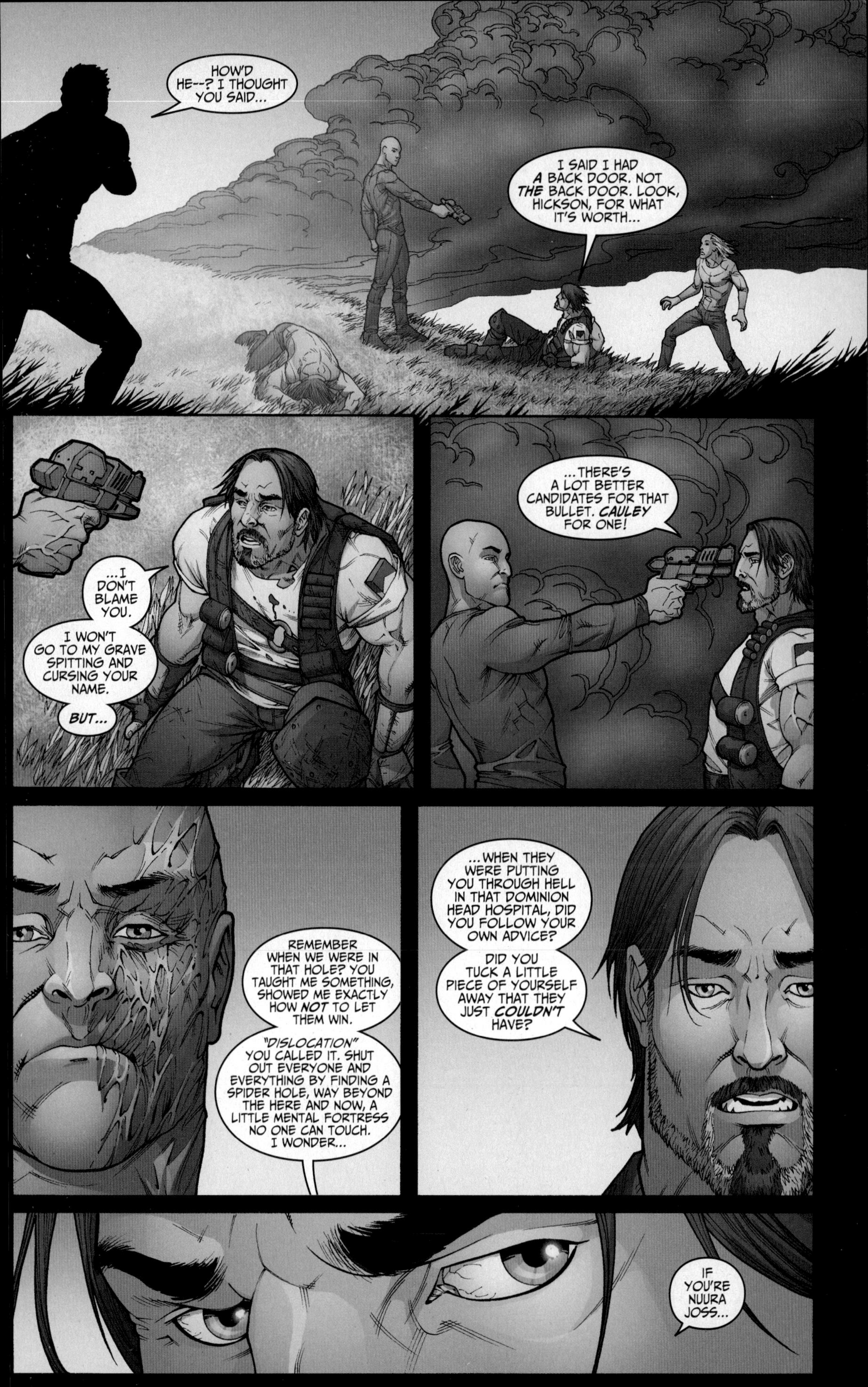
HOW'D HE--? I THOUGHT YOU SAID...
I SAID I HAD A BACK DOOR. NOT THE BACK DOOR. LOOK, HICKSON, FOR WHAT IT'S WORTH...
...I DON'T BLAME YOU.
I WON'T GO TO MY GRAVE SPITTING AND CURSING YOUR NAME.
BUT...
...THERE'S A LOT BETTER CANDIDATES FOR THAT BULLET. CAULEY FOR ONE!
REMEMBER WHEN WE WERE IN THAT HOLE? YOU TAUGHT ME SOMETHING, SHOWED ME EXACTLY HOW NOT TO LET THEM WIN.
"DISLOCATION" YOU CALLED IT. SHUT OUT EVERYONE AND EVERYTHING BY FINDING A SPIDER HOLE, WAY BEYOND THE HERE AND NOW, A LITTLE MENTAL FORTRESS NO ONE CAN TOUCH. I WONDER...
...WHEN THEY WERE PUTTING YOU THROUGH HELL IN THAT DOMINION HEAD HOSPITAL, DID YOU FOLLOW YOUR OWN ADVICE?
DID YOU TUCK A LITTLE PIECE OF YOURSELF AWAY THAT THEY JUST COULDN'T HAVE?
IF YOU'RE NUURA JOSS...

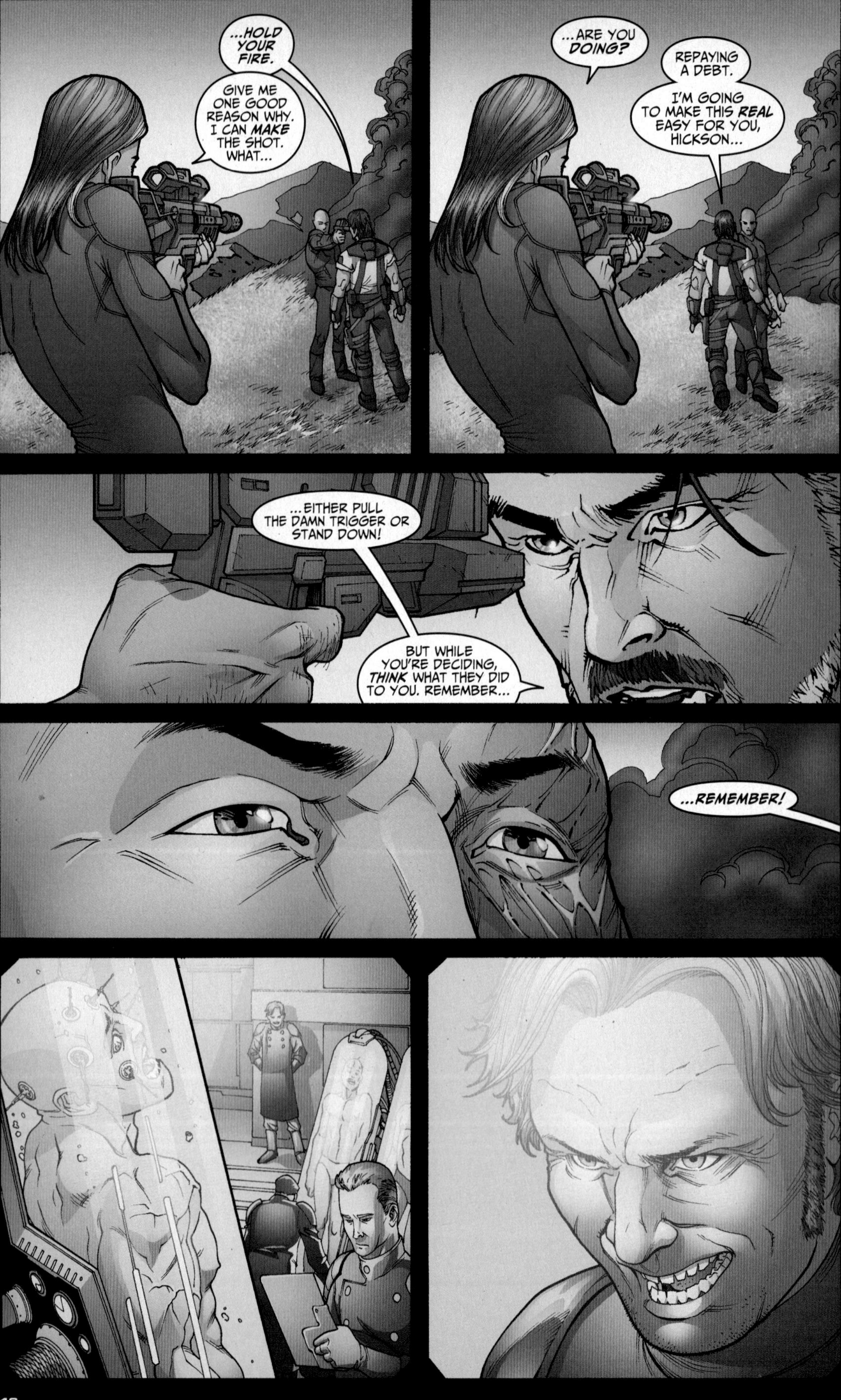
...HOLD YOUR FIRE.
GIVE ME ONE GOOD REASON WHY. I CAN MAKE THE SHOT. WHAT...
...ARE YOU DOING?
REPAYING A DEBT.
I'M GOING TO MAKE THIS REAL EASY FOR YOU, HICKSON...
...EITHER PULL THE DAMN TRIGGER OR STAND DOWN!
BUT WHILE YOU'RE DECIDING, THINK WHAT THEY DID TO YOU. REMEMBER...
...REMEMBER!

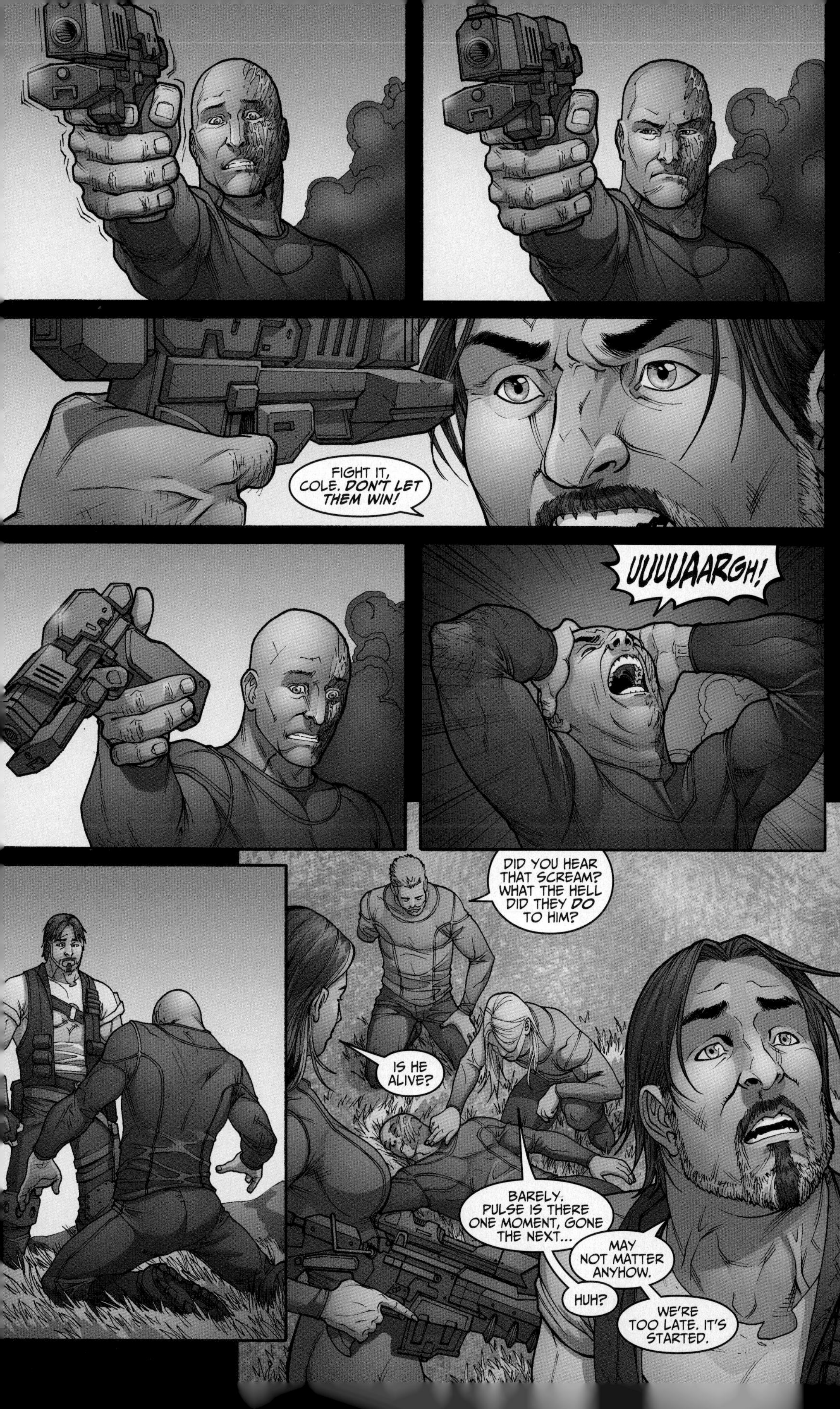

FIGHT IT, COLE. DON'T LET THEM WIN!
UUUUAARGH!
DID YOU HEAR THAT SCREAM? WHAT THE HELL DID THEY DO TO HIM?
IS HE ALIVE?
BARELY. PULSE IS THERE ONE MOMENT, GONE THE NEXT...
MAY NOT MATTER ANYHOW.
HUH?
WE'RE TOO LATE. IT'S STARTED.

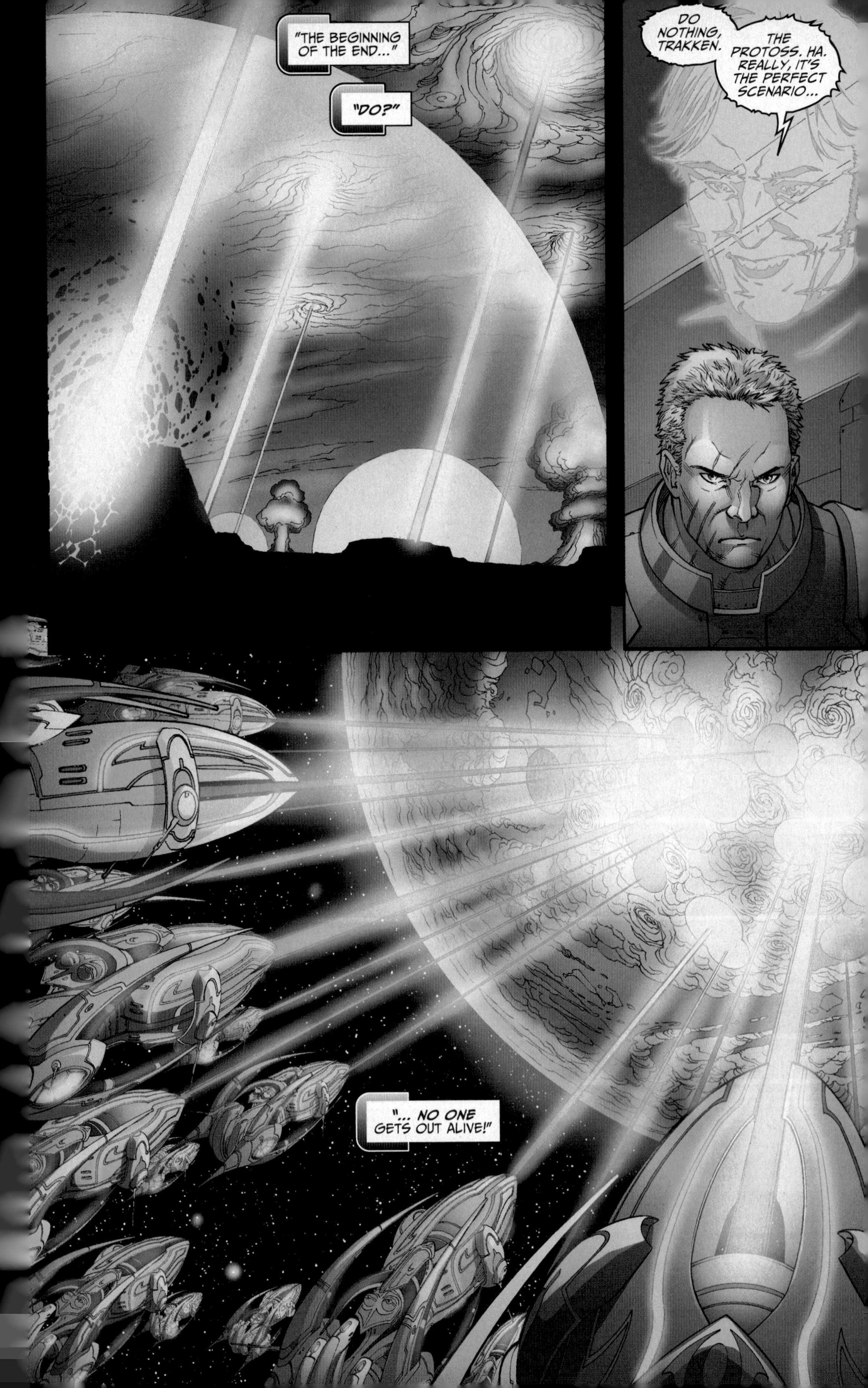
"THE BEGINNING OF THE END..."
"DO?"
DO NOTHING, TRAKKEN.
THE PROTOSS. HA. REALLY, IT'S THE PERFECT SCENARIO...
"... NO ONE GETS OUT ALIVE!"

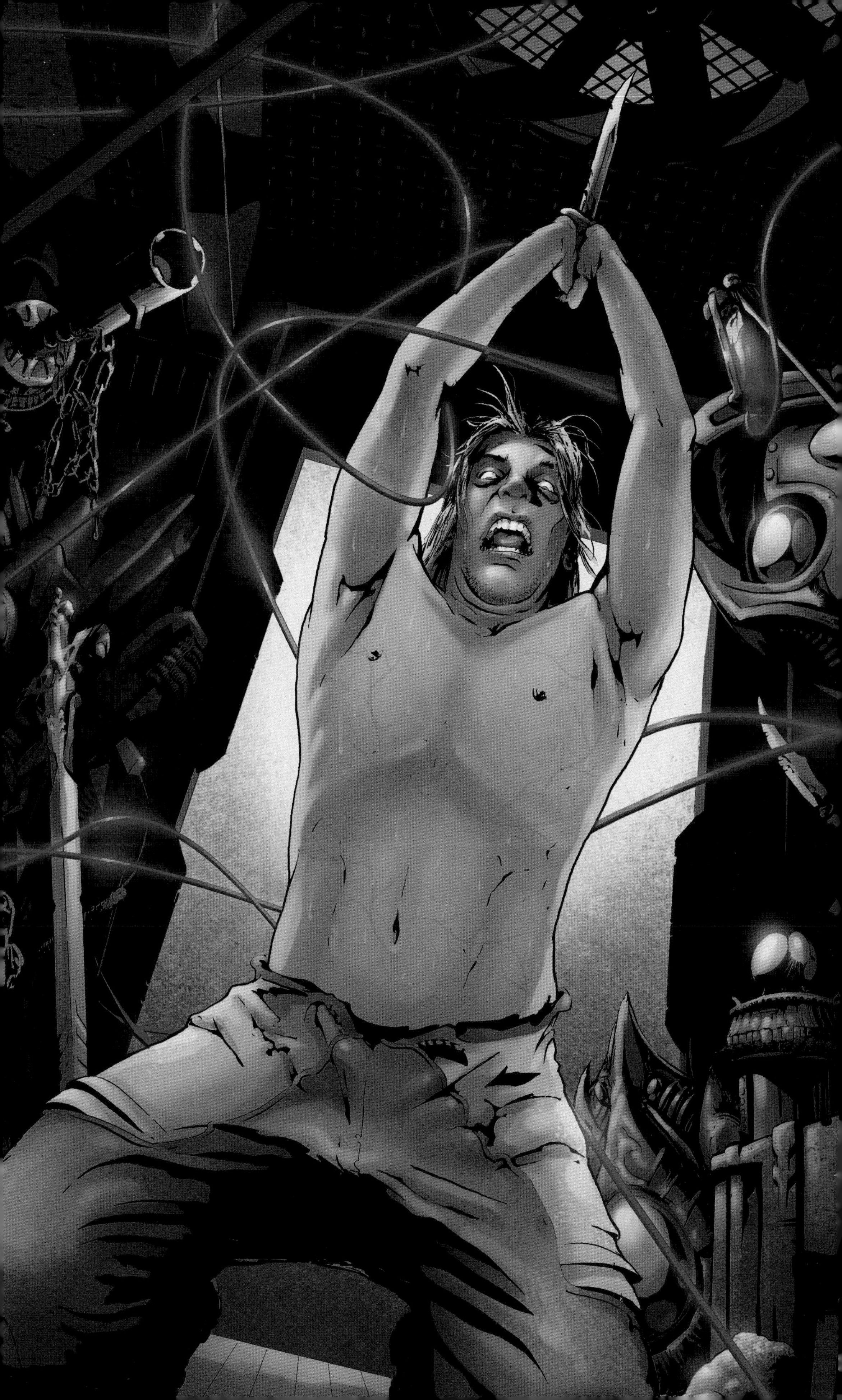

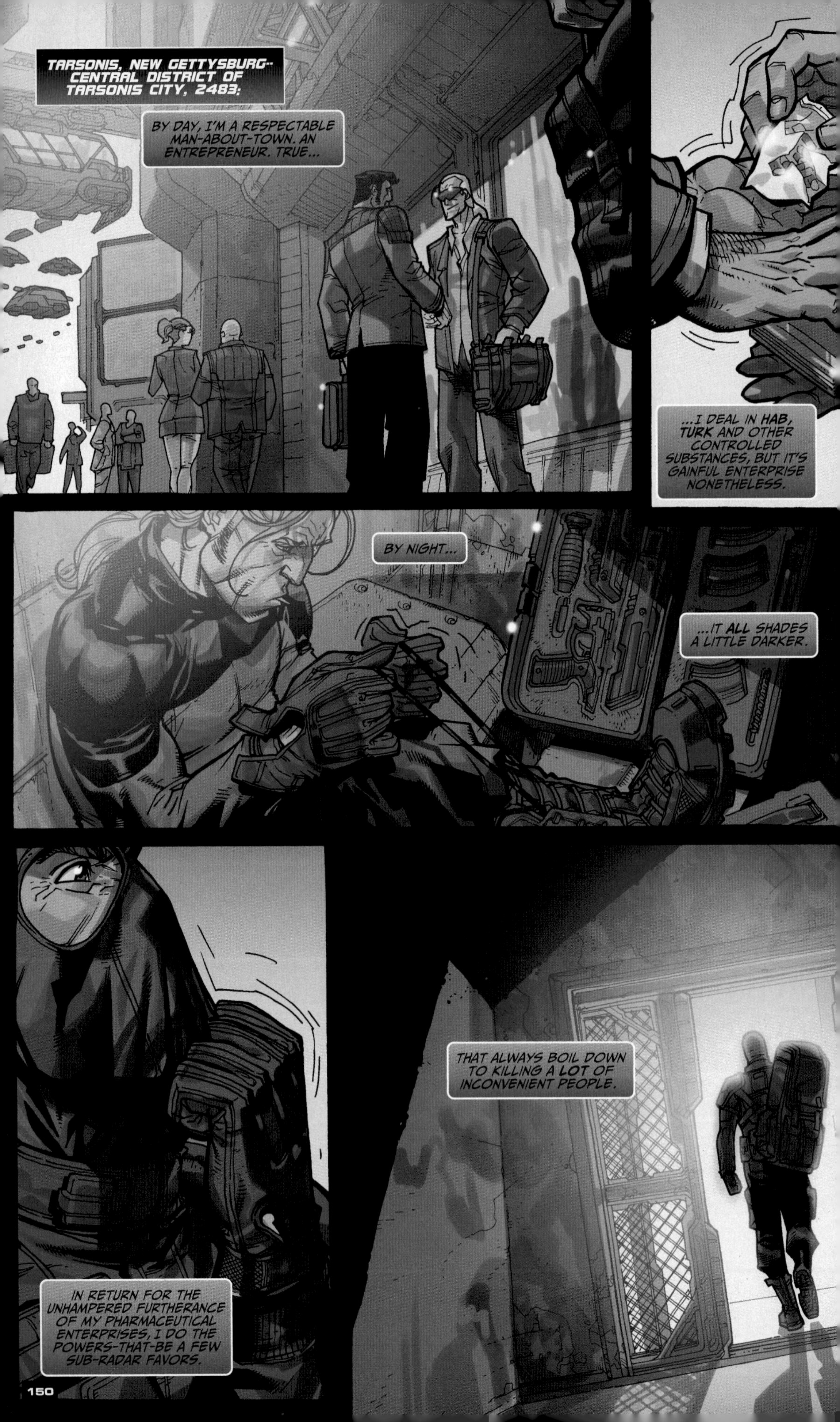
TARSONIS, NEW GETTYSBURG--
CENTRAL DISTRICT OF
TARSONIS CITY, 2483:
BY DAY, I'M A RESPECTABLE MAN-ABOUT-TOWN. AN ENTREPRENEUR. TRUE...
...I DEAL IN HAB, TURK AND OTHER CONTROLLED SUBSTANCES, BUT IT'S GAINFUL ENTERPRISE NONETHELESS.
BY NIGHT...
...IT ALL SHADES A LITTLE DARKER.
IN RETURN FOR THE UNHAMPERED FURTHERANCE OF MY PHARMACEUTICAL ENTERPRISES, I DO THE POWERS-THAT-BE A FEW SUB-RADAR FAVORS.
THAT ALWAYS BOIL DOWN TO KILLING A LOT OF INCONVENIENT PEOPLE.

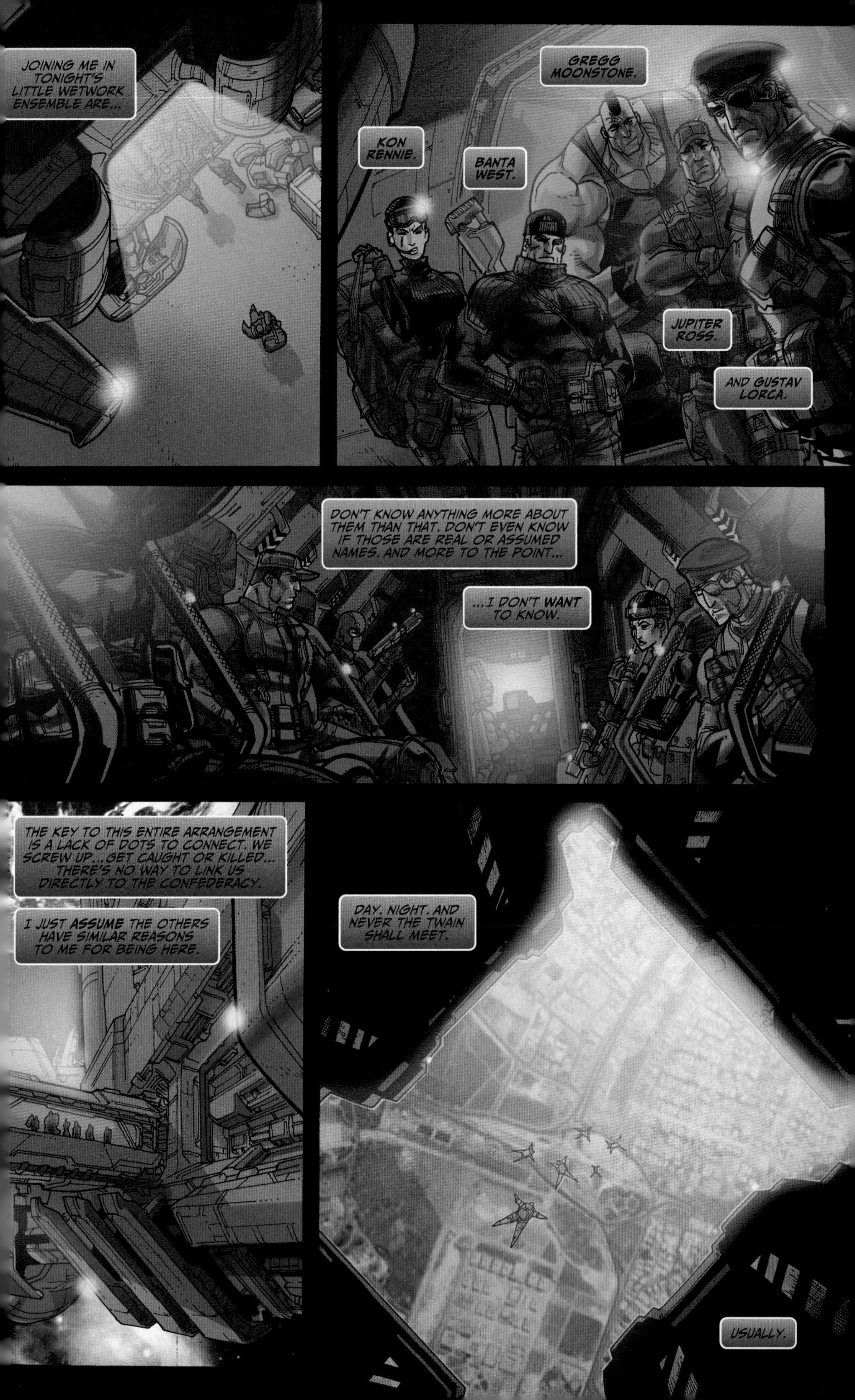
JOINING ME IN TONIGHT'S LITTLE WETWORK ENSEMBLE ARE...
GREGG MOONSTONE.
KON RENNIE.
BANTA WEST.
JUPITER ROSS.
AND GUSTAV LORCA.
DON'T KNOW ANYTHING MORE ABOUT THEM THAN THAT. DON'T EVEN KNOW IF THOSE ARE REAL OR ASSUMED NAMES. AND MORE TO THE POINT...
...I DON'T WANT TO KNOW.
THE KEY TO THIS ENTIRE ARRANGEMENT IS A LACK OF DOTS TO CONNECT. WE SCREW UP...GET CAUGHT OR KILLED... THERE'S NO WAY TO LINK US DIRECTLY TO THE CONFEDERACY.
I JUST ASSUME THE OTHERS HAVE SIMILAR REASONS TO ME FOR BEING HERE.
DAY. NIGHT. AND NEVER THE TWAIN SHALL MEET.
USUALLY.

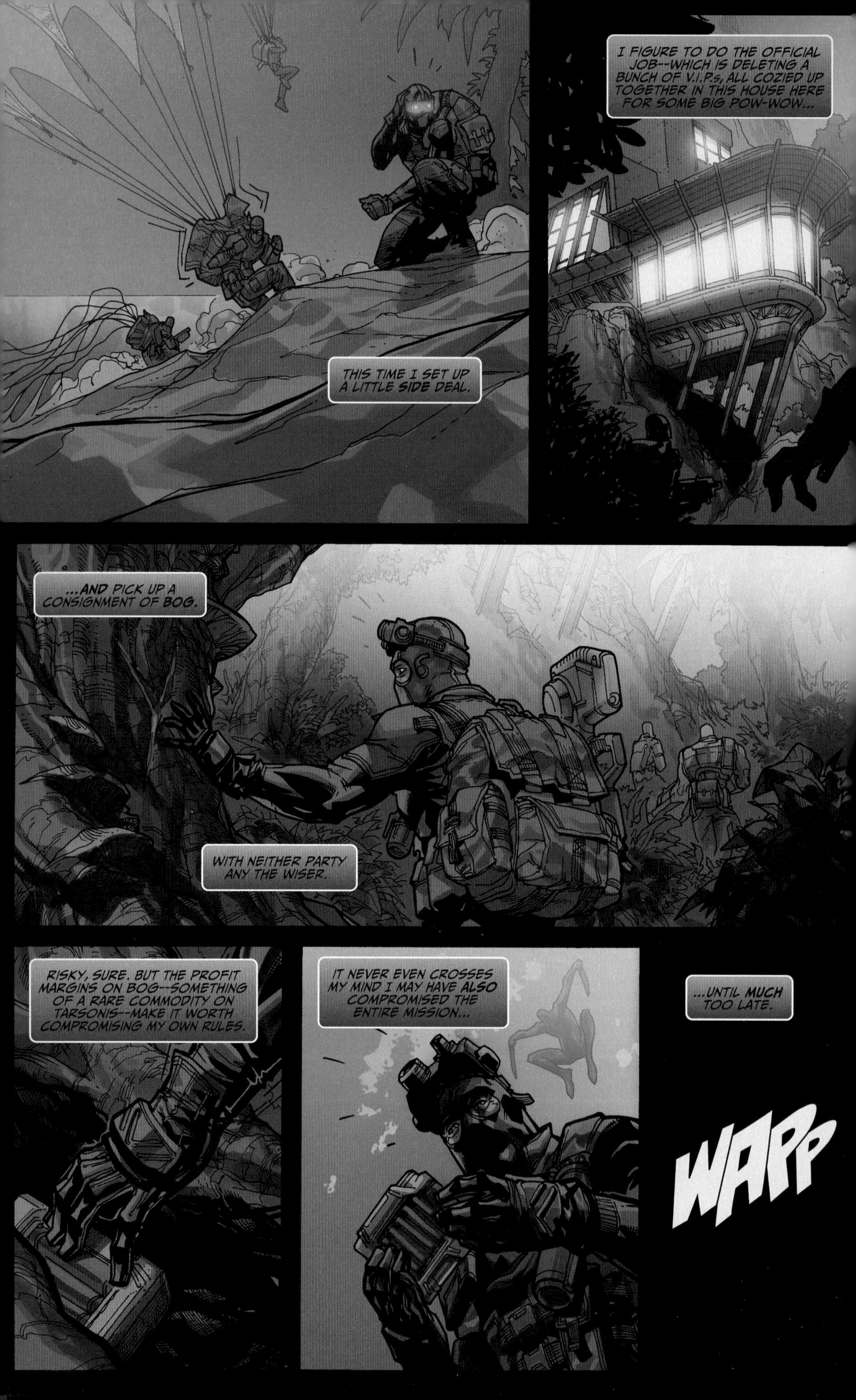
THIS TIME I SET UP A LITTLE SIDE DEAL.
I FIGURE TO DO THE OFFICIAL JOB--WHICH IS DELETING A BUNCH OF V.I.P.s, ALL COZIED UP TOGETHER IN THIS HOUSE HERE FOR SOME BIG POW-WOW...
...AND PICK UP A CONSIGNMENT OF BOG.
WITH NEITHER PARTY ANY THE WISER.
RISKY, SURE. BUT THE PROFIT MARGINS ON BOG--SOMETHING OF A RARE COMMODITY ON TARSONIS--MAKE IT WORTH COMPROMISING MY OWN RULES.
IT NEVER EVEN CROSSES MY MIND I MAY HAVE ALSO COMPROMISED THE ENTIRE MISSION...
...UNTIL MUCH TOO LATE.
WAPP

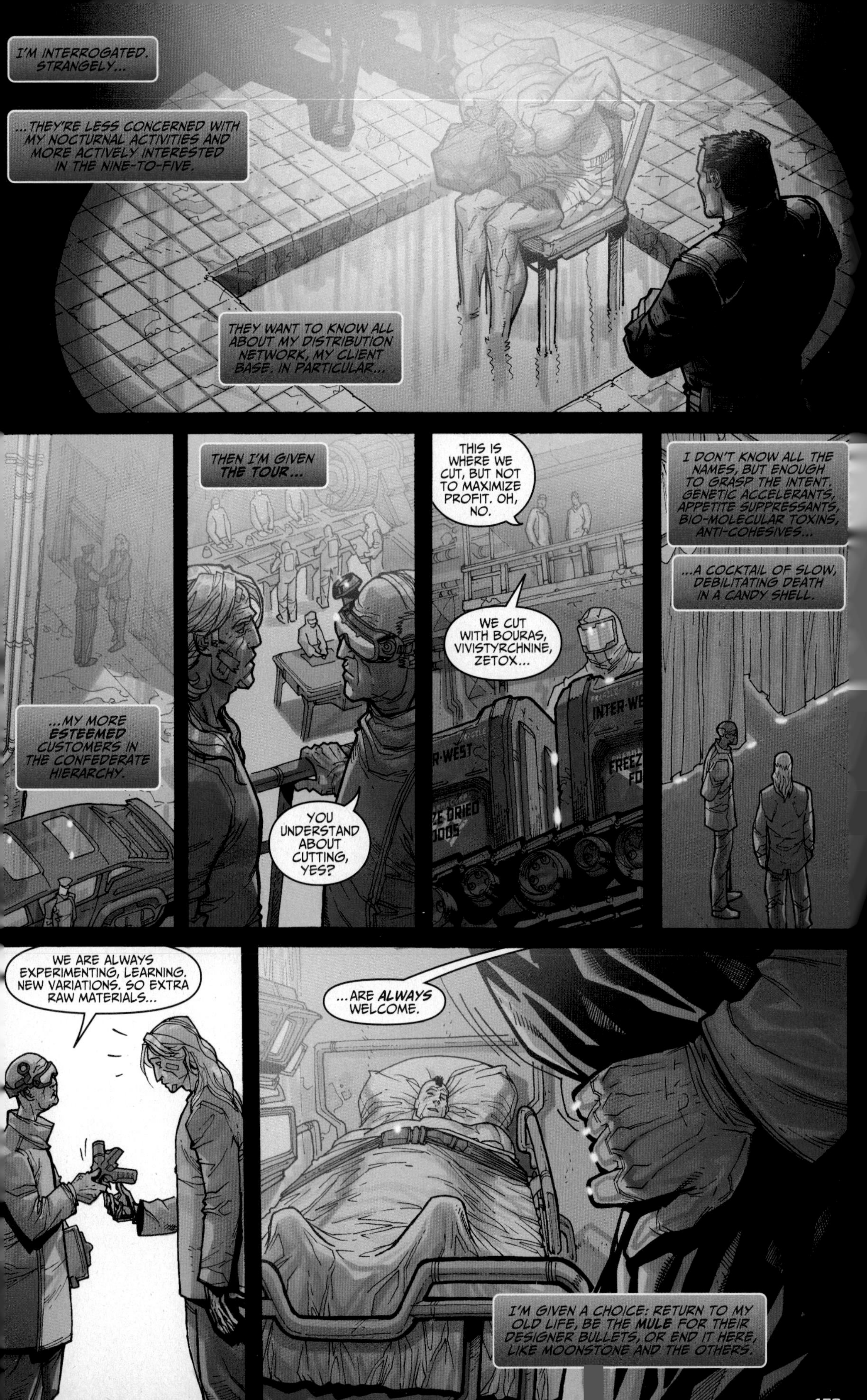

I'M INTERROGATED. STRANGELY...
...THEY'RE LESS CONCERNED WITH MY NOCTURNAL ACTIVITIES AND MORE ACTIVELY INTERESTED IN THE NINE-TO-FIVE.
THEY WANT TO KNOW ALL ABOUT MY DISTRIBUTION NETWORK, MY CLIENT BASE. IN PARTICULAR...
...MY MORE ESTEEMED CUSTOMERS IN THE CONFEDERATE HIERARCHY.
THEN I'M GIVEN THE TOUR...
YOU UNDERSTAND ABOUT CUTTING, YES?
THIS IS WHERE WE CUT, BUT NOT TO MAXIMIZE PROFIT. OH, NO.
WE CUT WITH BOURAS, VIVISTYRCHNINE, ZETOX...
INTER-WE
R-WEST
FREEZ
ZE DRIED
OODS
I DON'T KNOW ALL THE NAMES, BUT ENOUGH TO GRASP THE INTENT. GENETIC ACCELERANTS, APPETITE SUPPRESSANTS, BIO-MOLECULAR TOXINS, ANTI-COHESIVES...
...A COCKTAIL OF SLOW, DEBILITATING DEATH IN A CANDY SHELL.
WE ARE ALWAYS EXPERIMENTING, LEARNING. NEW VARIATIONS. SO EXTRA RAW MATERIALS...
...ARE ALWAYS WELCOME.
I'M GIVEN A CHOICE: RETURN TO MY OLD LIFE, BE THE MULE FOR THEIR DESIGNER BULLETS, OR END IT HERE, LIKE MOONSTONE AND THE OTHERS.

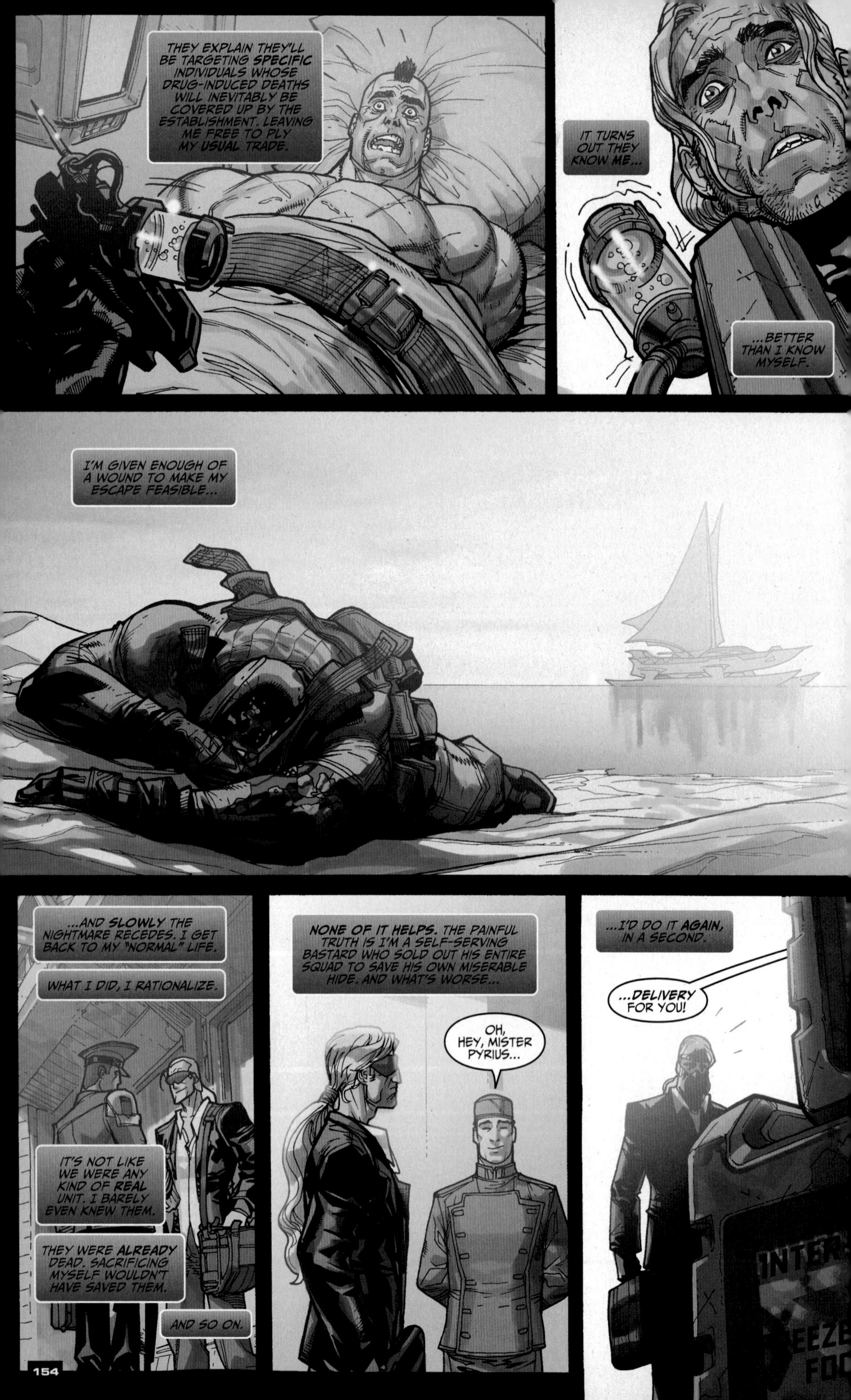
THEY EXPLAIN THEY'LL BE TARGETING SPECIFIC INDIVIDUALS WHOSE DRUG-INDUCED DEATHS WILL INEVITABLY BE COVERED UP BY THE ESTABLISHMENT, LEAVING ME FREE TO PLY MY USUAL TRADE.
IT TURNS OUT THEY KNOW ME...
...BETTER THAN I KNOW MYSELF.
I'M GIVEN ENOUGH OF A WOUND TO MAKE MY ESCAPE FEASIBLE...
...AND SLOWLY THE NIGHTMARE RECEDES. I GET BACK TO MY "NORMAL" LIFE.
WHAT I DID, I RATIONALIZE.
IT'S NOT LIKE WE WERE ANY KIND OF REAL UNIT. I BARELY EVEN KNEW THEM.
THEY WERE ALREADY DEAD. SACRIFICING MYSELF WOULDN'T HAVE SAVED THEM.
AND SO ON.
NONE OF IT HELPS. THE PAINFUL TRUTH IS I'M A SELF-SERVING BASTARD WHO SOLD OUT HIS ENTIRE SQUAD TO SAVE HIS OWN MISERABLE HIDE. AND WHAT'S WORSE...
OH, HEY, MISTER PYRIUS...
...I'D DO IT AGAIN, IN A SECOND.
...DELIVERY FOR YOU!

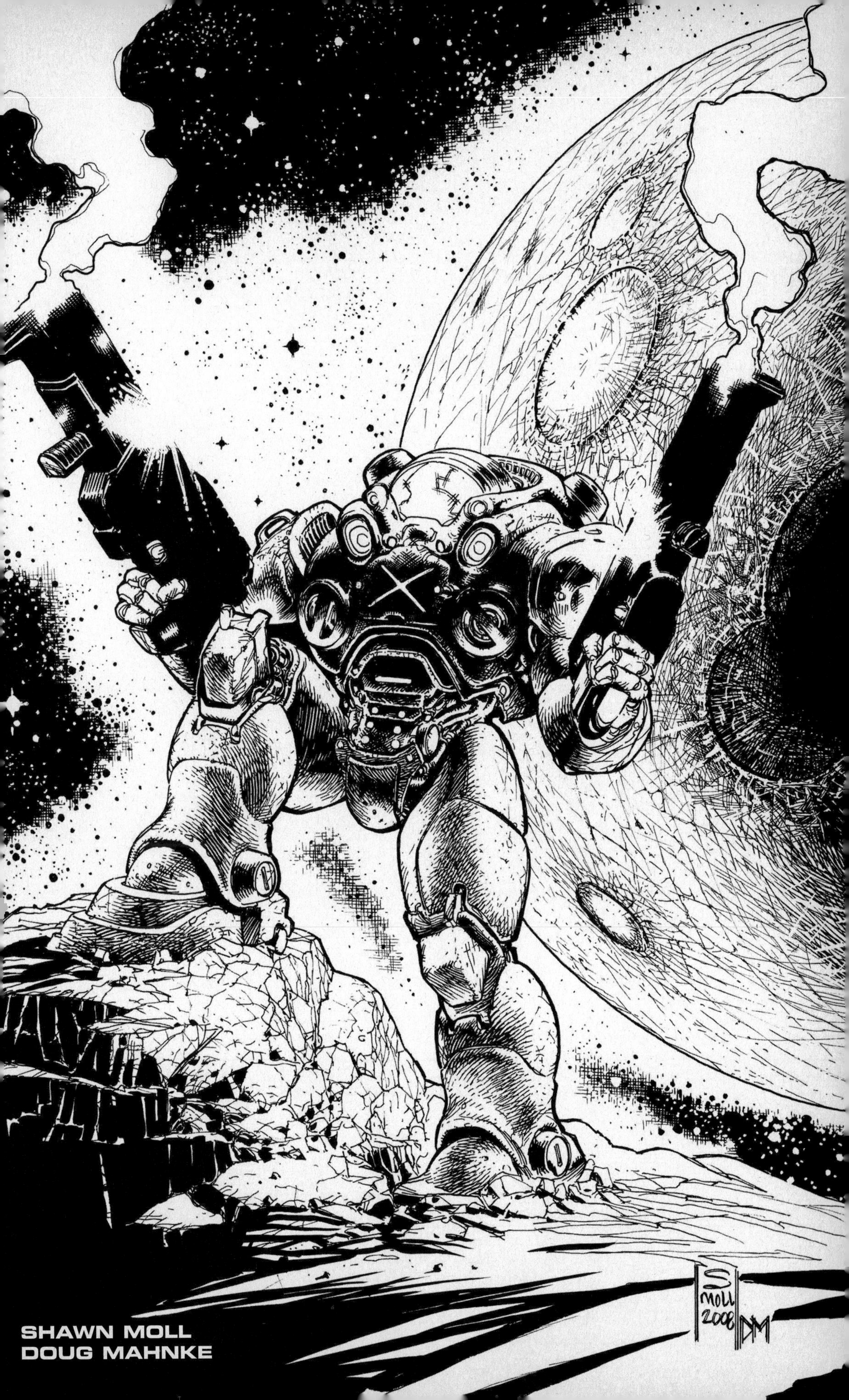
S MOLL 2008
DM

SHAWN MOLL
DOUG MAHNKE

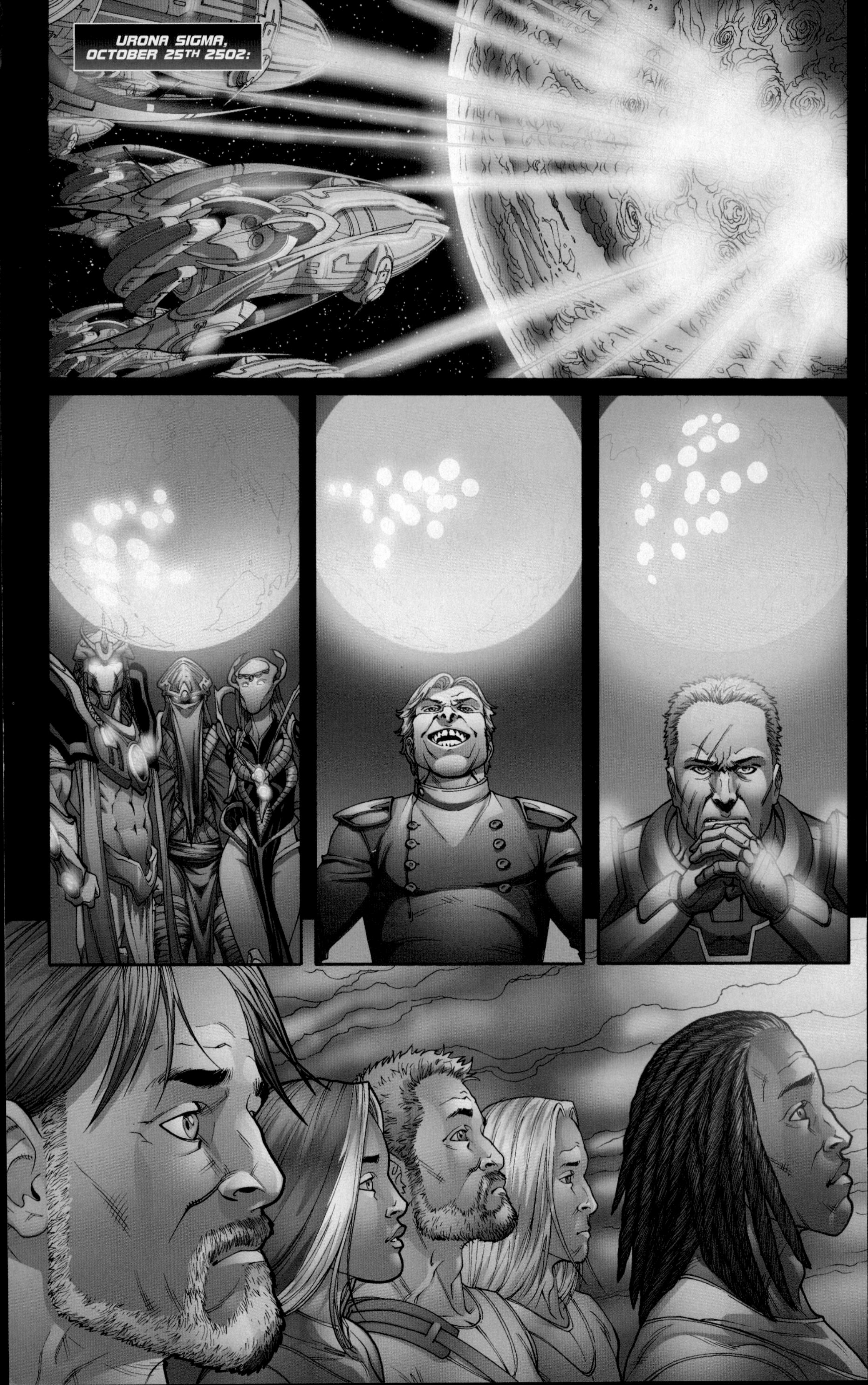
URONA SIGMA, OCTOBER 25TH 2502:

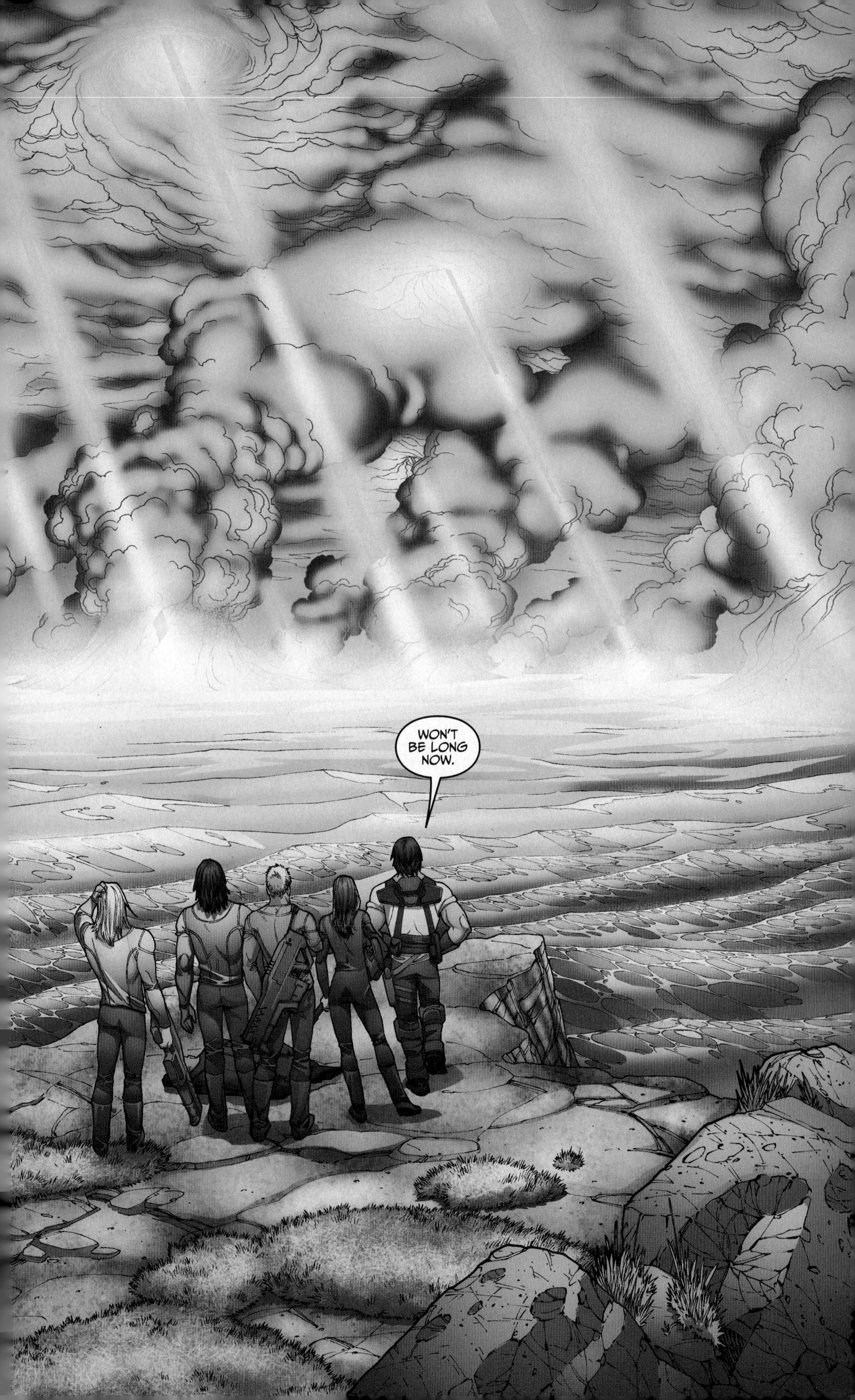
WON'T BE LONG NOW.

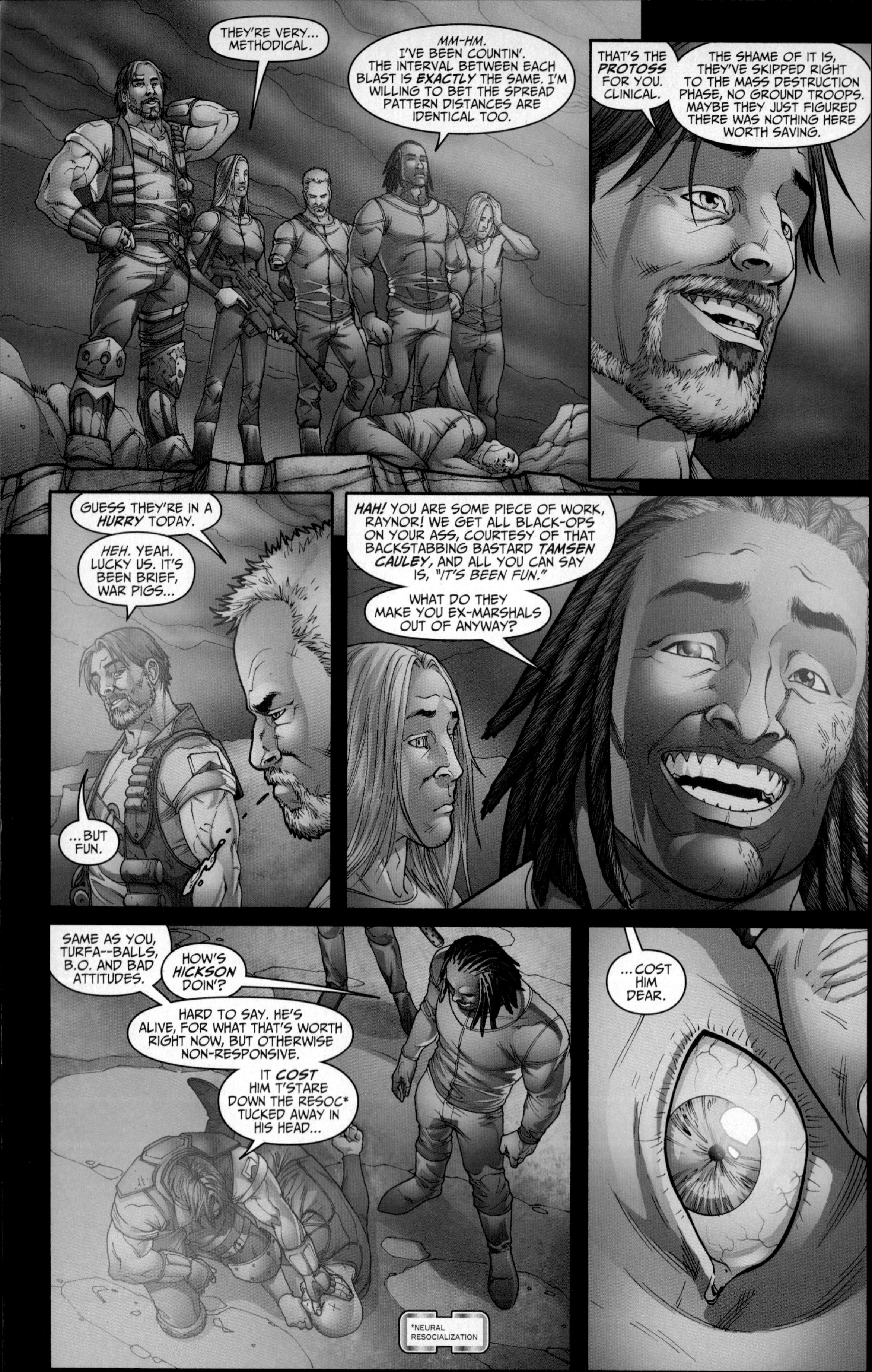
THEY'RE VERY... METHODICAL.
MM-HM. I'VE BEEN COUNTIN'. THE INTERVAL BETWEEN EACH BLAST IS EXACTLY THE SAME. I'M WILLING TO BET THE SPREAD PATTERN DISTANCES ARE IDENTICAL TOO.
THAT'S THE PROTOSS FOR YOU. CLINICAL.
THE SHAME OF IT IS, THEY'VE SKIPPED RIGHT TO THE MASS DESTRUCTION PHASE, NO GROUND TROOPS. MAYBE THEY JUST FIGURED THERE WAS NOTHING HERE WORTH SAVING.
GUESS THEY'RE IN A HURRY TODAY.
HEH. YEAH. LUCKY US. IT'S BEEN BRIEF, WAR PIGS...
...BUT FUN.
HAH! YOU ARE SOME PIECE OF WORK, RAYNOR! WE GET ALL BLACK-OPS ON YOUR ASS, COURTESY OF THAT BACKSTABBING BASTARD TAMSEN CAULEY, AND ALL YOU CAN SAY IS, "IT'S BEEN FUN."
WHAT DO THEY MAKE YOU EX-MARSHALS OUT OF ANYWAY?
SAME AS YOU, TURFA--BALLS, B.O. AND BAD ATTITUDES.
HOW'S HICKSON DOIN'?
HARD TO SAY. HE'S ALIVE, FOR WHAT THAT'S WORTH RIGHT NOW, BUT OTHERWISE NON-RESPONSIVE.
IT COST HIM T'STARE DOWN THE RESOC* TUCKED AWAY IN HIS HEAD...
...COST HIM DEAR.
*NEURAL RESOCIALIZATION

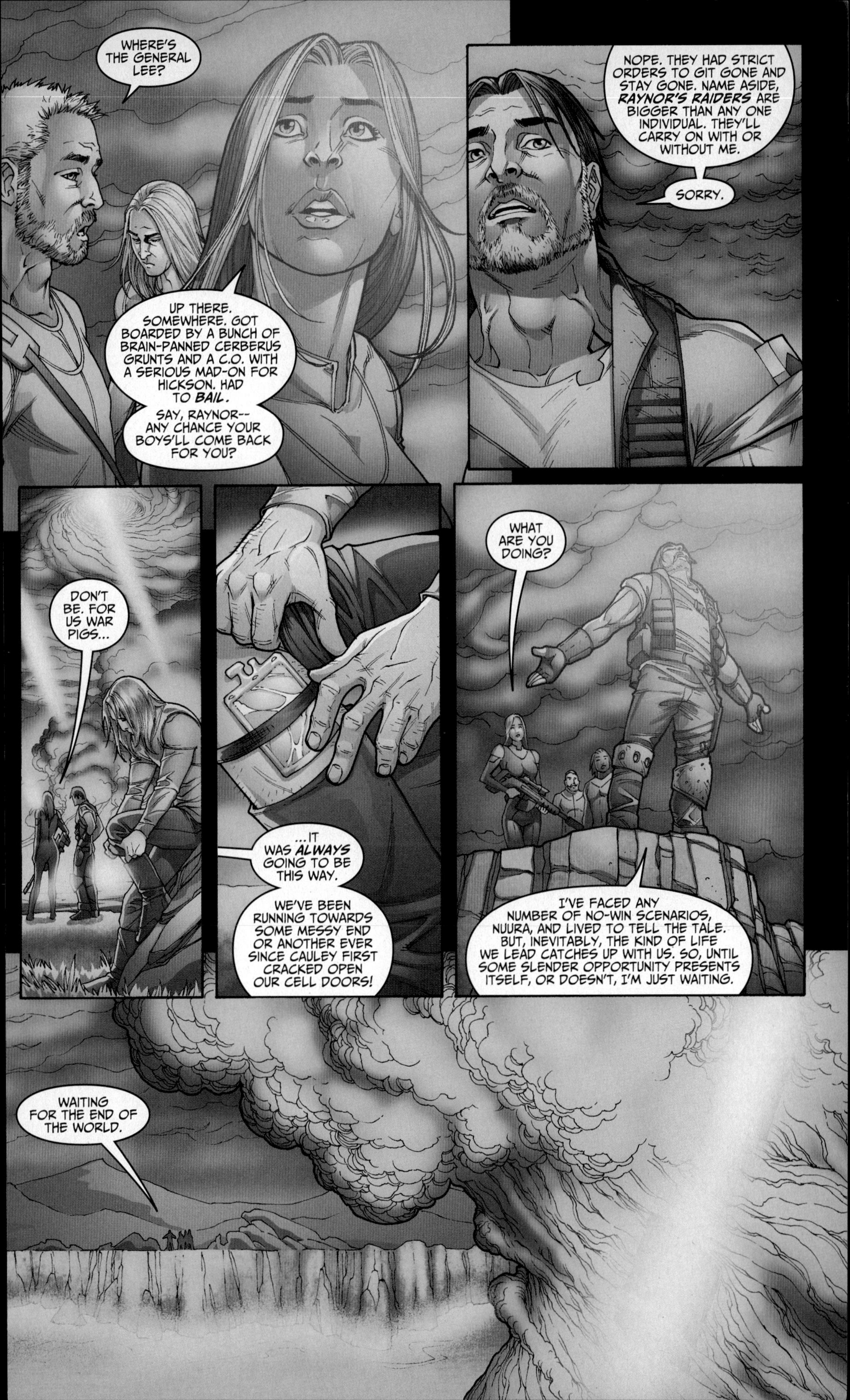
WHERE'S THE GENERAL LEE?
UP THERE. SOMEWHERE. GOT BOARDED BY A BUNCH OF BRAIN-PANNED CERBERUS GRUNTS AND A C.O. WITH A SERIOUS MAD-ON FOR HICKSON. HAD TO BAIL.
SAY, RAYNOR-- ANY CHANCE YOUR BOYS'LL COME BACK FOR YOU?
NOPE. THEY HAD STRICT ORDERS TO GIT GONE AND STAY GONE. NAME ASIDE, RAYNOR'S RAIDERS ARE BIGGER THAN ANY ONE INDIVIDUAL. THEY'LL CARRY ON WITH OR WITHOUT ME.
SORRY.
DON'T BE. FOR US WAR PIGS...
...IT WAS ALWAYS GOING TO BE THIS WAY.
WE'VE BEEN RUNNING TOWARDS SOME MESSY END OR ANOTHER EVER SINCE CAULEY FIRST CRACKED OPEN OUR CELL DOORS!
WHAT ARE YOU DOING?
I'VE FACED ANY NUMBER OF NO-WIN SCENARIOS, NUURA, AND LIVED TO TELL THE TALE. BUT, INEVITABLY, THE KIND OF LIFE WE LEAD CATCHES UP WITH US. SO, UNTIL SOME SLENDER OPPORTUNITY PRESENTS ITSELF, OR DOESN'T, I'M JUST WAITING.
WAITING FOR THE END OF THE WORLD.

SCREW CAULEY!

HE MAY BE CONTENT TO SIT BACK AND WATCH THIS PLAY OUT FROM A SAFE DISTANCE, BUT I'M *NOT!* GET ME A DROPSHIP PREPPED FOR LAUNCH.

I'VE WAITED YEARS FOR THIS OPPORTUNITY. AND NOW IT'S FINALLY COME, I NEED TO SEE HICKSON'S EYES POP AS MY HANDS CLOSE ON HIS NECK, HEAR VERTEBRAE CRACK AS I TWIST.

THE MILITARY SHRINKS WHO POKED AND PRODDED ME AFTER LOS ANDARES HAD A WORD FOR IT...

"...CLOSURE."

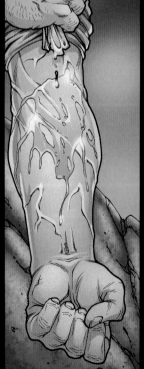

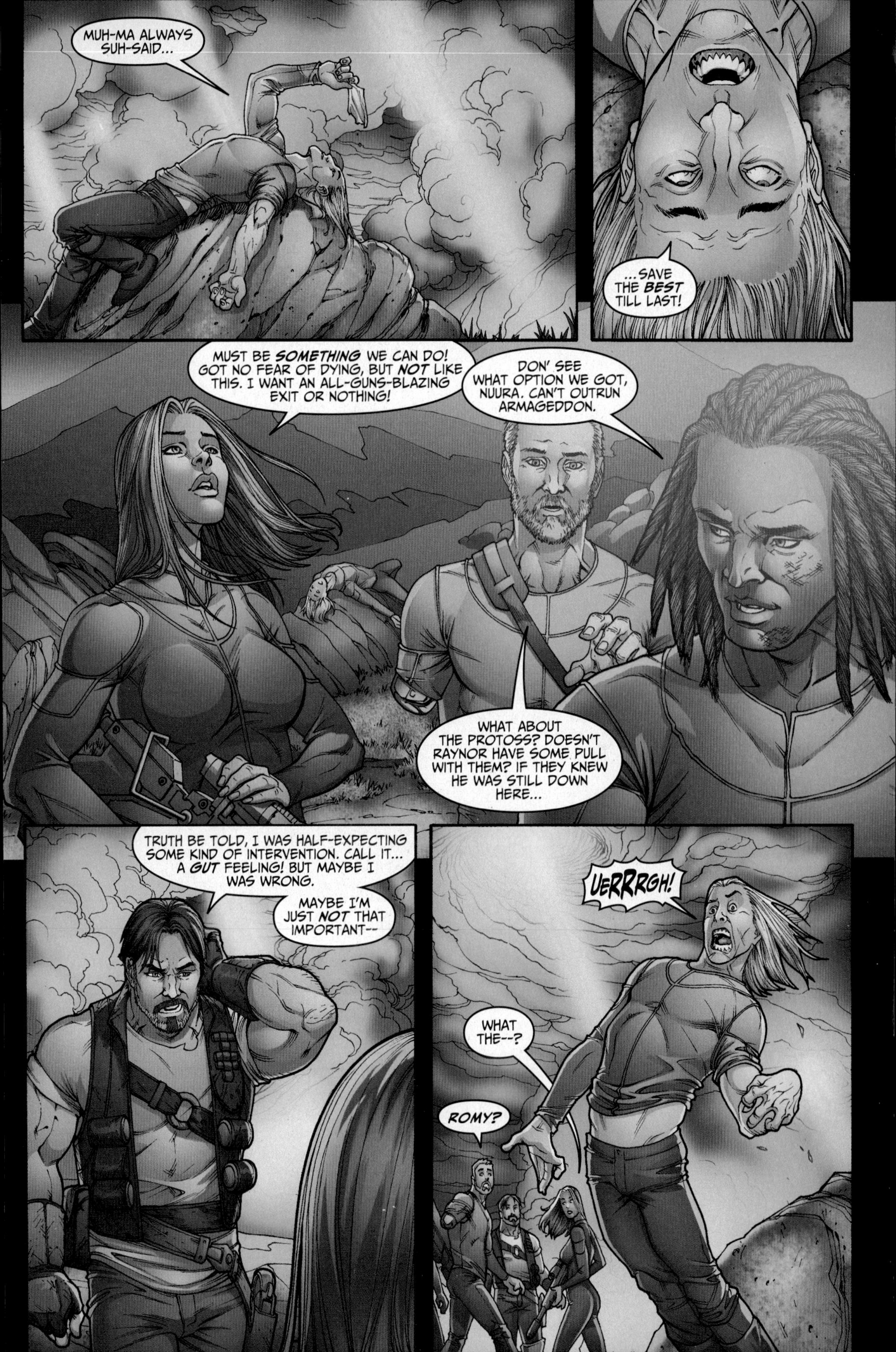
MUH-MA ALWAYS SUH-SAID...
...SAVE THE BEST TILL LAST!
MUST BE SOMETHING WE CAN DO! GOT NO FEAR OF DYING, BUT NOT LIKE THIS. I WANT AN ALL-GUNS-BLAZING EXIT OR NOTHING!
DON' SEE WHAT OPTION WE GOT, NUURA. CAN'T OUTRUN ARMAGEDDON.
WHAT ABOUT THE PROTOSS? DOESN'T RAYNOR HAVE SOME PULL WITH THEM? IF THEY KNEW HE WAS STILL DOWN HERE...
TRUTH BE TOLD, I WAS HALF-EXPECTING SOME KIND OF INTERVENTION. CALL IT... A GUT FEELING! BUT MAYBE I WAS WRONG.
MAYBE I'M JUST NOT THAT IMPORTANT--
UERRRGH!
WHAT THE--?
ROMY?

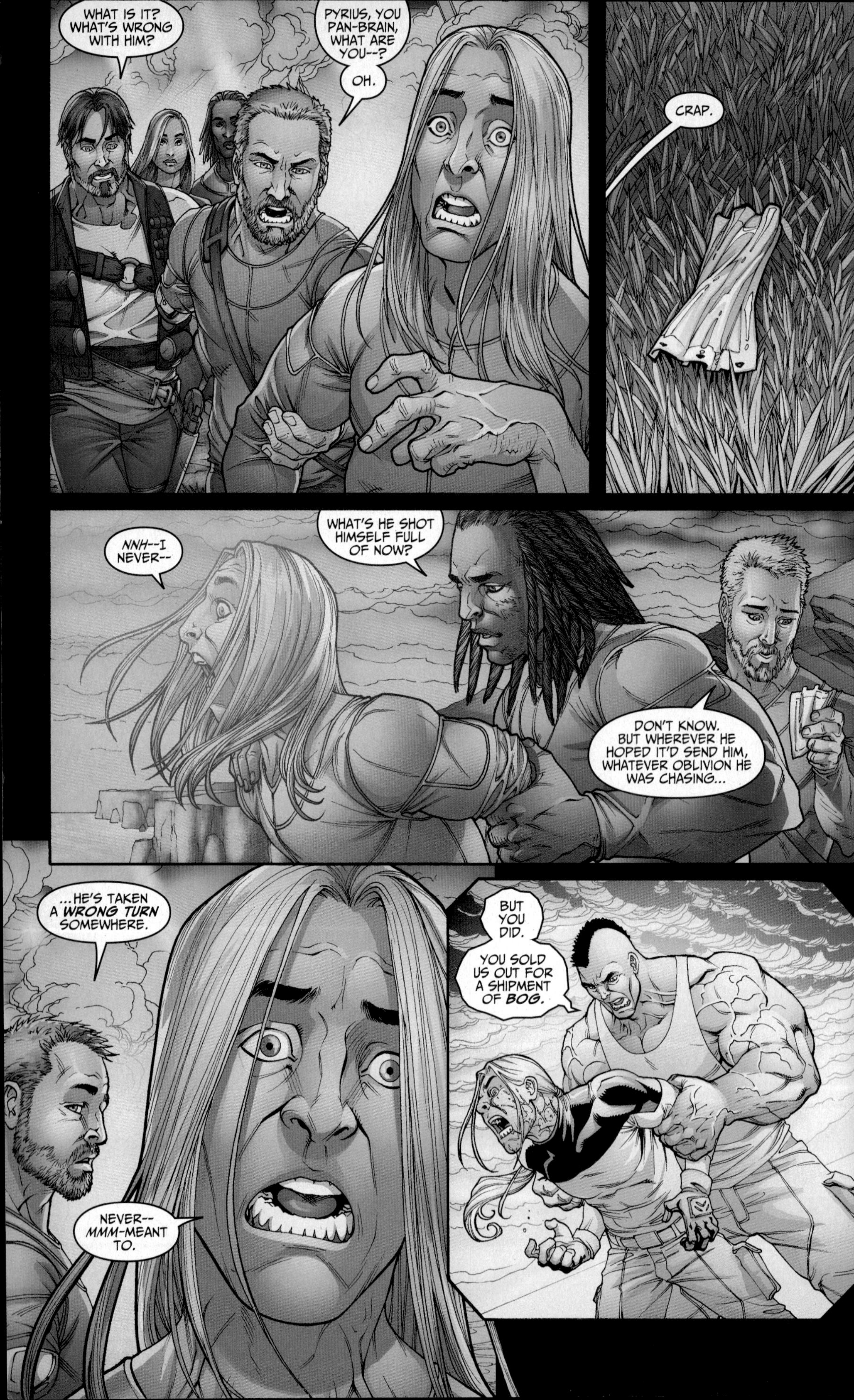
WHAT IS IT? WHAT'S WRONG WITH HIM?
PYRIUS, YOU PAN-BRAIN, WHAT ARE YOU--?
OH.
CRAP.
NNH--I NEVER--
WHAT'S HE SHOT HIMSELF FULL OF NOW?
DON'T KNOW. BUT WHEREVER HE HOPED IT'D SEND HIM, WHATEVER OBLIVION HE WAS CHASING...
...HE'S TAKEN A WRONG TURN SOMEWHERE.
NEVER-- MMM-MEANT TO.
BUT YOU DID.
YOU SOLD US OUT FOR A SHIPMENT OF BOG.

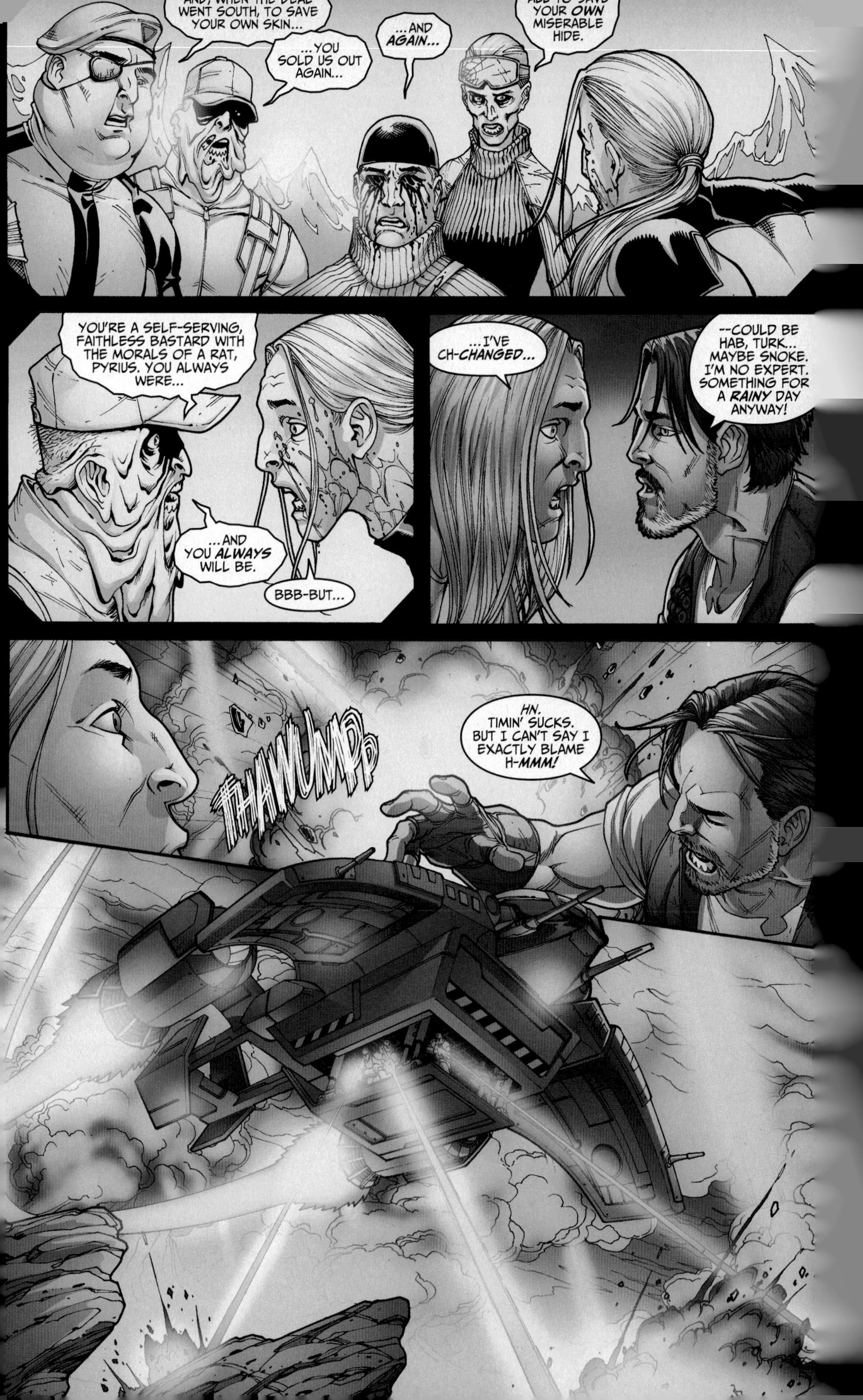
AND, WHEN THE DEAL WENT SOUTH, TO SAVE YOUR OWN SKIN...
...YOU SOLD US OUT AGAIN...
...AND AGAIN...
ALL TO SAVE YOUR OWN MISERABLE HIDE.
YOU'RE A SELF-SERVING, FAITHLESS BASTARD WITH THE MORALS OF A RAT, PYRIUS. YOU ALWAYS WERE...
...AND YOU ALWAYS WILL BE.
BBB-BUT...
...I'VE CH-CHANGED...
--COULD BE HAB, TURK... MAYBE SNOKE. I'M NO EXPERT. SOMETHING FOR A RAINY DAY ANYWAY!
THAWUMP
HN. TIMIN' SUCKS. BUT I CAN'T SAY I EXACTLY BLAME H-MMM!

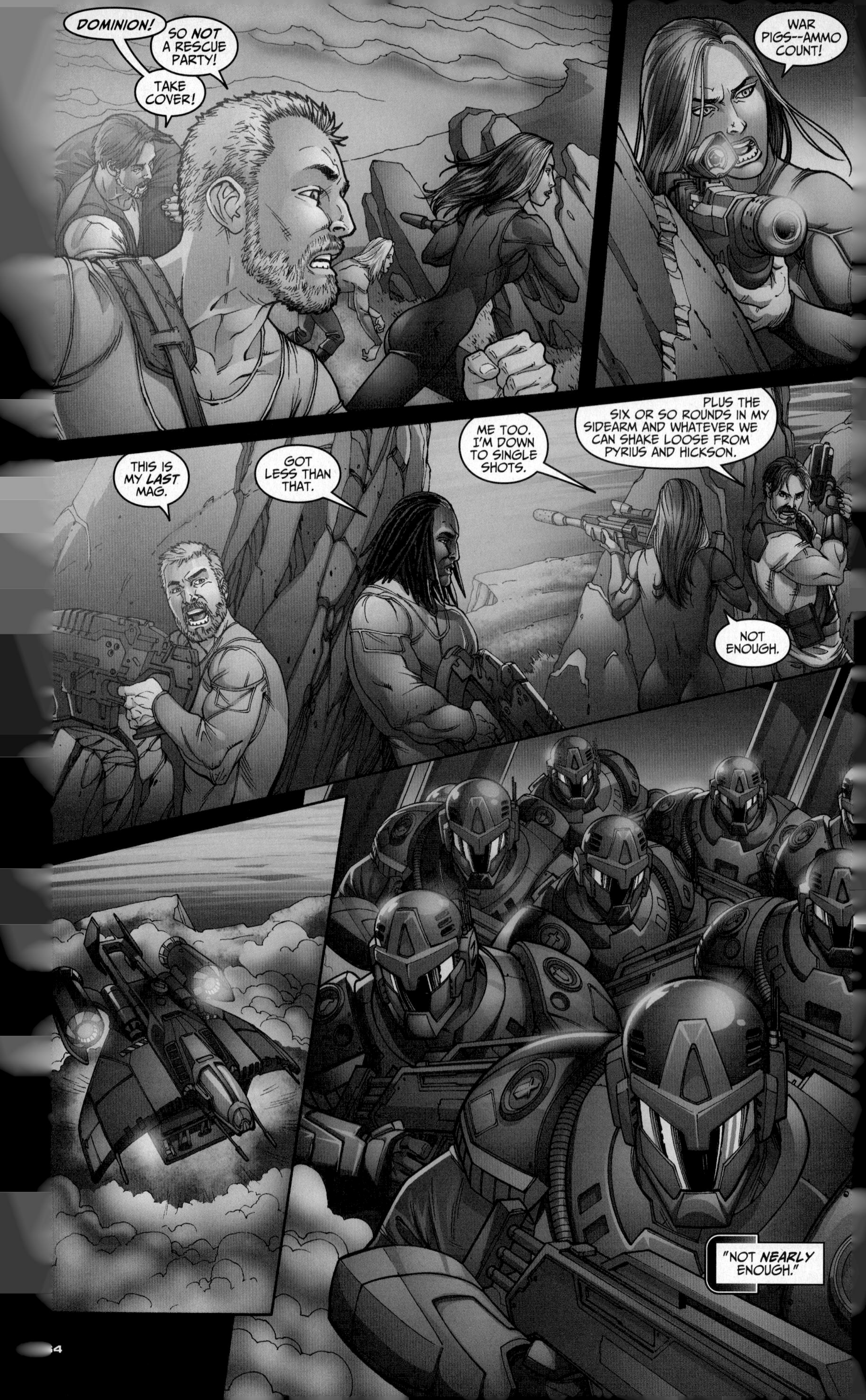
DOMINION!
SO NOT A RESCUE PARTY!
TAKE COVER!
WAR PIGS--AMMO COUNT!
THIS IS MY LAST MAG.
GOT LESS THAN THAT.
ME TOO. I'M DOWN TO SINGLE SHOTS.
PLUS THE SIX OR SO ROUNDS IN MY SIDEARM AND WHATEVER WE CAN SHAKE LOOSE FROM PYRIUS AND HICKSON.
NOT ENOUGH.
"NOT NEARLY ENOUGH."

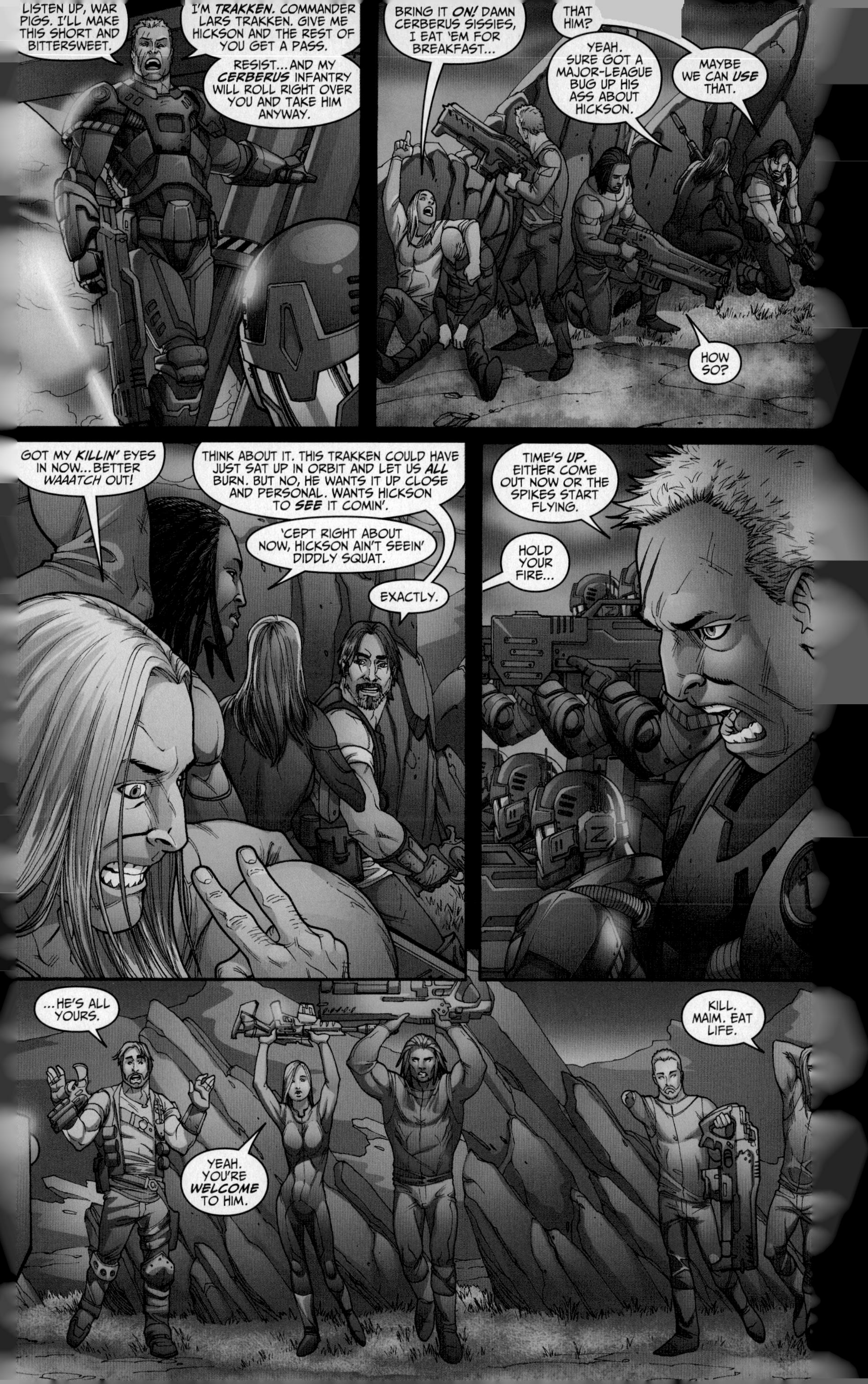
LISTEN UP, WAR PIGS. I'LL MAKE THIS SHORT AND BITTERSWEET.
I'M TRAKKEN. COMMANDER LARS TRAKKEN. GIVE ME HICKSON AND THE REST OF YOU GET A PASS.
RESIST...AND MY CERBERUS INFANTRY WILL ROLL RIGHT OVER YOU AND TAKE HIM ANYWAY.
BRING IT ON! DAMN CERBERUS SISSIES, I EAT 'EM FOR BREAKFAST...
THAT HIM?
YEAH. SURE GOT A MAJOR-LEAGUE BUG UP HIS ASS ABOUT HICKSON.
MAYBE WE CAN USE THAT.
HOW SO?
GOT MY KILLIN' EYES IN NOW...BETTER WAAATCH OUT!
THINK ABOUT IT. THIS TRAKKEN COULD HAVE JUST SAT UP IN ORBIT AND LET US ALL BURN. BUT NO, HE WANTS IT UP CLOSE AND PERSONAL. WANTS HICKSON TO SEE IT COMIN'.
'CEPT RIGHT ABOUT NOW, HICKSON AIN'T SEEIN' DIDDLY SQUAT.
EXACTLY.
TIME'S UP. EITHER COME OUT NOW OR THE SPIKES START FLYING.
HOLD YOUR FIRE...
...HE'S ALL YOURS.
YEAH. YOU'RE WELCOME TO HIM.
KILL. MAIM. EAT LIFE.

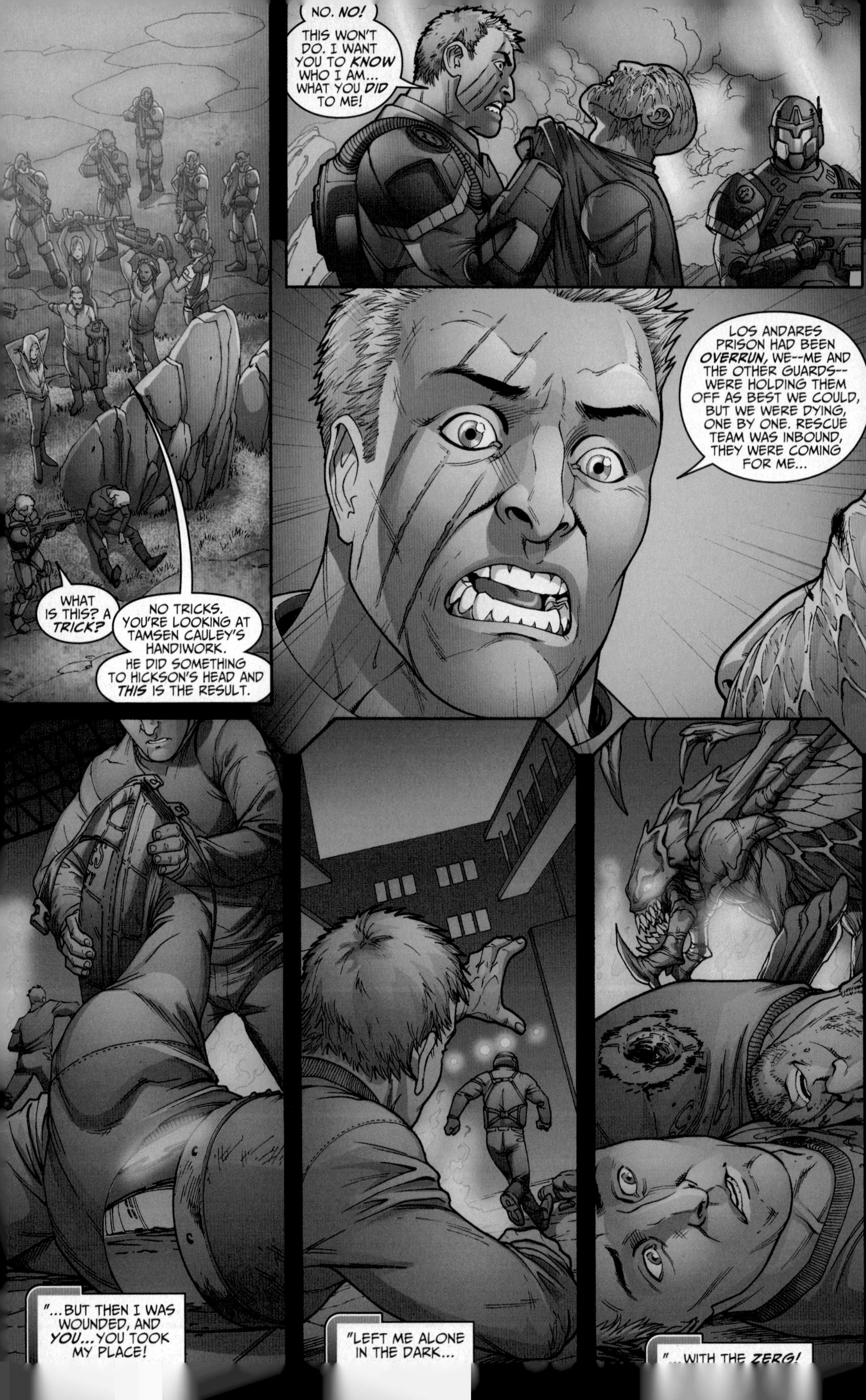
WHAT IS THIS? A TRICK?
NO TRICKS. YOU'RE LOOKING AT TAMSEN CAULEY'S HANDIWORK.
HE DID SOMETHING TO HICKSON'S HEAD AND THIS IS THE RESULT.
NO. NO!
THIS WON'T DO. I WANT YOU TO KNOW WHO I AM... WHAT YOU DID TO ME!
LOS ANDARES PRISON HAD BEEN OVERRUN, WE--ME AND THE OTHER GUARDS--WERE HOLDING THEM OFF AS BEST WE COULD, BUT WE WERE DYING, ONE BY ONE. RESCUE TEAM WAS INBOUND, THEY WERE COMING FOR ME...
"...BUT THEN I WAS WOUNDED, AND YOU...YOU TOOK MY PLACE!
"LEFT ME ALONE IN THE DARK...
"...WITH THE ZERG!

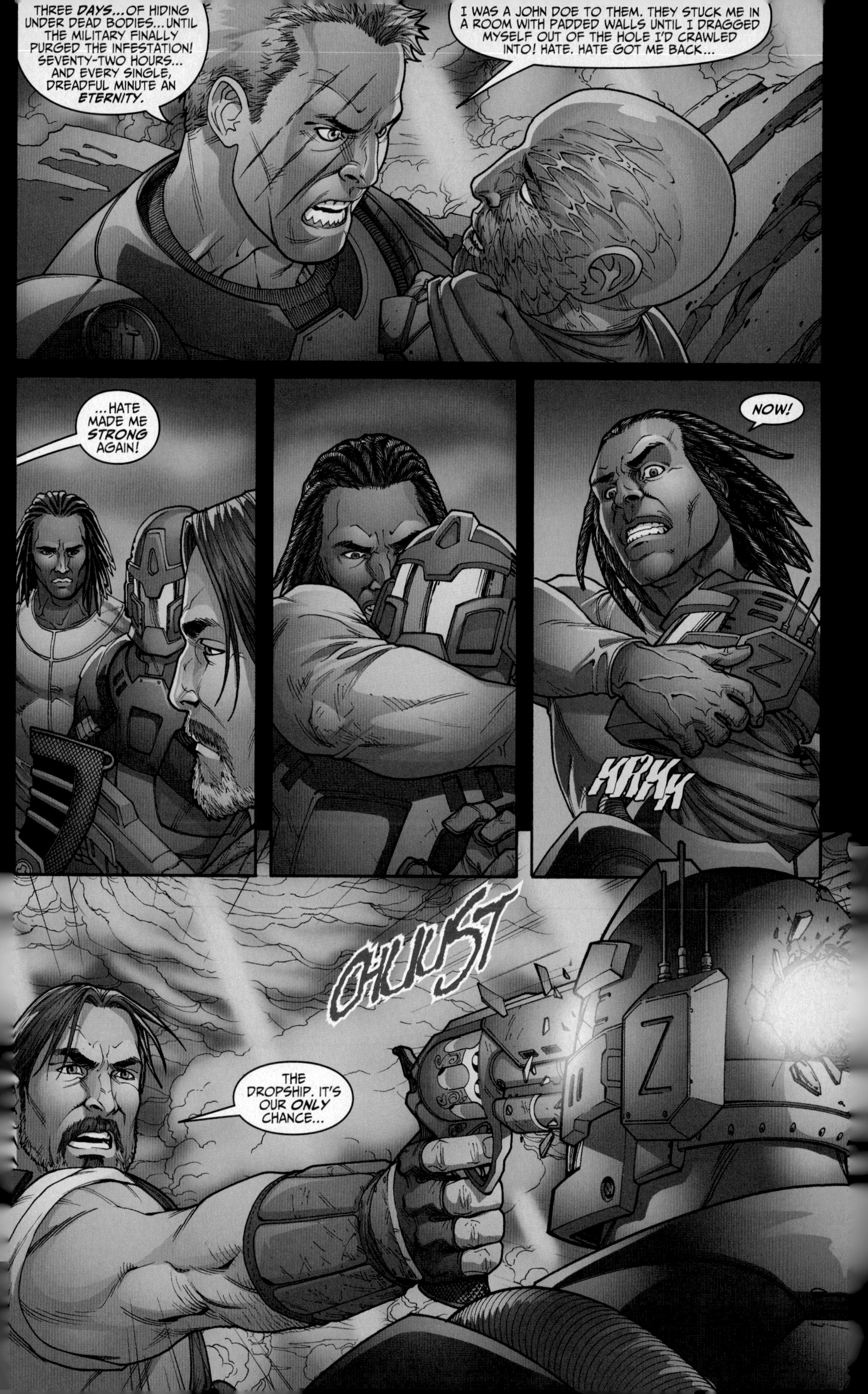
THREE DAYS...OF HIDING UNDER DEAD BODIES...UNTIL THE MILITARY FINALLY PURGED THE INFESTATION! SEVENTY-TWO HOURS... AND EVERY SINGLE, DREADFUL MINUTE AN ETERNITY.
I WAS A JOHN DOE TO THEM. THEY STUCK ME IN A ROOM WITH PADDED WALLS UNTIL I DRAGGED MYSELF OUT OF THE HOLE I'D CRAWLED INTO! HATE. HATE GOT ME BACK...
...HATE MADE ME STRONG AGAIN!
NOW!
KRKK
CHUKST
THE DROPSHIP. IT'S OUR ONLY CHANCE...

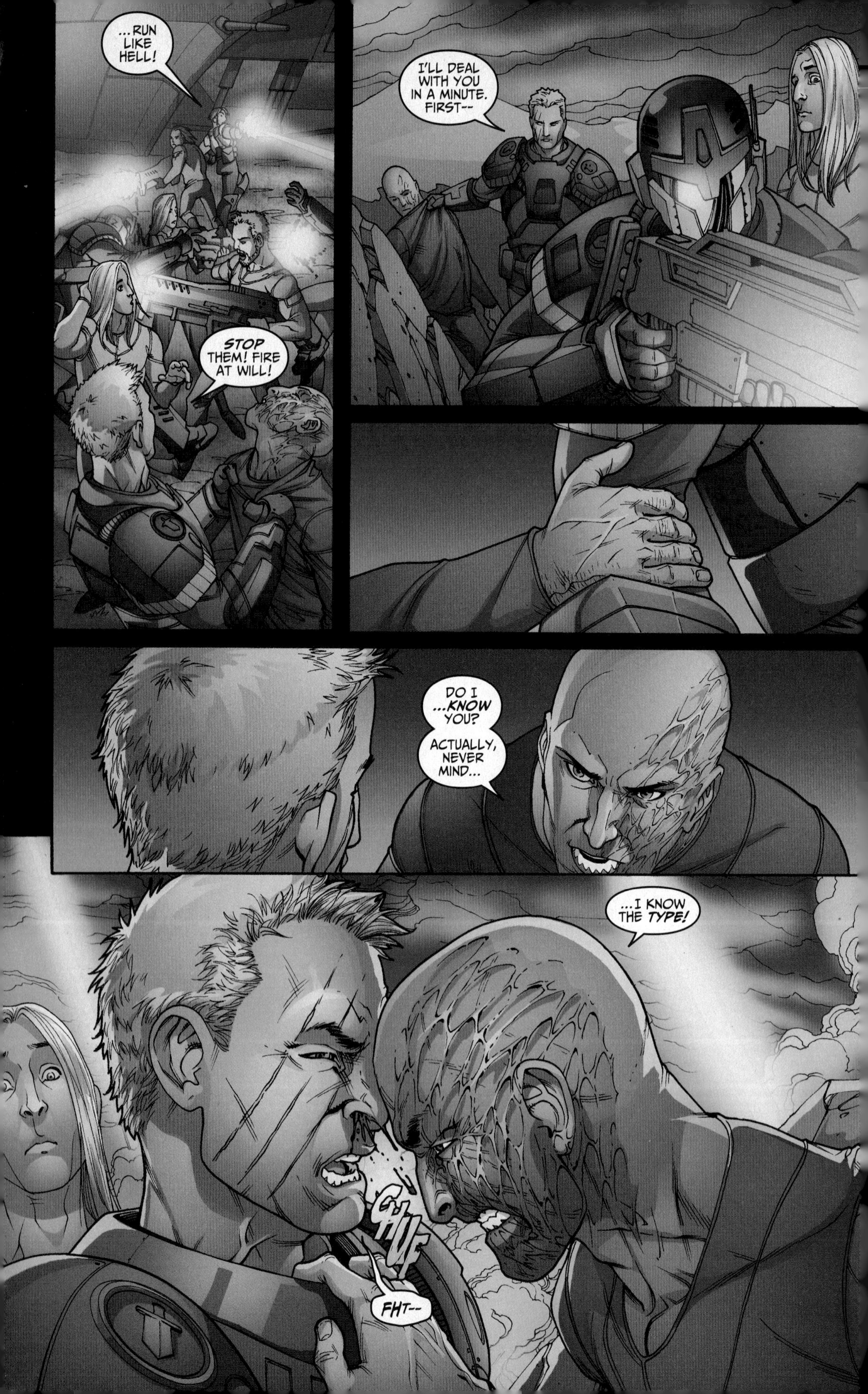
...RUN LIKE HELL!
STOP THEM! FIRE AT WILL!
I'LL DEAL WITH YOU IN A MINUTE. FIRST--
DO I ...KNOW YOU?
ACTUALLY, NEVER MIND...
...I KNOW THE TYPE!
FHT--

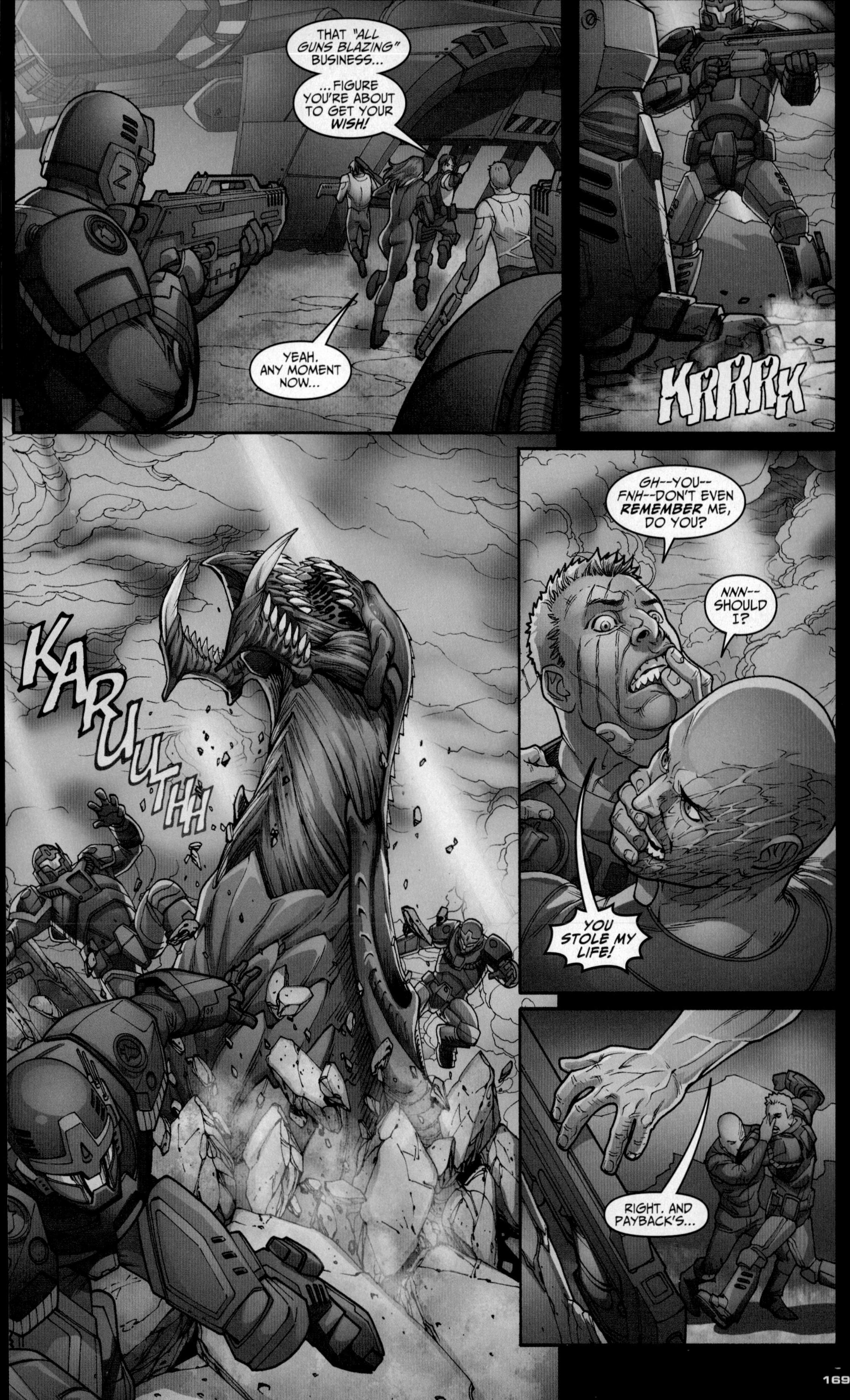

THAT "ALL GUNS BLAZING" BUSINESS...
...FIGURE YOU'RE ABOUT TO GET YOUR WISH!
YEAH. ANY MOMENT NOW...
KRRRK
KARUULTHH
GH--YOU--FNH--DON'T EVEN REMEMBER ME, DO YOU?
NNN--SHOULD I?
YOU STOLE MY LIFE!
RIGHT. AND PAYBACK'S...

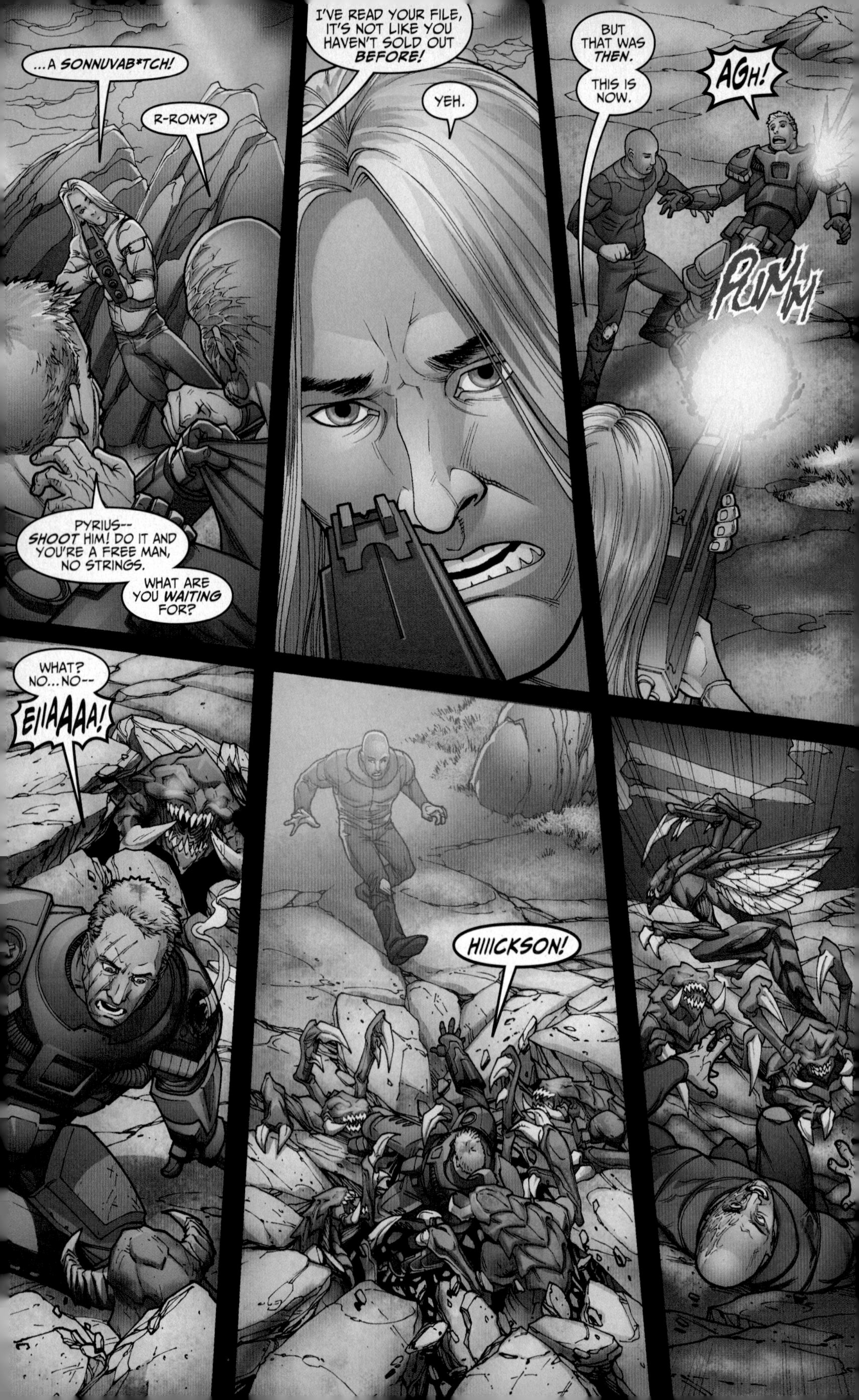
...A SONNUVAB*TCH!
R-ROMY?
PYRIUS-- SHOOT HIM! DO IT AND YOU'RE A FREE MAN, NO STRINGS.
WHAT ARE YOU WAITING FOR?
I'VE READ YOUR FILE, IT'S NOT LIKE YOU HAVEN'T SOLD OUT BEFORE!
YEH.
BUT THAT WAS THEN.
THIS IS NOW.
AGH!
WHAT? NO...NO--
EIIAAAA!
HIIICKSON!

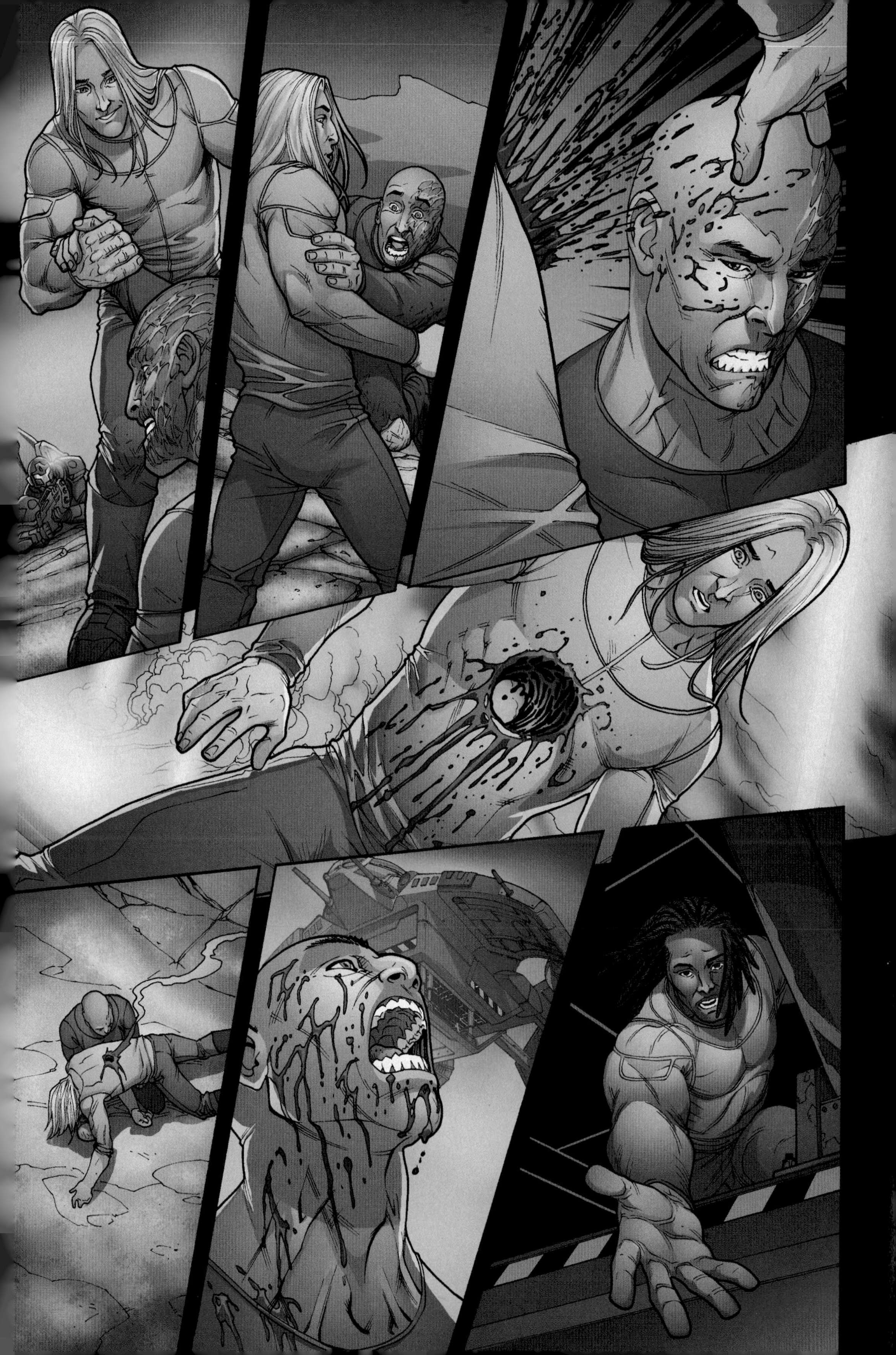

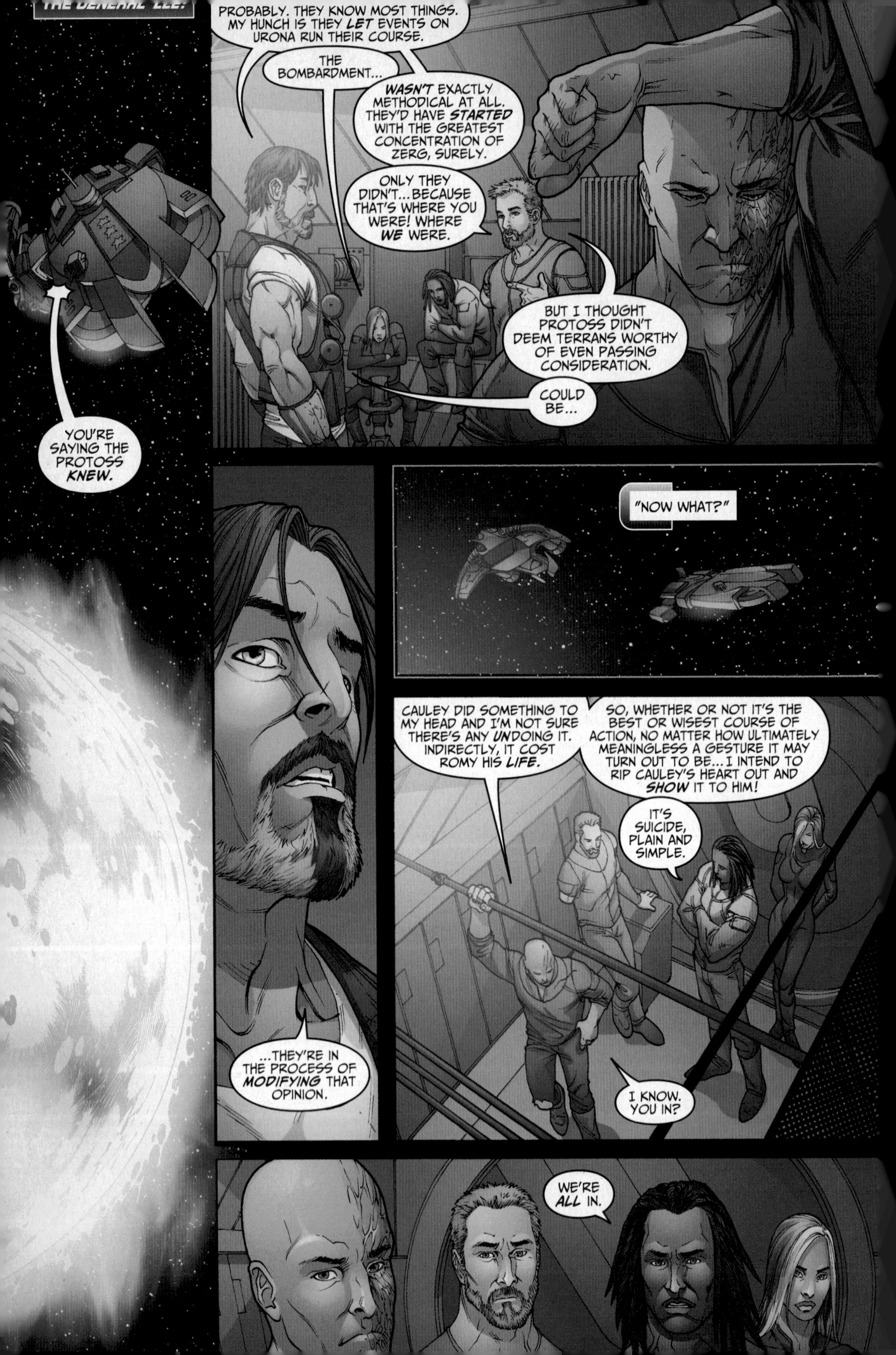

YOU'RE SAYING THE PROTOSS KNEW.
PROBABLY. THEY KNOW MOST THINGS. MY HUNCH IS THEY LET EVENTS ON URONA RUN THEIR COURSE.
THE BOMBARDMENT...
WASN'T EXACTLY METHODICAL AT ALL. THEY'D HAVE STARTED WITH THE GREATEST CONCENTRATION OF ZERG, SURELY.
ONLY THEY DIDN'T...BECAUSE THAT'S WHERE YOU WERE! WHERE WE WERE.
BUT I THOUGHT PROTOSS DIDN'T DEEM TERRANS WORTHY OF EVEN PASSING CONSIDERATION.
COULD BE...
...THEY'RE IN THE PROCESS OF MODIFYING THAT OPINION.
"NOW WHAT?"
CAULEY DID SOMETHING TO MY HEAD AND I'M NOT SURE THERE'S ANY UNDOING IT. INDIRECTLY, IT COST ROMY HIS LIFE.
SO, WHETHER OR NOT IT'S THE BEST OR WISEST COURSE OF ACTION, NO MATTER HOW ULTIMATELY MEANINGLESS A GESTURE IT MAY TURN OUT TO BE...I INTEND TO RIP CAULEY'S HEART OUT AND SHOW IT TO HIM!
IT'S SUICIDE, PLAIN AND SIMPLE.
I KNOW. YOU IN?
WE'RE ALL IN.

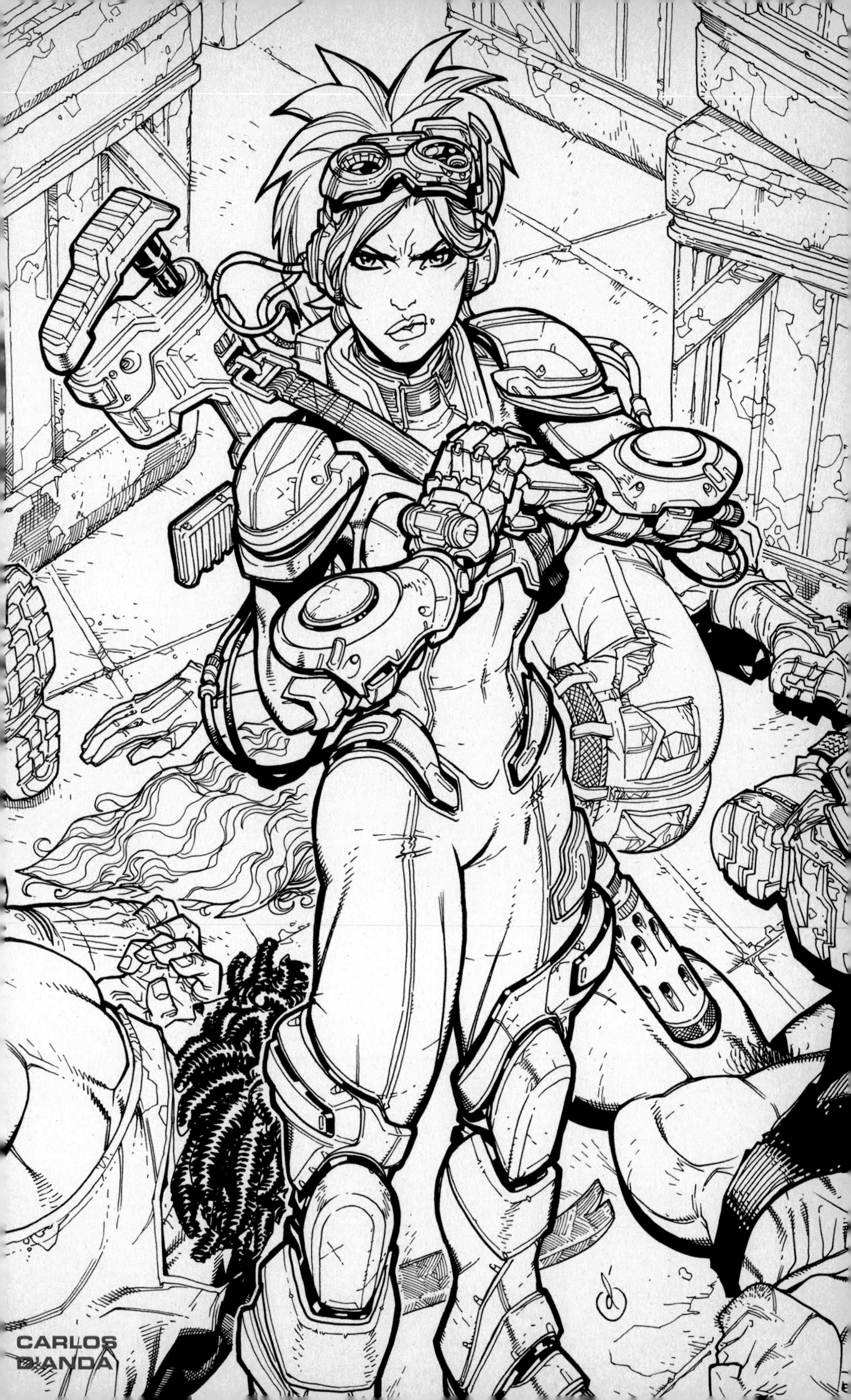

CARLOS D'ANDA

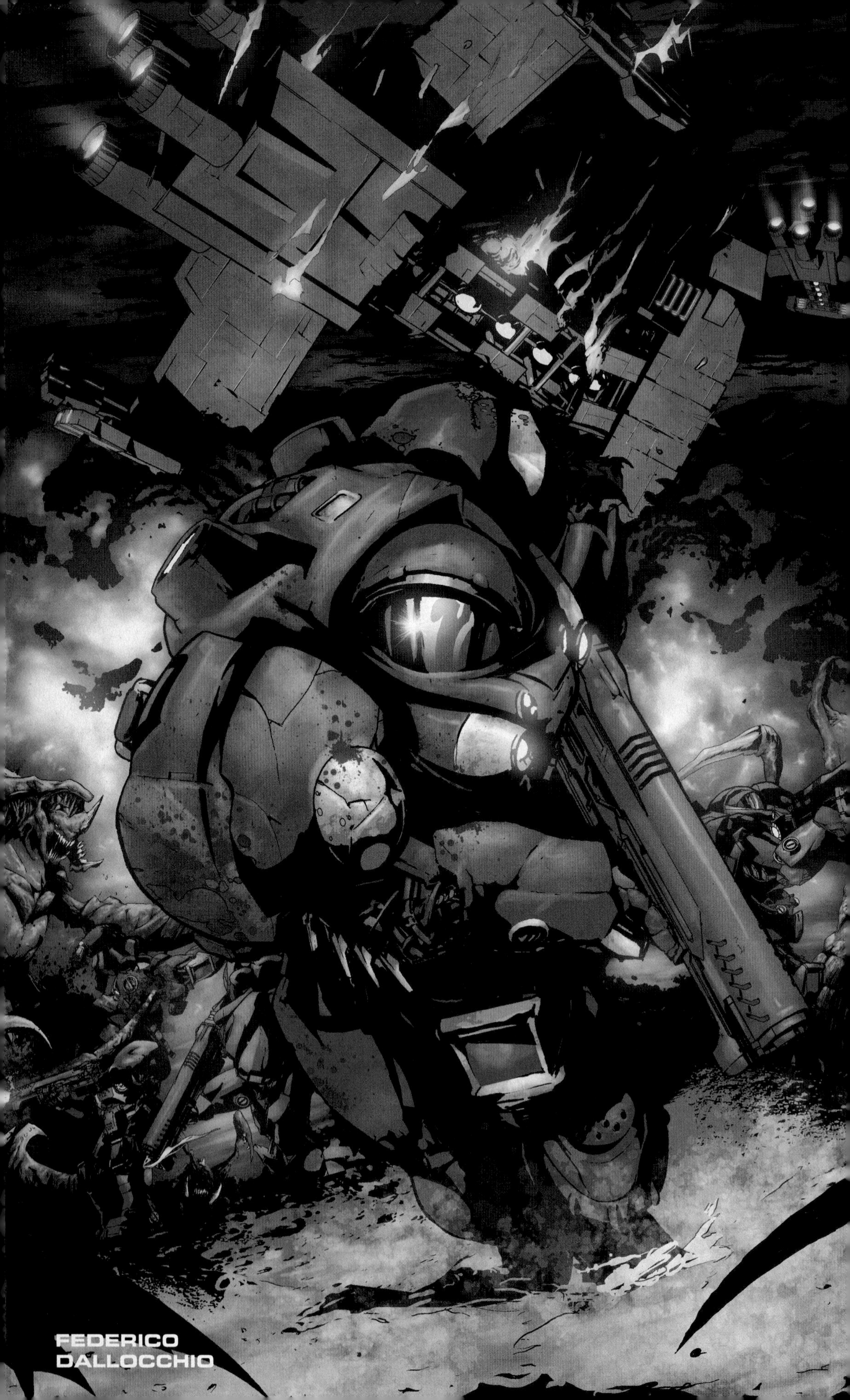
FEDERICO
DALLOCCHIO